DIZZY

This is the fascinating and compelling story of Disraeli's struggles and his triumph over his opposition, the saga of his rise to Chancellor of the Exchequer, then to Prime Minister and Leader of the Opposition. Here are the political coups that became legend . . . who but Dizzy could manage a loan of four million pounds from Louis de Rothschild to buy the Suez Canal?

But this is also the intensely moving personal story of a man supported through victory and defeat by his adored and adoring wife, Mary Anne, and, after her death, by his ever-deepening friendship with Queen Victoria.

**A magnificent novel of courage
and ambition, politics and passion
by the author of Lillie, David Butler.**

ABOUT THE AUTHOR

David Butler was born in Scotland. Son of a headmaster, he was educated at Larkhall Academy and St. Andrews University. After studying at the Royal Academy of Dramatic Art, he became popular as an actor on television, starting with the long-running series "Emergency—Ward 10." During "Ward 10" he began to write for the stage and television. Among his many successes are *The Strauss Family, Helen, A Woman of Today, Within These Walls, The Adventures of Black Beauty* and *Edward VII.*

David Butler is married and lives in Hampstead with his wife, Mary.

DISRAELI: Portrait of a Romantic

by
David Butler

WARNER BOOKS

A Warner Communications Company

WARNER BOOKS EDITION

Novelization copyright © 1978, 1980 by David Butler.

This work has been condensed from a two-volume work first
published in Great Britain by Futura Publications Limited,
originally titled: Volume I *Disraeli: The Adventurer* and Volume II
Disraeli: The Great Game. It was adapted from a television series
first produced in Great Britain. Series format and television scripts
copyright © 1978 by ATV Network Limited.

ISBN: 0-446-85776-9

This Warner Books Edition is published by arrangement with
Futura Publications Limited, 110 Warner Road, Camberwell,
London SE5.

Cover art by Paul Davis

Warner Books, Inc., 75 Rockefeller Plaza, New York, N.Y. 10019

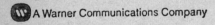 A Warner Communications Company

Printed in the United States of America

First U.S. Printing: May, 1980

10 9 8 7 6 5 4 3 2 1

DISRAELI:

Portrait of
a Romantic

DISRAELI:
The Adventurer

chapter one

It was the bells that woke him.

Half sleeping, half awake, he lay listening to the first, faint tinkling from the far off villages like the sound of sheepbells drifting down from the high slopes of a valley, soothing, insubstantial. But then, too soon, the bells of the nearer churches broke in, louder, more insistent, their timing staggered so that not one single carillon could be heard but all mingled in one great discordance. Soon the bells of all the churches, chapels and missions in the city joined in the clangor until the air itself seemed to vibrate in a clashing, peeling conflict of bells with each one striving to blot out the others.

On the first morning, they had shocked Ben out of sleep. The noise had seemed deafening and impenetrable. But already, in a few days, he had begun to make out some of the voices in the battle, one deep steady resonance that came from the direction of the Grand Harbor, another, an irregular, unmelodious clunk like an old cracked gong that came from toward St. Elmo's, and carrying musically through the din, the clear, silvery chimes from the twin belfries of St. John's, summoning the faithful, wooing the stragglers, to early morning mass.

The shutters were still drawn and streaks of sunlight slanted across the whitewashed walls of the room, picking out the colors in the deep-fringed Spanish shawl flung over the bed. For a moment, Ben imagined Clara lying there, covered only by a shawl, the long slope of her haunch, the curve of her waist, her shoulders rising sleekly from the richly colored silk, but her teasing, malicious features blurred and, instead, he saw the madonna face of the little Spanish gypsy girl who had gazed and gazed at him that night in camp on the road from Cordova to Granada. Her skin was dusky and would smell of musk. Her hair, not coiffured and gleaming like Clara's, but loose and dark as a cobweb, veiling the lift of her breasts.

"Ben!" The knock at the door startled him. "Ben, are you awake?" It was William. As he saw the latch move, Ben closed his eyes. He heard the door open and close softly. He was alone again. But the gypsy girl was gone, and so was Clara. The moment was over.

He stretched both arms high above his head and brought them down with a smack on the single sheet. He smiled. It was just as well William was with him. William Meredith, goodlooking, serious and studious, the best of fellows. They had both left England depressed and unwell, but the voyage and two months travelling in Spain, the sun, the riding and the sights to be seen had transformed them. Ben had never felt so alive. For the past two years he had been tortured by constant, nervous headaches that made him sometimes doubt his sanity. The future seemed empty and hopeless, but now each day was a delight and the past was forgotten. The cure had begun in Gibraltar. By the time they reached Andalusia, he was so confident, so sure of his place in the universe that soldiers saluted him in the street and grandees bowed to him. In Granada, the old woman who showed them round the superb Alhambra had been certain he was a

Moorish Prince come back to claim his own. "Yes," he told her, "this is my palace," and she curtsied as he sat, as of right, on the throne of the Caliphs.

The trip had begun as a quixotic gesture to help William. For nearly six years, William Meredith, a sensible and intelligent young man, a Fellow of the Royal Academy, had been unofficially engaged to Ben's equally sensible and intelligent elder sister Sarah. Both families were pleased but there was one problem. An old uncle of William's who had named him his heir, objected to the marriage. Although, like Ben, Sarah had been baptized into the Church of England in her teens, she was by birth a Jew. It had taken those years of steadfast devotion and determination to win the uncle around. The engagement was at last official, but Ben was angered on behalf of his sister, the person he loved most in the world, for a final condition was set, that the wedding could not take place for another year. Meredith chose to spend the year visiting and studying the countries around the Mediterranean, and Ben decided to borrow enough money to go with him. In twenty-five years of making rash decisions, he realized now it was the first sensible one he had taken. Not only was Meredith an ideal travelling companion, but his quiet, scholarly personality was just strong enough to restrain Ben's recklessness and hunger for experience. Besides, he made all the practical arrangements.

Now they had reached Valletta, capital of Malta, the little island poised like a steppingstone to the East. The next step would take them to Turkey or Greece, the Holy Land or Egypt. Ben's mind raced from images of one to the other. He wanted to see each first and all together.

As his head turned on the pillow, he caught sight of the table under the ornate, gold-framed mirror, the only opulent touch in the otherwise plain room. The waterjug which he had placed outside the door last night was on the table, with a bowl of fruit beside it. He had missed her again. The chambermaid must have crept in and out before the bells woke him. Slim, dark, the epitome of a Saracen maiden, he had been enchanted by her on his

11

first day at the inn and had tried to keep her in conversation when she brought his waterjug and basin. But she was demure and shy like all the native girls of Malta and since then had slipped in and out on little, silent feet. Do I frighten her? he wondered. I would so like to help converse with her . . . congress . . . ingress. He smiled, imagining William's face if he came in to find the chambermaid in bed with him. It would almost be worth bribing her to jump in, with all her clothes on and the covers pulled up to her chin.

He threw the sheet back and got out of bed. Last night he had gone to sleep wearing only his white, ruffled shirt. It covered him enough to be decent. He moved quickly to the window and threw the shutters back, then turned to the table with the mirror above it and looked at himself as he poured the water from the jug into the basin. The face he saw was narrow, vivid, handsome, slightly olive-skinned, his long black hair a mass of ringlets falling to his shoulders. The lines left by his illness were less strongly etched and only made it more interesting. Bending, he washed his face, then plunged his whole head into the water. He straightened, smiling, and shook the wet strands of hair back from his cheeks, shivering as trickles of water ran down inside his open shirt. He drank what was left in the jug, took a huge, golden orange from the fruitbowl and moved back to sit cross-legged on the broad windowsill. William distrusted the water, but Ben made a point of drinking from wells and springs and fountains wherever they went. He refused to believe that anything could harm him. The closer they came to Jerusalem, the more he felt physically as well as spiritually at home.

As he split and peeled the orange, he thought of the Holy City. Holy not only to his adopted religion, but to his race. He longed to be there, to stand in the steps of the Master, to cross the Kidron to the Garden of Gethsemane. Just as eagerly, he longed to see the ruins of the Temple and the hill of Zion. In his mind the two religions were one, the younger a more directly sanctioned and

12

purified refinement of the older. Part of his mission in life, he was convinced, was to explain the one to the other, to show their inseparable relationship. He was planning a new novel, the epic tale of David Alroy, the medieval hero of the Jews. It was to be a compound of mysticism and faith, history and romance, moral purpose, high adventure and love. Already he had sketched out a few key passages. Alroy's furious defense of his sister's honor when, unarmed, he snatched up a young tree by the roots and struck down her ravisher—a tender scene between his hero and the Arabian princess Schirene to the throb of nightingales—and Alroy's victorious entry into Bagdad. With half-shut eyes and juice from the orange sweet on his lips, Ben heard the faint murmur of the streets as the frenzied acclamation of an army.

He wiped juice from his chin and shook his head again, combing out his drying hair with his fingers. Daydreams, he thought. If daydreams were achievement, by now I would be Emperor of the West. Not for the first time, he decided to take stock of himself, Benjamin D'Israeli, twenty-five, unmarried, novelist.

At the age of twenty, after a series of brilliant schemes which impressed serious men much older than himself and all ending in disaster, he had found himself crippled with debts it would take him a lifetime to repay. He did not dare to tell his family. His father, though in comfortable circumstances, was not wealthy. Facing bankruptcy and the debtor's prison, other young men might have given in, but not Ben. He had already tried Law, journalism and the Stock Exchange. Now he left London for his parents' home in the country and there, in a few short months, he produced his first novel. *Vivian Grey* was finished in secret before his twenty-first birthday, the story of a penniless but talented young man, who conquers society and the political world by the sheer force of his personality. His sister and Mrs. Austen, the pretty and intellectual wife of his father's solicitor, were the only two to read the manuscript. Mrs. Austen, who expected great things of Ben, was enthusiastic and gave the novel to

13

Henry Colburn, a publisher, refusing to tell him who had written it. Colburn brought it out with the announcement that he was not permitted to reveal the author's name and, soon, everyone was reading it. It was daring, romantic and satirical. Ben was fascinated by politics and had seen just enough of fashionable society to be able to describe it.

The game was to guess which politician or titled wit was the author. Clues were said to be hidden in the names of the characters and places described. It is not impossible, it was whispered, that royalty is involved. When the news leaked that the writer was a penniless, unknown Vivian Grey, himself, a former lawyer's clerk who hovered on the fringe of the literary set thanks to his father, the critics and the public turned on Ben. For months he had basked in his secret glory, but now he found himself ridiculed. As extravagantly as the book had been praised before, it was now condemned as shallow and juvenile, indecent, the work of an ignorant upstart with no breeding.

Dazed and horrified, he retreated to his parent's quiet home for a while to lick his wounds. His father, Isaac D'Israeli, a kind, scholarly man who passed his days in bookshops and his library compiling anecdotes and literary reminiscences, was amused and sympathetic. "Ben," he always said, "could never do like the angels, but always rushed in, head first." You are too impatient for fame, he told him. Work slowly, prove yourself, then in time it may come. The advice added to Ben's despair. His sister Sarah, dear Sa, was one of the few who understood. With Mrs. Austen, she championed him fiercely, outraged by the injustice of his critics. And Colburn wanted a second volume.

Gradually Ben realized that, if not famous, he was at least notorious. If the public expected him to be daring and insolent, that is what he would be. Always a dandy in appearance, his clothes became more extravagant. As he strolled up Regent Street in a blue frockcoat, light blue military trousers, black stockings with red stripes and buckled shoes, he caused a sensation. The shoppers stood aside to gaze at him. "It was like the parting of the Red Sea," he told William, "which I now perfectly believe from experience." Since men affected to despise him, he concentrated on women, who responded eagerly to his wit and charm and intense good looks. Mrs. Austen became quite jealous of the way other women threw themselves at him. Her feelings for him had grown more intimate. In her fantasy, he became her boy lover. Being cosseted by her Ben found highly pleasing and soothing, for the mask of the dandy hid real hurt. And the headaches and nervous exhaustion had begun. The second volume of *Vivian Grey* was not a success, but the advance from the publisher helped to ward off his creditors.

He was treated by a fashionable doctor, whose wife added to Ben's problems by seducing him. Clara, a bewitching, ambitious, secret voluptuary, loved the feeling of power that intimacy with well known and promising young men gave her. Intrigued by Ben's obsession with politics in his writing, she encouraged his dreams of power, urging him to enter the political arena, feeding him tidbits of gossip from the bedchambers of Westminster. When his third novel, *Popanilla,* a satire on corrupt government, was also a failure, she cooled, his creditors closed in and he had to borrow from moneylenders at ruinous rates to keep them at bay.

Once again, he took refuge with his family. His father had bought a charming old house at Bradenham near High Wycombe and Ben spent the next year there with his parents, his sister and two younger brothers, resting and dodging the debt-collectors. Then came Meredith's decision to travel to the East and the longing to escape with him for a whole year filled Ben until there was no room for anything else. Isaac could not pay for the trip, so he talked his publisher into giving him an advance on a new novel, *The Young Duke,* to be as daring and romantic as his first. "What on earth does Ben know of dukes?" his father sighed, but he finished it in record speed and Colburn handed over five hundred pounds in advance.

15

With another two hundred borrowed from Mrs. Austen's husband, he was ready to join Meredith. They left London on 25 May 1830. From that day dates the renaissance, Ben told himself.

William Meredith had strolled out and down the broad Kingsway to take coffee and rolls in Great Siege Square, where he was joined by James Clay, an old acquaintance from Oxford, of whom he did not entirely approve. Clay was a raffish young man of some wealth and dubious morals. He had chartered a yacht, the *Susan,* to sail the Mediterranean in search of pleasure and was about to leave Malta, having exhausted its possibilities, when Ben and William arrived. William he liked, but he recognized Ben at once as an amusing fellow spirit, ready for anything. He admired his style and envied his reputation.

In Gibraltar, as a visiting novelist, D'Israeli had been lionized by the families of the garrison. The younger officers had marvelled at his elegance and copied his mannerisms. They had never seen such a dandy. He owned two canes, one plain ebony for the morning, one silver-headed for the afternoon. His reputation had preceded him and, while the officers of the Malta garrison were happy to accept Clay and Meredith in their mess, they were determined not to invite "that damned bumptious Jew boy." Apparently unaware of their disapproval, Ben called on the notoriously haughty Governor in his residence. Within a quarter of an hour, he had him rolling about the sofa with laughter. That afternoon he received an invitation to dine with the Governor and his lady.

When Meredith and Clay reached the inn, they found Ben finishing dressing in his room. William's mouth opened in astonishment. Ben's costume was made up of bits and pieces he had collected on the trip. He wore a blood red shirt with silver studs the size of shillings, striped trousers and red Turkish slippers. The Spanish shawl was tied round his waist. He stood at the mirror, adjusting a red neckscarf. "Flowing, I think—not tied. What do you think, William?"

"That it will make no difference," Meredith protested.

"Either way is altogether too much. We're going to a tennis match, not a fancy dress ball!"

Clay chuckled as Ben put on a blue-striped Spanish jacket sewn with ribbons. "You look like a cross between a matador and a Greek pirate," he said.

Ben shrugged. "I am determined to be remembered in Malta."

"You'll be lucky if you're not arrested," William muttered.

"My dear Willie, the officers and their ladies have ignored us so far."

"After you've dined with the Governor tonight, the other doors will open."

"I prefer not to wait. Obviously, they think a satirical novelist can only be a useless fop. So I'm determined to give them their money's worth." He picked up a broad-brimmed straw hat with a red ribbon round the crown. "Oh, and today I have made a momentous decision. I shall drop the apostrophe in my name. From this moment, I am simply Disraeli. It will look more English, I fancy."

"Oh, very English," Clay said drily.

Ben smiled. "Quite so." He perched the straw hat on top of his gleaming curls, tilted it. Selecting the ebony walking cane, he turned and bowed. "Shall we?"

They had been invited to the officers' sports enclosure because of Clay's reputation as a sportsman, but they were greeted with frigid politeness. The match had already begun and they took their seats in silence. Ben sat with his legs crossed, his hands folded over the top of his cane. He appeared quite indifferent to the stiffness of the army and naval officers around him, who neither acknowledged him nor spoke to him, although he was aware that among them some of the ladies were glancing at him covertly. William mopped his face, uncomfortable, wishing he had left off his waistcoat in this heat. Clay applauded the players loudly and smiled, waving to people he knew, hoping to lighten the atmosphere. But it persisted.

After a time, he saw Ben yawn and look at the sky, unmistakably bored. "You might at least pretend to be interested," he whispered. "It's the only way to win them over."

"To govern men, you must either excel them in their accomplishments, as you do," Ben murmured, "or despise them, as I do. Affectation will have more effect here than wit." A very pretty girl in front of them turned and smiled. He touched his hat and bowed to her, seated, smiling in response. The older woman beside the girl nudged her and she turned back.

"You're making a hit with the fillies, anyway," Clay said.

"The first step in my campaign," Ben nodded. "I have always found, once they are on my side, the battle is won." Just then, one of the players swinging at a high ball hit it with the edge of his racquet and it flew out of court, striking Ben lightly on the shoulder and dropping at his feet. He gazed at it for a second or two and picked it up. Conscious of everyone watching him, he turned to the stiff-necked and disapproving subaltern sitting next to him, speaking clearly enough for everyone to hear. "Pray advise me—what should I do with this object?"

"Why, throw it back, sir," the subaltern answered distantly.

"Ah—then could you kindly assist its passage back to the court? For you see, I have never thrown a ball in my life." He handed the tennis ball to the subaltern, who stared at him, then tossed the ball back. Ben applauded his feat politely. The officers around them were even more scandalized, but some of the ladies laughed quietly, realizing at last that he was playing a game. Clay bit his lower lip, bursting with suppressed laughter.

"Ben—?" William pleaded, agonized.

"Quite right, William," Ben agreed. "Yes, it is time to go."

He stood and led Clay and William toward the exit. As they passed an attractive older lady whom he had noticed glancing at him, cool, fair and amused, she lowered her

18

parasol and rose. "Mr. Disraeli—my husband and I would like very much to make your acquaintance. Perhaps you and your companions would care to join us for refreshment before lunch?"

Ben hesitated, reluctantly. "Alas, Madam, perhaps another time? You see, I have brought my morning cane. As it is now past midday, I must return to my lodgings to exchange it for my afternoon one." He bowed and moved on, leaving the lady surprised but amused. Clay followed him, fighting back laughter, and William hurried after them.

As they reached the wide stone bridge across the moat outside Kingsgate, Clay could finally laugh aloud. He leaned on the parapet, shaking and spluttering. "Your afternoon cane . . . I thought I'd die!"

"He means it." William shook his head. "I've seen him walk back four miles to change canes."

"I'll never forget their faces," Clay laughed. "Mind you, Ben, that was a devilish pretty woman you turned down. And she might have had friends."

"Have no fear, James. I fancy she'll be even more eager next time we meet." Ben smiled. "By tonight, we shall be awash with invitations."

They stopped at the inn where he changed canes. When he came down again, he saw with pleasure that they had been joined by Clay's Venetian servant, Battista Falcieri. Known as Tita, he was enormously tall with a fierce expression, drooping moustaches and a pair of daggers thrust into his waist sash. Having Tita as his man was the one thing that made Ben envy Clay. For his idol, his hero, was Byron and the huge, former gondolier had been Byron's servant. The poet had died in his arms at Missolonghi. His appearance was deceptive. He was good-natured and devoted, although in his youth he had killed two or three men and led a rebel regiment in the Greek War of Independence. With Tita at his side, Clay was never troubled by thieves or footpads in his night escapades and by day beggars kept their distance. He especially pleased Ben by telling him how Byron always carried a favorite book in his luggage, *Curiosities of Literature* by Isaac D'Israeli, a friend of his youth.

"Where are you off to next?" Clay asked.

"Well, we thought of going to Sicily," William told him, "but with the smallpox, it means three to four weeks quarantine."

"Look, I have an idea," Clay said. "I have my own yacht, the *Susan*. She's fifty-five tons, crew of seven. Why don't we join forces?"

William hesitated. "I'm not sure what . . ."

"If only we could!" Ben broke in excitedly. "But I don't have much money."

Clay smiled. "I'll be sailing on, anyway, in a day or two. I'd only charge you a nominal sum. Where do you want to go?"

"Jerusalem," Ben said. "That's our goal."

"Surely you don't want to go straight there? You have the rest of the year. I'd planned to sail to Albania, then Athens, Constantinople, the Holy Land and Egypt. It's not much fun travelling alone." Clay could see that Ben was for it and that William was tempted. "Let's shake hands on it," he said.

William paused. With two such travelling companions, no one knew what might happen, yet having their own ship would be a real adventure. He smiled and took Clay's outstretched hand.

"There is one thing," Ben said solemnly. "I refuse to cross the Homeric sea and into the mysterious passage of the Dardanelles on a vessel named *Susan*."

"Well, we can't change it," Clay chuckled. "But for your sake, we'll paint it out."

Ben laughed and smacked his hand down on top of theirs.

At Bradenham, Isaac D'Israeli's pleasant, old country home in Buckinghamshire, the group gathered in the sittingroom waiting eagerly while Sarah unfolded Ben's latest letter. It was a ritual in which each of them had played the leading part in turn, for all had had letters from him and shared them with the others. His short-sighted, erudite father Isaac, oval silver-rimmed spectacles perched on his nose, sat next to his delicate, waspish mother, Maria. She was still pretty, her hair dressed in three fat ringlets on each side of her brow, her shoulders covered by a lace fichu. His younger brother, Ralph, stood at the window.

Isaac smiled to their attractive neighbor, Mrs. Austen. Only the nervous movement of her foot under the hem of her muslin day dress betrayed her impatience for Sarah to begin. Often their letters overlapped and this was the only way to hear everything. He had told them of their hazardous trip through a rebellion from Corfu to Yanina, the capital of Turkish Albania, carrying despatches to Mehemet Pasha and of his delight at being made much of by a man who was daily decapitating half the Province. Of exchanging presents with a young Bey with whom they could not communicate until they were all dead drunk and passing out on the sacred carpets of the divan. Of the splendors of ancient Athens, untouched although the modern town had been devastated in the War of Independence. Of having to arm and keep a look-out for pirates. Of Navarino, Marathon, the Bosphorus and Constantinople with its mosques and bazaars, a teeming population of traders, all in their national costumes, the meanest merchant in the covered market looking like a king in an Eastern fairy tale. Clay and Ben had become so taken up by the diplomatic world, with balls and dinners, flirtations and visits to the Sultan and the Embassies that William Meredith gave up his idle companions and travelled on alone, overland. Ben had acquired his own servant, a Cypriot Greek who wore a Mameluke dress of crimson and gold, a white turban and a damascened sabre.

Sarah, a self-contained young woman of twenty-seven, interesting and intelligent rather than pretty, smoothed out the pages on her lap. Ben's last letter to their father had said that, with Clay, he was setting out from Jaffa in a party of six, well mounted and well armed, in a state of

21

growing excitement. As she read, the others listened intently, seeing what he had seen, feeling they were really there with him as they always did through his letters.

In the distance rose a chain of severe and savage mountains. I was soon wandering, and for hours, in the wild, stony ravines. At length, I reached the top of a high mountain. On an opposite height, forming with the elevation on which I stood a dark and narrow gorge, I behold a city entirely surrounded by an old feudal wall, with towers and gates. The city was built upon an ascent and, from the height on which I stood, I could discern the terrace and cupola of almost every house. In the front was a magnificent mosque with beautiful gardens, and many light and lofty gates of triumph. A variety of domes and towers rose in all directions from the buildings of bright stone. Nothing could be conceived more wild and terrible than the surrounding scenery, more dark and stormy, and severe. Except Athens, I had never witnessed any scene more essentially impressive. Athens and the Holy City must have been the finest representations of the beautiful and the sublime. The Holy City. For the elevation on which I stood was the Mount of Olives and the city on which I gazed . . . was JERUSALEM.

She paused. Mrs. Austen's sigh echoed inside them all. "At last," Isaac grunted. "Well, if his head was not turned before he left, it certainly will be now."

"Father!" Sarah protested, laughing.

"Ben has written to me that he had a profound mystical experience at Jerusalem and has plunged into work on his new novel," Mrs. Austen said, "more serious for a change."

"Indeed?" Isaac commented, dubiously. "What was his last effusion—*The Young Duke?* I fear that Ben's knowledge of mystical experience will prove as convincing as his knowledge of Dukes."

Ralph and Mrs. D'Israeli laughed.

"You are too severe on him," Mrs. Austen protested. "The reviewers may not like his books, but they have made him a celebrity."

"If Ben has a fault—and I criticize him because I love him—it is that he is determined to become a great man in too great a hurry."

"I wouldn't have him any other way, Papa," Sarah said.

Isaac smiled. "Nor, I suppose, would I."

Ben and James Clay had not yet met up again with William Meredith, who was to make some studies in Syria before meeting them in Cairo. Despite the mystical experience, they had stayed only a week in Jerusalem before sailing on to Alexandria. Egypt beckoned them irresistibly and they surrendered immediately to its scents and colors and lazy, sensuous charm. They were there for four months.

Cosmopolitan Alexandria had something for all appetites and, in slaking theirs, they both contracted a disease which might have cut short their pleasures—one of the thorns with which Venus guards her roses, as Clay said— but fortunately it yielded to doses of rest and Mercury. They rode across the desert to Rosetta, then sailed downstream to Cairo, where Ben climbed the great pyramid of Cheops and stood in silent adoration before the bland, unreadable face of the Sphinx. For weeks they drifted slowly down the Nile at the wind's pace, with the desert closing in gradually around them. In places, the valley was only a narrow strip of palms, then suddenly, lush green fields would stretch to the enclosing hills, with dense forests of papyrus, groves of cocoa trees and oranges. They were followed for days by naked *fellaheen* armed with reed spears and learned to avoid the half-submerged sandbanks where bull crocodiles roared at night. Dendera and Thebes made the wonders of Italy and Greece seem like toys. To Ben it was a mirage of triumphal arches, interminable walls of sculpture, avenues of sphinxes, obelisks and colossi, of gods and kings and the mysteries of the tomb paintings revealing the daily life of a whole unknowable world in colors preserved by the dry air as fresh as the instant they were finished. Their eyes and minds ached.

They journeyed to the borders of Nubia, where they spent one night in a black-walled Bedouin tent, lit by tiny hanging lamps. They had recovered from the grandeur and given themselves up completely to enjoyment. Wearing a burnous, Ben lay on a pile of perfumed cushions with a Bedu dancing girl crouching beside him, listening and watching as he smoked a water-pipe. She was slim and delicately featured, her eyes outlined with kohl. A dash of green was painted on her dark chin, her lower lip a brilliant blue. Her thin bodice was sewn with gold coins. Her billowing trousers were made up of separate leggings attached to her belt by ribbons and gathered at the calves, silk interwoven with gold thread. Her feet were bare, the soles dyed with henna, and around her ankles were silver chains with little tinkling bells.

Clay was seated cross-legged on the carpeted floor, his arm around another dancing girl. With a great show of modesty she had let him unclip her bodice and draw it aside to show the tattoo spiralling from her painted nipples to the cleft of her breasts. He was drinking, laughing uproariously as he listened to Ben and his girl.

"You have guessed correctly, my fair one," Ben admitted. "He is a mighty sheikh. Jamsk El Ay—master of many camels. His tents cover the hills of the golden land of Surrey."

Clay choked on his drink as the girls looked at him with new respect, then back to Ben. "And you, Lord?" his girl asked.

"I?" Ben shrugged. "I am an Emir, Disra El I, Lord of a kingdom of romance and poetry."

"Where is this kingdom, Lord?"

"Cloud Cuckoo Land," Clay laughed.

When Ben returned to Cairo, confident and relaxed, the first real tragedy of his life was waiting for him.

Clay and Tita were both worn out and had decided to rest for a month before sailing back to Venice. Ben's Cypriot servant had to go home to nurse his ailing father. William Meredith was expected any day and, reluctantly, Ben began to make the arrangements for their return trip via Malta. He had missed William and was glad when he finally arrived. William looked well, but was tired and suffering from headaches. He had a slight rash and found it difficult to sleep, but he was pleased with the room Ben had kept for him in the only decent hotel and settled down for a few days to recover and write up the notes of his studies. Ben was keen to hear of everything he had seen and done and to compare notes. Still, they had the whole trip home for that.

Coming back one evening from a visit to the Turkish Viceroy of Egypt, the ferocious Mehemet Ali, Ben collected Clay and they went together to coax William into joining them for a farewell supper in the old quarter of the city. As they crossed the verandah to the door of his room, an Egyptian servant squatting beside it rose and stopped them from going in.

"Is this not Mr. Meredith's room?" Clay asked, surprised.

"Yes, Effendi."

"We are friends of his," Ben said.

"No. No one to go in." They could see that he was worried, even frightened.

"What is it, man?" Clay demanded. "Is he ill?"

The servant nodded. "Doctor say—no one to go in. All things, all clothes burned."

Clay stepped back, afraid. But Ben was concerned. He pushed the servant aside and opened the door.

The room was bare, stripped of all its contents. On the bed, William lay in delirium, covered by a sheet that was slick with sweat. A Greek doctor wearing European dress and a red fez stood near the bed, watching. He turned quickly as Ben came in. "It is forbidden—"

"Please," Ben said, "I must see him." He looked around, alarmed by the bare room and by William's muttering, words too weak and broken to make out. He was wheezing for breath, his face disfigured by patches of eruption. "What is it?"

"Smallpox," the doctor said. "He was struck down very suddenly."

Ben's mind lurched, could not accept it. "But he'll recover."

The doctor shrugged. "Inshallah."

"He must!" Ben insisted.

"His throat is affected, his lungs. There is pneumonia," the doctor explained, almost apologetically. "After each crisis, he is weaker. If he survives the next . . . perhaps." Ben moved closer to the bed. "Do not go near him, sir!"

Ben paid no attention. He knelt by the bed, gazing at William, conquering his revulsion. William was still muttering, his eyes open but glazed, unaware of him. Ben could only think of Sarah. If William died her happiness, her life would be over, with his. He saw William's tongue moving, trying to wet his dry lips. There was a beaker of water on the small, cane table by the bed. Ben took it and sat on the edge of the bed, raising William's head.

"Sir—" the doctor pleaded.

Ben put the beaker to William's lips. The water trickled from his slack mouth but he had swallowed some and the desperate breathing slowed.

"William—it's Ben. Ben!" William's head jerked, and his eyes tried to focus. "I am here. I'll look after you."

"Ben?" William whispered.

Ben was relieved. "Yes, I am here."

William gasped. "Don't . . . don't leave me," he begged.

"Never. I'll take care of you. As soon as you are well again, we'll leave for England. For Sarah, William."

"Sarah," William whispered.

Ben smoothed the matted hair back from William's forehead. "She loves you and is waiting for you."

"Sarah . . ." William smiled faintly and his eyes closed. His harsh breathing died away.

"All you have to do is get better," Ben promised him.

"Then we'll go home. And oh, I have such marvels to tell you . . . Come, drink a little more, then sleep."

He held the beaker again to William's lips, but this time all the water ran out of his mouth. Ben raised his shoulders higher, holding him up with his free arm. The Greek doctor came to them and took the beaker from Ben's hand. William's head fell to the side. Ben was beginning to realize. He looked up, wide-eyed.

The doctor shrugged. William was dead.

chapter two

The long journey home, alone, was a nightmare, made unendurable by weeks of quarantine. Ben had written at once to his father, then to Sarah, though he could hardly remember what he had said. He could not sleep, nor even rest, for thinking of her. William had been the kindest, truest, gentlest of men and he would have given his own life for his, to save her from the pain she must be suffering.

He thought of the injustice of it, the years of waiting, of devotion in spite of prejudice, and at first he blamed himself for letting his friend die, for having caused his death. His reason cured him of that black thought, yet he realized one fact, that his life, his own career, had ended with William Meredith's. From now on he could only live for his sister. He would devote himself to her.

Although he was impatient to be back at Bradenham, when he saw the trees of the drive from the carriage window, Ben felt a surge of panic. He composed himself,

29

paid the driver and went inside. His father was in the study. Although they knew he was coming, Ben had not been expected on this day. Isaac seemed to have aged. Unable to speak, he hugged Ben and nodded toward the sitting-room.

Sarah was there alone. Wearing a high-necked mourning dress, pale, drawn, she sat on the windowseat, looking blankly down at her folded hands. She did not look up for a moment when Ben came in, then rose, incredulous at seeing him standing by the door, also in black mourning. Suffering had made her quite beautiful, Ben thought. He moved towards her and stopped. She ran to him and he held her, her head on his breast. Miraculously, she did not break down. After a time, she eased back, still holding his arms, gazing up at him. "I have longed for you to be here."

"Oh, my dearest Sa . . ."

"No, please," she whispered. "Don't—don't speak about it now. Later, when I'm used to having you home." She kissed his cheek and moved from him. In the months since the death, she had learned to accept it. Part of her had dreaded Ben's return because the wounds would be reopened and she would feel again the unbearable anguish of the first days. A sensible young woman, she had never believed tales of broken hearts, yet now she knew they were true, for she had felt hers creaking. She knew that soon they would have to talk about William, that she would weep and Ben would comfort her—and she would appear to be consoled, for his sake, while inside herself she carried a grief that no one's words and no sympathy could ever heal. She managed to smile. "I have no idea—I can't tell you what it means to see you. How long can you stay?"

"Forever," Ben said simply.

Sarah was puzzled. "You plan to live here in the country, instead of London?"

"To be with you. I have made up my mind never to leave you, to live only for you." Sarah could not quite understand, yet she saw he was deadly serious. She made to protest. "No, listen, Sarah. I have no wife, no be-

30

trothed. You have said that now you will never marry. Nor shall I. I dedicate my life to your happiness."

As she realized at last what he meant, she was shaken. "Ben—I could not accept—"

"Be my genius, my solace, my companion. My joy!"

Seeing him smiling to her, completely sincere, Sarah nearly cried out. More than anything, she needed Ben's warmth and companionship. Now that William was dead, her only remaining wish was to see her brother achieve success and recognition. To find that he was ready, determined, to give up everything for her, made her love him all the more deeply. "To live for me? To give up everything—" she began.

"I would lose nothing! And gain a whole world of peace!"

"To live in obscurity, denying yourself for my sake, you would destroy yourself," she corrected him gently.

"No," Ben shook his head smiling to her.

As she tried to think what to say, the door opened. Sarah was troubled and glad of the interruption.

It was Mrs. Austen who came in. In a light blue day dress with a rounded, lacy neck, a little blue bonnet, she was flushed and radiant. "I came by chance—when I heard you were here—" She moved to Ben as he bowed to her. "So formal?" She laughed quietly and kissed him, patting his cheek. "Over a year away—we lived for your letters." She was close to him, holding his hand. He felt her fingers grip his convulsively. He was very conscious of Sarah watching.

It was quite clear to Sarah at last. She did not know how much had passed between them, but Sara Austen obviously loved her brother. She saw his embarrassment. "Mrs. Austen has been in constant touch with your publisher, Ben," she said evenly. "To protect your interests."

"It was the least I could do—for my protegé." Mrs. Austen smiled. "If you call on me tomorrow, I shall hope to satisfy you—on all points."

It was at once discreetly provocative and explicit. But Ben's relationship with this woman was part of the life he

31

meant to put behind him. He was even more conscious of Sa and stepped away. "I intended to call on you and Mr. Austen as soon as possible."

"Mind that you do," Mrs. Austen urged him. "Though I expect that, secretly, you can't wait to get back to London."

"I plan to stay here."

"To finish your new book?"

"It is finished." Mrs. Austen and Sarah were startled. "And another I wrote while I was in quarantine is almost done."

Mrs. Austen clapped her hands. "That's wonderful!"

"Is it? The last two were mangled by the critics."

"The public loved them."

"But not the ones who matter. Every line he writes shows his lack of breeding, they said. Let the impudent mongrel go back to the kennel he came from."

Mrs. Austen glanced at Sarah and back to Ben, alarmed by his bitterness. "You would not think of giving up? Ben—you cannot!"

"I have promised Sarah—"

"It is a sacrifice I cannot accept," Sarah interrupted, firmly. "You wish to give my life meaning again? That will only come with your success. It is all I live for now."

Mrs. Austen watched Ben tensely, seeing the struggle inside him, waiting for him to speak. She wanted to hold him, mother him. All her dreams for him were in the balance. She had heard enough to guess what had been said before she arrived and recognized that everything depended on Sa. The strength must come from her.

"You must return to London," Mrs. Austen insisted. "We—my husband will help."

He could feel Sarah moving closer to him. "Adventure is to the adventurous. Your old motto," she said. "It is still true for you!"

He shook his head. "It would mean beginning again. I know no one I could trust, nowhere I'd be welcome."

"You have a standing invitation to visit Edward Bulwer." Edward Lytton Bulwer was a young novelist who had appeared about the same time as Ben. They had read and admired each other's books. Both were dandies, with wit, good looks and immense ambition. They could easily have been rivals but, when they met, they took an instant liking to each other. During Ben's absence, Bulwer's reputation had become more secure. He had become a Member of Parliament, acquired respectability, a wife and a fashionable home in Mayfair. "He is prepared to help you. If you do not accept because of me, I should never forgive myself," Sarah said. She could tell now that Ben was already half-convinced. "I cannot believe you are afraid. All you need is one open door. It is waiting for you."

With another loan and a small advance from his publisher, Ben returned to London and took a bachelor apartment in St. James's. The rooms were fairly cheap and poorly furnished, but he gave them a touch of the exotic by hanging on the wall of his sitting-room a pair of silver-hilted daggers and a curved scimitar in its scabbard, which he had brought back from his travels. The Spanish shawl was draped over the dingy sofa and an open, ivory-inlaid fan pinned above it. Against the fireplace rested a six-foot Turkish tobacco pipe with an amber mouthpiece and a porcelain bowl, which was his pride. Sarah brought him pots of red geraniums for his window-sills and his writing desk.

He did not, however, take up Bulwer's invitation, nor go out much during the day. He had to correct and revise the first of his new books for publication, and there was another reason. The first to learn he had returned were the moneylenders. Their duns followed him in the street and waited for him at his apartment house.

One afternoon in the spring of 1832 he was sitting at his desk writing, trying to ignore an intermittent knocking at the outside door. He heard a voice shouting, "Open up! You're in there, all right!" The knocking was repeated louder. Ben hunched over his manuscript, carrying on writing as the knocks became an angry pounding.

Outside in the stone passage stood a group of bailiffs

and debt collectors. The one beating on the door held a sheaf of bills. "He'll have to come out one day."

Another man scoffed. "But will he have any money when 'e does? This bill's been outstandin' two years!" He moved in and kicked at the door. The others muttered. Their heads turned as they heard footsteps on the stairs.

An elegant young man came up from the stairs into the passage. A glossy top hat added to his height. His hair was golden brown. Light whiskers outlined a long, sensitive face, which was saved from weakness by clear hazel eyes, shrewd and humorous. He was dressed with deliberate style, his tan frockcoat narrow in the waist, long in the skirts, his linen immaculate, the high stock at his neck of black satin, secured by an amethyst pin. He was Edward Bulwer. He hesitated briefly, seeing the group outside the door, then walked on past them, taking no more notice.

"Beg pardon, sir," the man at the door said, touching his hat. "Do you 'appen to know the gent that lives in 'ere? Would you 'appen to know if he's at 'ome?"

Bulwer seemed to be trying to place the name. When he spoke, he had a noticeable speech impediment. "M-Mr. Disraeli, I saw him just now at the corner of the street."

The debt collectors waited to see who would be the first to move, then left in a rush, each one trying to get there first. When he heard the last of them clatter down the stairs, Bulwer smiled. He stepped back to Disraeli's door and tapped on it lightly. He waited, but there was no answer from inside. He knocked again, took an envelope from inside his coat and slipped it underneath the door.

The long, tasteful drawing-room of the Bulwers' house in Hertford Street was filled with animated guests that evening. The lights sparkled on the jewels of the ladies, whose arms and shoulders were dazzling against the black dress suits of the men.

Bulwer stood with his appealing, vivacious wife, Rosina, an Irish girl in her middle twenties. They were talking to Wyndham Lewis, the Tory Member of Parliament for Maidstone, a good-natured, kindly man, who admired Bulwer in spite of his radical opinions. With him was his wife, Mary Anne. Frivolous, pretty, delicately featured, she looked much younger than her thirty-nine years. Many people pitied Lewis for being married to such an empty-headed chatterbox. She was notorious for her lack of education and tact, but in all the years of their marriage they had never had a hurtful argument and only Lewis knew how much of his success he owed to her.

"Are you sure he'll be here?" Mary Anne asked eagerly.

"I can't promise," Bulwer said. "We've sent Disraeli invitation after invitation, but he's dropped out of sight."

Rosina saw him glance toward the hall door. The soft, Irish charm was deceptive; he had already discovered her tongue could be acid. "I can't imagine why you're so keen," she said. "He's just another conceited writer."

"Poodle, please," Bulwer begged. "Not again." Although she enjoyed her husband's popularity, Rosina despised his profession and had begun to object to him inviting literary men to their home. She either ignored them or was rude, concentrating on the other guests. Bulwer was relieved when he saw Disraeli beyond her, hesitating in the doorway. "Here he is, the most elusive man in London."

Ben was dressed at his most dandified in a black velvet jacket, purple trousers with gold stripes down the sides, a scarlet waistcoat strung with gold chains, flowing lace ruffles at his wrists and white gloves with jewelled rings worn outside. He had nearly thrown away Bulwer's note, thinking it was another bill, and had only made up his mind to come at the last minute. He was tense and on his guard as Bulwer came to meet him.

Bulwer shook his hand warmly. "I can't tell you how much I've looked forward to seeing you again."

"I've been abroad for some time, Mr. Bulwer."

"Edward, please," Bulwer smiled. "And we have heard something of your travels."

There was a murmur of interest in the room as he led

Ben to Rosina. Rosina had been prepared to dislike him but found herself responding in a completely feminine way as he bowed and kissed her hand. She smiled, to Bulwer's relief. "At last. Now perhaps my husband will stop talking about you. I own I was almost jealous."

"Now, now, Poodle," Bulwer laughed.

"It's true! You are the only living writer, besides himself, that he really admires."

"You do me too much honor," Ben said.

"Impossible," Bulwer assured him. "Besides, the world is too slow to recognize genius. We must at least praise each other."

Ben smiled briefly. The tension in him was easing, thanks to the sincerity of Bulwer's welcome. He had known, as soon as he had decided to come, that this would be a testing time for him. On how he behaved, on what he said, a great deal would depend. He forced himself to relax, yet as he looked around the room, his neck stiffened. A woman had paused near them and was smiling.

"Mrs. Bolton," Rosina said, "may I introduce Mr. Disraeli, the author of *Vivian Grey* and *The Young Duke*?"

The woman's smile deepened. It was a smile Ben remembered so well. She was tawny-haired, sexually provocative, in her thirties. Clara. "I know them well," she said, "and indeed, I know Mr. Disraeli."

He bowed. "Mrs. Bolton . . ."

"You have been touring the Middle East, I hear."

"Until recently. Pray give my regards to Dr. Bolton."

Clara inclined her head, smiled again and moved on.

"Now, who else do you know?" Bulwer asked.

"No one, I'm afraid." Bulwer was surprised. "I confess, my acquaintance with society so far has been in respectable but less exalted circles."

"Yet they all know you."

Rosina saw his disbelief. "Most of our guests are here because they are eager to meet you."

Ben realized they were serious. "But I thought—"

"That you had outraged all London?" Bulwer laughed. "Only the stuffy and the petty-minded. Since then, tales of your wit, your daring—"

Rosina giggled. "Your morning cane."

"Oh, it's started quite a fashion," Bulwer agreed. "The makers of walking sticks may take you as their patron saint."

"And friends in the United States write that you are required reading there," Rosina added.

Ben smiled. "No, no, please. You overwhelm me."

"Well, then, come and meet some of your admirers," Bulwer said. "You'll excuse me for introducing a disagreeable subject—but what are your politics?"

"If Pups is getting on to his hobbyhorse, I'll leave you," Rosina said. "Do sympathize with him, Mr. Disraeli. He's so dreadfully disappointed there hasn't been a revolution."

Bulwer frowned briefly as she left. "Rosina does not entirely support my political beliefs. What are yours?"

Ben hesitated. "It depends who I'm talking to."

Bulwer was thrown. In his books, Disraeli had shown an awareness of social conditions and their problems, satirized the callous exploiters of the industrial revolution. "No convictions?"

Ben wondered briefly if he should give Bulwer the pleasure of appearing to share his opinions. Instead, he decided to be honest. "Many," he said. "But I am neither Whig nor Tory nor Radical. No one party has a monopoly on the truth."

Bulwer nodded. "So you're uncommitted. But not indifferent?"

"Far from it. I am as obsessed by politics as some men are by drink or women. Sometimes I think it is only there I could really make my mark." He shrugged. "But politics is an occupation for gentlemen of leisure. And without noble connections or wealth or political friends to help me . . ."

"Then we must do something about it. Whom would you prefer to meet first?" He nodded across the room toward a tall, heavyset Irishman, Daniel O'Connell, lead-

37

er of the Irish Radical MPs. "Daniel O'Connell—or the Prince of the Dandies, Count Alfred D'Orsay?"

Ben was impressed. "D'Orsay . . ." He began looking around.

"Over there, with the long necked beauty."

"Exquisite."

"And influential. Lord Melbourne's friend, Mrs. Caroline Norton." He led Ben toward the couple at the center of a group in the far corner. D'Orsay was in his early thirties, tall, slim, so handsome he was almost beautiful, yet his build was masculine and athletic. He wore a slight beard and his chestnut hair was a mass of casually disordered waves and curls. Unlike Ben's, his evening clothes were not flamboyant, but exquisitely fitting, with the perfect cut that had made his tailor's fortune. A Frenchman, the brother of the Duchesse de Guiche, he was the arbiter of elegance, a connoisseur of art and himself an accomplished artist. With so many advantages it was natural that he had many enemies, yet even they admitted that his legendary charm was unforced and genuine. The woman with him was dark and strikingly attractive, with dark, compelling eyes. She was Caroline Norton, the acknowledged mistress of the leading Whig statesman, Lord Melbourne. As he was introduced and bowed, Ben was shaken by their unreserved pleasure at meeting him.

On the other side of the room, O'Connell watched sourly. He did not care either for Jews or dandies. He was joined by a younger and more dashing Irishman, Daniel Maclise, whose talent for making his sitters recognizable, though idealized, had made him a fashionable portrait painter. He already knew and liked Ben. In fact, he had sketched both him and Sarah.

"Who's that tinselled coxcomb they're all cooing over?" O'Connell growled.

"Disraeli, the novelist. Do you wish to meet him?" It was an encounter Maclise would like to see.

"Not if he were the last man in England," O'Connell said. "I can't abide these flashy Israelites." He grimaced as the people around Ben laughed.

38

"I hear we are to have a new book from you soon," D'Orsay was saying.

Ben nodded. "Yes, it should complete the corruption of the public's taste."

They laughed. "But you have become a great traveller," Caroline Norton said. "You must tell us about everything you have seen."

"Alas," Ben sighed, "like all great travellers, I have seen more than I remember. And remember more than I have seen."

Bulwer joined in the laughter. He was gratified. His new friend was more than living up to his expectations. Rosina joined them with Mr. and Mrs. Wyndham Lewis.

"Mr. Disraeli?"

Ben turned, trying to identify the unknown voice. Mary Anne smiled to him radiantly.

"Mrs. Wyndham Lewis and Wyndham Lewis, Member of Parliament for Maidstone," Bulwer said.

Ben and Lewis bowed.

"You have been very cruel," Mary Anne said disapprovingly. "I wonder I can even talk to you."

"Madam?"

"Not to come earlier."

"My wife is an admirer of yours, Mr. Disraeli," Lewis explained.

Mary Anne agreed. "I am one of—no, no qualifications. I am your *greatest* admirer. I have read everything you have ever written."

"Then some of my correspondents have been extremely indiscreet," Ben answered drily.

Mary Anne laughed delightedly. "That was very humorous. Is it from one of your books?"

"I try not to quote myself, Madam."

The others were moving away as unobtrusively as possible. Ben caught D'Orsay's eye, but D'Orsay smiled and shrugged, leaving him alone with her. How am I to extricate myself without offending her? he asked himself.

Mary Anne tapped his arm. "Well, I'll try to remember it. I can't promise, though. For I'm such an empty-head.

39

Sometimes I think there's so much space inside my skull, things just get lost in it." She laughed, expecting him to join in.

"Madam, there's no need—"

"Oh, please—not Madam," she protested. "It makes me feel so very ancient. You shall call me Mary Anne."

"If you insist, Madam."

"Mary Anne." He repeated her name and she laughed happily. "There, I knew we would get on famously. I know you far better than you realize. I'm sure I could tell you things about yourself that would surprise you."

"I am convinced of it."

"You are mocking me again," she teased.

"I assure you . . ."

"I don't mind a bit," she said. "You see, I can tell when you are serious—which is nearly all the time. For you say serious things in a funny way, so that people won't think you are too solemn." Ben was startled by her unexpected shrewdness. "Especially about politics. I think you are obsessed by politics, even when you write about love."

"Surely politics is the great Romance?"

"Oh, Wyndham doesn't think so. He finds it all deadly dull. But he's a Tory, of course. Are you a Tory?"

"At the moment I incline to the more liberal party. They give much better dinners and are more amusing!"

"Then you must give me a chance to convert you, by coming to dine with us."

"I . . ." He sought for an escape, but he was trapped.

"I insist."

"In which case you leave me no alternative. Now if you will excuse me, I have something urgent to tell Bulwer."

She was thrilled at his acceptance of her invitation and disappointed that he should leave her so soon.

"Oh—well, only on condition that you do not forget me."

"You may depend on it," he assured her.

He bowed and crossed to join Bulwer, who was with

Daniel O'Connell. "Excuse me," he said quietly, "I had to escape from that intolerable woman."

"It is the price of fame," O'Connell said flatly.

"I have never heard such a rattle. I could not get a word in edgeways." As he looked back he tensed slightly, finding himself facing Clara Bolton.

"How long have you been home?" she asked, deceptively casual.

"About three weeks."

"And you have not come to see me?" Her eyebrows arched.

"I have been with my family in the country."

"And now?"

"I've taken rooms in St. James's—Duke Street."

"How convenient," Clara murmured. Her smile was scarcely visible, yet its promise was unmistakable.

Bulwer, D'Orsay and Caroline Norton came over to them and Clara moved on. D'Orsay said in his liquid French accent, "We have been trying to guess which university you were at. Was it Oxford or Cambridge?"

"Neither. I left school at fifteen."

"Fifteen?" D'Orsay was astonished.

"And completed my education at home, in my father's library."

"Did you never wish to go to university?" inquired Caroline.

In his youthful arrogance, Ben had rejected the idea as insultingly unsuitable for someone of his genius, though sometimes, now, he wished he had been at one of the seats of learning, if only for the sake of a conventional, approved background. It was something he would never admit. He felt very relaxed and could feel himself growing expansive, sure of his audience. Others had gathered around to listen and watch. His hands rose expressively. "I thought of it, but I burned for action. I wanted to enter Parliament, or publish a newspaper, to be a soldier, a saint, or a poet like Byron. All of them at once. Instead my father had me articled to a firm of solicitors in the City."

41

"So you became a barrister?" said Caroline.

"Alas, no. I gave it up."

"Why?"

"I was more interested in life. And the Bar? Law and bad jokes until you are forty and then, with the most brilliant success, the prospect of gout and a coronet."

His listeners laughed delightedly. Beyond them, other people were heading in twos toward the door, prompted by Rosina. She came to them, as he went on. "I was secretary to the senior partner. Instead of life, for three years I heard of nothing but death and divorce." He made it sound amusing, but they had been years of frustrating boredom, beginning just before his seventeenth birthday. One of the partners was a friend of Isaac's and had a daughter. Ben was encouraged to consider their home as his own and saw that his entire future had been planned for him. However, the temptations of marriage and easy advancement in the firm were not enough to sweeten the thought of spending the rest of his days penned up in a sunless office in Old Jewry, patching over the shabby cracks in other people's lives. Determined to leave, shortly before his twentieth birthday, he announced a sudden desire to read for the Bar, and escaped.

His new friends were keen to hear more, but Rosina interrupted. "I think we can go in now. Mr. Disraeli, I have promised Mary Anne Wyndham Lewis that you will take her in to dinner and sit with her."

Ben's head swivelled. Mary Anne was already advancing on him. "Anything rather than that insufferable woman!" he beseeched. Rosina drew herself up. He looked around the group, pleadingly. Bulwer's mouth twitched. D'Orsay made a moue of sympathy and left with Mrs. Norton. Ben submitted. "Well—Allah is great."

Mary Anne had arrived to claim him. "There you are, my perfect knight. And looking so solemn." He bowed. "You must have guessed that I like silent, melancholy men."

"I have no doubt of it." Ben said, sincerely.

He could hear Bulwer and O'Connell chuckling. Mary

Anne smiled sunnily to him. With her rose-satin dress cut low to reveal the slope of her narrow shoulders, the yellow diamonds at her throat, her hair in bright, girlish bunches of ringlets over her ears, her great, eager eyes, she was almost unbearably winsome and so proud of having captured him. The room had been filled with beautiful, sophisticated women, yet he was sacrificed to the ego of a flirtatious rattle. It is for my sins, he thought. He offered her his arm and led her out.

In the next few months, the friendship between Ben and Bulwer developed rapidly. They were a foil and complement to each other and became inseparable, to Rosina's annoyance. She liked to be the focus of attention at her lavish parties and resented the ever-widening circles which grew around Disraeli. He was soon working hard merely to keep up with his invitations, no longer on the fringe of society, but much closer to its center.

The change in his fortunes impressed Clara Bolton. The promise that had been implied was kept. She lived with her elderly, complaisant husband, Dr. Buckley Bolton, in King Street, off St. James's Square, just around the corner from Duke Street. She could walk from her door to Ben's in three minutes. She would have been prepared to go much further. It gave her intense excitement to hear her husband's distinguished patients and guests talk about the new rising star and to know that only an hour or two before she had most ardently satisfied him in bed.

Ben had intended to avoid Clara and tried to discourage her visits. She merely came more often, letting herself in by the rear door of his apartment which he used to avoid his creditors. It was entirely an accident that his rooms were so close to her home, but she would not believe it. To her it was a sign that, consciously or unconsciously, he had needed her. Her ambitions for him were rekindled.

It was a time of unrest, following the rejection of the second Reform Bill by the House of Lords. The parliamentary parties were preparing to do battle, welcoming new recruits and promising young men. Bulwer had al-

43

ready embarked on a political career. Ben had always been tempted by the idea of it, yet had realized, reluctantly, that there were too many difficulties in his way.

His father had had no particular feeling for religion. He was part of the Jewish community by birth, but resisted every attempt by the Elders to involve him in the rituals and observances of the synagogue. He had arranged for his children to be baptized not through any conviction, simply to make it possible for them in later life, if they chose, to adopt one of the professions from which Jews were barred by law. Technically, there was nothing to prevent Ben from entering parliament. However, although baptized, he was still a Jew and would have to offer himself to a suspicious and deeply prejudiced electorate.

Under the influence of Clara's enthusiasm, the obstacles gradually seemed less insurmountable and his ambitions revived. He began to visit the gallery of the House of Commons again to listen to the debates, particularly when the party leaders were speaking, Peel for the Tories whom he had renamed "Conservatives," and Russell and Palmerston for the Whigs, whose younger members called themselves "Liberals." Amongst the Radicals, he admired Cobden and appreciated O'Connell's vigor. Bulwer was listened to with respect, but his speech impediment hindered him from being a really effective speaker. Privately, in his letters to Sarah, Ben was sure he could outshine them all. Sometimes, in his rooms, he declaimed as though addressing both Houses, one style for the Commons, another for the Lords. With Clara urging him on, applauding, it was easy to imagine himself rallying the members of his party with his oratory, winning all to his side as he championed some noble cause. He had told her of his vision of her sprawled on his bed, veiled only in the Spanish shawl, and she used it. Lying on the sofa with the shawl drawn around her, the fringes trailing over her long, pale thighs, she brought his fantasy to life, exciting herself and him as she reawakened his belief in his destiny at the same time as his desire.

Yet Ben had no pride in his association with Clara.

It was not that he felt guilty about deceiving the amiable Dr. Bolton, he had to admit. It was something about Clara herself. She was using him in her own strange way, as she used everyone. He was glad their affair was secret for he could tell that his friends neither liked nor trusted her. When her husband had treated him before his journey to the East, she had visited his family at Bradenham. Both Sarah and his father had warned him against seeing too much of her. He did not trust her himself, though he found her sexually stimulating and flattering in her avid praise. He had no illusions that she was in love with him. If he did not fulfil her expectations for him, and soon, she would drop him as she had dropped him before.

Much more important to him was his acceptance by old Lady Cork. In her eighties, still passionately interested in anything new, she presided over one of the leading literary and political salons in London. She was captivated by Ben and saw a prodigious future for him. Through her introductions, he was at last able to mix with the kind of wealthy and titled figures who peopled his novels. From now on he could describe them at firsthand. When his new book came out, *Contarini Fleming,* again imaginatively biographical, she considered it his masterpiece. The critics were not so kind but, as she was a relic of the previous century and had been admired by Dr. Johnson, Ben was happy to accept her verdict.

Perhaps inevitably, his success with men was not so complete. Intelligent women, whose only defense in a male-dominated age was to adopt masks of intellectual superiority and moral seriousness, made prodigious demands on their suitors of unbending devotion, visible achievements and lofty ideals, yet became playful kittens when Ben appeared. They clustered around him, lapping up his flow of serio-comic nonsense, learning whole pages of his works by heart, accepting his views on art and government and society as if they were oracular. To the men's suspicion of him was added resentment of his apparently effortless conquests. They sensed rather than knew that, although he adored women, his approach was quite calculated. He had absorbed his own advice. "Talk to women, talk to women as much as you can," he had written. "This is the best school. This is the way to gain fluency, because you need not care what you say, and had better not be sensible." In any gathering, he knew what was expected of him. However, he did not immediately try to hold the floor nor monopolize the conversation like others. He waited, assessing moods and interests, until a subject was mentioned which offered possibilities. Then he would begin, in his rich, expressive voice, spilling out his thoughts in a stream of delicately wrought images, sometimes profound, sometimes amusing, mingled with facts and anecdotes and personal observations, till he had his listeners spellbound. He was at his best when Bulwer joined him, needing relaxation after a late sitting at the House, the only man who could match his wit, and each would draw fresh brilliance from the other. The formidable hostesses of Mayfair began to compete to have him as a guest and the first stage of his campaign was won. Their influence on public and private opinion, in the making of reputations, was immense and the men of power were being forced to take notice of him.

The most intimate, though platonic, of his friendships was with Caroline Norton. She lived with her mean, coarse husband, who virtually ignored her apart from occasional moments of violence, in a small house in Storey's Gate, off St. James's Park. Dynamic, alluring, she had had a play produced at Covent Garden, wrote dashing Byronic poetry and newspaper articles as well as editing a magazine. In addition, she was strikingly beautiful, with classic features, raven hair and black sloe eyes, a dazzlingly fair complexion and a full figure. Ben worshipped her and became a constant visitor at Storey's Gate. He would sit on the floor in her miniature drawing-room, leaning back against the sofa on which she sat caressing his hair. The drawing-room was so tiny that the sofa seemed to fill it, and the celebrities who called to see her were often crowded shoulder to shoulder. She was one of the queens of fashion and had great influence because of her liaison with the Whig Home Secretary,

Lord Melbourne. Each morning she would stand on her little balcony to wave to him as he rode past on his way to his office in Westminster.

The evenings Ben most looked forward to were when she was joined by her two sisters. The three together created an almost overwhelming impression of charm and beauty. They were the granddaughters of Sheridan, the playwright, and had inherited his frankness of speech as well as his looks. When they said the most outrageous things, which was often, their long eyelashes would lower modestly, their voices demure. The effect was devastating.

Caroline invited Ben to dinner before a party to celebrate her eldest brother's birthday. "He's the only respectable one in the family," she told him. "And that's because he has a liver complaint."

Ben was honored. He was the only one not a member of the family. Rarely at his ease with beauty, he was soon completely at home, as he found they were all firm admirers of his. Looking from Mrs. Norton to her mother, old Mrs. Sheridan, and to her sisters, Mrs. Blackwood and the adorable Georgina, Lady Seymour, he felt unfaithful to Caroline, since he had to confess that she was not the loveliest. He confided in Mrs. Blackwood who sat next to him. "Oh, you can rule me out," she sighed. "I'm nothing. You see, Georgy's the beauty, and Carrie's the wit, and I ought to be the good one. But then I'm not."

He was enchanted with them all. The only unpleasantness was the surly manners of the host, Caroline's husband. He resented the social prominence of the Sheridans and tolerated his wife's sentimental association with Melbourne for the benefits it might bring. He had been drinking too much and, toward the end of the meal, began pressing Ben to help him finish the wine. "Here," he insisted, pouring another glass, "I've never tasted anything so good before." Ben sipped his glass and agreed the wine was very good. He could see that Caroline and the others were embarrassed. "Good?" Norton boasted. "I've got wine twenty times as good in my cellar."

"No doubt," Ben drawled, looking around the table.

"But, my dear fellow, this is quite good enough for such *canaille* as you have here today."

Norton laughed loudly, thinking he had demolished his wife's relations, and was not quite sure why they joined in the laughter. Afterward, Caroline told Ben he had endeared himself to her for ever. With her or one of her lovely sisters on his arm, he went to theaters, dinners, balls, at which he met everyone of importance.

With the sudden noticeable upsurge in his fortunes, the moneylenders lessened their pressure on him, to see what might happen. As a permanent guest, the entertainments cost him nothing and it was not impossible he might make a wealthy marriage. Marriage was not, however, on his mind. The financial failure of his new novel had convinced him that now was the time, if ever, to take a positive step into politics. He had made progress, but knew that many difficulties still remained. While finishing his epic Jewish tale of *Alroy,* he thought more and more about political questions, assessing his chances, the contacts he had made, considering with which of the parties he should ally himself. There was little to choose between the two main parties. The Whigs were strongly in power, though his family had always supported the Tories. Both seemed to have forgotten their original principles and to be run by old men, who wanted no change in the status quo. Reform was in the air and he recognized the need for it, but he could not bring himself to give wholehearted support to the Radicals or the Reform group in the Whigs.

With his increased social life and concentrated periods of work, he saw less and less of Clara Bolton. He did not attend her parties, nor answer her notes. He was often not at home when she called. At first it irritated her, then infuriated her. She felt she had a right to his attention whenever she demanded it. On an evening in early June, she told her husband she was going to ride in the Park. She slipped around the corner and let herself into Ben's apartment. He was in his shirtsleeves, writing at his desk.

Ben had hoped that his affair with Clara would die a

painless death and was not prepared for her anger. "Two weeks without a word—not even a note!" she said accusingly.

"I have been busy, Clara."

"Not too busy to spend time with Mrs. Norton. You sit at her feet and take crumbs from her fingers—like a pet monkey!"

Ben controlled himself. He had promised himself he would not lose his temper. "Clara—let us not quarrel."

At his reasonable tone, her anger was checked. She had not come to argue with him. She had taken pains with her appearance. The close-cut, black riding habit and wide-brimmed hat suited her lithe figure. Her first annoyance had been because he had not commented on it. He had simply seemed surprised when she came in. She laid her riding crop on the table and began to strip off her gloves. "Do you wonder I am hurt? Twice—you have been to see me twice in a month."

Seeing her take off her gloves, Ben came to a decision. The affair must end now. He rose, yet hesitated at saying the words. "I have been trying to finish my new book."

Clara smiled. "You used to say I was your inspiration." When he did not reply on cue, her smile faded. "But that was a year ago."

"As you say," he began. Her eyes searched his face. "What has taken place recently has had little meaning for either of us. You must know that what was between us is over."

Clara had tensed. "I will not be discarded," she warned.

"You may remember," Ben said gently, "it was you who discarded me."

"You had become a laughing stock. It was ruin to be seen with you." Her anger was flaring again. She had come prepared to forgive him, to accept his contrition. In spite of the disappointment he was to her she had meant to give him another chance to prove himself. His books were failures. None of the political fixers she had approached would find a place for him. And he was presuming to drop *her?* She nearly laughed. "Well, I'll lose no

49

sleep over you. You're amusing enough for an hour or two, but what are you? Just a penniless scribbler with a great opinion of himself." She could see that her words had their effect. There was something else which she had intended to keep to herself, to prepare him for. "You applied to become a member of the Athenaeum. It may interest you to know you've been blackballed. They don't want your sort there."

The news shook Ben. His father had been a founder member of the Athenaeum Club. He did not doubt what she had said. Her information was always correct. He stepped back as she picked up her riding crop.

Clara noticed his reaction and sneered. She would like to have struck him, but it was better to leave with dignity. She moved to the front door and paused. "You may be taken up by some fools in society now, but they'll forget you when the novelty wears off. In a year or two, no one will even remember your name." She went out, slamming the door behind her.

Ben was relieved she had gone but she had hurt him deeply. In spite of the veneer of nonchalance, he was very vulnerable. To be turned down by the Athenaeum . . . it made a mockery of the acceptance he had won. Perhaps Clara was right? People might see him as only a kind of jester, a hired buffoon.

He sat again at his desk. It was no use running after her. At least he was glad about that. She was out of his life. Yet perhaps he was a fool to have antagonized her. She could be very dangerous. He tried to put her out of his mind and picked up the page on which he had been working. He read through the words, but was overcome by doubt and self-criticism. He crumpled up the sheet of paper and threw it away.

Behind him, he heard the handle of the door and turned quickly, thinking Clara had come back. But it was Edward Bulwer. He breathed out.

Bulwer looked at him curiously. "Was that Mrs. Bolton I saw leaving? You should be more discreet."

Ben nodded. "She will not come here again."

Bulwer smiled. "I am delighted to hear it. I'd hate to

think of you as just another of the little flies who dangle on her web."

Ben had no wish to keep secrets from Bulwer. It was better, anyway, that he knew, if Clara spread any poison. "I was once."

"Like many a man before you. She is none too sparing with her favors." From hints she could not resist dropping, he had already partly guessed that Clara had taken Ben as a lover. "How did you meet her?"

"Through her husband."

"She is of more value to Dr. Bolton's practice than a hundred signed testimonials." Ben smiled briefly, grateful for his friend's blunt humor. "Still, I mustn't malign her," Bulwer went on. "She has taste—only men of wealth or promise appeal to her."

"Then she made an error of judgment with me," Ben said.

He was clearly depressed. Bulwer realized that whatever had happened had affected Ben badly. Badly enough for the façade to crack. "How so?" he asked gently.

Ben moved to the window. The light outside was changing, matching his somber mood. "It's a cautionary tale," he said. "I thought, not having an influential family, I must have riches to succeed. At nineteen I gambled on the Stock Exchange, with money I did not own. And lost, crippled myself with debts that I have been paying off ever since." It had seemed so easy. When Ben left the solicitor's office, the Spanish colonies in South America had been in revolt. Companies were formed to exploit the new countries, if they became republics, which seemed unlikely. With one of his fellow clerks and a young friend in the City, Ben began to speculate in the shares of mining companies. His instincts told him the companies were unsound but, when the new republics were unexpectedly recognized by the British Government, the value of shares rose rapidly. He and his companions waited and, since the market continued to boom, finally began to buy as many shares as they could. Ironically, it was partly because of pamphlets Ben had been commissioned to write on the untapped resources of the newly formed state

51

of Mexico and the great profits to be made. Shortly after their shares were bought, the market slumped as many of the impressive sounding companies were discovered to exist only on paper. Ben was faced with repaying thousands of pounds and had nothing. "Since then, I have not known a quiet hour," he finished.

"Couldn't your father settle your debts?" Bulwer asked.

"He thinks he has. I couldn't tell him the full amount."

Bulwer could sympathize with financial problems. His own existence was a continual struggle and, already, Rosina's extravagance and improvidence were causing bitter rows between them. He had always rather envied Ben. "Surely your books sell well?"

Ben shook his head ruefully. "Not even enough to pay the interest on what I owe. Every year I have to borrow more, so every year the mountain on my back grows bigger." Over the rooftops across the street the clouds were tinged with fire from the sunset. He thought of the Valley of the Kings. How right he had been to feel dwarfed . . . Dreams were always mocked by reality. "I burn to write great drama, poetry that will live—instead I have to turn out romantic novels to satisfy my creditors! And one bad review brings them beating at the door."

"A problem we share," Bulwer said. When Ben turned, he smiled. "Oh, admittedly my reviews are not as bad as yours . . . yet at the moment I have not six shillings in the bank."

Ben was surprised. He in turn had been envying Bulwer. "But I thought—"

"A pose, my dear Ben. The pose is everything. In society it is not what you are but what you seem to be that matters. Like a travelling salesman."

Only an hour ago, Ben would have agreed with him, but Clara's words had burnt into him. She had made him doubt himself, and only the smallest touch of self doubt was enough to make it impossible for him to go on. "Well, I have precious little to sell."

Bulwer had never seen him so down. He was glad he

had come and of the reason that brought him. It was, perhaps, the only remedy that would answer the case. He laughed lightly, again surprising Ben. "You have forgotten your most valuable asset."

"What is that?"

"Yourself, man! You have shown just enough of yourself in your books for people to want to know more."

Ben tried to respond, but could not. "So I told myself," he said quietly, "I wish I could believe it."

" 'All belief is the result of wishing to believe.' Now who said that?" Bulwer murmured. He was relieved when Ben smiled. "You set out to conquer society. What you have done so far is only hand in your visiting card. Now you must storm the salons."

"But Clara said—"

"Let the Bolton woman go hang!" Bulwer said vehemently. It was time for the medicine. "All she wanted was to rise on your coat tails. I have been sent to bring you to the shrine of Art and Fashion." Ben was intrigued. "To Lady Blessington's. Where the lovely Marguerite holds court with D'Orsay."

Ben's hands were unsteady with excitement as he tied his stock. He had met D'Orsay occasionally since that first evening at Bulwer's and their appreciation of each other had increased. D'Orsay was everything he would like to have been. He had even cut his own ringlets shorter, less like a cavalier, in imitation of him. He could never hope to match the quiet perfection of D'Orsay's style. In any case, his own taste ran more to flamboyance. Yet he had learned from his coolness and detachment, the lurking amusement of the perfect dandy. That was what to strive for.

Like everyone he had heard of the superb mansion in Seamore Place, and its hostess's salon. His ancient admirer, Lady Cork, mentioned it so often that her contempt was very obviously mixed with envy. He had for so long had an ambition to be invited there that the mere expectation drove all thoughts of Clara out of his head.

Lord Blessington, a fabulously rich dilettante, had met a spiritual, delicately lovely Irish girl, married to a drunken boor. He had brought her to England, arranged a divorce and married her. Margaret. A discerning collector, he loved to display his possessions. Margaret was the rarest. Some time later he acquired another, a ravishing boy from an impoverished French family, who had an eye for beauty and would help him in his collecting and, with his lively fancy, devise new ways for the Earl to enjoy himself and spend more money, which was all he asked from life. The young man was Alfred D'Orsay. Soon, Blessington considered him as something more than a son. He already had several children, of whom only the youngest, Harriet, was legitimate. A strange, capricious man, he arranged in his will to leave everything to her, if she was married to D'Orsay.

Thrown together, Margaret and D'Orsay fell deeply in love. She agreed to his marriage to her step-daughter, who was fifteen, provided it was not consummated until the girl was nineteen. Two years later, Blessington died. For a time, Margaret lived with D'Orsay and his virgin wife in Italy, then they moved to London, redecorating and refurnishing the house in Seamore Place like a palace. Advised by her father's family, Harriet reluctantly left D'Orsay, leaving him alone with her stepmother, while her relatives fought the will. The scandal was tremendous. The ranks of respectable society closed. The couple were shunned, asked nowhere, their own invitations icily refused. Sensitive, highly intelligent, with a genuine appreciation of literature and the arts, Lady Blessington defended herself by attacking. She opened her own salon. Curiosity brought some of the bolder spirits. Their report of her quick sympathy and understanding, of the unrivalled elegance of her home and its lavish hospitality, brought others. Most men of any pretension or distinction in the arts began to call and, soon, to be invited there was almost a sign of success. They seldom, if ever, brought their wives. However, other ladies, writers and poets, or those interested in writers and poets, and young, less conventional members of the aristocracy were to be met there. The righteous fumed, but were without power to stop it. Margaret, Lady Blessington, with D'Orsay smiling at her side had scored an almost total triumph.

The house at Seamore Place was even more wonderful than Ben had imagined. Everywhere he looked there were treasures to ravish the eye and stir the heart. Antique statues graced niches and carved, gilded pedestals. Crystal mirrors reflected the light of superb chandeliers. Marie Antoinette's blue Sèvres clock from the Petit Trianon.

Ben was as striking as ever when he arrived with Bulwer, in a plum velvet suit, canary-colored waistcoat strung with gold chains and red rosettes on his shoes. D'Orsay came to welcome them. "At last," he smiled. "I had almost given you up."

"My fault, I'm afraid," Ben explained. "I was delayed by a moment of self-criticism."

D'Orsay was intrigued. "Nothing too serious, I hope?"

Ben shrugged. "Try as I might, I could not get the bow in my cravat to come out evenly."

They laughed. D'Orsay looked to Bulwer for confirmation and he nodded. He bowed to Ben. "It is the only excuse I would have accepted."

As always, Ben had nothing but admiration for the Count's own appearance. The high, slightly rolled collar of his dark blue dress coat was bound to set a new style. Over his silk embroidered waistcoat he wore only one gold chain, but in it was mounted a magnificent turquoise. Beyond his shoulder he could see a throng of people, some ladies but mainly gentlemen, many of them exquisitely dressed disciples of D'Orsay. He heard laughter. Somewhere a small orchestra was playing an air by Rossini. His spirits rose with the lights, gaiety and music. He felt a sense of elation faintly tinged with amazement. This was not a special occasion, only a normal evening. Once admitted here, a guest could come as often as he chose, without invitation. Every night of the week, the doors were open. Was it possible for anyone to be rich enough to entertain on such a scale?

A woman was coming toward them. Her dress of blue

satin overlaid with lace had huge puffed sleeves, ending at the elbows, and was cut off the shoulders and very low to emphasize the fair texture of her skin and the splendid curves of her throat and bosom. Now in her early forties, the famous line of Lady Blessington's chin had rounded without slackening. Her hair was a dark, lustrous brown, dressed close to her head, parted above her forehead and looped back above the ears to form an intricately coiled knot behind. She wore no jewelry to mar the line of her throat, only diamond drop earrings and above her brow, in the parting of her hair, a gold *ferroniere* with a turquoise that matched D'Orsay's.

The men had seen her and bowed. D'Orsay led Ben forward. "Marguerite, may I present Mr. Benjamin Disraeli."

Ben bowed again and kissed Lady Blessington's hand. "I shall never listen to rumor again," he murmured.

"Why is that?"

"It only told me that Lady Blessington was beautiful. Not that she dimmed all other beauties."

Lady Blessington smiled, but her eyes held a challenge. "I warn you, Mr. Disraeli, I am not susceptible to flattery."

"I am glad to hear it," Ben replied, with patent sincerity. "All my life, my most earnest study has been to tell the truth."

She considered him. "Then I see I must not confide any secrets in you."

Ben's left hand rose in a gesture of explanation. "Truth, not tempered with discretion," he said, "I hold to be the height of rudeness."

They laughed. D'Orsay could tell that she liked him. "I wanted to ask you—" he began, but Marguerite stopped him. "No, no, Alfred. Later you may ask anything you wish. For the moment, he is mine." She took Ben's arm and led him through the crowd in the drawing-room to the white and gold library, which served as her boudoir.

She led him to a group of ladies, among whom he was pleased to see Caroline Norton and the popular poetess,

Letty Landon. He bowed and kissed Caroline. "Do you find Mrs. Norton beautiful also?" Lady Blessington asked.

"A Grecian statue brought to life," Ben said. "With all the wisdom of Athene."

"How ungallant to make me jealous already," Lady Blessington protested, teasing.

From the doorway, D'Orsay and Bulwer watched the ladies laugh and pose as Ben was introduced. He was absolutely in his element. Debonair, expansive, he might have existed in such surroundings all his life. "I thought you said he was in despair?" D'Orsay commented quietly.

"I assure you he w-was," Bulwer told him. "Only an hour ago."

D'Orsay watched, approvingly. "Part genius, part dandy—and part actor. An irresistible combination."

"And last, because youngest, Selina Forester," Lady Blessington was saying. "Is she beautiful, too?"

Selina was a slender girl, with a bewitching, elfin face, newly out. Ben knew her family slightly. She bit her lip as he thought of a description for her. "A wood nymph," he decided. "Or rather, a fawn half fearful of the wind across the glade."

Selina was thrilled by the compliment, but did not like to show it. "I'm afraid Mr. Disraeli is too kind," she demurred. "He finds all ladies beautiful."

"I cannot deny it," Ben admitted, smiling. "In this company." It was not mere flattery, although he had become very adept at turning phrases in praise of beauty. The ivory swell of breasts from gorgeous silks and taffetas, laughing eyes, hair gathered into Apollo knots and decorated with flowers, feathers, combs or jewels, and the new, short, wider skirts, raised quite clear of the floor, altogether enough to stir an anchorite.

"Well, say like Paris you had to choose," Caroline Norton proposed, "not between three goddesses, but between the six of us. To which would you give the golden apple?"

The ladies smiled, waiting eagerly for his answer. The

question was not entirely ingenuous, he realized, but he did not intend to fall into a trap. He laid his hand on his heart. "I'd divide it into six equal parts, and present one part to each."

They laughed, insisting that he give a less diplomatic answer. He smiled, shaking his head, and they were disappointed when D'Orsay came to take him away. "If you'll pardon us, Marguerite—ladies," D'Orsay said, holding up his hand. "We must circulate." They watched, as he led Ben back to the drawing-room, then clustered around Caroline Norton to question her.

In the drawing-room Bulwer was talking earnestly to Daniel O'Connell. Broad-shouldered, deep-chested, a reckless fighter for Ireland and the Radical cause, O'Connell stood with his feet apart, his hands clasped beneath his coat-tails. They paused as D'Orsay brought Ben to them. O'Connell had met Ben several times and, although he still did not care for his flamboyant style, had been forced to concede that there was something to him. He could not be dismissed as a mere coxcomb. "Bulwer tells me it's you who's been writing those political articles in the *Times*," he said, then added bluntly, "very perceptive. It only goes to show one should not judge a candy by its wrapping."

"Or a diamond by its roughness?" Ben suggested mildly.

Bulwer held his breath then was startled as O'Connell chuckled. "Well, well, well." He liked a fighter. "I was warned about the quickness of your wit. I see I must be careful."

"I can just hear Ben in the House," Bulwer cut in. "No one could speak more effectively."

O'Connell stopped smiling. "Are you thinking of standing for parliament, Mr. Disraeli?" he asked, surprised.

Ben saw D'Orsay look at him, also surprised, expecting a jest. But it was not the moment to be flippant. "I have thought of little else for years," he answered seriously. "My secret ambition—if you will. Although I realize it will be difficult."

58

"Indeed, it will be," O'Connell agreed. "Which side would you support?"

"As a careerist, I suppose I should back the Government. The Whigs look like being in forever," Ben said, and smiled. "But unfortunately, I dislike their policies. Then again, by upbringing I am a Tory—yet I am sympathetic to the Radicals. It's a pity there isn't one party that combines all three."

O'Connell laughed with the others. "You'd have to look for that in Utopia," he said. Yes, there was definitely more to the Jewboy than he had thought. He was not precisely the type that O'Connell wanted for his party, but Disraeli had a style that impressed the upper crust and that could be useful. He bowed affably. "Well, I'll be interested to watch your progress. I wish you luck in whatever you decide." He moved on.

It was the first sign of even partial acceptance that Ben had had from any of the leading political figures. "You're winning them over!" Bulwer told him elatedly. "I've never seen O'Connell so friendly."

"Still, *mon ami*," D'Orsay warned, "you must not put all your eggs in one basket. Having met the leader of the Radicals, would you like to meet the leader of the Tories?"

"Sir Robert Peel? Is he here?" Ben felt a surge of new excitement.

"Over there, with Maclise the painter."

A tall, superior man was standing with the artist, surveying the other guests with an aloof disdain. With his clear-cut features, strong nose and red-gold hair, he had once been thought commandingly handsome.

"Do you know him?" asked D'Orsay.

"No. But I've seen debates at the House of Commons and heard him speak."

D'Orsay took him over and presented him to Peel. Ben bowed.

"It is an honor, Sir Robert. I was brought up to revere the names of Peel and Canning."

Peel, who was haughty by temperament, inclined his

head a fraction, icily. He surveyed the Hebrew standing deferentially before him and did not at all like what he saw. He took particular exception to the swags of golden links which spanned his canary breast and to the scented glossy ringlets.

Bulwer, at once guessing the impression made, attempted to vindicate him. "Mr. Disraeli is one of our most distinguished younger novelists, Sir Robert."

Peel cleared his throat. "I was recommended to read one of his books. I did not finish it." His voice was harsh, with a noticeable Lancashire accent.

Ben, although wounded, did not show it. D'Orsay went on blandly, as though no insult had been offered. "Mr. Disraeli is also a student of politics. He has heard you speak in the House."

"Indeed?" Peel's interest was faintly aroused. "What was the debate?"

"I'm afraid I cannot remember. I did not stay to the end," Ben answered smoothly.

D'Orsay only just managed to control his mirth. Peel said evenly, "A most interesting evening." He nodded to Bulwer, looked briefly at Disraeli, his face a mask, and moved on.

"Touché," smiled D'Orsay. "Though not the way to win powerful friends."

"There's not an ounce of humanity in him," Maclise said.

"It was a moment you should immortalize on canvas, Maclise: Dignity confronted by Impudence."

"Provided you made it quite clear who was being impudent," Ben added, and they laughed.

D'Orsay turned. "Here come the ladies again. If you take my advice you should concentrate on them for the moment."

"I intend to," Ben assured him. "One thing I have learned is that they have more influence than anyone else on public opinion."

"Mr. Disraeli," said Lady Blessington as the fair group came up, "we have been trying to decide on a name for you."

"We just cannot get used to calling you 'Ben,' " Letty Landon explained.

"Why not?" he asked.

"Benjamin, perhaps. But Ben is the name of a prize-fighter," Caroline protested. They laughed.

"Then what shall we call him?" begged Lady Blessington.

"Something out of his own books?" Caroline suggested. "Vivian?" As the novel had been based on the author himself then that name should serve very well.

"Alroy," was an alternative put forward by Selina, shyly.

As a footman passed with a tray of glasses D'Orsay summoned him with a smile. "Here we are. Champagne for a christening."

He took two glasses, handed one to Ben while the others took glasses from the tray and waited expectantly. "You may all do as you please," D'Orsay announced, "but with his permission, I shall call him 'Dizzy.' "

There was a chorus of delighted agreement. "Yes, of course!"

"Perfect!"

"Dizzy!"

Raising his glass in a toast D'Orsay proposed, "To Dizzy!"

They all laughed and drank the toast while Disraeli smiled, not at all displeased.

chapter three

Disraeli was with his family in their sitting room at Bradenham. As they listened to him, Sarah and his mother were in a considerable state of excitement while his father remained dubious.

"It is the most wonderful thing I have ever heard!" Mrs. Disraeli exclaimed.

"It depends in which sense you use the word 'wonderful'," Isaac murmured.

"But Father, isn't it exciting for Ben to be fighting a by-election at Wycombe, only a few miles from here?" Sarah could scarcely hide her pride.

"It is certainly an improvement on the incessant round of parties, balls and dinners which appear to have been his only occupation for the past year."

Disraeli was stung. "I may have seemed to be a social butterfly, Father, but I have not been wasting my time."

"I am relieved to hear it." A succession of routs, assemblies, levees and soirees was scarcely a serious occupation for an intelligent man. "Dizzy . . . I don't care for your new nickname, Ben. I'm afraid that may be what you've become." —

"All Society is governed by a few influential hostesses. Everyone of any importance in the fashionable world, in literature, in Government, is to be seen at their receptions. Not to be invited there is not to exist!"

"Debatable," Isaac commented.

"A fact of life. At least, now I am known and have many people who may be of use in my career." He had expected his father to be more understanding.

"In politics?"

"Yes. It is with their encouragement that I offer myself as a parliamentary candidate."

"With their encouragement, but no one's actual support," Isaac reminded him.

"First, I must prove myself. I am standing as an independent."

"Ben, let me remind you of the *political* facts of life. There are very few electoral seats in this country and all are controlled, directly controlled, by one or other of the two main parties."

"Then the voters must be given an alternative! I shall present myself as a candidate totally dedicated to their interests—not to any party."

"Exactly!" Mrs. Disraeli agreed warmly.

"Before we are all carried away," said Isaac, "let me remind you that in Wycombe there are at most only thirty or forty men eligible to vote. And most of them are told whom to elect by the landowners and businessmen who employ them."

"But if they listen to my arguments . . ." Disraeli began.

"They will still have no choice. They will still have to stand up in public on polling day and announce their votes, with their employers watching."

"Then I shall appeal to the unattached!"

"Who give their votes, quite simply, to the man who offers the highest bribe. Where are you to find enough money?"

Disraeli paused. "I shall win on merit, not through bribery."

"Admirable, but . . ."

"I offer new blood and new ideas. As a Member of Parliament I will have a chance to speak to the people and show them that Government need not be heavy and dull, clinging to the past, but alive, creative and exciting."

Sarah knew that the excitement came from Ben's enthusiasm, but she felt herself caught up by it. She smiled, her eyes shining. How confident he was . . . She could already see him standing, proud yet humble, before the bar of the House of Commons.

The enthusiasm carried over into the streets of High Wycombe. Isaac D'Israeli was well-liked locally and so his son was certain at least of a polite hearing. The warmth of the response was entirely due to Ben. His unconventional appearance, his charm and good humor delighted the townsfolk, who were used to candidates who presented themselves as serious and sober minded, models of all the virtues. Their election addresses were plodding and unimaginative, while his speeches struck fire and laughter. He was found to have a deft manner of dealing with hecklers, always courteous and unruffled, even when their shouted comments became grossly personal. His approach was direct, talking to people in the streets, in their shops and houses, and support for him grew rapidly.

It was true that his supporters were never sure exactly which policies he would back if he were elected. He refused to adopt any of the old Party slogans, which might have given a hint where his true loyalties lay. Independence, complete independence of thought and action on behalf of the voters, was what he promised. Of course, he was standing against a Whig—but only because Bulwer had not managed to convince the Whig leaders that he should be given the seat unopposed. He had brought with him strong letters of recommendation from the most influential Radicals, O'Connell and Joseph Hume, although they were allied to the Whigs. It was very puzzling. There was no clue in the fact that the Tories were not contesting the seat. Whig landlords had always controlled the few voters at Wycombe, so there was little chance of upsetting their candidate. Yet as the day of the election drew closer and the enthusiasm for the younger Disraeli grew, it began to look as if, for the first time, the result would not be a foregone conclusion.

As she strolled down the High Street of Wycombe on Ben's arm, Mrs. Austen was impressed and felt more than a touch of his own excitement. He wore a suit of bottle-green velvet, his canary waistcoat strung with even more gold chains than usual and lace ruffles spouting from his cuffs. The brim of his tall, black hat had a slight, indefinably rakish curve at the sides. "The height of elegance," sighed the younger ladies. "The sign of a coxcomb," growled their fathers. On his lapel was fixed a huge rosette in pink and white, his chosen campaign colors. Mrs. Austen hugged his arm tighter to feel its hardness against her breast, agitated by the proud beating of her heart, as people applauded him and passers-by stopped to shake his hand. She was proud because she had made his triumph possible. The money to pay for his office and pamphlets and to hire meeting halls had come from her husband. Now she could see with her own eyes how well spent it had been. "But, Ben," she whispered, "everyone is so friendly."

He smiled. "They say there's never been anything like it. They say that, at one stroke, I have captured the seat." His opponent, Colonel Grey, had been rushed down to meet the challenge, but his stammering incompetence had become obvious in the first meeting to which he spoke. The Whig organizers were nervous.

"We'll show the landlords!" a small shopkeeper shouted from the door of his soap and candle shop.

"That we shall!" Ben called back, smiling.

A burly chimney sweep, his face grimed with soot, in a round, flat hat and leather apron, with his brushes slung at his back, came forward to grasp Ben's hand. "You'll shake 'em up in parlymint, sir," he said.

"I shall certainly try, my friend," Ben promised. "And

I'll touch you for luck." He clapped the sweep on his shoulder and the crowd laughed.

A pretty girl appeared at an upstairs window beyond. She leaned out, waving two cloths, one white and one pink. Ben smiled up and blew her a kiss.

That night the crowd was entertained by a band and a torchlight procession led by the hesitant Colonel Grey with a mob paid to cheer him and boost his popularity. When they had passed and people still stood with torches and placards, arguing and debating, their attention was caught by a sudden cheer from Ben's supporters. He had climbed up on to the stone portico over the entrance to the Red Lion Inn, with its larger than lifesize effigy of a red lion. Bareheaded, wearing his green velvet, rings and chains, his rosette on his breast, he stood smiling down at them with his left hand resting on the beast's head. There was amusement and a surge of wonder at his daring. The crowd had been brought together by Grey and Ben was using it to make his own last-minute speech.

They moved forward as he began, impassioned and compelling. The boos and protests of his opponents were lessened by cries of "Let's hear him! Give him a chance!" and cheers from his supporters, "Dizzy! Dizzy!" Soon the area around the portico was thronged with people laughing and applauding, as they gazed up at the flamboyant figure lit by torches held up from below.

"Yes, I am a true Independent!" he harangued them. "Your needs, *your* interests are the only party badge I wear. For Toryism is worn out ... and I cannot condescend to be a Whig!" His audience rocked. "I understand the people because I have sprung from the people!"

"Like Moses from the bullrushes!" a heckler shouted coarsely.

"I ask no better fate, my friend. For he was lifted by the hand of a princess and rose to be ruler of his adopted land!" Some boos were still mingled with the cheers and laughter. They stilled as he raised his hand. "I have no noble blood—nor have I ever taken a penny of public money. If—or rather, when—I am elected, as I am certain to be, I promise not to support the privileges of the few, but to work for the good of the whole nation! My policy can be summed up in one word and that word is England!" The boos of Grey's supporters were completely drowned by loud applause and cheering. "Yes, my friends, when the poll is declared I shall be there." He pointed to the head of the lion. "And my opponent will be there!" He pointed to its hindquarters and the mob roared with laughter.

Outside Wycombe Town Hall on 27 June 1832, Disraeli waited with his opponent, Colonel Grey. The military man was soberly dressed and nervous. Disraeli appeared supremely confident, still wearing his pink and white rosette. From time to time he waved to his boisterous admirers. The returning officer stood near both men, holding up his hand for silence while people in the watching crowd shouted "Disraeli! Dizzy!" and others "Grey!" with cheers and counter-cheers.

Ben could see that most of the women sported his colors. A large group of his supporters were holding up a chair, especially made for him in pink and white wood. He nodded to Sarah and Mrs. Austen who were with them, carrying bouquets of pink and white flowers. He smiled, hiding the nervousness he could not conceal for himself. He had won popular favor but all depended on the few men eligible to vote, who had to do so in public. He had private promises from many of them, some of which had been kept. But he could see the others waiting to declare their votes and that, among them, only two were looking at him.

The raucous voices quieted as the seller of soap and candles came up on to the platform. In spite of the local magnates who stood at the front and stared relentlessly at the electors, flanked by squads of hired bullies, Ben was sure of him and smiled, then noticed with a sense of shock that the man was wearing a yellow rosette, the Whig colors. "I cast my vote . . . for Colonel Grey," the shopkeeper said, looking rigidly ahead. With the cheers of the Whig supporters still ringing, the next elector stepped up. He glanced apologetically at Ben. His vote was announced in so low a voice it could hardly be heard, but it, too, was for Grey.

Ben had begun to realize that it was all over. He was deeply and bitterly disappointed. He stood, smiling and confident to the last, while the cheers of his followers fell away and those of his opponents increased. He shrugged to Sarah and Mrs. Austen when the final totals were declared, twenty to Colonel Grey, twelve to Benjamin Disraeli, Esquire, then thanked his supporters and turned and bowed courteously to Grey who nodded stiffly, seemingly even more embarrassed and nervous at winning.

The special chair could be put away.

Disraeli's friends were more downcast by his defeat than he himself. Its principal effect was to turn him into even more of a dandy than ever. The mask of mockery became more fixed. With Bulwer, who had begun to find Rosina's increasing jealousies unbearable, he spent a few weeks in Bath at the end of the season. Together they were irresistible. The pulses of maidens raced and the eyes of young matrons sparkled whenever the two elegant figures appeared at the routs and assemblies. It was a month of sheer pleasure, of sighs and conquests, then Bulwer returned to his shrewish wife and his duties at Westminster and Dizzy to his writing desk and the demands of his creditors.

The brightest moment in the weeks that followed was the arrival one day of Tita, Byron's former servant. He brought Dizzy a lock of the dead poet's hair. He had left James Clay's services and was destitute in London. Disraeli longed to engage him as his own man, but it was out of the question. Instead, he took him down to Bradenham where Isaac happily welcomed him into his household, delighting in the tales of his past life. The tall, menacing ex-gondolier with his drooping moustaches caused consternation in the streets of Wycombe and in the local public houses, but he was soon found to be friendly and good-natured and was accepted in the district almost as quickly as he became indispensable to Isaac.

Maclise's studio had high, sloping windows facing

north for a steady light. Greek and Roman busts and headless torsos were strategically placed about the chamber. Lady Blessington sat in a gilt chair on a dais. At his easel was Maclise, painting her portrait, relaxed and handsome in an open-necked smock. Disraeli stood near the window, leaning nonchalantly on one hand while D'Orsay sketched him in profile, with a fine line, drawing the calm face with its sensual mouth and heavy lidded eyes and the black cravat high up against the resolute chin. A few other guests, writers and artists all, moved about, admiring their host's work. Some stopped to listen as D'Orsay asked to be reminded of the election results.

"Twenty votes for Grey—only twelve for me." Dizzy told him.

D'Orsay shrugged. "I can't say I'm really surprised. The Government has more than enough money and influence to make sure their own man was elected."

"And Charles Grey *is* the son of the prime Minister," Lady Blessington added.

"That's hardly a recommendation," said Disraeli, puffing on his cheroot.

An older guest, Colonel Webster, happened to be passing and paused as they laughed. He tapped Disraeli's shoulder. "Take care, my good fellow, I lost the most beautiful woman in the world by smoking. She could not bear it."

"Really?" Disraeli murmured.

"Believe me, it has prevented more liaisons than the fear of a duel or divorce."

"You have just proved that it is a very moral habit." The others laughed as he continued to draw smoothly on his cheroot. Webster moved off, shaking his head and smiling.

"Stand still if you want to be immortalized," D'Orsay complained.

"It's all right, I've already sketched him," said Maclise and D'Orsay chuckled. "And his sister. A remarkably intelligent young woman, Sarah. She's started canvassing Wycombe for the next round already."

Lady Blessington swivelled around in her throne-like

chair, surprised. "Are you going to stand again?" she asked.

"Of course. At the general election."

Maclise squeezed a little more flake white on his palette. "The Reform Bill will have come into force by then and there will be two hundred or so more voters. He'll have a better chance."

"Yes, but is all the effort worth it?" D'Orsay wondered, as surprised as Marguerite at Dizzy's persistence.

"This life of pleasure, idleness and occasional literary work is delightful," Dizzy said. "The years slip by in a dream. But every so often my ambition pricks me awake and whispers that I am achieving nothing."

"Remember what you said yourself," Lady Blessington reminded him. "Without noble birth, powerful friends or a fortune behind you what can you hope to achieve?"

"Everything," Dizzy answered simply. "If I did not believe I could reach the top I would not step on the ladder. The election at Wycombe is only the first rung."

Maclise nodded. "Well, each of the two hundred new electors has two votes and it's a two-candidate seat. You are bound to get one of them."

"Yes. The only problem is where am I to find the money?" Dizzy sighed.

"Simple," D'Orsay smiled. "Borrow more from your creditors. If you win it will be their only chance of getting their money back."

The hustings once more found Disraeli magnetic and impassioned in his addresses to the electors. Again he wore his pink and white rosette. As was becoming his custom when he spoke, he had his thumbs in the armholes of his waistcoat, using his expressive hands only occasionally for an eloquent gesture.

"I care for no party! I stand here without party. I plead for the cause of the people and I care not whose policy I denounce!" He had learned from his first adventure. It was not enough to denounce what he was against. He also had to state clearly the principles for which he stood. "You ask what I support? I support the secret ballot—the repeal of the taxes on knowledge—the greatest reduction of taxation consistent with maintaining the real efficiency of the Government and the improvement of the condition of the poor!" There were cheers from his Radical supporters and, to some people's astonishment, warm applause from the local Tories who were again without an official candidate. They had recognized that Disraeli's Radicalism was, in fact, a return to basic Tory doctrines. He went on to a swelling tide of cheers. "The farmer in doubt, our markets without trade and our manufacturers without markets, and pauperism prostrate in our once contented cottages. Englishmen, behold the unparalleled Empire raised by the heroic energies of your fathers! Rouse yourselves in this hour of doubt and danger!"

Disraeli, this time totally confident, stood once more opposite the plainly dressed Colonel Grey and a third contender called Smith. The returning officer was reading out the results over the hubbub of the excited crowd.

"The honorable Robert Smith, 179 votes. Colonel Charles Grey, 140. Benjamin Disraeli, Esquire, 119. I therefore declare the said Robert Smith and the said Colonel Charles Grey elected as Members of Parliament for this constituency."

Once again, the special chair would not be needed.

Disraeli sat with his sister Sarah and father in the sitting-room at Bradenham later that evening. He was sobered and bitter.

"It is not easy to have to accept defeat for the second time."

"That third man took votes from you. It was very close," Sarah said comfortingly.

Disraeli shook his head. "That's little consolation. So many said they supported me, yet I come last. Bottom of the poll."

"Your election expenses must have been very heavy," said Isaac more practically. "Can you pay them?"

Dizzy hesitated. "I have not a penny left in the bank." He moved away to stand with his back to them. It had cost him dearly to confess it. Sarah made a move toward him but Isaac stopped her. "Sarah . . ." He nodded to the door. She understood and went out quietly. Isaac watched his son for a moment. When he spoke, his voice was gentle. "Ben, you are not to worry. I shall take care of it. And I know you must have other debts. I'll settle the most urgent of them."

Dizzy turned. "Father, I can't ask you . . ."

"It will come out of what I hoped to leave you," Isaac told him with a slight smile.

Disraeli was moved by his kindness. "Father—" he began.

"No thanks, now," Isaac commanded. "It's little enough I can do for you. I wish I could do more. Sarah was right, you know. You have done well."

"To come last?"

"But closer than anyone could have expected."

Dizzy was hurt. "You doubt my ability?"

Isaac shook his head. "Never that. I know that with a little more self-discipline you could succeed in anything you put your mind to. But in trying to become a politician, a public figure, you have not taken into account the effect of hidden prejudice."

"I am an Englishman. A member of the Church of England," Dizzy protested.

"But you are still by birth a Jew," his father said softly.

Disraeli drew himself up. "And proud of my race. I have never denied or concealed it."

He had, for a time in his youth, been ashamed of his blood, but this had slowly turned to pride. Had not his race produced Christ and the prophets? Poets, artists, great thinkers? And men of action. Warriors, financiers, advisers to most of the civilized governments of the world?

"Precisely," Isaac agreed. "You do not deny your race. So even to be elected to the House of Commons without anything else, would have been a triumph. You must not take it to heart, because the times and the centuries are against you."

"My only regret," Disraeli said slowly, "is that it may be months or years before there is another by-election."

Isaac was confounded. "You mean to try again?" he breathed.

"And again." Isaac wondered at the absolute determination in his son as he went on. "Yes, Father, I shall fight on. And now not only from ambition, but from pride. I refuse to let myself be beaten!"

Once again in London, Dizzy found that his attempts to enter parliament, though unsuccessful, had earned him notoriety instead of respect. Some of his fashionable friends who had been concerned by his championing of the democratic cause, were relieved by an address he wrote to the voters of Buckinghamshire when he thought briefly of standing for that seat immediately after his defeat at Wycombe. Aimed at a settled, rural community, the tone of the address was much more conservative, expanding his earlier theme of the need to protect the farmers and agricultural workers, and to prevent rash experiments in legislation that would tear apart the fabric of British society. His financial problems forced him to withdraw from the contest. Then his friends were confused when it seemed likely that a by-election would be held in the constituency of Marylebone in London and he published another address, this time meant for a very different, city community. Again, he described himself as a militant Independent, unattached to either of "the aristocratic parties," who "had already fought the battle of the people."

"Just what is he?" they asked. *Town* magazine said, "Someone asked Disraeli, in offering himself for Marylebone, on what he intended to stand. 'On my head,' was the reply." In an attempt to explain himself, he brought out a phamphlet which called for the formation of a National Party, a natural alliance between forward-thinking Tories and sensible Radicals. Never having belonged to either of the main parties, he did not share their passions and prejudices. Far from explaining his independent position, the pamphlet won for him the reputation of cynical political adventurer.

Some of his closer friends tried to convince him that he could not remain independent, with the freedom to approve or criticize as he chose, and still succeed in politics. With the backing of either party, he would by now have been in parliament. His natural frankness was taken for arrogance and his belief in his destiny for overwhelming conceit.

Caroline Norton wished to help him and, at the same time, to win him over to the party she supported. One night she arranged for him to meet her admirer, Lord Melbourne, in a small gathering at her house in Storey's Gate.

Melbourne, a deceptively indolent patrician nearing 60, had become Home Secretary again after the massive Whig victory in the General Election. The unfortunate and understanding husband of Lady Caroline Lamb, driven mad by her passion for Byron, he had seen much in his time and his knowledge of men and of the world was profound. During dinner, the beautiful sisters exerted themselves to create a lighthearted atmosphere and Caroline was relieved when Melbourne responded. He had expected to dislike Disraeli as bumptious and pretentious, but found the young man more gentlemanly than he had imagined, in spite of his rings and perfume, modest in expressing his opinions and even interesting on the subjects of history and his foreign travels. He drew him out on his political contacts and was encouraged to learn that the link with O'Connell was slight. He was not surprised to hear that Peel had been abrupt and distant. "I thought you'd get a nasty kick from Peel," he nodded. "He is not a horse into whose stall you should go unadvisedly, or without speaking to him first."

Afterward, in the tiny drawing-room, there came the after-dinner lull and he tried to help by continuing the conversation about the countries Caroline's protege had visited. Disraeli sat on the floor by Caroline's feet, listening as Melbourne held forth on the difficulties of dealing with the Foreign Ministries of the Eastern Mediterranean and the Ottoman Empire, the unbridgeable differences in attitude between industrialized Europe and the traditionalist Moslem nations. He expected Dizzy to confirm what he said. "Your Lordship," Disraeli murmured, "appears to have derived all your notions of Oriental matters from the Arabian Nights Entertainment."

There was a breathless hush, then Melbourne clapped and rubbed his hands together. "And a devilish good source, too!" he chuckled. As they talked, he was impressed by the soundness of many of Disraeli's views on the questions that vexed government; the Irish Church, the reform of voting procedures, the rights of manual workers. He knew, of course, that Caroline was anxious he should like the boy and do what he could to help him. He found himself more and more willing, especially as it would please her. At last, he leaned forward. "What can I do to advance you?" he asked. "Do you have a genuine desire to go into politics—for, mind you, it's a damned dishonest business." This was the moment Caroline had worked for and she held her breath as Dizzy assured Melbourne that he had no other desire in life. Melbourne nodded. "Well, would you like to be private secretary to one of the Ministers?"

Dizzy hesitated. "I would rather be a Minister."

Melbourne laughed. "No doubt, no doubt. But tell me, what do you really want to be? What is your ultimate aim?"

"To be Prime Minister," Disraeli said simply.

There was no mistaking his total sincerity, yet the mere thought was ridiculous. Melbourne's mouth opened briefly in astonishment. He closed it firmly. He glanced at Caroline, who smiled and bit her lower lip, but Melbourne felt too concerned for the boy to let the statement pass. He did not wish to see a promising life wasted. "No chance of that in our time," he said gruffly. "If you are going into politics and mean to stick to it, I daresay you will do very well, for you have ability and enterprise. And if you are careful how you steer, no doubt you will get into port at last. But you must put all those foolish notions out of your head. They won't do at all. In any case, Stanley will be the next Prime Minister, you will see. Nobody can compete with him. He rises like a young eagle above them all."

The conversation ended. Caroline knew Dizzy had lost his chance of advancement with the Whigs. An aristocratic party, they liked each of their adherents to know his place. A post might have been found for Dizzy, if he were prepared to accept it and to show his gratitude by working for the party's interests. His ambition made that impossible.

Although shaken by Melbourne's seriousness, Disraeli did not resent what he had said and remembered it for the rest of his life. His advice had been roughly the same as his father's, but neither had reckoned with the untapped power he felt inside himself. In any case, his principles would not have allowed him to accept any alliance with the Whigs. It was natural that the old statesman should see his party carrying on in power forever but Dizzy felt that would be a great disaster for the country. It was also natural that Melbourne would see the successor to himself, Russell and Palmerston as the rising young star, Lord Stanley, backed by rank, wealth and ability.

He bowed to Melbourne as the older man said a not unkindly goodnight, kissed Caroline's hand and left. Then Caroline and her two sisters, Helen Blackwood and Lady Seymour, turned to him, half scolding him and half sympathizing. "Oh, Dizzy," Caroline said, "I'm sorry, but it's true. There *are* too many obstacles in your way. Listen to him——he is very experienced."

"But not infallible," Disraeli said quietly.

"What do you mean?" Mrs. Blackwood asked.

"That I intend to prove him wrong as soon as possible."

It was a perfect day. The sun seemed to shine with a more richly golden radiance in the gardens of Seamore Place where a small orchestra, the musicians incongruous among the flowers, played for the *fête champêtre*. Laughing groups had formed. In the arbors were strolling couples. Delicacies were laid out on trestle tables and footmen hovered discreetly with trays of ice-cooled wine.

D'Orsay sauntered along with Bulwer and Disraeli, looking for Lady Blessington to pay their respects. Not a few feminine hearts lifted at the sight of them. On their way across the main lawn they met Sir Robert Peel, who was with Mary Anne Wyndham Lewis and her husband. Bows and greetings were exchanged, although Peel did not at first acknowledge Disraeli. He coughed. "May I compliment you, Mr. Bulwer, on your speech yesterday?"

"I thank you, Sir Robert."

"There was, I believe, only one thing wrong with it."

"M-may I ask what that was?"

"That it did not come from my side of the House." It was a rare pleasantry and drew light, polite laughter. Then Peel affected to notice Disraeli. "Ah, Mr. Disraeli. I have not seen you to congratulate you on your showing at High Wycombe."

"On being defeated?" Dizzy had stiffened.

"We must all admire your . . . perseverance." It was the closest Peel could come to being affable. He nodded and moved off with Wyndham Lewis.

Mary Anne was left for a moment with Disraeli. "You must not feel disheartened," she said gently.

Dizzy smiled. "I assure you I do not. I tell myself I shall be like the old Italian general who was asked why he was always victorious and replied, 'Because I was always beaten when I was younger.'"

Smiling, his fair admirer said, "Now that I *have* read before. I have had copies made of all your speeches. I tell everyone how brilliant they are."

"I am flattered to have such a champion."

"Enough to come and dine with us again?" Mary Anne teased.

"Whenever I am invited." Dizzy had dined once with the Wyndham Lewises and found it surprisingly enjoyable. If he had won the seat, he reflected, he might not have accepted with such alacrity but he needed sympathy and Mary Anne's outrageous flattery would dull, at least

78

for a moment or two, the memory of so many slights and disappointments.

"I am giving a special dejeuner on the twenty-second. I shall expect you there without fail. But mind you do not flirt with all my lady guests in turn. It makes them all jealous. Your duty is to flirt with me, for I am the hostess," she told him.

He bowed. "You understand the art of turning pleasure into duty." The woman was not such a fool as he had first thought. Beneath all the gush and chatter there was a lively mind. Was she after an affair with him, he wondered. Mary Anne laughed delightedly and tilted her head coquettishly like a young girl as she moved on to join her husband and Bulwer. He played a mildly amusing game with her, he the worshipful knight and she the fair, magnanimous lady. He must be careful not to let it develop too far.

As he turned away he caught sight of someone watching him across the lawn. It was a woman standing beside Lady Blessington. She was sensually beautiful, full figured, in her early thirties, with large, dark eyes. Her heart-shaped face was framed in lustrous dark hair coiled about her ears in loops. They gazed at each other for a moment until Lady Blessington asked her a question. She turned to the much older man with them.

D'Orsay came up to Disraeli, who was taut with excitement. "Alfred—there she is! The woman I saw at the opera last night."

"*La belle inconnue.* Where?"

"Over there. Talking to Marguerite and the older man."

"Ah . . . the fair Henrietta."

"Henrietta—is that her name?" Disraeli had only glimpsed her as she left Lady Blessington's box, yet the memory of that almost secret smile had robbed him of sleep.

"Lady Henrietta Sykes. The man is Lord Lyndhurst, famous as former Tory Chancellor and even more as a roué. She must like the type."

"How?"

"Her husband, in spite of ill health, is also known as a womanizer."

"I must meet her!" Dizzy demanded.

"So that's how it is?" D'Orsay surveyed him, smiling.

"I have been unable to think of anything else since I saw her."

"Come, then. But first there is someone else you must meet."

They moved in the general direction of Henrietta. En route was a slim, sharp featured man talking quietly to a woman who had her back to them, her face concealed within her bonnet.

"May I introduce Mr. Benjamin Disraeli?" said D'Orsay. "Sir Francis Sykes."

"How d'ye do?" Sykes nodded, in answer to Disraeli's bow.

The woman with him turned. Disraeli nearly stepped back in shock. It was Clara Bolton.

"Mrs. Bolton I believe you already know," D'Orsay could not resist adding.

"Oh yes, we are old playfellows," Clara smiled.

Sykes chuckled. "Knows everyone, Clara. Disraeli? Now, my wife was talking about you."

"Indeed sir?" Dizzy tried to keep his voice calm, but he knew Clara was aware of the tension in him.

"Read some of your novels. Very taken with them."

"I am honored, sir," he said, his heart pounding.

"Beware, Sir Francis. Dizzy has quite a collection of fair admirers." There was a hint of malice in Clara's voice.

"We are all collectors in our own way," D'Orsay said smoothly.

Sykes chuckled again and the two dandies moved on. D'Orsay was vastly amused. "What a piquant situation!" He wanted to laugh, but restrained himself for Dizzy's sake.

"I'd sooner have met the devil with him than Clara!"

Disraeli muttered. He had to force himself not to look back.

"Reassure yourself. She is too clever to say anything. At least you know Henrietta has heard of you."

"She's gone," said Disraeli, his heart sinking.

D'Orsay shook his head. "Not far, I imagine." He looked about. "Yes, in the rose garden with Marguerite."

Dizzy hurried to present himself to Marguerite and to be presented to her companion. It gave Marguerite a chance to move on and, in a few moments, he found himself alone with Henrietta. She was seated on a stone bench in a bower of white roses and the perfume wrapped itself around them, almost too heady to breathe. Close up, she was even more beautiful. He had found her voice low and musical, but now she was silent. Her eyes were cast down. He was desperate to impress her and began to talk animatedly, gesturing. When her great, dark eyes turned up to him, he was thrown and what he was saying seemed empty and futile. She smiled, that secret, enigmatic smile he remembered, and he sank to the bench beside her.

Watching, D'Orsay felt almost jealous. He had never seen two people reach such a complete understanding in so short a time. It was the absolute *coup de foudre,* for both of them. They sat, without moving, gazing at each other, with no need for words.

The concert had just finished. Henrietta and Clara were seated in the front of the box, with Sykes and Disraeli behind them. All evening Disraeli had watched Henrietta's profile, his eyes devouring her. She was acutely aware of him. As the music crashed to its finale there was loud applause, the four joining in. When they rose, Disraeli was standing behind Henrietta's chair. She dropped her fan and he hastened to pick it up. As he gave it to her, their fingers touched and they held the contact, gazing at each other. Disraeli glanced round to see Clara watching them, smiling maliciously. He stood back as Sykes turned, offering his arm mechanically to Henrietta, who rested her hand lightly on it and went out with him. Still smiling, Clara waited for Disraeli to offer her his arm, but he refused to play her game and merely bowed stiffly. She laughed and walked out.

A fashionable buffet supper was held in Bulwer's drawing-room to celebrate the success of his latest novel. Present, among others, were Rosina, Maclise, Lyndhurst, D'Orsay, Caroline Norton. As they swirled around him, Bulwer prayed that Rosina would not make a scene. In Naples, where they had been together while he worked on his book, she had had to be locked up for a few weeks because of her instability.

Henrietta stood with Sykes, Clara Bolton and Dr. Bolton, a mild-mannered, short-sighted man in his early sixties. Henrietta was watching Disraeli, who was with Bulwer, D'Orsay and Caroline Norton.

"I really must congratulate you, Edward," said Disraeli. *The Last Days of Pompeii* has brought ancient Rome alive, as no other work."

"A masterpiece," D'Orsay confirmed.

"I cried so much reading it," said Caroline, "I was afraid I would not be fit to be seen at your party."

They laughed. Disraeli glanced around to see Henrietta watching him.

"Be an angel, my dear," Clara cooed to Dr. Bolton, "and fetch me another glass of punch." He nodded and went off obediently to the buffet table.

"You have your husband deucedly well trained, Clara," Sykes observed.

"He will do anything to please me."

"Who would not?" he murmured. "Do you use kindness or cruelty?"

Clara smiled. "A delicate mixture of both." The sexual innuendo was unmistakable. They spoke directly to each other, as if unaware of Henrietta.

"Irresistible," Sykes breathed.

As Henrietta saw his right hand close tightly over Clara's, she flushed with shame and anger. She moved away, pretending to look at a full-length portrait of Bulwer above the fireplace. She sensed that someone had come to stand beside her and dreaded the thought of being forced to make polite conversation. Then she saw, to her relief, that it was Disraeli.

"I had not expected you to be here," he said quietly.

She glanced back at her husband and Clara, who were absorbed in each other. All at once she saw no reason why she should deny her own feelings any longer. "I only came because . . . because I knew you would be."

For a glorious moment, Disraeli's head spun. "When may I come to you?"

Henrietta looked again at her husband who was whispering to Clara. The woman was laughing, completely ignoring her own husband who stood holding two glasses of punch patiently. "Soon," she promised. "I shall send you word."

Rosina had come to Bulwer. Her once pretty face was pinched and flushed, her mouth set. "Rosina, please!" he begged.

"It is disgraceful!" she protested in a hissed whisper. "How could you invite them to our home?"

She had clearly been drinking again and her own morbid jealousy made her continually suspect infidelity in everyone she saw, yet Bulwer was troubled. He noticed others looking from Sykes and Clara Bolton to Dizzy and Henrietta. There would soon be a full harvest of scandal.

Henrietta obsessed Disraeli to an extent he had never before believed possible. Until he met her, love had been a pastime, an elaborate game of advances and retreats, seduction and surrender where it did not much matter to him if he won or lost. Now for the first time, he believed the old tales of sorcery. All his schemes and ambitions were forgotten and replaced by one single longing, to be with her, to hear her voice, feel her touch, be part of her.

For once, he had found a woman whose passion matched his own. Well-bred, reared to observe the proprieties, Henrietta in public was a model of virtue, the perfect lady. In private, alone with the man she loved, she

83

was insatiable, demanding and inventive, matching his moods with her own. Her desire for him was total and shameless in its totality, by turns playful and imperious, carnal and sentimental.

Such love, that expected and gave all, was a revelation to Disraeli, a poetic concept brought to life. The only flaw was the need to keep up the social pretenses in front of her husband. Sykes welcomed her association with Disraeli, which made it easier for him to spend time with Clara. Yet he did not intend to appear to the world as a cuckold, nor a complaisant pimp like Dr. Bolton. He made the rules, which were tacitly accepted by all of them, and forced Henrietta and Dizzy to keep to them. She detested Clara Bolton, but had to receive her whenever she called. Dizzy did not have automatic right of entry to their house in Upper Grosvenor Street, nor their country home at Basildon. He had to be invited and to come and leave at the customary hours. A more striking figure than Clara, it was more difficult for Henrietta to visit his room unseen. The restrictions placed on their desire made it even more precious and consuming.

Disraeli began a novel, the story of his love for her. She appeared in it as herself and he as the hero, Armine. A version of that—Ammin—became her pet name for him. She used it in her letters and in their most tender moments when he lay exhausted, like a child on her breast. She was five or six years older than her Ammin and it sometimes amused her to mother him and scold him for not taking care of himself and smoking too much. He responded to each of her fancies, playing the lover or teacher or child with equal relish. The novel became too personal for him to think of publishing it. It was put away, unfinished.

Still hounded by creditors, he reluctantly had to leave her for a few months and take refuge at Bradenham. They lived for each other's letters, but Dizzy found that, free from the immediate spell of her presence, he could begin to think of work again. Pacing the Yew Terrace, he conceived a project for a poem, Homeric in scope, to be called *The Revolutionary Epick*. Daringly, it was to tell the story of the French Revolution and its hero was Napoleon.

The opening sections went well and he soon saw that it was his most important work. When finished, it would run to over thirty thousand lines and stand comparison with the greatest of all ages. Yet, without Henrietta, his inspiration dried up and what had begun as excitement became sheer labor. Then an invitation arrived from her, backed by one from Sykes. They had taken a house at Southend for the spring of 1834. Their little daughter Eva was with them and their house guests were Clara and Dr. Bolton. Dizzy knew how difficult such a situation must be for Henrietta and did not hesitate to accept the invitation to join them.

Once again it was torture for them to be together and yet play the game of hostess and guest, watched sardonically by Clara, to be always in other's company and to separate at night. Dizzy to his small bedroom off the dining-room and Henrietta with her ailing, unfaithful husband. Dr. Bolton seemed to enjoy it all hugely. Yet, just being near Henrietta was a consolation after months of separation and Dizzy was able to work again. Lines flowed from him and the setting of the house helped him to frame his mood to the national tempest he was describing.

He had his writing and the adoration of the little girl who had taken to him at once, but Henrietta became increasingly tense. More and more she loathed Clara and the falsely innocent but sly Dr. Bolton. Whenever she managed to snatch a moment with Ammin, one of them would appear, anxious not to have the easy existence which Sykes paid for destroyed by a possible scene. She began to think of Clara as a serpent and Bolton as a toad. Her own husband she saw as a spiteful tomcat, playing with them all as so many mice.

One day she arranged a picnic and had the servants carry hampers and wine coolers to a sheltered spot near the cliffs. As the party walked there, enjoying the spring sunshine, she was able to draw ahead with Disraeli. They passed the site of the picnic and, temporarily out of view of the others, hurried on through thick clumps of gorse to the top of the headland beyond. They paused in a secluded hollow near the edge of the cliffs, with the sea breaking on the rocks below them. It was the moment for which Henrietta had planned. They were together at last. Dizzy turned to her and took her in his arms and she strained herself against him, as they kissed. She panted and her arms held him more tightly as she felt his instant arousal. One of his hands forced its way between them and cupped her breast. She broke her mouth from his and swayed back slightly, gazing up at him.

"My dearest," he whispered.

"I have so longed to be alone with you . . . Love me . . . please. Please . . ." she begged. She drew her arms from him and, slipping them under his velvet coat, pulled him to her again. But now her hands were only separated by the fine material of his shirt from his slim body.

As he pressed his body again to hers, they heard a rustle in the gorse bushes behind them. They started and stepped apart guiltily. She tugged at the lace fichu at her throat which his hand had displaced. Disraeli swung away, staring sightlessly out to sea, sucking in air to control his breathing. They had scarcely time, before Sykes sauntered around the bushes with Clara Bolton on his arm.

There was a strained pause which Sykes and Clara both rather enjoyed. As Disraeli turned to face them, Sykes smiled blandly. "Doctor Bolton thought he saw you heading this way."

"We . . . came to see the view," Henrietta told him.

"We were afraid you might have strayed," Clara said with a hint of irony.

Disraeli was about to answer her sharply, but a silent plea from Henrietta stopped him.

Sykes glanced toward the horizon. "Exquisite, isn't it?"

"Did it inspire you, Ben?" Clara asked, well aware that he resented her calling him by that name, now used only by his family and oldest friends. "I do hope so. The whole idea of you joining us all on this little holiday is for you to be able to work on your epic."

"I have been more inspired than ever before in my life," he replied levelly.

Clara laughed. "I cannot wait to read it. Can you, Francis?"

"Very keen," Sykes said drily. "Now perhaps we'd better be getting back."

"You needn't worry," Clara said. "My husband is seeing to the picnic arrangements."

"Will he notice you have gone?" Henrietta asked sweetly.

Clara smiled. "Eventually, Lady Sykes. Eventually."

The more open tension between them which had begun at Southend continued when they all met again in London. Everything they said when they were together seemed to have a double edge.

The intervening weeks had seen the publication of the first book of *The Revolutionary Epick*, which Dizzy's admirers praised extravagantly and which the critics and public found almost unreadable in places. His inspiration was said to be labored, to proceed by fits and starts, a criticism which Clara could not resist alluding to when they all met for tea in the drawing-room of the Sykes' house in Upper Grosvenor Street. "But then, you had so many distractions," she added consolingly.

"Another cup, Mrs. Bolton?" Henrietta asked.

"No thank you, Lady Sykes. That was delightful. But then, you are always so welcoming."

"I am always happy to welcome my husband's friends," Henrietta said, pointedly.

Sykes chuckled. "And I yours, my dear." More like a sleek, malicious tomcat than ever, he noticed Disraeli shift uncomfortably in his chair. He did not dislike Disraeli, even found him good company when the women were not around. He glanced at his wife, so poised and well-mannered, only the faintest flush on her fine-boned cheeks betraying the control she had to keep over herself.

That new afternoon gown with its tight waist suited her rounded figure. Then at Clara, more flashily dressed, with her vulgar style and insolent smile. She couldn't hold a candle to Henrietta, really. "All one big happy family, eh?" he muttered.

"I particularly liked our holiday together at Southend," said Clara. "It reminded me of the happy days I spent visiting your dear parents at Bradenham, Ben."

"Yes," Sykes agreed, "Henrietta and I must call on them next time we're in Buckinghamshire."

Disraeli dreaded the thought of this war of poisoned darts being carried to Bradenham. There was a momentary pause, then Clara sighed, "I'm so sorry to break up our little tea party, but I'm afraid I have to go." She rose. Disraeli and Sykes rose with her. "Must you, Clara?" Sykes asked.

"I must put in an appearance at home. Thank you, dear Lady Sykes. Goodbye . . . Ben."

"I'll see you to your carriage," Sykes said. He took her arm as they left.

As soon as the door was shut, Disraeli turned to Henrietta, distraught and passionate. "How long is this to go on?" he pleaded. "It is torment to me to see you alone only for moments."

"Oh, my dear," Henrietta breathed.

"I cannot work for thinking of you, Henrietta! To have you with me . . ."

"It is even worse for me, for the hours without you have no meaning. I have nothing else to fill my days but to think of you."

Disraeli drew her to him and they kissed. But she pushed him nervously away and glanced at the door. "Francis will be back any moment," she said, in anguish. When Disraeli reluctantly released her, she went on, "Yes, it's worse for me. My marriage is a sham."

"Leave him!" Disraeli commanded.

"If only I could! He plays cat and mouse with me. And all the time I know he has been with her! That woman . . ."

"My darling—my own heart's darling," he muttered. He could bear his own pain more easily than the sight of hers.

"Only say you love me," she begged.

"Can you doubt it? I would give my life, my future—all friends, duty, my hope of heaven itself for you!"

As he moved again to take her in his arms, the door opened. Disraeli stopped short. Sykes was watching them both from the door. "Well," he said, "I think our little comedy has gone on long enough, don't you?"

Disraeli turned to face him. At last, it was in the open. He felt surprisingly calm. "I would sooner call it a tragedy—if it did not contain so many elements of farce."

"Quite so."

Henrietta drew closer to Disraeli as if to seek protection as Sykes came forward. But she was also no longer afraid. Like Disraeli, her voice was level. "I can no longer hide my feelings—which you have encouraged—because, having me still under your roof allowed you to carry on your affair with Mrs. Bolton without open scandal."

"Quite so," her husband repeated coldly. "An ideal arrangement for us all. However, for me too it has become an intolerable situation, which I intend to resolve."

Disraeli suddenly had the wildest hope. "Divorce? You would give Henrietta a divorce?"

Sykes shook his head. "There is no question of divorce. I shall simply go abroad for a year or so, and take Clara with me. How you will then avoid giving rise to scandal is your own concern." He turned back to the door, paused and glanced at them. "I trust you will be discreet. However, knowing Henrietta's willful disposition, I very much doubt it." He bowed slightly, coldly, and left.

Disraeli gazed at Henrietta, still unable to accept the suddenness with which it had happened.

"Free . . ." Henrietta whispered. Her mind swirled in a turmoil of emotion, elation, an almost irresistible desire to shout aloud. And yet it was tinged with uncertainty, when she saw Ammin looking at her so tensely.

"He is right," Disraeli said. "The two of us alone will be targets for gossip, society will censure us." He hesitated. "Are you prepared to risk that for me?"

Henrietta felt at that instant she could die for him. "What is the world to me without you?" she told him simply. "Only love me, and I will belong to you completely—if that is what you want."

Disraeli swept her into his arms.

chapter four

A new life began for Disraeli and Henrietta. With Sir Francis Sykes travelling abroad, they became inseparable. The most censorious members of society considered their behavior shameless but, in the freer world of their friends, they were soon acknowledged as a couple. For most of the time Dizzy lived at Upper Grosvenor Street, as master of the house. Henrietta would accept nothing else. For so long she had wanted him to belong to her, and herself to him, that she could not now bear to be without him even for an hour. They went everywhere together, the theater, the opera, to balls and soirées, oblivious of the effect their liaison had on others, in a perpetual honeymoon.

It was a year of political unrest. The old maxim that the most dangerous time for a government is not when its majority is small but when it is overwhelmingly large was seen to be true. With no need to keep a united front to stay in power, the Whig party began to split apart, leading to a series of sensational resignations, including that of the "young eagle" Stanley, who disapproved of the influence of the party's radicals.

Near the end of 1834, King William summarily dismissed the Whig government and Sir Robert Peel found himself Prime Minister at the head of a Tory minority. With no hope of staying in power unless he had a mandate from the country, Peel called another general election. He was given just enough encouragement to try to stay in office. And once again, Disraeli stood as an independent Radical at Wycombe. Again he had no backing from the official Radicals and the Tories tacitly supported him and again, in spite of brilliant speeches, local enthusiasm and promises, the heavy bribes of the Whig agents were more convincing. He came third.

This was his only separation of any length from Henrietta and she did not know how she survived it. She resented anything and anyone taking his attention from her.

When he returned from High Wycombe, after the ecstasy of their reunion she could sense that he was unsettled. Early in the new year, she woke one afternoon in her blue and gold bedroom and saw him seated at the table by the window, writing. He had pulled on a pair of trousers and, in his open white shirt with flowing sleeves and a fall of lace at the cuffs, she thought he looked extraordinarily like his hero, Byron.

She shifted languorously, comfortably naked, as she watched him. How handsome he looked as his head lifted momentarily in thought . . . "Shall we go to Lady Blessington's tonight?" she asked.

"H'm? . . . Why not?" He went on writing, not even taking his quill from the paper.

"No," Henrietta decided. "I think it would be safer to go to the opera." He carried on writing. "I said, I think it would be safer to go to the opera."

He glanced at her. "Why?"

"Because you will only flirt with all the other ladies— as you always do."

He smiled. "I flirt because it would be an insult to the

beauty of your sex, if I did not. But all the time I think—not one of them can be compared to you."

Henrietta snatched up a book of Keats's poems that was lying on the bed and threw it at him. "You beast!" she laughed.

He caught it. "Now, do be quiet, Henrietta, and let me get on. I must finish my poem."

"Why?"

"Because if I do not, what are we to live on?" The first book of the *Epick* had brought in practically nothing, but any fears Disraeli may have had of being despised as a kept man were eased when Sara Austen's patient husband finally, after much persuasion, agreed to lend him another twelve hundred pounds for a year, at low interest. The money lasted a much shorter time than Dizzy had expected. Now the year was up and Austen was becoming impatient. Henrietta had no income of her own. She could expect no help from her parents or family, who cut her because of her relationship with Disraeli, while the allowance that Sykes made her was barely enough to cover the unkeep of her two houses. They had to depend on whatever credit could still be raised by his prospects and her social position.

"Pooh . . ." she shrugged. "Write it some other time."

"I cannot, my love. For over a year, I have finished nothing, published nothing. Let me concentrate."

As he began to turn away, she protested. "You should concentrate on me."

He paused. "I do. There has scarcely been a day we have not spent every moment together."

"That's not true," she pouted. "You're always going down to see your family—or talking boring politics with people. Only two months ago you spent weeks away from me." She was hurt that he had not come at once to kiss her when he realized she was awake. Once he would have done it.

"My darling," he said with a smile. "I was fighting an election. I have to take every chance that comes."

"I can't think why you bother. You never win." She

saw at once that she had wounded him. "Oh, my dearest, I didn't mean it," she said quickly. "It's only that it's so hurtful that people don't see your genius like I do. Come —come here. Show me you forgive me." She raised her arms to him and the sheet slithered from the tips of her splendid breasts to lie crumpled over her waist.

He laid down his pen and rose. Crossing to the bed, he sat on the side of it and kissed her gently. When her arms began to close around him, he eased back. She frowned again. "I don't see why you're so determined to get into Parliament. Just to be with me should be enough."

"Of course, it is," he assured her. She tried to hold him again and he caught her wrists, smiling. "Henrietta, we must talk seriously. I have to find a profitable way to spend my days."

"What do you mean?"

"Our debts—you know more ways to spend money than anyone I have ever known." She laughed, but he still tried to make her understand. "We cannot go out by daylight. We are besieged by creditors again. We have to stay at home with the door locked." Even a visit to the opera would be hazardous. Any one of the loungers outside the portico of Covent Garden could be a process server waiting for him with a writ.

"How perfect," Henrietta murmured. "It gives us more time to be alone together." This time her hands caught his shoulders and when she drew him down he could not resist. She kissed him, open-mouthed, her body moving beneath him. When their lips parted, she did not let him go. He lowered his head to cradle his cheek on her breasts. With one hand, she played with his black curls.

"Dearest, dearest Ammin . . ." she breathed. Her fingers closed around his head, then slipped down to stroke his face, tracing the contours of his cheeks, his mouth.

"Life would be ideal, if only—if only I had some hope of success."

"Your next book—" she began.

"Oh, not just books! I don't want only to write about

94

great events—I want to act them, to bring them into being." He pushed himself up to sit, still leaning over her. "Henrietta, don't you see? My love for you has rekindled, redoubled all my ambitions. There are days when I feel I could guide the destinies of nations—move thrones and continents . . ."

The warm urgency of his voice sent a thrill through her that made her feel . . . made her feel . . . "All for me?" He was gazing down at her, his eyes dark and tender. "And that is all that prevents our life together from being totally happy?" she whispered. "Then I must wave my wand and do something about it."

"What do you mean," he asked, puzzled.

She kissed him and smiled. "Wait and see." She squirmed softly, drawing the sheet aside, and her body was suddenly revealed, nude and golden.

"No," he protested. "Henrietta, what did—?"

His words were cut off as she smiled and her back arched, her arms rising to catch him around the neck. She hung on him with her whole weight and he toppled over to lie with his face on the pillow beside her. He was laughing, still trying to question her, but her kisses silenced him.

One afternoon, a few days later, Disraeli returned from a visit to Edward Bulwer. It had left him thoughtful. Peel had been forced to accept the impossibility of carrying on in office and once more there was a Whig government under Melbourne with a strong majority. The easygoing, sensible Melbourne had proved surprisingly capable during his previous short months as Prime Minister and was obviously set for a long term of power, especially if he could bridge the gap that had opened between his party and the Radicals. Bulwer's news was that Melbourne had done it and there was now a firm alliance between him and O'Connell who, until recently, had been denounced by the Whigs as a traitor.

Bulwer's advice was for Disraeli to recommend himself again to Melbourne through Caroline Norton. At his lowest ebb of fortune, Disraeli was tempted, but it would mean going back on the most consistent point in his political creed, total opposition to the Whigs, the party of privilege. He could not do it. Also, a surprising thing had happened. Always a Tory at heart, he had put himself forward as a reformer because he disliked the weakness, the disorganization and the reactionary morass into which the Tory party had fallen. Now Sir Robert Peel had issued a manifesto, the Tamworth manifesto, committing his party to a policy of controlled social and industrial reform. In parts it uncannily echoed Disraeli's own stated beliefs although without the practical proposals he had made, and showed that the Tories were capable of responding to the spirit of the times and of returning to their own basic principles. There was no longer any reason for him to carry on his stand as an independent.

When he entered the drawing-room in Upper Grosvenor Street, he was disconcerted for a moment to find a man with Henrietta. He was tall, strongly built and distinguished. The first impression was one of youth, but Disraeli quickly realized that he was much older than he looked. His face was hawk-like and could have been severe, except for the laughter lines at the corners of the mouth and eyes, which showed that, again, he was not what he seemed. He turned as Disraeli paused in the doorway.

"And here is the very man," Henrietta said. "Lord Lyndhurst, you remember my Dizzy?"

"But of course." He smiled as Disraeli bowed. "At the moment, the man in London I most envy."

Henrietta inclined her head at the compliment. Disraeli had also remembered his brief glimpse of Lyndhurst with Henrietta and Lady Blessington a year before. He could see at once why the former Tory Lord Chancellor was so attractive to women, but he had not been prepared for the shrewdness of his eyes nor the directness of his approach.

"Well, then," Lyndhurst said, considering him. "Henrietta has been telling me about your political ambitions. We have all seen your determination. How many times have you stood for parliament now?"

Disraeli closed the door and came forward. "Three times for Wycombe. And once for Marylebone, but I withdrew from that election."

"And you stood as a Radical."

"As an Independent."

Lyndhurst shrugged. "Yet in the first of those contests, you were backed by O'Connell, and Bulwer asked the Whigs to let you in unopposed—both Radicals. Whatever you are, you are certainly not a Tory."

"No, I am not," Disraeli admitted. He could see Henrietta bite her lip, worried, but he had realized it was dangerous to be anything less than absolutely candid with this man. "If by the Tories you mean stagnant reactionaries. So like the Whigs you can scarcely tell the difference between them."

"Well, you see my difficulty," Lyndhurst sighed, with a glance to Henrietta. "If I tell Wellington and Peel and all the others at the Carlton Club that you now wish us to help you, they will say, He must have a very flexible political conscience."

"I have never changed my basic beliefs nor claimed to be what I am not," Disraeli said stiffly.

Lyndhurst nodded. "Very commendable. But what are you?"

Disraeli hesitated. It was the moment to break off the conversation, or to commit himself forever. "I am a conservative," he said slowly. "A conservative to preserve what is good in the constitution, a radical only to change what is wrong. If I have to choose a party—as I realize I must—yours would be the only one I could join."

Henrietta held her breath as Lyndhurst glanced at her again and back to Dizzy. "I think I like that," he chuckled.

"I would call myself, if anything, a Progressive Conservative," Disraeli went on.

"Then you're not very different from Peel," Lyndhurst said, smiling. He paused. "I think we could use you. We need new, younger spirits to counter those new young Whigs who call themselves Liberals. I'll do what I can."

Henrietta gasped with relief when she saw him hold out his hand and Dizzy clasped it. "I don't know how to thank you, Lord Lyndhurst," she said.

"Let's see what happens. First, we must get him elected to the Carlton Club."

"Will that be possible?" she asked.

Dizzy heard the uncertainty in her voice. It hurt him to realize she meant, will they accept a Jew? He had his own bitter memory of being blackballed at the Athenaeum. He looked at Lyndhurst. "You said yourself they would doubt my sincerity."

Lyndhurst's smile was shrewd. "Not if I take you on as my unofficial secretary—to work up speeches, write letters for me and so on. That's if you'd care for the job."

"I—I'd be honored," Disraeli told him, overcome.

Lyndhurst smiled more fully. He had come only in response to Henrietta's appeal, but he was a swift judge of character and he saw distinct possibilities in this young man, in spite of his bizarre appearance. He would certainly be useful, and might turn into an amusing companion. "That's agreed, then," he said. "Then we must find you a seat in Parliament. Not for Wycombe, I think. There's a by-election coming up at Taunton. We need a good man to fight that against Labouchere. We'll put you up as . . . 'Conservative' candidate."

Dizzy could not speak. It was so swift, so simple when one had the power of one of the great parties.

Henrietta was elated. It had gone even better than she had dared to hope. "Do you think Dizzy will get in?" she asked, excitedly.

"With his own brilliance and official Party backing?" Lyndhurst smiled. "It's the best chance he's had yet."

For the first time, Disraeli appeared on the hustings wearing a blue rosette. He knew it would be a hard fight, for Henry Labouchere, the Whig candidate, had already represented Taunton, was popular and politically experienced. And was ready to make capital out of Disraeli's apparent conversion to Toryism.

Disraeli, however, had expected this and had his arguments ready. In his first major speech, he proved his consistency to his supporters and drew cheers with his insistence that he would still work for the union of conservatives and independent Reformers. With two major speeches every day, in the midst of nine or ten hours canvassing, he won over doubters and worked up his supporters from interest to outright enthusiasm. Bareheaded, his raven-black ringlets falling over his right temple, wearing his bottle-green velvet, his chains and rings, he was the most unlikely Tory candidate anyone could imagine, but the response to him was even greater than it had been at Wycombe.

At the hustings on the first day of the poll, he gained the show of hands, which no blue candidate had ever done before. But on the second day, when the poll was closed, he stood on the platform to hear the Returning Officer declare Labouchere the winner, by 452 votes to 282. He had changed his rosette but not his fortune.

The disappointment of yet another defeat, when he had seemed so close to victory, was sweetened by a reception and dinner which the local Conservatives gave in his honor immediately after. Win or lose, they were delighted with their candidate. The speech he made that night, declaring his belief in democracy, in the constitutional monarchy and the possibility of true prosperity under a Conservative administration, was widely reported in the national newspapers. He flayed the Whigs for clinging on to power by making concessions to O'Connell whom they considered a traitor, by extending the duration of each Parliament and by denying the liberty of the individual. It won him many new admirers and ensured his election to the Carlton, founded by the Duke of Wellington as the social hub of the Tory party.

A few days later, Disraeli and his family met in the sitting-room at Bradenham. He needed all his strength of will to control his anger. Mrs. D'Israeli looked from him to her husband, whom she could see was troubled and puzzled. Her two younger sons, Ralph and James, were pale, silent, as was Sarah, who stood holding a folded copy of the *Times*.

"No, Mother," Disraeli said, "even with official support at last, I knew there was little real chance of winning. It's not being beaten again that makes me angry."

"What is it, this thing in the paper?" Isaac demanded. "My eyes—I cannot make out newsprint any more. But Sarah will not read it to me." When no one answered, he peered at her. "Well?"

"It is a report of a speech, Father," she told him reluctantly, "which O'Connell made in Dublin."

"Daniel O'Connell? About Ben's defeat?"

"More personal," Disraeli said. "Much more." A version of his remarks at Taunton had been reported to O'Connell who had not paused to check that Disraeli was not giving his own opinions, only quoting what had been said about the Irish demagogue by his temporary Whig allies. Furious, O'Connell had strode on to the platform at a packed political meeting and electrified his listeners with a vicious, intemperate savaging of Disraeli's background, character and reputation, accusing him of gross ingratitude. Disraeli took the paper from Sarah. "By joining the Conservatives, he says, I have proved I have all the necessary qualities of selfishness, depravity and lack of principle. He calls me a blackguard, a ruffian, a reptile." He opened the paper and read aloud. " 'He is a liar both in action and words. Shall such a vile creature be tolerated in England? The British Empire is degraded by tolerating a miscreant of his abominable description ... His name shows that he is of Jewish origin. I do not use it as a term of reproach; there are many most respectable Jews. But there are, as in every other people, some of the lowest and most disgusting grade of moral turpitude. And of those I look upon Mr. Disraeli as the worst. He has just the qualities of the impenitent thief on the Cross, and I verily believe, if Mr. Disraeli's family tree were to be examined and his genealogy traced, he would be discovered to be the heir at law of the exalted individual to whom I allude. I forgive him now and, as the lineal descent of the blasphemous robber, I leave the gentleman to the enjoyment of his infamous distinction and family honors.' " He paused and threw the paper into the fireplace. "I apologize for reading out this filth." The speech had been even more widely reported than Disraeli's. It had been reprinted in almost every newspaper throughout the country, causing a sensation.

Isaac was horrified. "Did his audience shout him down?"

"The speech was greeted with laughter and applause," Sarah told him, bitterly.

Isaac nodded. Although his son was a Christian, the very name "Jew" was considered enough with which to insult him. "This is what I was afraid of," he muttered. It was inevitable and absurd, really, to be wounded. Yet the pain was there. The pain, for himself and his son, was there.

"It shall not go unanswered!" Disraeli promised.

His father shook his head. "There is no answer that will not make it worse." His head was bowed and the color had drained from his face. He crossed the room slowly and went out into his study.

"Follow him, Ben," Sarah urged.

"No." He had straightened as he watched his father leave and the line of his mouth had grown hard. "He would only tell me to turn the other cheek. It is too late for that."

His mother was alarmed. "What are you going to do?"

Disraeli saw his brothers and sister watching him intently. "The only thing I can," he said. "Send him a public challenge to prove his words."

Henrietta had never been so agitated. She drew him into the drawing-room, out of the servants' hearing. "A duel? What are you thinking of?"

Disraeli took her hands and, folding them in his, kissed them. "It is the only way I can answer this insult to myself and my family. He must give me satisfaction."

101

She pulled her hands from his. "You might be killed!" she gasped.

"It won't come to that," Disraeli assured her, touched by her concern. "O'Connell is hiding behind a vow he has taken never to fight another duel and his son has apologized for him indirectly. I have won already."

What Henrietta was feeling was not simple concern, but alarm for her own position. "And saved your precious name," she said scornfully. "What about mine?"

"Henrietta—"

When he moved to take her in his arms, she swung away from him. "You never think of me!" she accused. "As if the shame of being cut by most of society were not enough, my own family has disowned me because of you. And now you make yourself more notorious!"

"What should I have done?" he protested, stung. "Accepted his insults? I would have lost my pride and all hope in the future."

"You lose more of your pride with every election," she said cuttingly.

"One day I shall win," he replied, trying to remain calm.

She stared at him. "Why is it so important? Am I not enough . . . ? I'll never understand you."

He smiled. "Lyndhurst will understand." The older, pleasure-loving peer had become his closest confidant, although there was always a faint suggestion of teacher and pupil. The delicate work which Disraeli did for him, drafting speeches and official letters and carrying even more vital, verbal messages to members of both Houses of Parliament, was repaid by the priceless, political education given to him by Lyndhurst. Through him, Disraeli learned how Parliament actually worked and heard all the backstairs gossip and secrets of government for the past thirty years. He met everyone of consequence in his chosen party, some of whom became friendly, although most were surprised by the older statesman selecting him as his aide. At a dinner at Lyndhurst's he met some of the younger Tories, among whom was the wealthy, striking

William Ewart Gladstone. The two men had little in common and took scant notice of each other.

"Lyndhurst?" Henrietta laughed. "He only supported you because I asked him to. He will do anything for me."

There was a tone in her voice which disturbed Disraeli. "Why?" he asked.

"Do you think you're the only man who ever loved me?" Henrietta snapped.

He was shaken by what she implied. "You were his mistress?" Her face became haughty and she looked away. Her silence answered him. "You used his affection for you," he whispered, "to buy me favors . . . ?"

She looked back, realizing she had said too much. He was hurt and shocked, beginning to be angry. When she spoke, her voice was more gentle. "Of course not, Ammin. You mustn't believe that."

"Then why did you say it?"

"I was upset," she explained. "Ever since I saw that open letter of yours in the papers, I've been unable to sleep—for fear you would be hurt. I couldn't bear it, if anything happened to you."

The appeal in her eyes and the note of contrition soothed him, yet he still had doubts. "And Lyndhurst?" he insisted.

"You mustn't take it so seriously," she smiled. "I only said that. He told me he admires you, sincerely admires you."

"But he has claims on you."

She laughed. "No . . . only of friendship. Oh, I flirted with him once—but that's all in the past. Don't look so stern—you had friends, too, before we met . . . It's not fair when I've been so worried about you."

She had pricked his conscience and he felt in the wrong. Somehow, he had misunderstood. "I'm sorry, Henrietta," he began.

"No, I'm sorry," she said contritely, moving on him. "You know I live for you. Don't ever doubt me."

Her arms were half raised as though asking for forgiveness. He stepped forward and drew her to him. "My darling . . . How could I?" he smiled.

She sighed in relief and clung to him as he kissed her. She pulled him down to sit with her on the sofa, moving against him. "How I've missed you," she breathed, her lips touching his mouth, his eyes, in little warm kisses. "Every minute, I've longed for you. And I promise—I promise to be better. Not to resent your work and having to be away from me. Not to be jealous."

He kissed her again. "You need never be. We are one. You are the beating of my heart."

She murmured and her hands pressed on the back of his neck, urging his body to follow hers as she leaned back. "My soul . . ." she whispered, loving the pressure of his lean body as he lay partly over her. He kissed under her ear and down to the tiny crease he adored, where her neck joined her smooth shoulder. She gasped and her throat arched at the caress she remembered so well, then her body became more yielding, welcoming him.

There was a soft knock at the door.

They did not hear it, until it was repeated. Disraeli straightened, and helped Henrietta to sit up. Her breathing was unsteady and she was flushed, ruffled by the interruption. "Yes?" she called, sharply.

The door opened and the handsome, well-built Daniel Maclise came in. He stopped, seeing them both together.

"Danny!" Disraeli said, surprised. He rose.

Maclise bowed. "Am I intruding? The girl sent me straight up."

"It's quite all right, Danny," Henrietta told him, smiling. "I didn't know we had a sitting today."

"We don't," he told her. He was painting Henrietta's portrait in her robes of state. "It's not you I'm calling on, really. I was hoping to see himself."

"Does someone want to commission my portrait?" Disraeli asked.

Maclise chuckled. "O'Connell might want a memorial stone." Even Henrietta laughed. "No, I was looking for you. D'Orsay is desperate to see you."

"What about?"

"He wouldn't tell me," Maclise shrugged. "But it's urgent—important news."

"What could it be?" Disraeli wondered, intrigued.

When Disraeli was shown into Lady Blessington's drawing-room, she jumped up and came forward. She seemed unusually excited to see him. "Here you are at last!" she exclaimed.

Dizzy bowed and kissed her hand. He saw that D'Orsay had also risen, only his studied, dandy's sangfroid keeping his own excitement in check. Dizzy bowed to him. "Maclise gave me your message."

"Maclise?" D'Orsay repeated. "Oh, yes. I asked him to pass it on, since he'd be seeing Henrietta."

"We weren't sure if you were even back in town," Lady Blessington said.

Disraeli spread his arms at the sides. "Here I am before you," he smiled, "burning with curiosity."

Lady Blessington took his hand and led him to the divan. "It's about that horrid challenge of yours in the newspapers."

"For which I was proud to make all the arrangements," D'Orsay interrupted.

"Which—thank Heavens—were not needed," Lady Blessington said. She sat, with Disraeli beside her. "Yet I am told you have refused to accept the apology from O'Connell's son. Why?"

"It was too serious a matter, both for my family and myself, to be settled so simply."

"And O'Connell's side had received so much publicity," D'Orsay added.

"Exactly," Disraeli agreed. "If I had accepted his apology, it would have looked like a retreat. I have told him that I shall keep on insulting his father, until one or the other gives me satisfaction."

"But that will force him to fight a duel with you."

Disraeli paused. "I do not think so. He has already fought one duel on his father's behalf and is not ready to risk another. My object is to show that, while he is ready

105

to apologize for his father's conduct, he is not prepared to fight for him."

D'Orsay laughed quietly. Margaret Blessington shook her head. She could not approve of men arranging to murder each other in public, although she had to admit that Disraeli's action had been both daring and romantic and that he had provocation. "Anyway," she said, "it has had the most extraordinary effect."

"The Duke of Wellington—," D'Orsay began.

"Alfred! Please, don't keep interrupting," she complained. He bowed and sat again in his chair, then leaned his head on one hand in an attitude of profound attention. She shook her head at him and turned back to Disraeli. "The Duke has been greatly impressed by your courage. And has written to Peel to say they must do something for you."

The announcement, now it had come, had sounded so casual that Disraeli had to repeat it to himself before he really took it in. He slowly sat upright. Wellington, The Iron Duke, the victor of Waterloo, was the most revered hero and statesman in England. The real leader of the Conservative party, whoever was nominally at the helm. He had met the Duke only in passing, though for years he had tried to bring himself to his notice. Having won his favor, everything was possible. He could feel excitement bubbling up inside himself. It increased when Lady Blessington added, "Peel wants you to dine with him."

He realized that he was smiling inanely. He wanted to hug them both and looked from Marguerite to D'Orsay, who nodded. "And Lyndhurst says you have squabashed the O'Connells," he drawled. ". . . whatever that means."

They laughed. Lady Blessington laid her hand over his. "Everyone speaks of you with new respect. There's no doubting your sincerity now."

"The sword *is,* sometimes, mightier than the pen, you see," D'Orsay said.

Dizzy laughed and looked from one to the other as they went on. "All over town, people speak of nothing

106

but your stand against the Radicals. You should hear Wyndham Lewis—"

"And pretty little Mrs. Wyndham. You would think she had molded you herself out of clay."

Disraeli felt almost dazed. He passed a hand over his forehead and rose. "This is true?" he asked. "All true?"

"If you doubt my word, I shall have to challenge you," D'Orsay threatened, smiling.

"Don't you dare!" Lady Blessington protested.

D'Orsay laughed and rose, too. "Instead, I shall walk with him to the Carlton Club and allow the members to buy us champagne till dinner in honor of Dizzy's triumph."

Part of Disraeli was eager to accept. A friendly reception at the Carlton, rather than the chill politeness to which he was accustomed, would be enormously satisfying and final proof that all this was real. But there was someone else who would be as excited as himself. "I would love to," He told D'Orsay hesitantly, "but—if you'll forgive me—no. It is so rare to have good news . . . I must get home. I can't wait to tell Henrietta."

He hurried into the drawing-room where he had left her. He had come straight from Seamore Place, spending the last coins in his pocket on a cab. But Henrietta was not in the room.

He paused, smiling to himself. Would he tell her right away, or pretend that nothing had happened of importance, or hint and let her cajole the news out of him? Yes, he would hint at it with pretended indifference. Only a meeting with Wellington and dinner with Peel. He laughed, imagining her reaction.

He went out quickly and hurried up the stairs. Her dress and most of her underclothes were draped over the chaise-longue in her boudoir which he passed through to reach the bedroom. He opened the bedroom door.

He stopped in shock, about to say her name.

Henrietta lay on the bed, naked and eager. His friend,

Maclise, was leaning over her, wearing only his linen shirt. He was laughing, teasing her. She was laughing, too, while she pleaded and her hands caught at his arms, trying to draw him down to her.

The second for which the play continued, until the couple realized that the door had opened, seemed to Disraeli to last for minutes. Then Maclise turned and saw him and froze, staring. Henrietta was still absorbed in her needs and her realization was slower. When she glanced at the door, her mouth fell open, almost stupidly. A sound like a questioning sob came from her throat and she threw one arm over her eyes to shut out the sight of Disraeli gazing at her, stricken and disbelieving.

He stepped back and closed the door. By the time Maclise had pulled on some clothes to follow him, he had gone from the house.

Disraeli was never sure how he spent the days immediately following. For some of them, he sat alone in his rooms which he had not given up, unable to think clearly, unable to sleep, unable even to drink, for brandy instead of blotting out his memories only seemed to bring those last, horrifying moments into sharper focus. He did not answer Henrietta's piteous, self-accusing attempts at explanation and pleas for forgiveness. Maclise knew better the hopelessness of trying to apologize.

At last, Bulwer and D'Orsay came to find him and gradually their practical, masculine approach, sympathetic but sensible, brought him out again into the world. Bulwer's opinion was that he was fortunate to be rid of Henrietta, who could only have become more of a liability to him as their affaire continued. D'Orsay agreed. He knew at first hand the problems of living in open scandal, which, for example, would make a career in politics impossible. Although Disraeli could not wholly agree, it was what he needed to hear.

They took him to Lady Blessington who was wise and experienced and let him talk and talk until he had lanced the wound. Because she had always defended Henrietta in the past, she would not condemn her, even for his sake.

She chided him gently for expecting faithfulness from someone who was incapable of it. She had loved him as much and for as long as she was able. Disraeli's bitterness had made him suspect others in their circle of being her occasional lovers. He could not even believe now that her relationship with Lyndhurst had been as innocent as she had claimed. He remembered discussing platonic friendships between men and women with Lyndhurst some months before. "Don't you think it's possible?" he had asked, when the older man seemed skeptical. "After," Lyndhurst had said. "But not before." Lady Blessington smiled. However, she had one very serious point to make. It would be ruinous for Disraeli to let this business cause a breach between himself and Lord Lyndhurst. The suggestion of their both being involved in an unpleasant scandal could be highly damaging.

Disraeli took her advice and found Lyndhurst to be sympathetic and understanding. The bond between them was strengthened, rather than dissolved. Work, Lyndhurst prescribed, was the antidote to melancholy. Sorrows and jealousies breed in inaction. The quarrel between Disraeli and the O'Connells had been brought to an official end when a police officer arrived one morning at his rooms, arrested Disraeli in his bed and took him to Marylebone Police Court, where he was bound over to keep the peace on a surety of five hundred pounds. Lyndhurst pointed out that, while everyone agreed he had won his battle, he now had a reputation for being hot-tempered, even dangerous. It was the perfect time, while his name was still so much in the public eye, to make a clear statement of his political position.

At that time, the Radicals were mounting a ferocious attack on the House of Lords, led by O'Connell. It gave Disraeli his theme and opportunity. In a comparatively short time, he wrote his first purely political book, *A Vindication of the English Constitution*. Writing it enabled him not only to codify his own opinions, it established him as a political thinker who could not be ignored. The stronger the government in the House of Commons, he said, the more essential was the need for a

109

Second Chamber to control it and prevent it from becoming the master of the people whom it was elected to serve. "I cannot force from my mind the conviction that a House of Commons, concentrating in itself the whole power of the State, might—I should rather say would—establish in this country a despotism of the most formidable and dangerous character." As well as vindicating the existence of the House of Lords, he restated his belief that the Conservatives were the natural party of democracy. The book brought him many new admirers. Isaac called it his "political birth." Even Peel wrote to thank him for the pleasure that reading it had given him.

Yet all the time Disraeli thought of Henrietta. He tried to convince himself that, long before the betrayal, he had tired of her and to agree with Bulwer that he was well rid of her. In public he smiled and flirted and talked with his usual brilliance, but at night he lay sleepless and lonely, longing for the days of the year to be turned back like the hands of a clock and to have her warm in his arms and her sweet breath on his face, to have again the time when he believed in love and woman's faithfulness.

He envied D'Orsay more and more. He envied the perfect poise, the half smile with which the dandy accepted success or failure, praise or blame, the amused indifference with which he won a hundred pounds on the turn of a card or lost a thousand. Schooling himself to adopt the same manner, he managed to convince nearly everyone that he was completely unaffected by what had happened. The scandal-mongers were disappointed, but D'Orsay was pleased. "Feel slightly, think little, never plan, never brood," he had counselled Dizzy. "Everything depends upon the circulation; take care of it. Take the world as you find it; enjoy everything. Vive la bagatelle!" He was gratified that Disraeli had achieved the cool detachment which he would need to survive thwarted ambition and lost love. But D'Orsay was wrong.

Wretched, unable to find comfort or to keep up the pose any longer, Disraeli had to get away from London where so much reminded him of Henrietta. His family welcomed him back to the old house at Bradenham, accepting his explanation that he needed peace to write. His mother scolded him for not having taken care of himself. He looked so drawn and pale. Only Sarah suspected that he had not merely been overworking.

He could not hide anything from her and, slowly, she drew out of him the whole account. She had guessed that it involved Lady Sykes, whom she had met and not liked. The year before, Ben had startled them by bringing Henrietta to spend a few days at Bradenham. They were accompanied by Lord Lyndhurst. The county had been scandalized and could not understand why Isaac had allowed his son's mistress and her former lover to cross his doorstep. But Isaac was unworldly and unsuspicious. He had only been worried that his style of living might be too simple for Ben's fashionable friends. They were, in fact, delighted and the visit was a success, although Sarah was troubled by the intimacy which she detected between her brother and Henrietta Sykes, whom she thought shallow and insincere. She warned him against becoming too attached to her and it caused the only coolness that ever came between them. Over and again now, he told himself how right she had been. Yet perhaps, he too, was to blame—for expecting her to respect a man who was unsuccessful and half drowned in debts, for not spending every minute with her as she had begged, for not giving her the satisfaction she needed. For weeks he tortured himself with self-doubts and accusations until he feared for his own reason.

Again he turned to Lyndhurst's antidote of work. The need for him to do something constructive had become extremely urgent. His novels had proved to have only a limited appeal and it was years since the last had appeared. That and his series of election defeats alarmed the moneylenders, who began to refuse to extend his credit. Some were demanding immediate repayment. Once, fortunately when his father was out, he had to hide in the well in the garden while Tita, in his best broken English, explained to the Sheriff's officers who had come to arrest him that the young Mr. Disraeli had left on an extended journey through France and Italy. From then,

111

he lived in fear of every stranger. The situation was made worse by Benjamin Austen's patience finally running out. Always before he could depend on Sara Austen to speak up for him, but she was hurt at being neglected by him over the past two years and made jealous by the rumors. He promised to repay her husband as soon as he was able. "Which you will keep like all your other promises," she said bitterly. "We wanted to help you. I thought I had helped you. Everything we gave you you have spent on that—that woman!"

Among his papers, Disraeli discovered the unfinished story he had written for himself and Henrietta, into which he had poured all his passion and joy and belief in the power of love. Like a man suffering from vertigo who forces himself to climb a high tower, he made himself read it again, although it was an ordeal to be plunged back into that time, the painful ecstasy of love at first sight with its hopes and certainties. It was intensely personal, but he knew that what he had written was too good to throw away. He decided against revising it. His first thought was to leave the opening chapters as they were, then to turn the second half into a tragedy with the hero, Ferdinand Armine, sinking gradually into ruin and degradation after the discovery that he has been betrayed. Yet that again might be too obviously personal and give ammunition to his enemies. As he worked on it through the autumn months, the reality of the lovers he had created and the charm of the idealized Henrietta worked their spell on him. The lovers were torn apart and each promised to be married to others, so that he could describe Armine's anguish, but the romantic in him took over and the story ended, as he would have wished, with the hero saved from bankruptcy, the lovers reunited and all explained and forgiven. He called the novel *Henrietta Temple* and dedicated it to Count D'Orsay.

He began work immediately on another, *Venetia,* a historical romance based on the lives of Byron and Shelley. Before he had progressed very far, his financial problems reached a crisis. Mrs. Austen's husband decided he would wait no longer and insisted on all the loans he had made being repaid at once, even threatening to take him to court. Disraeli had to swallow his pride and ask his father to help him again. Austen would not even take a partial settlement from Isaac. Every penny had to be produced at once.

Henrietta Temple appeared at Christmas and was his most popular success since his very first novel, especially with younger readers who knew the emotions were not exaggerated. It was ironic that some critics thought the scenes in the sponging-houses overdrawn and could not have been based on experience, for Disraeli's share of the proceeds went straight to the moneylenders. Again he had been unable to confess the full extent of his debts to his father. He had been sworn in as a Justice of the Peace for Buckinghamshire in October and to be arrested for debt now would have ruined him completely. The possibility of it preyed on his mind so much that his nervous system was affected and he finished *Venetia* only with the greatest difficulty. With the advance from his publisher he gained another few weeks of peace, but he had nothing with which to fill them, no prospects except a repetition of the failure of the past. He began to dread the thought of the future and the endless struggle, and was almost ready to give up.

Isaac became anxious about his son, seeing him retreat into himself. He was not a rich man and settling Ben's debts had strained his finances. He hoped he had not let his concern show too much nor spoken too sharply and that that was what had affected his son. Yet the more he thought about it, the more he was convinced the trouble was something other than money. He could not think of a way to bring up the subject, himself. Then one day, Tita told him he had taken Ben out a tray, since he had stayed in the garden and not come in for lunch. Two hours later, the food was still untouched. It was not the first time. Isaac went to find Sarah. "Something is gnawing at him," he said. "I don't know what it is. You probably do."

"Perhaps writing *Henrietta Temple* took more out of him than we realize," she answered carefully. "Perhaps he has to recover."

113

Isaac nodded, beginning to understand. "Ah—that might explain why it is so much more real than his other books. I don't wish to be told the details. But you are closer to him than anyone, Sarah. You must do what you can."

The arbor in the garden was screened from the house by close-trimmed hedges. In front of it was the wilder part of the lawn with scattered clusters of late daffodils and the last primroses of spring. Disraeli sat alone on a rustic seat, empty, detached, a book of Milton's poems open on his knees. He gazed ahead, his eyes unfocused, lost in thought.

Becoming aware that he was not alone, he glanced round and saw Sarah standing watching him. She looked at him for a long moment, then came into the arbor. "Father says I have to comfort you," she said.

"Does he know?" Disraeli asked quickly.

"Not everything. Only that something happened."

He relaxed slightly. "You don't have to worry, Sa. I appreciate your concern." He picked up the book and pretended to read, dismissing her.

"If you treat me like one of your ladies in London," she said evenly, "I shall pull your ears and break your hobbyhorse."

He looked up in surprise and then laughed. "How right you are, my dear sister. I am wallowing in self pity and behaving like a child. Yet I *am* over her."

"I am very glad," Sarah said, and sat on the wooden seat beside him. "You should not hate her, either. I do not think she could help her nature."

He was surprised again. For a studious young woman brought up in the country, Sarah was remarkably perceptive and tolerant. What she had said almost echoed Lady Blessington, but they were in the minority. He smiled. "I wish more of our London ladies had your understanding, Sa. . . . No, I don't hate her. She was passionate, wilful. Even her husband tried to warn me. She had to possess me utterly and, when she feared she was becoming no longer the most important part of my life, she prepared a way of escape from her own disappointment. Writing the

114

book released me from her. Nearly all the pain I felt is gone."

Sarah was relieved, although still puzzled. "Then why are you so bitter? Why do you hide yourself here and only go to London for a few days at a time?"

It was not a question he wanted to answer, but her candid eyes were intent on him and he could not evade it. ". . . Because I thought I had reached another turning point in my life—and find that I am exactly where I was three years ago," he said quietly. "No, not three—further back. After all that time with Henrietta, all I had left was a larger mountain of debts. Once again I had to ask Father to pay off the worst."

"He did it willingly," Sarah told him.

He rose abruptly and stood looking out towards the grove of beeches across the lawn. "But I am not a boy any more! I am nearly thirty-three. It is shaming."

The hurt in his voice touched Sarah, but she would not let herself be weak. "How can you say you are no further forward?" she protested. "Your speeches are reported in the papers. You are a close friend of Lyndhurst. Wellington favors you. Peel speaks highly of you."

"Because they have learned they cannot ignore me, and are afraid I will move to the other side." He turned to face her and shrugged. "They still do not trust me."

"Then you must prove to them they can!" she said positively. She rose to face him. "Great things are happening. They say the old King is dying. If he does there will be a new reign and another General Election. You must be ready. You owe it to yourself . . . and to me, to everyone who believes in you, to try and try again."

Her spirit worked on him as it had done so often in the past. As she gazed at him, he felt the faint stirring of his old confidence and knew he could not betray her belief in him.

Having given up his rooms, Disraeli had nowhere to live in London and Count D'Orsay came to his rescue. Lady Blessington had moved from Seamore Place to William Wilberforce's former home, Gore House, in three acres of quiet gardens to the south of Hyde Park. It was set back behind a high wall, ensuring more privacy, and was spacious, with more rooms, superbly decorated with her usual perfect taste, really a Georgian country house a few hundred yards from Hyde Park Corner. Because of the continuing legal battle over her husband's will and his equivocal position, D'Orsay did not live with her but in a smaller, very elegant house adjoining, looking out on to Kensington Gore, with a private gate at the side into her gardens.

Due to the success of his two latest novels, Dizzy was more in demand socially than ever. Accompanied by D'Orsay or Bulwer he went everywhere and could sense that the town was in a ferment. The rumors that the King was dying were true, but the bluff old sailor refused to surrender to death and the weeks dragged on with the political parties already maneuvering and campaigning for the inevitable general election. Lord Lyndhurst arrived back from a long stay in Paris and took Disraeli with him on a round of visits to Peel and Wellington and the other Conservative leaders. There was a flurry of local elections at which Dizzy spoke on behalf of the Tory candidates and increased his reputation as a highly effective speech-maker. Although he felt revitalized, he had still not fully recovered from his nervous exhaustion and once, having rushed down to speak at Aylesbury, he fainted and collapsed in the street.

He was hailed as one of the coming men and approached by several constituencies, asking him to be their candidate. It was a strange, almost unreal month of mounting excitement. Through Lyndhurst, he was close to the real centers of power for the first time and behind the scenes at many secret conferences. Attempts were made to win the influential young Lord Stanley back to the Liberal camp, but he had reached an agreement with Peel and stayed true to his new allegiance. The maneuvering and speculations went on and, suddenly, the excitement reached its peak on the evening of 19 June 1837, when news came from Windsor Castle that the King's life was nearing its end. He died two hours after

116

midnight and, as soon as the prayers had been said and the orders for the lying in state given, the Archbishop of Canterbury rode off with the Lord Chamberlain and the royal physician. They galloped through the night toward London and reached Kensington Palace just before dawn, to kneel before the little, virtually unknown Princess Victoria, the late King's niece, who came to them in her nightdress and dressing-gown to be told that she was now Queen, at the age of eighteen.

Early on the following morning, Disraeli was summoned by Lord Lyndhurst and drove with him to Kensington Palace where all the chief personages of the realm were assembling for the accession council. Disraeli only had one brief sight of the slim, small girl in her plain black mourning dress, but was impressed like everyone else by her dignity. Afterward, Lyndhurst told him that she delivered her speech and accepted the oath of loyalty from each of her councillors with the same natural dignity and sweetness, so that the words of the oath took on fresh meaning and the worldly Lord Melbourne was not alone in having tears in his eyes.

The next day, Edward Bulwer came to see him, and D'Orsay and he insisted on Disraeli taking a walk with them. They strolled through Hyde Park to Park Lane, until they reached the townhouse on the corner of Grosvenor Gate. Dizzy knew it reasonably well from previous visits, the home of Wyndham Lewis and his rattle-brained, flirtatious wife, Mary Anne. It was Mary Anne whom his two friends had brought him to meet. Over his protests, they knocked and were shown into the L-shaped drawing-room overlooking the park.

Disraeli was impatient as they waited. Bulwer checked his fobwatch against the ormolu clock on the mantelpiece. D'Orsay was watching a cabriolet that passed down Park Lane, carrying a rather attractive lady. Dizzy looked from one to the other. There were few secrets between them and they knew his situation. "I cannot think why we had to come here!" he protested again. "There are ten hundred places I'd rather be than listening to Mary Anne Lewis's chatter."

117

"She is devoted to you," D'Orsay murmured.

"And I to her—for ten minutes of frivolity. But the world is turning out there."

"She asked me most particularly, as a friend, to bring you," Bulwer told him. "She wishes to speak to you, on some urgent matter."

Dizzy snorted. "The only matter of urgency to me is that there is an election afoot and I have not a penny to stand as a candidate."

D'Orsay smiled. "You are welcome to my entire fortune—which amounts to three shillings in ready cash."

"And I have barely enough to pay for my own campaign," Bulwer said.

"Then we all have more important matters to deal with," Disraeli answered. "Why are we here?"

He broke off as Mary Anne came in, smiling radiantly. She was dressed in a pink satin gown with lacy sleeves and ribbon bows down the front. Although pretty, it was a style that was much too young for her. She was followed in by her pleasant, businesslike husband. As the three friends bowed to them, she clapped her hands happily. "Here they are, the three champions! They are all quite beautiful, don't you think so, Wyndham?"

Lewis smiled. "I hardly see them with the same eyes, my dear."

She laughed. "For which I should be profoundly grateful." She concentrated on Disraeli. "Edward tells me you were really there, at Kensington Palace. Did you see the new Queen?"

"Only a glimpse. I was not, of course, in the chamber for the Accession Council."

"How was little Victoria?" Lewis asked.

"A revelation," Dizzy said sincerely. "Turned overnight from a girl into a woman. Tiny, pale but very composed, a Queen to the tips of her toes."

Mary Anne sighed. "It's all so exciting," she began. There was a sudden loud crash of cannon from an artillery battery across the road in the park and she squeaked and jumped. The men laughed.

"It's only a salute, my dear," Lewis said, smiling.

"Yes, I know," she giggled, "but artillery always makes me jump. And I always think it's going to break the windows." She moved to the nearest window and touched the panes reassuringly, looking out.

A footman had followed them in and stood waiting, with a bottle of champagne and glasses. Lewis signed to him to serve. "Oh, look, Wyndham! The Household Cavalry," Mary Anne exclaimed and he moved to join her at the window. There was the sound of hooves and the jingle of harness as a detachment of the superb cavalry in their glittering helmets and cuirasses trotted past outside.

Bulwer and D'Orsay had closed in to stand with Disraeli. "As soon as you are settled, we shall go," Bulwer told him quietly.

Dizzy was horrified. "And leave me alone with them?" he whispered, protestingly. "I'll never get away!"

The footman had served Lewis and Mary Anne. They turned at the window and Lewis raised his glass. "To our new Queen, Victoria," he proposed. "May God prosper her." They repeated the toast and drank.

Mary Anne surveyed them, her eyes shining. "Look at them—the three handsomest men in England! You must agree, Wyndham. I assure you, I should like to have them all cast in bronze."

They laughed. "Then before that metallic fate overtakes us," D'Orsay suggested, "perhaps you will permit Bulwer and myself to withdraw? We only brought Dizzy as requested."

"Well—if you must," Mary Anne said. Her delight at their leaving was transparent. They bowed to her.

"I trust we may have longer at our next m-meeting," Bulwer said. He managed to catch Disraeli's eye and winked as the footman showed D'Orsay and himself out.

Disraeli was aware of Mary Anne smiling at him conspiratorially and waiting. He finished the champagne in his glass. They heard the sound of the front door closing. "At last," she sighed. "How delicious to have you to ourselves! No disrespect to Edward and Count D'Orsay, but they are not of our party."

119

Lewis smiled. "My wife has become quite a raging Conservative, thanks to you, Mr. Disraeli."

"He is the nonpareil!" she exclaimed. Then, directly to Disraeli, "and how wonderful for you to be recognized officially, at last! I have followed your career, read your speeches and admired your courage ever since we first met."

He was flattered and touched by her enthusiasm, and bowed to her. "I am not worthy of so much kindness."

"Kindness, my foot," she said. "Anyone will tell you I only back winners. Which brings me to the point. I have not heard that you have been chosen as a candidate in any constituency yet."

He hesitated. "I must confess to a slight embarrassment of choice. I have been asked to contest not one, but seven different seats."

"Seven?" Lewis repeated, astounded. "That's unheard of!"

"Have you chosen one?" Mary Anne asked.

". . . That is the embarrassment."

"Would you excuse me for a moment?" she said. She smiled to him and went out, leaving him alone with Lewis.

After a slightly awkward pause, Lewis coughed. "Remarkable woman, Mary Anne."

"She is indeed, sir."

Lewis paused again, glancing at him and away. "You'll forgive me, but do I take it your embarrassment is financial?"

"Total."

Lewis, who already had a fair idea of the situation, nodded. "I myself am one of the two MPs for Maidstone. The second is a Liberal who is retiring at this election, and a Radical is standing in his place."

"I see," Disraeli said politely.

"It would be a great stroke to have two Tory members. And my wife and I wondered if you would care to stand with me? If you have not chosen somewhere else."

"No, I—I have not," Disraeli answered slowly. He knew that Lewis and his wife meant to be kind. It was an honor to be asked to be his running mate and he was genuinely grateful. The gesture, however, had merely increased his sense of embarrassment.

"The electors of Maidstone, unfortunately, are notoriously corrupt," Lewis told him confidentially. "Expenses could be high—perhaps adding up to thousands of pounds."

It was time for Dizzy to make his confession. "I am flattered, sir—but I have already told you—"

"Perhaps you have not understood," Lewis broke in. "I am offering to pay the bulk of your election expenses."

Disraeli could not believe for a moment that he had heard correctly. For once he was at a loss for words. Offering . . .? "I—my dear sir, I am overwhelmed." It was so unexpected, he could think of no suitable phrases, yet realized that simple words of thanks were not enough. Lewis was totally honest and straightforward and deserved equal frankness. "But I must warn you, on my past record, it is very unlikely that I shall be successful."

It was Lewis's turn to be surprised. He had been pressed and wheedled by Mary Anne, although he himself had not been wholly convinced of Disraeli's suitability. He saw now that appearances might have been deceptive. "I admire you for saying that, sir," he said with sincerity, then smiled. "However, I have learned to trust Mary Anne's judgment. And I want another Conservative in the borough, a younger man who will write the letters, handle most of the constituency business and make the speeches. What d'ye say? Do you accept?"

"With both hands, sir!" Disraeli said eagerly.

As they shook hands, Mary Anne came back in. She had clearly been listening and beamed with pleasure as they turned to her. "Well, my dear," Lewis chuckled, "did I put it right?"

"Perfect, Wyndham," she assured him and kissed his cheek.

"Mrs. Lewis—Mary Anne, I thank you from the bottom of my heart," Disraeli said. "I shall not fail you for want of trying."

"I know," she said confidently.

He gazed at her. How strange that it was she, the last person on his mind, who would have given him this chance. How often he had laughed about her. Whatever her failings and oddities, she was generous and affectionate and he swore to himself never to cease to be grateful to her for the path she had opened up. He bowed. "If I succeed, it will be thanks to you."

"Nonsense!" she contradicted, smiling. "It will be thanks to your genius, and to Wyndham's money."

Disraeli left almost immediately for Maidstone, the county town of Kent on the River Medway, to begin his campaign. It was all new territory to him, but the town, with a few light industries, was set in the middle of a large agricultural community whose needs and interests he understood very well.

True to his word, Wyndham Lewis left him to make most of the speeches. It was a deliberate policy. Lewis was already well known and respected. He introduced his fellow candidate, then left him to make his own impression. There were less than four weeks to go to polling day. From the start, Disraeli amazed the Tory party workers with his brilliance and energy. He absorbed the problems and conditions of the area within a few days and, thereafter, was able to refer to them in his speeches with complete authority. His ability to handle large audiences was astonishing. His speeches were more direct and constructive than ever before, dealing with local issues, yet widening them to embrace the whole country, so that his listeners felt an indefinable sense of increased importance and of privilege at his concern for their affairs. It was headier and on a higher plane than the petty local electioneering to which they were accustomed and the response was tremendous.

Disraeli knew he had to make the strongest possible effect. His opponent was Colonel Perronet Thompson, a popular and prominent Radical, the editor of the *Westminster Review*. Thompson and his supporters made great play with Disraeli's exotic way of dressing, his name

122

and Jewish ancestry. In addition to the legitimate, open campaign, there was another, more vicious and underhand, aimed at destroying his credibility by publicizing his scandalous friends, his love of married women, his quarrel with O'Connell and his debts. The result was that more people were keen to see this extraordinary candidate and the numbers at his meetings swelled. Among them were organized bands of Whigs and Radicals who jeered and catcalled, shouting out "Shylock! Shylock!" and "Any old clothes!" He was taunted with forsaking his reformist principles. The speech he made in reply routed his opponents and parts of it were widely quoted. It was directed not at Maidstone, but at Westminster, an attack on the Poor Law which had been passed three years before by the Whigs, with the support of Wellington and Peel, a harsh law which drove the poor into workhouses, splitting up families and forcing the old to end their days in institutions more like prisons than homes, without the comfort of friends or children. Disraeli in his own county and another magistrate in Berkshire were the first to speak out against it. He called the first meeting to oppose it and was the first to sign the petition to both Houses of Parliament calling for its abolition. "It is not to elicit an electioneering cheer, it is not to gain a single vote that I tell you this . . . That Bill bears fearful tidings for the poor. It goes on the principle that relief to the poor is a *charity*. I maintain that it is a *right!* To sum up my feelings in a sentence—I consider that this Act has disgraced the country more than any other upon record. Both a moral and a political blunder, it announces to the world that in England poverty is a crime."

In the weeks leading up to the election, he wrote regularly to Sarah and to Mrs. Wyndham Lewis, reporting his progress. To both he sounded unfailingly confident. Yet as polling day came nearer, he was irresistibly reminded of High Wycombe and Taunton, where he had been greeted with the same cheers and enthusiasm. On the day itself, when the poll was declared, he felt like a puppet as he smiled and waved to his supporters. Neither he nor they seemed real to him any longer. His

123

nerves were stretched to such tightness that his mind seemed to have become blank, his actions mechanical. Then he was following Wyndham Lewis and Thompson, the Radical candidate, into the main room of the town hall, where the party managers and the Returning Officer stood on the platform.

The hall was jammed with people, some seated, others crowded around the walls. Excitement was intense and, as Lewis and Thompson came out, they were welcomed with cheers and counter-cheers. The sight of Disraeli in his green velvet frock coat, embroidered waistcoat spanned by gold chains, his tight, check trousers and ringed fingers brought a shout of derision from Thompson's supporters who packed the sides and rear of the hall. Disraeli was hardly conscious of the familiar, raucous cries of "Jew-boy! Shylock! Old clothes!" as he took his place beside Lewis. He was as pale as the lace at his throat, trying to appear detached and not to tremble, nerving himself for the humiliation of another defeat.

Mary Anne Lewis was seated near the front of the hall, in the rows reserved for candidates' families and local dignitaries. She was tense, listening to the violent shouts of Disraeli's opponents. She had not heard this kind of abuse ever before and was anxious when she saw how deathly pale he was. Beside him, Wyndham and Thompson were relaxed and smiling, waving to the crowd.

The Returning Officer had been signalling for silence and there was a breathless hush as it was at last achieved and he raised the paper he was holding. "As Returning Officer for the Borough of Maidstone, I hereby declare the total of votes cast in the general election of 27 July, 1837, to be as follows," he announced. "Wyndham Lewis, Esquire, 706. Benjamin Disraeli, Esquire, 616. Colonel Perronet Thompson, 412." There was a storm of cheering, through which the Returning Officer continued. "I therefore declare that the aforesaid Wyndham Lewis and the aforesaid Benjamin Disraeli are duly elected Members of Parliament for the Constituency of Maidstone."

Mary Anne rose to her feet with the others around her, applauding. She was nearly in tears with her excitement and delight. She saw Disraeli's head jerk as though he had come awake. He stared at Wyndham Lewis who smiled and shook his hand.

On the platform, Disraeli felt the grip of Lewis's hand and heard the noise of the crowd and their names being shouted, but everything was distanced, as in a dream. He turned automatically with Lewis to shake hands with Thompson, the defeated candidate, and the Returning Officer, but still could not catch what they said. Then he turned to face the hall again and a wall of sound struck him and shocked him into full awareness. He saw Mary Anne and his local agents and supporters cheering and applauding and an immense feeling of elation flooded into him. He glanced at Wyndham Lewis who was hanging back and nodded to him to make their speech of thanks and acceptance.

As he stepped forward and bowed, there was a renewed chorus of boos and shouts of "Shylock!" Almost at once they were drowned out by cheers and louder applause. He bowed to Mary Anne and then, with ironic grace, to the most clamorous group of his jeering, disappointed opponents. There was a huge burst of laughter. He held up his hand, his emerald rings catching the light. "My friends, voters of Maidstone—" But his words could not be heard for the roars of "Dizzy! Dizzy!"

Pushed forward by a surge in the mass behind her, Mary Anne stood just below the edge of the platform, gazing up at him, watching him as he acknowledged the cheers and boos with equal impartiality, confident and commanding, in his true element at last.

chapter five

As his first parliament and the first of Victoria's reign would not assemble for another three months, Disraeli returned to Bradenham. The news had preceded him. To his astonishment, at Wycombe he found his old colors of pink and white hanging and pink placards everywhere, announcing his victory at Maidstone. He was cheered at the Red Lion and surrounded by well-wishers who told him that, on the previous day, a market day, when the news of his election had arrived, there had been a demonstration in the streets. Money was collected to illuminate the town in the evening, church bells were rung and a band paraded until after midnight. He was deeply moved to realize that, although he could not capture the seat against the power of the local magnates, he had taken the peoples' hearts.

His family was extremely proud. Sarah wept and clung to him, and Isaac coughed and polished his glasses to cover his own emotion when they met. He was amused to see Tita bow to him, as low as to a Venetian signior. And for the first time in years, he felt really at ease in the open among strangers.

At Maidstone he had engaged a lawyer friend to protect him against writs and debt-collectors during the election. With his new dignity as an MP, he had been given a breathing space. Members of Parliament were paid no salary, although reformers were agitating for one to make it possible for candidates from the poorer classes to stand for election, but Dizzy now had prospects and the money lenders called off their hounds.

Isaac was as grateful to the Wyndham Lewises as his son, and readily agreed to invite them to Bradenham. They came for a few days at the end of August and, in spite of disappointing weather, enjoyed their visit enormously. The more Disraeli saw of them, the more he liked them. Lewis was an odd, silent man who fitted amiably into almost any company, as unobtrusive as his wife was noticeable. She was so natural and warmhearted, no one could resist her. She struck up an immediate rapport with old Isaac, brightening up his rather monotonously bookish life. His children were amazed to see him chuckling with her and joining happily in her love for guessing games and childish conundrums. Sarah was relieved to see her brother's affection for the older couple. After the visits of Clara and Henrietta she had been secretly afraid, but she could tell that his attitude to Mrs. Lewis was one of pure friendship and gratitude.

Life seemed strangely flat after they had gone.

Success and a temporary freedom from care worked wonders on Disraeli's health. The constant feeling of exhaustion of the past year vanished. He was so alive, he had to force himself to conserve his energy, limiting the number of books he read, the number of political meetings he attended and visits he paid, and making himself rest for the two weeks before he returned to London in November.

Parliament was assembling in temporary quarters. A disastrous fire three years before had burned out sections of the Palace of Westminster and the Lords were meeting in the Painted Chamber, the Commons in the former House of Lords. Stepped wooden benches lined the sides of the hall, with its massive, medieval beams. It was already filled with members, who were chatting noisily and greeting friends. The atmosphere was informal, like a genial club, but the appearance of most members was very sober. Many wore top hats and some still had on their dark outdoor greatcoats. All but a few were wearing black frock coats and strapped trousers. Some county members deliberately kept to the old fashioned, rustic dress of a decade or so before, wide brown coats with huge pockets, breeches, boots and linen waistcoats reaching almost to their knees. They wore wide-brimmed hats and white handkerchiefs tied in a bow round their necks. A group of them had just strolled in from Bellamy's and were eating meat pies. To look at them, they might have been prosperous farmers or country gentlemen at a market, with the same blunt manners. Their way of dressing, in spite of variations, was almost a uniform and proclaimed that they disliked change and innovation. Fairly evenly spread on both sides, they had considerable influence in the House.

At the far end of the hall, new members were going through the ritual of taking the oath and being sworn in by the clerk, with the chaplain and uniformed ushers. The Speaker's chair was empty until his appointment was confirmed. Already seated on the Government front bench was the small, sharp-featured Lord John Russell, the Home Secretary. Next to him lounged the watchful, popular Lord Palmerston, Foreign Secretary, nodding to acquaintances as they passed. Russell and Palmerston led the Whigs in the Commons, Melbourne in the Lords.

In front of them was the huge, wooden Treasury table, with a scarlet despatch box lying before Russell. Separated from them by the table was the Opposition front bench. In the aisle up from it stood the leader of the Opposition, the aloof and handsome Sir Robert Peel, with dapper Lord Stanley and the bluffly good-looking racing man, Lord George Bentinck. In spite of Conservative hopes, the election had brought the Whigs back to power, supported still by the Radicals. Bentinck glanced round at a buzz of surprise in the crowd and stared over Stanley's shoulder. "What on earth is that—with Wyndham Lewis?" he spluttered.

Moving to the Opposition benches at that moment was the sedate Wyndham Lewis. With him and in startling contrast to everyone else was Benjamin Disraeli, entering Parliament for the first time. He was wearing his bottle green velvet suit and from its sleeves, as usual, cascaded sprays of lace which reached to his fingertips, without concealing his white gloves and, over them, his full assortment of rings. His yellow waistcoat was strung with the customary swags of gold chains. Hatless, his black, perfumed ringlets were arranged with exquisite care. Peel watched him, expressionlessly; Stanley, turning, said distastefully, "It is the Oriental adventurer—Disraeli the novelist."

"Here, in Parliament?" Bentinck grunted, incredulous. Next they would be admitting Gypsies.

"Lewis's fellow MP for Maidstone," Stanley told him laconically.

"You mean he's one of ours?"

"Conservative. Or so he says. With Radical ideas. Bit of a weathercock."

"He's fought five elections in five years to get here," Peel said drily. "Nothing, it seems, could keep him out."

The heavily built Daniel O'Connell had stopped in mid-sentence and tensed at the sight of Disraeli, a fit of rage at once seizing him. Beside him, his diminutive and elderly lieutenant, R.L. Sheil, laid a trembing and restraining hand on his arm. "Let him be, Danny," he murmured.

Disraeli was all too well aware of O'Connell, but affected to ignore him. He paused and looked round as Lewis climbed up to the Conservative back benches. O'Connell and Sheil moved to their places at the far end of the Government benches by the Bar of the House, where the block of Irish MPs were taking their seats. Disraeli was conscious of many eyes on him. He surveyed the crowded back benches on his own side, then nonchalantly, and with an air of bravado, took his seat immediately behind his own Party leader, Peel, on the second front bench.

There was a whirring of astonishment and muffled derision. Bentinck, seated on the back benches, glanced at Wyndham Lewis. "In Parliament one minute," he growled, "and the back benches aren't good enough for him. Flashy upstart!"

On the front bench, seated next to Peel and Stanley, dressed soberly in black, was the rich young Tory MP, William Ewart Gladstone. He looked round at Disraeli and it took only an instant to see what had caused the commotion. The peacock Disraeli was sitting in the row usually reserved for senior members of the party. He could not have declared his ambition and his arrogance more clearly. Recognizing him, Disraeli smiled and bowed from where he sat. Gladstone gave only the most frigid nod in reply and looked away. There were cries of "Order, order!" The rest of those members still standing hurried to take their seats and the House prepared to elect its new Speaker.

A few days later, Disraeli was in the rush to the Painted Chamber to join the Lords for the Queen's Speech. Since before dawn, people had begun to fill the streets between Buckingham Palace and Westminster, until the whole route was lined with dense crowds agog to see the girl Queen as she passed in her coach of state for the Opening of Parliament. With the cheering and infectious excitement of the crowds, anticipation in the Commons had risen to an extraordinary height. Not all members of the Commons would be able to fit into the Painted Chamber and, when the summons came, everyone rose at once to be among the first at the door. Eagerness to be part of a truly historic moment turned the rush into a stampede, with members jostling and thrusting one another aside. The elderly Speaker, Abercromby, was knocked over and would have been trampled on, if he had not been hauled back to his feet by his mace-bearer, who cleared a way for him by banging members' heads roughly with his gorgeous mace.

Dizzy was determined not to miss the spectacle and

managed to push his way through and to find himself a place as the Commons thronged into the Lords' Chamber. There, the hubbub died away and he forgot the bodies pressing round him as he gazed at a scene from one of his own novels brought to life. The Lords assembled, the peers and peeresses in their sumptuous robes, coronets, stars, ribbons, the great officers of State and the ladies and gentlemen of the Queen's Household flanking the dais on which she stood, with Lord Melbourne on her right in scarlet and ermine. How frail and tiny she seemed, wearing not a crown but a diamond tiara. With her golden brown hair, pale, oval face and huge, blue eyes, she looked almost beautiful and he saw that her composure, at which everyone had marvelled, was truly remarkable. She read her Speech from the Throne without a tremor, every word carefully enunciated in her clear, sweet voice. Afterwards, involuntarily, she glanced at Melbourne and he gave her the smallest nod of approval. It was over in a fraction of a second but, for as acute an observer as Disraeli, it was enough to tell him that already the young Queen had placed her full confidence in her aging, worldly Prime Minister. Melbourne was highly conscious of his responsibility for educating her in the intricacies of being a constitutional monarch. Through his affection for her he lost his cynicism and advised her, as impartially as possible, with wisdom and tolerance. Disraeli had glimpsed the start of one of the most tender of all romances.

He went straight from Westminster to the house in Grosvenor Gate where Mary Anne was waiting for him to come as he had promised, to tell her every detail of what had happened. He paced about the room, too stimulated to sit. "To be part of such a scene in real life—after waiting so long!" he enthused. "Perhaps only you can know how I felt."

"Oh, I'm so proud! But who will form the Government? Peel?"

"No chance of that, unfortunately. We outnumber the Liberals in Parliament, but the Radicals and Irish will vote with them and keep them in office."

"Then you must attack—split them up."

"I intend to," he promised. "The first chance I get."

She bit her lip. "Your maiden speech—how I wish I could be there!"

"I have composed it already."

"Is that possible?" she asked, puzzled.

"There will be a debate of reforms in the Irish election system. Daniel O'Connell is bound to speak, denouncing any changes. I shall follow him."

Mary Anne's smile faltered. "Is that wise? He is your bitterest enemy."

Disraeli paused and turned, his face serious. "The whole House knows that. If I did not challenge him, they would think I was afraid. I have prepared my arguments most carefully."

"I am certain," she nodded, reassured by his confidence.

He smiled to her. "I must make a successful speech as soon as possible. The impact of this one will be tremendous!"

There was pandemonium in the House. Disraeli was on his feet trying to deliver his maiden speech. But with the cacophony all about him it was difficult to hear. From the Government benches opposite, mainly from the Irish members, came a medley of hisses, groans, catcalls, drumming of feet, shouts and imitations of farm animals. Many on Disraeli's own side could not help laughing themselves. It was his manner of delivery which had caused it, more than the content of the speech. He had chosen to address the House in the style of an ancient orator, grandiloquent, with expansive gestures, in sharp contrast to his youthful, dandified appearance. Wyndham Lewis was appalled. Beside him, Bentinck chuckled openly. Among the jeering Radicals, Bulwer was disturbed for his friend and saw O'Connell smile triumphantly as his supporters and the Liberals shouted him down.

"I stand here tonight, Sir, not formally, but to some degree the representative of all new Members," Disraeli shouted amid roars of laughter. "Now why smile? Why envy me?" More laughter. "About that time, Sir, when the bell of our cathedral announced the death of the monarch . . ." Screams of laughter blanketed his words. "Nothing is so easy as to laugh!" He was shaking with nerves, but still struggled to make himself heard. Peel looked around and nodded encouragement. Disraeli took a fresh breath and tried again. "We remember the amatory ecologue between the noble Tityrus of the Treasure Bench and the learned Daphnis of Liskeard . . ." It became completely impossible to hear him as his words were drowned by moos, pig squeals, cockcrows, yelps and barking. "Now, Mr. Speaker, we see the philosophical prejudices of men!" The noise volume lowered slightly as the hecklers wished to hear something of what he said, if only to howl the more. "I think, Sir . . ." From the Whig benches came, "Question? Question?"

From the Conservatives, "Hear, Hear!"

"I am not at all surprised, Sir, at the reception I have received. I have begun several things many times and I have succeeded at last, although many have predicted that I must fail, as they had done before me." The only effect was to cause a crescendo of shouting, jeering and animal noises, some even from his own side. Suddenly, drawing himself up, in a voice that cut through the din, his hand thrown out in challenge, Disraeli became for a moment a dominating figure.

"Aye, sir, I sit down now—but the time will come when you *will* hear me!" He sat down in an increased tumult of hooting, boos and catcalls. The whole House seemed to have been given licence to take out its prejudice on him. He sat, indrawn, looking neither to left nor right. He did not even realize that Peel and some of the others had begun to cheer him for his courage. It had been a mistake to rise immediately after O'Connell. The Irishman's supporters had been lying in wait for him and not one section of his carefully prepared speech had been allowed to make its point.

The night before, he had written a jubilant letter to Sarah, promising to give her a full account of his triumph.

He would have to write very differently now. He was fully conscious that his maiden speech had not only not been a success, it had been an unprecedented disaster.

A group of Irish MPs were laughing, congratulating themselves, in the smokeroom at the Athenaeum Club. They had soundly smashed Disraeli. The Jew upstart's career had likely been ruined at its very outset. Knowing what was in store for him, he would never dare to open his mouth again. "We've settled him for good," one of them crowed. "That's the finish of him." The elderly Richard Lalor Sheil sat near them, astute, politically resourceful, the most influential of Ireland's politicians after O'Connell.

Bulwer had come in and stopped to listen. He was as startled as the others, when Sheil suddenly burst out, "You blathering idiots!" They looked at him in astonishment. "I heard his speech and I tell you this: if ever the spirit of oratory was in a man, it is in *that* man. Nothing can prevent him from being one of the finest speakers in the House of Commons."

They were surprised at the anger in his voice. "But, Mr. Sheil—" one of his colleagues protested.

"If there had not beeen those interruptions, Mr. Disraeli *might* have been a failure," Sheil said quietly. "But he was simply crushed, by ignorance and bad manners." He turned away in disgust.

The next evening in Bulwer's drawing-room, a few guests had gathered, friends of himself and Disraeli. It was an affectionate gesture on Bulwer's part, as he was a member of the faction which had begun the demonstration. Disraeli was grateful. After his humiliation, he had been nearly in despair and needed the sympathy of his friends. He stood apart, talking quietly to Lord Lyndhurst.

The other guests also spoke quietly, recognizing the harmful effect the events of the day before might have on Disraeli's future. Among them was the young Tory MP, William Gladstone. Tall, severely handsome, with expres-

135

sive, dark eyes and an athletic figure, he would have stood out in any society.

He had accepted Bulwer's invitation with some reluctance and only because his conscience had driven him. Although horrified by the behavior of the Whigs and low Radicals, he had experienced a sense of satisfaction when Disraeli had been forced to abandon his speech. It was not mere satisfaction that the fellow's Oriental arrogance had been shattered and his flashy shallowness exposed. He had realized with a faint flush of shame that what he felt was pleasure at the defeat of a possible rival in the Party. Some Tories had been prophesying that the novelist would soon be first among the younger members, a position which Gladstone had held himself for most of the past five years, since he entered Parliament at the age of twenty-three under the sponsorship of the Duke of Newcastle. He had already, under Peel, been Junior Lord of the Treasury and Under Secretary for the Colonies.

He had been educated at Eton and Oxford, where he was President of the Union and had won a Double First in Classics and Mathematics. Intensely religious, believing in the power of prayer and convinced that each decision he took in private and public life should be reached only after the most searching meditation to discern God's intention, he had for a time only one wish, to enter the Church. This alarmed his wealthy father, Sir John Gladstone, who had made a fortune out of sugar and slaves, and he advised his son to wait. His father's unenthusiastic reaction to what he had thought a sublime call turned Gladstone toward his second choice, politics. The thought of being in Parliament fascinated him and ambition flamed up in him, but he resisted it as a temptation, until he could convince himself that the Almighty had a purpose for him, "to oppose the increasing worldliness of modern political principles." In nearly every respect, Disraeli and he could not have been more different. Dizzy had begun his career with few, if any, advantages. He appeared to be tortuous and unprincipled, but was remarkably constant and fair-minded. Gladstone had entered Parliament at his first attempt, for a seat in which the votes were directly controlled by his sponsor. He appeared completely straightforward, but was a mass of complexes and contradictions. By racking his conscience, he could make himself believe almost anything. And his opinion was not be be altered by any argument, unless his conscience told him that he had misinterpreted the Divine will.

He had made himself come to Bulwer's as a punishment for the pleasure he had felt at Disraeli's failure. He had no liking for the man himself. In an effort to understand him, he had tried to read some of his novels but gave up, considering them flippant and overwritten, meant only to titillate, with no observable moral purpose. In the first instance, his antagonism had been caused by Disraeli's indolent, affected manner and gaudy dress. Gladstone would have said, "Typical," but he would not admit to any prejudice against Disraeli's race, as such. No, it was the fellow himself he could not like, yet charity for the less fortunate was an essential part of Christianity and must be dispensed.

He was with Wyndham Lewis and Mary Anne, to whom he was sincerely attached. He had at first been shocked by her frivolity and freeness of speech, but had soon come to see that her chatter was harmless. Her heart was innocent. He enjoyed her company and teasing ways. It gave him the illusion of flirtation and feminine involvement, without moral danger. This evening he had been touched by her concern for her "protegé," Disraeli, as she had defended him against Rosina Bulwer's slighting remarks.

The Bulwers were still near them and the scarcely concealed hostility between them was an added embarrassment. "I don't see what all the fuss is about," Rosina said, waspishly, appealing to the others.

"Really, Rosina!" her husband protested, signing to her not to talk so loudly.

"It was just a speech. He must have made hundreds."

A servant came to Bulwer and he left them, hurrying to the door.

"Yet never one so important," Gladstone said. His expression was earnest.

"In what way, Mr. Gladstone?" Rosina asked.

"You see, madam, one may speak well on many occasions and in many places, yet fail when one tries to speak in Parliament."

"That's why a new Member's first speech is so important," Mary Anne explained. "To ensure that when he rises again, he'll be listened to."

"No wonder Dizzy is so dizz-heartened," Rosina laughed. None of the others responded. Mary Anne glanced away.

Across the room, Disraeli stood with Lyndhurst by one of the window recesses. He was touched that Lyndhurst was here. The aged rake had recently, to everyone's consternation, married a much younger woman and he had hardly been seen for some weeks. But he had left his bride to offer his friend such aid and comfort as he could. "Nothing can alter the fact that it was a fiasco," Disraeli was saying. The hurt was still evident.

"No, my boy," Lyndhurst said soothingly, "Peel says that some of the party were disappointed—but not him. You did all you could under the circumstances."

"He's being kind."

"He could see the Radicals were determined not to let you be heard." As Lyndhurst spoke, he was facing the door. He paused for a moment and then muttered, "I don't believe it . . ." He had seen Bulwer in the doorway with R.L. Sheil.

"Oh, my stars!" Lewis ejaculated.

"What is it?" Mary Anne asked.

"Sheil," said Gladstone. "O'Connell's right-hand man. Coming in with Bulwer."

"You mean he's invited him?"

"I didn't think Pups had such a sense of humor," Rosina laughed.

Lyndhurst left Disraeli as Bulwer brought Sheil to him. Disraeli was taut.

"I don't believe you know each other," Bulwer remarked in introduction.

"Only by sight," Sheil said, smiling to Disraeli, who bowed. "I told Mr. Bulwer I longed to meet you. I wanted to congratulate you on your speech yesterday."

"You are pleased to be ironic, Sir," Disraeli said stiffly.

"Not at all, young man. I am quite sincere. I wished to apologize for the behavior of my fellow countrymen."

Disraeli hesitated for a moment, surprised. "Your pardon, Sir. It is I who should apologize."

Bulwer judged it time to withdraw and leave them to themselves. Sheil chuckled, "No doubt you've been going around in despair. But I say your reception yesterday was fortunate."

"How so?" Disraeli wondered. He had been startled by Sheil's arrival. Clearly, he was not here merely to apologize for the Radicals.

Sheil lowered his voice. "You must know that many of the Members have had misgivings about you. And not only among your opponents."

"I am aware there may be a certain amount of prejudice," Disraeli said carefully.

The little man shook his head. "It's not just a matter of race. They are suspicious of your reputation for wit and brilliance. No speech you could have made would have been listened to properly."

"Do you believe so?"

"I know it," Sheil asserted. "At the best you'd have been received coldly and your speech forgotten the next day. But the disgraceful behavior on my side has made the House feel ashamed and, next time you rise to speak, you'll be listened to with politeness."

Disraeli had not expected to be encouraged by one of his chief opponents. He was thankful. The little Irishman had come to bring him the benefit of his experience. "Now mark me," went on Sheil sagely, "you must surprise them. You must *not* be brilliant, but very short and simple. You've shown us you have a fine voice and a good temper. Now get rid of your genius for a while.

Speak often, but try to be dull. Stick to practical matters, quote figures and dates until you've earned a reputation for soundness."

"Yes," Disraeli agreed, thoughtfully.

"Remember—only subjects of detail until they're used to you," Sheil finished. "In a short time the members on both sides will sigh for the wit and eloquence they know is in you. Then you can pour them forth and you'll become a favorite speaker."

"It is perhaps the truest advice I have ever been given. I am deeply indebted," Disraeli said.

The others, watching at some distance, were surprised to see him take Sheil's hand and shake it warmly.

"Mind you," cautioned Sheil, with a touch of irony, "if you give me an opening, I'll tear you to pieces in the House."

Disraeli was with Mary Anne in the drawing room at Grosvenor Gate. "So you are following Mr. Sheil's prescription?" she surmised.

"As though he were the Queen's physician. Years ago my father gave me much the same advice. I wish I had listened to it then."

"Wyndham and I so enjoyed our visit with your family. How is your dear father?" she inquired.

"Well, I thank you, although his eyesight troubles him."

"And your sister?"

"Sarah also is well. My greatest sorrow in leaving Bradenham is always in parting with her."

Mary Anne sighed. "It is a pity you cannot visit them more often."

"Yes, it is like an oasis of calm. I always come away refreshed. When I was last there I rediscovered the poems of Milton."

"Milton?" she repeated, curious.

"John Milton. I wandered through the woods reading *Paradise Lost* aloud. What language, what a sublime concept!"

"Paradise Lost? Is it a poem?"

140

"Yes," he said blankly.

"I must make a note of it." She rose and moved to her escritoire. "And now you've plunged back into the prose world of politics," she said, when she had written the name in her notebook.

"Headlong," he chuckled. The gaps in her education continually shocked and amused him.

She looked at him fondly. "I am so grateful to you for taking over the constituency work for Wyndham. It cannot be neglected, yet he has all his business interests to attend to. And he is far from strong."

"I am only too happy to do it. I owe you both an unpayable debt."

She smiled. "There is no question of debt. I am more than content with my protegé."

"As always, you overwhelm me, Mary Anne." He bowed. "Now, if you will excuse me I should be at work." He turned toward the door.

"Of course. Oh—do you happen to know Mr. Milton's address?"

"Milton?" said Disraeli, puzzled. He could not imagine what she meant.

"I would like to invite him to dinner," she explained.

He began to laugh, but stopped himself. She was obviously sincere. He wondered how he could reply without embarrassing either her or himself. "He has been dead for some time," he said solemnly.

"Oh dear, I'm sorry to hear that. Was it unexpected?"

He paused. "Old age, I fancy."

He could not help smiling now. He was used to educated and beautiful women and Mary Anne was neither. And yet he found her enchanting.

The Members, seated in the House, listened attentively as Disraeli spoke. He stood in his place behind Peel, deliberately using the minimum of gesture and inflection. There had been a hush when he rose and caught the Speaker's eye, but he had surprised them with his calm, businesslike delivery.

"My point, Sir, is that the author's copyright, as the only legacy he leaves his heirs, should be protected for at least fifty years after his death."

"Hear, hear!" approved Peel loudly. He was echoed by the Conservatives.

"It has been the boast of the Liberal Party that in many brilliant periods of our literary annals they have been patrons of letters." It was a gesture to the Whigs and, on the Government front bench, Russell and Palmerston nodded agreement.

"Hear, hear!" Russell called.

As many Members of the House were authors in one way or another, there was general approval for Disraeli's proposal. His points had been concise and he was listened to with respect.

"And it will be honorable to the present Government if, under its auspices, it is succeeded by legislative protection," he concluded.

He sat down composedly to loud applause, led by Bulwer among the Radicals and by Peel and Gladstone. Seated among the Irish MPs Sheil folded his arms and smiled.

"Well, now he's back in the saddle he can ride on," Bentinck growled to Wyndham Lewis, who was applauding vigorously. How condescending, Lewis thought, coming from a country Member who had never been heard to utter a word in debate, in all his years in Parliament. . . .

The Disraelis were settled in the small, sheltered arbor in the garden of Bradenham. Mary Anne, on a visit, was sitting with Isaac and Maria. Sarah refilled their glasses from an earthenware pitcher of fresh lemonade on the table in front of them. They had all grown very close. Mary Anne was particularly attached to old Isaac, who was now nearly blind.

"So," Maria probed, "Ben is really making a name for himself?"

"A great name, Mrs. D'Israeli," Mary Anne assured her. "Peel often asks him to speak first in debates."

"So it is really true?" Isaac asked.

"He must have told you," Mary Anne said with a smile.

"Yes, but—well, you see, Mrs. Lewis, Ben is the soul of truthfulness, but he is also a romantic novelist and so inclined to embroider the facts a little."

"Especially when he is the hero of the story, himself," said Maria, who knew her son well.

"Mother!" Sarah objected, scandalized. "And you, Father! What will Mary Anne think?"

Mary Anne laughed. "That they are secretly almost as proud of my protegé as I am." She patted Isaac's hand.

"I have read that the other members crowd into the House to hear him," Sarah said.

"Yes, he followed some very sound advice, "Mary Anne confirmed, "and now the mere possibility of him speaking is enough to fill the House. Wyndham says that whenever he rises you could hear a pin drop."

"Well, well, well," Isaac said quietly. He was not an emotional man, but he could not conceal the growing sense of pride he took in his son.

Disraeli and Wyndham Lewis were coming to them from the house.

"Here they are," Maria told him.

When they reached the arbor, Lewis was seen to be breathing heavily. He had become grayer in those past months and any physical effort strained him. Mary Anne was concerned. "You look tired, my dear. I hope you haven't walked too far?"

"No, no, we took it very easily," he reassured her, sitting on the bench.

"You look hot, too, Ben. Sit down and have some lemonade."

In contrast to Lewis, Dizzy's cheeks were flushed. He seemed all energy and spirit. "No, thank you, Mama."

"Was that the postman I heard just now?" Isaac enquired.

"Indeed, it was," Disraeli said.

Sarah was intrigued by the emphasis. "Anything important?"

"The answer to our prayers," Disraeli announced.

143

"What?" Maria demanded. "Don't be a tease, Ben."

"Will someone tell me what is going on?" Isaac protested a little testily.

"A change of government, Mr. Disraeli," Lewis said.

"No!" Mary Anne gasped, thrilled. "The Whigs are out?"

Disraeli smiled to her. "Out. The agitation in the country has forced Melbourne to resign. The Queen has asked Peel to form a government with himself as Prime Minister."

The indications were clear to everyone except Maria. "What will it mean?" she asked.

Sarah's eyes were intent on her brother. "Will you be offered a post?"

When he hesitated, Lewis answered for him. "As one of the ablest of our younger men, it's not impossible. It's even likely."

Excited, Sarah rose and took Disraeli's arm. They both looked at Isaac. "What do you hope for?" he asked.

"Anything," Disraeli admitted truthfully. "However small."

Sarah hugged his arm. "All he needs is to set his other foot on the ladder!" she said.

Disraeli smiled and capped it. "Then what may happen next in the dazzling farce of life—the Fates only know."

"But I do, too," Mary Anne told him, confidently. "You shall climb so quickly, you will soar out of sight!"

As the others laughed, Disraeli smiled to her and she dimpled back. It was impossible for him now to believe that, once, he had thought her insufferable and vain and giddy. Next to Sa, no one had ever understood him so well nor worked so unselfishly on his behalf. She had no real intellect, yet he had seen that she was uncannily shrewd at times and he had not been surprised to learn from Wyndham Lewis that her advice had often been very useful in his business dealings. If he ever had the success he dreamed of, he promised himself to repay Wyndham and her tenfold.

"It's a pity we can only drink to Sir Robert in lemonade," Isaac was saying. He looked at his son and shook his head. "I don't know, Ben ... sometimes I wonder how an old hedge-sparrow like myself could have sired an eagle like you."

chapter six

The salon at Gore House, Lady Blessington's new home, was even more sumptuous than the one she had made famous before. Indeed, the whole house, once the visitor had turned in through the wrought-iron gates, might have been taken for a miniature French palace.

Normally, no reason was needed for a party at Gore House, but tonight was special. D'Orsay had just been granted a formal separation from his wife and the solution to the tangled legal situation which had for years kept him and Marguerite on the brink of financial disaster could not be long delayed. Although only a few knew the reason for celebration, half the notables of London seemed to be there. Among the most conspicuous was the fierce old critic and writer, Walter Savage Landor, whom Margaret Blessington with her usual generosity had helped to survive. He had caused some embarrassment at dinner by arguing with a fellow guest, a well known Catholic, over the Psalms. As a classical scholar, Landor attacked them as crude and repetitious, with no significance to modern life. He became so heated in his attack on their value even as poetry that everyone had become uncomfortable. It ended in a burst of laughter, when Lady Blessington smiled beautifully to him down the table and pleaded, "Do write something better, Mr. Landor."

Disraeli was still chuckling. He was sitting with Selina Forester. Next to her, D'Orsay murmured, "I do not think I would like to be criticized by Mr. Landor."

Disraeli agreed. "He is as ferocious as his middle name."

They were rising from the table. Those gentlemen who wished might remain with the port and brandy. Dizzy and D'Orsay chose, with some others, to go out with the ladies. They caught up with Lady Blessington and Lyndhurst as they entered the salon.

"Depend upon it, Count D'Orsay," Lyndhurst declared. "I say, if Dis continues to build on his new reputation as a serious practical thinker, he must be given office when we next form a government."

Disraeli bowed as Lyndhurst smiled and moved on with Lady Blessington. All through dinner he had been concentrating on Selina. Her elfin prettiness had turned into real beauty over the past few years and she had proved to be as intelligent as she was beautiful. He was intrigued by the hint of challenge in her smile. "Tell me, Dizzy," she said, "do you not find your head turning with all this praise? Or do you take it with a pinch of salt?"

He touched his heart. "My dear Selina, to me it is water in the desert—where salt is the last thing one wishes."

She laughed and considered him. "Why is it that you are so amusing outside Parliament, and so dull inside?"

He moved closer. "The secret is that I am never more serious than when I appear to be joking."

His eyes held hers and her lips parted slightly. "Oh, dear . . ." she whispered. "Now that the secret is out, I shall have to take you seriously all the time—and that, I fear, would be much too dangerous." She smiled teasingly

148

and left him to join Lady Blessington. He watched the sway of her slim figure as she crossed the room.

D'Orsay had been listening. *"Ravissante,"* he agreed. "You are épris—in love with her?"

"But, of course!" Dizzy assured him. Then as D'Orsay reacted, he added, "And with half a dozen others."

"So you are not about to propose?" D'Orsay laughed.

"Nothing is further from my mind. To tie oneself perpetually to one woman. . . ." Disraeli shuddered as they began to stroll round the room. "No, many people —my sister Sarah, Lyndhurst—they advise me to marry for the sake of my career. What a soulless reason!" D'Orsay laughed. They had the fearful example of Bulwer, who had fled to Europe to escape Rosina's relentless persecution. And there was D'Orsay's own experience of marriage. Disraeli shook his head. "Besides, it takes money to support a wife, and I have none."

"I am sorry. It is partly my fault," D'Orsay apologized. "Believe me, if I could repay—"

"No, no, please, Alfred!" Disraeli objected. He had lent him nearly half the earnings on his novel *Venetia*, to settle gambling losses which D'Orsay had not dared to mention to Marguerite.

"The cards do not run well," D'Orsay confided. "I lost three hundred and twenty-five pounds the night before last. If only I could assist you. But, if you think that I could be of any use to you in the way of security, I would do for you what I would do for any other."

Disraeli smiled. How like D'Orsay. Owing money, and borrowing more on top, was as natural to him as breathing. He never thought of the final reckoning, which at times haunted Dizzy, a bourgeois feeling of guilt which he could never quite lose, although he had learned to jest about it. "You are very kind. However—" he declined. "The more I borrow, the more impossible it becomes even to pay off the interest on what I owe."

"For all of us," D'Orsay laughed. "But we must find some means of clearing up your debts."

149

"I'm not sure I even want to," Disraeli told him. "I'm fond of them. For so long, they've been the source of my only real excitement. I owe all my knowledge of human nature to them. In dealing with my creditors, I have learned a diplomatic skill that, one day, shall confound and control cabinets."

D'Orsay's laughter was attracting attention and he restrained it. "That's very philosophical," he said. "You are indebted to your debts."

"They are my guardian angels," Dizzy told him. "If I become too confident, they make me stop and think. If I am lazy, they prick me into action. The two greatest stimulants in the world, Youth and Debt. One I shall soon lose, but not the other. What should I be without my debts? The dear companions of my life that never desert me."

"You should put it into a book," D'Orsay smiled.

"I could," Dizzy assured him. "I could write a whole treatise about it. The one thing I cannot do, is get rid of the damned things." He paused and bowed to Selina who was watching them from across the room.

"But, *mon cher,* you could solve your problems so easily," D'Orsay murmured.

"How?"

"By taking the inevitable step," D'Orsay said. "You could marry an heiress. Someone like Selina, she is obviously attracted to you." Dizzy was amused and shook his head. D'Orsay nodded toward an appealing, dark-haired young woman who was passing them and smiled. "What about Lady Charlotte Bertie?" he suggested. "Clever, twenty-five thousand pounds, and home-loving. She'd have you." He took Disraeli's arm and began to lead him toward Lady Charlotte.

Disraeli hung back. "No, no, I am not yet up for auction." D'Orsay laughed. "As for love, all my friends who married for that or beauty, either beat their wives or live apart from them."

D'Orsay gave up. "Like Edward and Rosina."

"Exactly," Disraeli stressed. "I may commit many follies, but I never intend to marry for 'love'—which I am sure is a guarantee of unhappiness."

Disraeli had been working in the library of the House of Commons. He was a familiar sight there, for when the House was not sitting he studied the parliamentary reports of earlier years in Hansard, to the amusement of some of the other members. But today he had been working on constituency business. He preferred to deal with it in the study at Grosvenor Gate, but Lewis had not been well for the last week and was in bed. He finished his last letter and took them out to the desk to be despatched.

As he waited, he saw Bulwer come in, look round and make for him. He had not seen Bulwer often since his return from his travels and was pleased, but hoped he would not have to listen to yet another saga of Rosina's tantrums.

Bulwer seemed very serious as he came to him. "I was terribly sorry to hear, Dis."

Disraeli smiled. "About what?"

"Don't you know? Wyndham Lewis."

"Wyndham?" Disraeli asked, puzzled.

"He is dead," Bulwer said.

The bluntness of the news shocked Disraeli. "How? When?"

"This morning," Bulwer told him. "Heart attack."

Up to this day, life had been kind to Mary Anne. Adored in childhood and by her wealthy, indulgent husband, she had known only affection and no real sorrow. Now she was distraught. She sent word to her husband's family and to her mother to join her. She felt desperately alone and nearly broke down when Dizzy arrived. She was wearing mourning and he had never seen anyone changed so much in so short a time. Yet the shock and the suffering had not aged her. Paradoxically, she looked younger and more fragile. He stood watching her.

She was seated on the sofa and his heart went out to

151

her as he saw how hard she was fighting not to weep. "We were married for . . . for seventeen years," she faltered. "I was in the room with him when he died."

"Yes."

"We were so close." She looked away, biting her lip. "All I can see ahead is loneliness—emptiness."

"It is natural," he said quietly. "But you must not imprison yourself in those feelings. You must try not to brood over the past." She caught her breath and shook her head. He sat beside her. "Mary Anne, you are too young to feel that life is over, that all happiness died with him."

"I try," she whispered. "But I have no one to turn to."

"I assure you," he said soothingly, "in myself and my family, you have sincere friends who have loved you from our first acquaintance."

She tried to smile to him. "I am grateful. So was Wyndham, for your attention to me."

"It is not only gratitude on my part," he told her. "But appreciation of the qualities I have come to see in you, the kindness and sweet temper, which will make me always your friend." The sincerity in his deep, gentle voice had begun its calming effect on her, as he meant. She took his hand and held it tight. "As far as my advice, and assistance and presence can contribute to your welfare or give you comfort, you may count on me."

"Dear Dizzy . . ." she breathed. She lowered her head and kissed his hand, then leaned her cheek against it. Moved and slightly disturbed, he sat looking at her bowed head.

They were motionless for a time, then he heard the door open. He released her and rose. Rosina Bulwer was being shown in. She looked at him coldly as he bowed to her, disliking him as a close friend of her estranged husband. She hurried past him without a word, to sit by Mary Anne and take her into her arms. Unable to control herself any longer, Mary Anne held her close, weeping quietly against her bosom.

A few weeks later, D'Orsay had come to Disraeli's temporary bachelor quarters to invite him to dinner. While he waited in the rather bare living-room, he tried the madeira in the decanter. It was passable. Dizzy had been down to Maidstone to answer some queries of the local committee. As always, D'Orsay had missed him and smiled when he came in, still wearing a black velvet frock coat in mourning and looping his choicest gold chains over the pearl buttons of his white, watered silk waistcoat. "Is Mary Anne bearing up?" D'Orsay enquired.

Disraeli nodded. "From her letters, I'd say she'd recovered her spirits wonderfully."

"Where is she now?"

"In Wales, attending to Wyndham's business affairs. There was a great deal to be sorted out, I believe."

"At least he left her well provided for," D'Orsay remarked innocently.

"Very well, I imagine. She has the house at Grosvenor Gate, and Wyndham had a fifth share of the profits of the ironworks. Some years that was nearly a hundred thousand pounds."

D'Orsay blinked and came perilously near being taken by surprise for once. He recovered quickly, and immediately thought, Dizzy will soon be able to afford better madeira. "And so, *mon ami,* your prayers are answered."

Dizzy was looping the last chain over its button. "How so?"

"For an end to your financial problems," D'Orsay explained. "Don't tell me it hasn't occurred to you? The answer all along was to find a rich widow who would support you. She could not be more ideal."

The chain fell from Disraeli's fingers and dangled below his waistcoat. He was momentarily quite shocked. ". . . Mary Anne? She's forty-five—forty-six! Thirteen years older than I."

"But she *is* rich," D'Orsay reminded him. "And young for her age and pretty. And you like her."

"Like her, yes!" Disraeli protested, still thrown by the

153

suggestion. "Admire her to an extent. I am genuinely fond of her. Oh, this is ridiculous! I've had no indication from her that she'd welcome anything more."

"No?" D'Orsay smiled. "How long did she tell you she'd been married? Seventeen years? By my reckoning, it must be at least twenty-two." He moved closer to Dizzy, lifted the dangling chain and looped it over the lowest button. "You do not need me to tell you that a woman who, at such a time, is still careful to hide her real age must have done so for a reason." He stepped back, not looking at Dizzy, but admiring the curves of the chain.

Disraeli could not argue against what he had said. Perhaps D'Orsay had meant it half in jest, but the more he thought about it, the less absurd it seemed.

Disraeli nearly missed the Queen's Coronation. Like all other MPs he had an invitation and a reserved seat in Westminster Abbey, but there was a condition which he could not fulfill. He did not have the obligatory court dress, nor the cash to buy or hire it. To confess it to anyone except his family was too embarrassing, so he contented himself with pretending that the thought of attending the ceremony bored him.

He was genuinely hard pressed again. The reason for his trip to Maidstone had been more serious than he had admitted. An accusation had been made locally that, during his election, he had offered massive bribes which he had neglected to pay. It was a clever move by his opponents, damaging him both with those voters who were against bribery and those who expected it. He rushed down to consult the committee and, to clear himself, published an open letter in the newspapers, attacking the barrister who had made the accusation and denying it as completely untrue. His defense was effective but the letter was so strongly worded that he found himself in court facing a charge of libel and only escaped heavy damages by making an "apology." The apology was really another skillfully worded attack but, fortunately, the Attorney-General accepted it.

It had all cost more money, which he did not have. Yet

it was worth it. The stories his family had heard of his success in parliamentary debates were not exaggerated. The House might be half empty on a dull evening after all the main speeches had been given, but if Disraeli rose to speak, it would soon fill, the Members crowding in to hear him, expecting and getting fireworks. He was unpredictable, speaking from time to time according to his own beliefs and not following the strict Party line. Sometimes he even drew cheers from the opposite side, yet a few minutes later he would lash them with such scorn and invective that they would squirm in their seats and his own side would be cheering him on. It was unsettling, especially for the older Tories, who liked to know exactly where a man stood. He was not expected to criticize his own Party, and they often wished he would take his brilliance somewhere else. They did not trust him. But he had made his mark and he could not let the false accusation at Maidstone go unanswered or it could be used later to destroy him.

His brother Ralph arrived the day before the Coronation with money from his father and they raced all over town, looking for a secondhand court costume, silk stockings and buckled shoes. He was finally fitted out at half-past two in the morning, in time to take his seat in the Abbey. He was immensely impressed by the spectacle, the most splendid he had ever seen, and again by the young queen with her grace and composure throughout the long ceremony. He was delighted by the beauty of his new friend Lady Londonderry, who sat among the peeresses, and by Lyndhurst's dignity in his robes. He chuckled at Melbourne with his coronet slipping down over his eyes. All the small details fascinated him. But most of all, the pageantry as the members of the five Orders of Nobility paid their homage appealed to his romantic soul. Like everyone else, he found himself cheering when the old Duke of Wellington climbed to the throne and knelt to take the oath of fealty to the girl queen. And he was moved when the aged Lord Rolle tripped and fell on the steps of the throne and Victoria, forgetting all etiquette, rose and helped him to his feet. At the end, when the drums beat and the trumpets sounded their fanfare, he joined full-heartedly in the shout, "God Save Queen Victoria! Long Live Queen Victoria! May the Queen live for ever!"

Mary Anne had returned from Wales. With a few others he watched the Coronation Review in Hyde Park from her windows. They had to stand well back, because she was still in mourning and must not be thought to be giving a party. He stayed behind, when the others left. All Members of Parliament were presented with a commemorative gold medal after the Coronation. He had given his to Mary Anne and was pleased to see she was wearing it. It was very effective as the only ornament on her chaste, black-trimmed dress.

"So you are going off to Lady Londonderry's," she remarked.

"Yes, she is giving a banquet for the Duke of Wellington and Marshal Soult. It is a historic occasion, an honor to be invited." He paused. "I wish you could be there."

She smiled. "Oh, you know I can't. Besides, I would never be asked." The color had come back to her cheeks and, after the weeks of rest and fresh air in Glamorgan, she looked remarkably youthful.

"I hate to leave you alone," he said.

"My mother will be back shortly," she told him. She touched the gold medal. "And you've already been more than kind. I should have known you'd be my first visitor on my return."

He took her hand and kissed it. "Could you doubt it?"

She was touched. "Some friends have scarcely called since Wyndham died," she said fondly. "But not you." She moved from him to sit near the central window, through which they could still see the vast crowds circulating in the park, a mosaic of summer dresses mingling with the scarlets, blues and greens of thousands of uniforms.

He followed and stood beside her. "I came as often as my duties allowed. And wrote whenever I could."

"And such letters," she smiled. "In all the trials of

156

these last months, with Wyndham's family being so difficult, they were the only things that lightened my
heart."

"I hoped a little gossip might amuse you."

"It was kind of you to think of me."

Now that the moment had come, he felt uneasy, and
hesitated.

"There has not been a moment when you have been
absent from my thoughts."

Like him, Mary Anne hesitated.

"If I were a girl I fear my head would be turned. Of
course, I understand that you write and speak as a poet,
saying more than you really intend."

He moved closer. "Why do you say that?"

"I mean—at first, I read your letters out loud. They
were so charming and amusing. But later I could not."

"Why not?"

She could not look at him. "They—they were more
like the letters of a lover than of a friend."

"But that is what I wish to be," he said simply. "And
not merely a lover—a husband."

She turned to him, startled and flustered. "You cannot
mean . . ." she whispered.

"I was never more serious," he assured her. "Surely
you cannot claim to be surprised? You must know I have
the most profound admiration for you?"

"As a friend . . . You have not thought . . ." She rose
and stepped away.

"Oh, but I have, Mary Anne. Long and deeply.
Your heart is warm. It is made to seek another with
which it may beat in time. And so is mine." He still
followed her and his arm went round her waist.

"Please . . ." she begged, frightened by her own reaction to his touch.

He turned her to face him. "We could waste months,
years of our lives in needless loneliness if I do not speak
now. I offer you constant, loving companionship and
unchanging devotion, if you will marry me."

Mary Anne was flattered and also tempted. She could
not deny that she thought of him constantly, sometimes

157

longed just to hear his voice. "What can I say? It is too soon." She broke away from him.

"Love is always unexpected. It knocks at the door without bidding."

She had expected him to follow her again, but he had not. She turned to him, torn. "What would people think?"

Disraeli smiled. "What they say already. The malicious among them see your kindness to me as partiality, my devotion to you as proof that we are already lovers."

"How shameful!" she exclaimed, shocked. Yet at the same moment, she felt a wild excitement that people should think of Dizzy as her lover.

"That the world should guess I love you?"

There was a suggestion of hurt in his voice that disturbed her even more. "No! I don't—you know my feelings for you have always—I am confused. I need time," she entreated.

He moved closer again. "I beg you for an answer."

She could not look at him. He was so intent, so handsome. Always before, she had controlled how far the game had gone. But it was no longer a game. "I could not think of marrying again so soon. I must have time to think, to consider your offer, to learn your true feelings," she protested.

"They will not change," he swore. "My heart is pledged. Say at least I may hope."

Mary Anne had to catch her breath. Thoughts were chasing through her mind, of her loneliness, of her dead husband, Dizzy's kindness to her, the difference in their ages. If only she knew that he was sincere! "If you will wait a year," she said quietly.

"I cannot!" he exclaimed. "I must have a sign before then. You are coming to visit my parents next month. You will still come?"

She hesitated, but could not refuse. "Yes."

He smiled for a second in relief, then she nearly trembled as he moved closer, his eyes fixed on hers. "Then say nothing to anyone. Listen only to your own heart. And if you find that you can love me, leave off your left glove when you arrive, so that I may clasp your hand and feel the soft warmth of it in mine. And no one but ourselves shall know what it means."

Mary Anne gazed at him, flushed, mesmerized by his hypnotic voice.

Disraeli waited on the dimly lit station platform with his father and Sarah. He stood apart from them, tense and excited, just out of the light of the flaring gas jets. They could hear the sound of an approaching train.

"Here it comes," Isaac smiled.

The locomotive appeared out of the blackness, belching smoke from its chimney stack, steam hissing from valves and joints as it came to a halt like a breathless dragon. The lights from the carriages passed across the group. A porter was shouting, "Maidenhead! This is Maidenhead!"

"There she is. Mary Anne!" cried Sarah.

Disraeli hurried forward and opened a carriage door. He bowed as Mary Anne stepped out onto the platform, hardly seeming to notice him. His eyes were on her hands and he was stricken to see she wore both gloves. She went straight to Sarah to kiss her, then to be kissed affectionately by Isaac.

Her mother had come with her and Disraeli helped her down, not noticing when she spoke to him and moved forward to be introduced. Isaac took the small boxes which Mary Anne was carrying and he and Sarah greeted her mother. "How lovely to see you. Did you have a good journey?" Sarah asked.

"The carriage is just outside," said Isaac. "I'll have Tita take care of your luggage."

Disraeli closed the carriage door and turned. Talking to Isaac and Sarah, apparently unaware of him Mary Anne was stripping off her left glove. He moved toward her.

"I'm so happy to be here," Mary Anne was saying. "I can't tell you how much I've been longing to see you all." Disraeli reached her. Her left arm was by her side.

"This way. It's not far," Isaac said, leading her mother toward the exit. Sarah was looking down the platform for

159

a porter. Disraeli's right hand touched Mary Anne's left and he clasped it tightly. The contact was erotic, highly charged, so much so that Mary Anne's eyes half closed and she swayed, her feelings almost insupportable.

Isaac D'Israeli sat in his study at Bradenham some months later. Ranged around him were the books which had given him so much interest and solace throughout his life. The studious old man was now very frail, his eyes worn out with studying innumerable lines of type. He was bent over a book on his desk, trying to read it with his glass. Disraeli was with him.

"I got through so much while Mrs. Lewis was staying here. She read to me every morning." Isaac muttered.

"Doesn't your magnifying glass help?"

"It's no use. The letters blur and dance." Isaac gave up and laid his glass aside, rubbing his eyes.

Disraeli was deeply concerned and said, "How can you work, Father?"

"Oh, Sarah makes my notes. My memory's as good as ever." He peered at his son. "What was your problem with your committee at Maidstone?"

"The usual—money. I raised enough."

"From Mrs. Lewis?"

"Yes," Disraeli admitted, reluctantly. Mary Anne had lent him enough to pay the expenses of his libel case.

"A pity. I hope you are not about to commit a great folly," Isaac sighed. "There is no fiercer hell on earth than a loveless marriage."

Disraeli was tense. "I know exactly what I am doing, Father."

"It is not you I am concerned about," Isaac declared, "but Mary Anne. She is gentle and vulnerable."

"Will you believe me when I say that my only fear is that I might not make her happy?" Disraeli said seriously.

Isaac nodded. "Well said. Yet there are those who will think your main interest is her money."

Disraeli knew that his father was really asking for

reassurance. He had not been able to keep his plans hidden from his family. His mother had hurt him. "Have you thought?" she insisted. "Really thought about it? She is far too old for you! While you are still in your forties, she will be sixty. While you are in your fifties, she will be seventy! And you will never—can never have any children. Have you realized that?" His father's reaction had been different. He was attached to Mary Anne and saw her as someone to be cherished. He was afraid that Ben had seen only the advantages to himself in the marriage, and not the responsibility toward her which it involved. There would be grave difficulties, over and above the difference in age. Not least, the attitude of other people, who would be bound to assume that Ben's affection for her, however sincere, was due solely to her wealth.

"It is not as much as I supposed, nor the world imagines," Disraeli said.

"But you continue as a suitor?"

"Even more. I have found, in these months since her visit, that I cannot bear to be without her," Disraeli told him. It was the simple truth. "I know she is silly and tactless and frivolous, but I do not care."

Isaac had been watching his son. He wished he could see his face clearly, but he was relieved by the honesty in his voice. If only he were not living another of his romantic fantasies . . . "It is a strange kind of love," he mused, then smiled faintly. "You are an enigma, Ben—even to me."

Disraeli moved to the study door and paused, glancing back. "And to myself at times, Father."

He went up to his room and he began a letter to Mary Anne. "I can tell you nothing, but that I love you and, indeed, am so ill and stupid that I should not be surprised if you doubted it from this very weak expression." He paused. He had already started another one. "The sun shines, and Bradenham looks beautiful; most green and fresh, and today even bright. But you are not here." He looked at them, troubled, and laid down his pen. Again, he felt a vague uneasiness. He had not lied to his father.

161

He had followed D'Orsay's advice deliberately at first, planning his campaign to win Mary Anne very carefully. Each step was worked out, the sentiments, the phrases, the tone of voice to be used. Once his first proposal had been made, after she had been convinced of his concern for her, she was to be given no pause to think. She would be overwhelmed with proofs of his love for her, desire if that was what she wanted, admiration if that was what she preferred. He was playing for high stakes. With this marriage, his future would be secure and he would have a solid base for the struggles that lay ahead in his career. He would keep his part of the bargain and treat her, if not with true love, at least with constant devotion.

Her unshakable insistence on waiting for a year before making her final decision had thrown his calculations out badly. He had counted on a short and triumphant campaign. Now, somehow, he had to survive the threat of bankruptcy for another twelve months. At the same time, he had been shaken to hear from her that Lewis's will had provided for her in a practical, rather than an open-handed way. His interest in the ironworks had been left to his brother, who was to make Mary Anne an annual payment of not less than £4000. She was to keep the house on the corner of Grosvenor Gate and Park Lane until her death, when it would revert to her husband's family. She would be comfortable, but it was not a fortune. Perhaps D'Orsay's original advice had been right? He should have set himself to marry a younger woman with a large dowry, which would be at his disposal.

While his mind still swayed one way and another, regretting his haste to propose, Mary Anne arrived for her visit to his parents. On the day she and her mother were due to come, he found to his own surprise that he was excited and increasingly anxious, in case she changed her mind. He told himself he had begun to believe his own protestations of love. But it was true, and he could not alter it. He knew he had to have her. And at Bradenham, her passion had answered his. It may have been the effect of having to restrain themselves in front of his family and her charming, old mother, but when they were alone she was like a girl in love, melting eagerly into his arms, whispering endearments, pausing out of sight of the house in their walks to kiss and be kissed and be told how much he adored her. Their loveplay had gone further than he had ever thought she would permit. After her companionable marriage to Wyndham and so many empty flirtations, she had found a man who roused feelings in her that she had never known before.

And yet with separation came coolness. Her first letters had been as warm and passionate as his, always speaking of the day they would meet again, longing for them to be together. Then they had become more formal and less frequent, mentioning visits and mutual friends, avoiding his questions and pleas for reassurance. He sensed that it was not coyness and it disturbed him. He could neither finish the letters nor work on his play. He went to find Sarah.

She sat at the table in the sitting-room, transcribing her father's notes. As her brother came in she looked up. "Is he all right?"

"As uncomplaining as usual. But it is a cruel irony for a man who has lived for his books to be unable to read any more."

"Yes." She watched him as he crossed to the garden window. "And you?"

"Me?" he turned.

"I hear you pacing your room at night. I know it is not only Father's health which troubles you."

He smiled. "Dear Sarah, how could I think I could ever keep anything from you?"

"What is wrong?" she asked. "Something to do with Mary Anne?"

He hesitated. "I am not sure. She insisted on our waiting. I agreed. Each week I feel for her more deeply, but instead of more affectionate, she has grown colder."

"You always dramatize things, Ben," Sarah said, fondly. "Are you sure it is not your imagination?"

"Her last letters have been formal, distant, I can't imagine why."

Sarah thought for a moment. "Her letters to me are the same as ever. There is one thing . . ."

"Yes?" he prompted.

"She seems to be seeing a great deal of Lady Bulwer."

"Rosina?" Even becoming "Lady Bulwer," when her husband had been made a baronet in the Coronation Honors List, had not altered Rosina's crazy hatred of his career.

"Since she and her husband parted, Mary Anne has often mentioned how cruelly he treated her."

"Rosina is mentally disturbed!" Disraeli protested. "She even appeared on the election platform to accuse him of infidelities which were untrue. She had to be locked up!"

"Well, she has succeeded in convincing Mary Anne that she is a martyr and her husband is a callous monster," Sarah informed him.

All at once, Disraeli realized he might have left it too late. "And I am one of Bulwer's closest friends. I have been a fool to wait. I must get back to London!"

When Rosina Bulwer had been released from the temporary restraining order in the asylum, she had had no one to turn to. Mary Anne had sheltered her as a friend and come to believe her delusions. The deed of separation between the Bulwers had been signed in the drawing-room at Grosvenor Gate. Rosina was there now with Mary Anne.

"His letters," said Mary Anne, very disturbed, "have been so ardent—so loving."

"Oh, no doubt," Rosina smirked maliciously. "He longs for your four thousand a year."

"But he knows that that and this house is all I have, and only while I live," Mary Anne argued, not wanting to believe her, yet half persuaded. "It could never come to him."

"Has he not told everyone you are to be his wife?"

"It proves he is serious. All our friends now expect it," Mary Anne insisted.

"And so do the debt collectors. He has made sure to tell them, too. They will not press him so hard, knowing he is to marry into money." Rosina shook her head as she looked at Mary Anne, as if genuinely sad that her friend had been so abused. She detested the Jew charlatan almost as much as she detested her own husband and was determined to do everything she could to split up this match. She wanted to shake Mary Anne out of her infatuation. Mary Anne was stricken with doubts and unhappiness as she gazed at her. Just then, there was a knock on the door and a manservant showed in Disraeli. Mary Anne rose to greet him, agitated.

"Is it your custom to walk in unannounced?" Rosina demanded sharply.

"Since when have I needed to be announced in this house, madam?" he asked. "And since when have my actions been accountable to you?"

Rosina, furious, turned to Mary Anne. "Are you going to allow him to speak like that under your roof?"

"Rosina, please . . ." said Mary Anne faintly, uncertain.

"Very well. I shall not call again until you send for me," Rosina declared coldly. "I only hope by then you have discovered whom you may depend on." She stalked out past Disraeli without even glancing at him.

When she had gone, Disraeli waited for Mary Anne to speak. "From your silence I trust you are not displeased to see me?"

"How could you think that?" she asked, trying to smile.

"Only too easily," he said levelly. "These last weeks have been the most miserable I have ever passed. All my hopes of happiness are centered in you."

"Oh, my dearest," she faltered. Seeing him here so unexpectedly, just after Rosina had been saying those things. . . . He looked so pale and saddened.

"I have written over and over again to tell you of my passion," he said. "But from you, nothing. Have you discarded me? Or do you wish merely to show your power over me?"

165

"Believe me, I would not put you to so mean a test," she swore. "But I cannot write my feelings down on paper like you. And I have been sorely troubled."

"How?"

His eyes were fixed on her and she could not confess her doubts. "By the thought of how much Rosina has suffered," she told him.

"One can only be sorry for her," Disraeli said.

"If the world only knew how cruelly her husband has treated her!" Mary Anne broke out. "For him to bring his mistresses to her very home!"

He spoke quietly, carefully. "Mary Anne, it is right for you, noble of you to defend your friends. But surely you realize that Rosina's stories are all lies?"

"How can you say that?" Mary Anne protested.

"Because I have seen Bulwer's despair," he said matter of factly, "and seen her change from a gentle girl into a poor creature driven by hysterical jealousy, until she is a danger to herself and others."

"Oh, yes, she warned me that you would take Bulwer's side—that you are no better than him!" she countered, becoming angry.

"And you believed her?"

"Not at the time," she snapped.

"But now you do, because you wish to!"

She had gone too far to stop herself. She sat on the sofa, not looking at him. "I am not blind! You may think me a stupid woman and laugh at me behind my back, but I know a fraud when I see one!"

"A fraud?" He was dangerously quiet.

She laughed shortly. "I am not so vain as to imagine it is my beauty that draws you here! You have no scruples when you see something you want: a seat in Parliament, a house and fortune to give you respectability."

He had drawn himself up. His voice was cold and direct. "Very well, madam, since you would have it, I admit that when I first proposed marriage to you I was prompted by no romantic feelings."

Mary Anne gasped, as though he had struck her. She had expected him to deny it, to make protestations. She

166

glanced at him. His face was stern, but his eyes were oddly tender, almost sad.

"A wife would have been convenient to me," he conceded. "I wished for a home without the tortures of romantic passion. So I was not blind to the advantage of our alliance. But I found you in sorrow and my heart was touched. Unexpected by me, I found you amiable, yet gifted. One whom I could look on with pride as the partner of my life. Who could console me in defeat and share in my triumph, my honor and happiness."

"Oh, yes, you know how to flatter!" His words were a snare. They had trapped her before. "All you want is this house and my yearly income! I will not be made a fool of. How could I have believed you could love a woman so much older than yourself? I should have known when you borrowed money from me!" Even as she said it, she wished she had not. But it was said, and his eyes, too, had gone cold.

He half turned as though to leave, but stopped. "I wondered if you would mention that," he said, surprisingly mild. He looked at her bleakly for a moment and she trembled as he began to speak. "Apparently all you wish to believe is what jealous friends tell you. Now hear the truth! Your so-called fortune is only enough to maintain this house and you. To eat and sleep here, is that sufficient reason to make me give up my liberty? Would I sell myself so cheap? I would not consent to be kept by a princess without love! But I cannot expect you to understand that. I thought my heart was inextricably linked to yours. Well, I only blame myself. On your conduct to me I make no comment. For a few years you may flutter in some frivolous circle, but the time will come when you will sigh for any heart that can be fond, and despair of one that can be faithful. Then perhaps you may remember me. I will not pretend to wish you happiness." He turned abruptly and strode to the door. Mary Anne was distracted, racked with doubts, fears and hurt pride, but the terror of losing him was suddenly greater than any other. As he opened the door, she found her voice and cried brokenly, "Dis! Oh! My love . . ." He hesitated, his back to her, and she ran to him sobbing, "Don't leave me, please!" She turned him to face her and clung to him, weeping. "I never, never wanted you to ... Only—I was afraid you were playing with me. I didn't mean any of it! I will be everything to you, everything you can wish. I love you, I love you beyond anything in the world." Her stumbling, desperate words touched his heart. He saw her embarrassment at having to confess her fears, her deepest feelings, and held her, laying his hand over her mouth. As she looked up at him, questioning, he took away his hand and kissed her gently, with great tenderness.

A few wedding guests hurried out to form two lines on the steps of the old church in Hanover Square. It was St. George's day, 1839. Disraeli led out Mary Anne, who was radiant, looking unbelievably young in her cream satin wedding gown and flowered bonnet. It had been a very quiet wedding, as both had wished. Isaac was not well enough to attend, and Mary Anne's relatives had declined the invitation. Bulwer and Lord Lyndhurst were the principal witnesses.

Disraeli and Mary Anne walked through the portico and down the little avenue of guests who threw confetti and Mary Anne laughed to see some of the tiny, colored paper stars, hearts and diamonds catch in his ringlets. An open bridal carriage was waiting. He shook hands with Lyndhurst and Bulwer, then lifted Mary Anne into the carriage in a cloud of rice and confetti, as the others closed in, laughing and applauding.

chapter seven

The honeymoon began in the Kentish Hotel at Tunbridge Wells. It rained incessantly, but they scarcely noticed. A week later they set off on a Continental tour, through Belgium and Germany, ending in Paris, where they dined at the Embassy and Dizzy helped Mary Anne choose some of the latest fashions. After nearly two months of loving and travelling and sightseeing, they returned to Grosvenor Gate to begin their life together. Dizzy was at last master of his own house.

Their happiness together was more complete than Mary Anne had ever thought possible. As a husband, Disraeli was loving and considerate, appreciative of everything she did for him. She was used to being the wife of an MP, but now it was much more exciting. Wyndham had never made any kind of stir in politics. Now she could read *her* husband's speeches which were always being reported in the papers, cut out cartoons of him and comments praising or abusing him, and see him pointed out when they walked together in the street. Her whole delight became to make life as easy, orderly and pleasant for him as she could. She studied all his wants, his clothes, his meals, his likes and dislikes. Every moment of her day was devoted to him. Without losing her sense of humor, she made herself be practical in running the house and arranging his appointments, and was always there, pretty and welcoming, no matter how late the debates in the House lasted. He would come back, tired and unsettled, to find a fire in the drawing-room and Mary Anne waiting with a snack prepared in case he was hungry. Within a very short time, many of those who had sneered at his marriage began to envy it.

With her, Disraeli himself had begun a new life. "My nature demands that my life should be perpetual love," he had said. And so it had become. She was that ideal combination of friend, lover, mother and wife, for which he had always sought. Gradually, he opened his heart and his dreams to her, more than he had ever done to anyone, even Sarah. There was only one area which was still secret, the dear companions of his youth, his debts. She had wanted to know about his finances and he had reluctantly tried to explain them to her, but in so involved a way that she had given up. How could he tell her that he was now paying forty percent interest on debts, some of which went back fifteen years? The thousand or two she gave him out of her capital to settle them may have seemed large to her. They were simply swallowed up, although they eased the pressure slightly. He did not want her to worry and spoil her happiness. She would have worried, indeed, if she had known that his latest loan to pay off back interest had the contents of their house as security.

Socially, being married brought some changes. He saw much less of Bulwer, who was not at ease with Mary Anne, although Rosina had now turned against her, too. He was dropped by some of his aristocratic friends, who did not consider Mary Anne acceptable. He did not miss them. He had his close relationship with the Tory lords, Lyndhurst and Chandos. He was amused to see that, since the wedding, Mary Anne half thought of herself as Jewish. He took her to a family dinner with his new friends, the Montefiores, to meet the Alberts and De Rothschilds. "Not a Christian among them," he wrote to Sarah, "but Mary Anne bears it like a philosopher."

And there was William Gladstone. Gladstone had married his wife, Catherine, only a month before the Disraelis' wedding. She was from a rich, Liberal family, tall, slim, blue-eyed and very attractive. Though also highly religious, she was as full of fun as her husband was solemn. It was natural that the wives of the two leading young Tories should meet. They liked each other at once and the two couples met frequently at each other's homes. Being newly married gave them another interest in common. The two wives became quite close friends, although Mary Anne was nearing fifty and Catherine was not yet thirty. They laughed at the same things and Mary Anne tried to help Catherine to organize her household. She had been brought up in a castle, staffed by efficient servants, and sometimes forgot that in running her own home she had to make arrangements and give orders. She was incurably unpunctual and Gladstone often scolded her gently for leaving things scattered about. She would laugh and say, "What a bore you would have been, if you had married someone as tidy as yourself." They lived rather grandly in Carlton House Terrace and, unlike the Disraelis, had no need to be concerned about money, as Gladstone's father had divided his extensive West Indian properties between his sons, making them all wealthy in their own right. Gladstone was as attached to Mary Anne, as was Disraeli to Catherine, yet the two men were never at ease together. They let their wives laugh and chatter and occasionally joined in but, between each other, they kept a wary, watchful distance like two young dogs on a street corner.

Disraeli had returned to Parliament with fresh vitality. He let no opportunity to speak pass and was often called for by the Conservatives immediately after Peel and Lord Stanley. While Gladstone was a powerful speaker in cer-

171

tain areas like finance and trade, Disraeli's interests were more varied. Sometimes he was asked to be ready to answer any major speech of the Government Ministers, in the absence of his Party Leaders. Mary Anne was proud when Peel invited him to a private dinner, at which all the other guests were members of the Shadow Cabinet. But nothing came of it. He was given no position inside the Party. Too many people were unsure of him.

They remembered how, at the end of the last session, he had shocked both sides of the House by rising to protest against the insultingly short time it had taken to reject the Charter which had been handed in, with two million signatures representing the hopes of millions more in the laboring classes, in the fields and factories, to be given some form of political rights and representation. He was speaking independently, as a progressive. Again in this session, he rose to defend the Chartists' leaders against harsh punishment and to protest against the raising of troops to put down the movement. Perhaps, he said, some of the reforms they demand are misguided, but it is the duty of Parliament to cure the grievances and the appalling conditions which had made them seem necessary. He could not understand why the Liberals who had brought in the first Reform Bill and the Conservativies who had backed the Poor Law were now both fighting controlled reforms. "I am not ashamed or afraid to say that I wish more sympathy had been shown on both sides toward the Chartists," he declared. "I am not ashamed to say that I sympathize with millions of my fellow-subjects."

Yet he won back many on his own side, who laughed and cheered at his reply to the Liberal Chancellor of the Exchequer and an Under Secretary who had both attacked him as "an advocate of riot." He could not let their comments pass, he said. "Indeed, from a Chancellor of the Exchequer to an Under Secretary of State is a descent from the sublime to the ridiculous—though the sublime is on this occasion rather ridiculous, and the ridiculous rather trashy. How he became Chancellor of the Exchequer, and how the Government to which he belongs became a Government, it would be difficult to tell. Like flies in amber, one wonders how the devil they got there."

Dizzy had always thought that all he needed was the chance to prove himself, that once he was in Parliament his superior powers would automatically be recognized by everyone, friend and enemy. His heroes proclaimed themselves. He believed in the Hero, winning through after setbacks and hardships to be universally admired and respected. It was only with the utmost unwillingness that he admitted to himself that many in his own Party disliked and distrusted him. It was partly caused by prejudice, partly by his alien appearance and gaudy clothes and the scandalous stories told about him, and partly by his obvious ambition. To be ambitious was right and proper, but it should not be so naked. He was clearly an outsider.

Even in his speeches, when the House rocked with laughter as he slowly built up a ludicrous image to demolish his opponents or finished them off with a dazzling rapier thrust, he never smiled at his own wit. He seemed to be unaware of the effect he was creating, his rich, full voice modulated only enough to make his point, his movements so restrained that the smallest lift of a hand became of enormous significance. Normally, he stood with his arms tucked in at the sides, his elbows slightly bent. In attack he would stand straight, his head raised, his thumbs tucked into the armholes of his waistcoat with the gold chains dangling and glittering between them. The moment everyone waited for was when his left hand reached for his hip pocket and fished out his white handkerchief. It was a signal they had come to appreciate. Whoever he was attacking would wince, others hunched forward in their seats as he passed the handkerchief slowly from left hand to right, then paused in passing it back, delivered the coup de grace, coughed gently and dabbed his lips before putting the handkerchief back in his pocket, while laughter sounded all around him and his victim writhed. When not speaking, he sat motionless on the bench behind Peel, arms folded, with his hat tilted forward over his eyebrows. It was a relief to him to be able to lay aside the mask at home with Mary Anne and in the company of old friends.

He had his own beliefs, and often wished he had not. It would have made it easier to follow the narrow party line. Just as he could not run with the pack, he could not bark with it. He knew that the standpoint he occasionally took in debates and the views he expressed were not held by most other Tories, yet he relied on them to respect his sincerity. In reality, he was adding to his reputation as a slippery, undependable mischief-maker. He had a genuine admiration for Sir Robert Peel, the most able politician of his day, and knowing his chief's eye was on him, carried out his obligation to vote with the Party. However, when the division was not crucial, he voted according to his own convictions. Characteristically, on the very day he dined with Peel, the vote was taken to reduce the sentences on the Chartists' leaders and he was in a minority of five against the entire rest of the House.

The Queen was married. Most of the eligible young princes and princelings of Europe had entered the marriage stakes, presenting themselves in London to be considered as her consort. The prize was worth having, a vivacious, not unattractive girl, a vast fortune in goods and palaces and the position as second most important person in a gigantic empire. It was won by Prince Albert of Saxe-Coburg in Germany, Victoria's tall, handsome cousin who was nearly exactly the same age, with the same golden brown hair and blue eyes. He was intelligent and sensitive and, from the moment she saw him, she would have no one else. They had their first child, named Victoria after her mother, within the first year. Everything was perfect, except that Albert had a distressing wish to make decisions about the way they lived and to be involved in the work of running the country.

Times were bad and agitation increased. In spite of the Queen's support, Melbourne's government lost the confidence of Parliament. Instead of resigning, he went to the country and Disraeli had to fight in another general election.

The demands of the voters of Maidstone were more rapacious than ever. Because of that and the bad feeling left by the charges made against him, he began to look for another seat. Selina's father, Lord Forester, offered to nominate him for Shrewsbury and he accepted gladly. In a rural area with a Tory history, he was fairly certain of a majority without bribery. For the campaign he had his own banner made, choosing as his crest the Castle of Castile on a blue background with the motto, *Forti nihil difficile*. To the brave nothing is too difficult. His opponents translated it as, The impudence of some men sticks at nothing. He was prepared for the usual attacks but, this time, they were potentially more damaging. Anonymous placards were posted up, accusing him of trying to get into parliament only to avoid being declared bankrupt or sent to prison, and listing the legal demands for repayment of debts made against him over the last three years, amounting to £22,000. His back to the wall, Disraeli issued a declaration to the electors that the statements were utterly false, that he had paid every shilling he owed and would not have put himself up as a candidate if he had not had "that ample independence which renders the attainment of any office in the state, except as the recognition of public service, to me a matter of complete indifference." The voters were taken in by his splendid indignation, and so was Mary Anne, who had been alarmed.

There had just been a domestic crisis. In his absence, a writ had been delivered and read by Mary Anne. It was for £5000. For once she would not accept his reassuring explanation and they had their first and only major row. It took all his most skilful juggling to appease her, to satisfy his creditors and to keep news of the writ from being made public. Afterward, when he was to be away from home, he took care to have his business letters sent to Bradenham for Sarah to handle.

The election at Shrewsbury was all over in five days.

He won decisively, was chaired through the town by his supporters, had his health drunk at forty different stopping places and returned in time for the celebrations at the Carlton Club. The Whigs had been turned out and the Tories had their first real majority for many years. Melbourne's main achievement had been to teach the Queen how to rule justly and impartially. He had done his work superbly, but had left the problems of the country to cure themselves. Now Victoria had to ask Peel to form a government. He was afraid of another clash with her, another Bedchamber Plot, but the way had been prepared. Prince Albert had shown surprising firmness and succeeded in his battle to advise his headstrong wife. With Melbourne's resignation, he became the true power behind the throne, and saw to it that Peel, for whom he had a sincere respect, was given every assistance to make his coming to power easy and efficient.

All over London, prominent Tories and former Ministers waited for the summons to Downing Street as Peel began to construct his cabinet. The number of places was limited, but room could always be made for the most promising of the younger men.

Two days after Peel returned from Windsor, Lord Lyndhurst and William Gladstone called on the Disraelis at Grosvenor Gate. Lyndhurst was in excellent spirits after a week of suspense. If the Queen had refused to accept Peel, there had been just a chance he would have been asked to be Prime Minister.

"But I understand you are once again to be Lord Chancellor," Disraeli said. "I couldn't be more pleased."

"I hope to show there's still some life in the old dog," Lyndhurst chuckled. "Have you heard from him yet?"

Disraeli hesitated briefly. "Not yet. You, Mr. Gladstone?"

Gladstone coughed. "Vice-President of the Board of Trade has been mentioned. But nothing definite as yet."

"My sincere congratulations."

"Catherine will be so proud," Mary Anne exclaimed. Gladstone smiled faintly, but was clearly embarrassed.

"Well, we only looked in to see if you'd been sent for, Dizzy," Lyndhurst said. "Patience, eh? There are still posts to be filled."

Disraeli nodded. "Many, I fancy."

"Yes. Now, don't bother, we'll see ourselves out. Your servant, Ma'am." Lyndhurst bowed to Mary Anne and left with Gladstone.

Mary Anne's eyes were shining. "Isn't it exciting?" She hurried to the window to see them as they got into Lyndhurst's carriage. "Sir Robert sitting in Downing Street choosing his team. Waiting to hear what you'll be offered."

"Lyndhurst is uneasy," Disraeli muttered. "I could tell."

Mary Anne sensed that he was worried and turned. "What is it?"

"I should have heard by now," he told her and went out.

She followed him across the passage into the study and watched him as he crossed to his desk. He was no longer hiding his anxiety. "Not to be chosen, when you are one of their best men?" she said indignantly. "When Peel himself has often praised your ability? It is unthinkable!"

"Yesterday I would have agreed," Disraeli told her gently. He sat at the desk and she moved closer. "I have only been able to bear the struggle, the prejudice, in the expectation that one day I would be given official recognition by my Party. To be passed over now would be overwhelming."

Mary Anne stroked his hair. "It would be too unjust, my darling. Sir Robert must know that."

"I wish I were so sure." Peel was so reserved, it was impossible to guess what went on in his mind. True, he had gone out of his way to be friendly on occasion, had congratulated Disraeli warmly after several of his speeches, an unusual sign of favor. He had repaid it by

177

giving Peel his loyalty. Yet what did that proud, distant man really think of him? Disraeli was most effective in attack. Now that he no longer needed him, in those past days had Peel even thought of him at all?

"What can you do?" Mary Anne asked, troubled.

"Humiliate myself," Disraeli said bitterly, "by writing to ask him not to destroy my career. All day I have fought against it."

"But you must write," Mary Anne declared. She squeezed his shoulder. "What does pride matter? There is no one else to speak for you." He was heartened and kissed her hand. As she saw him reach for the paper, she knew she was wrong. There was someone else. She would write to Peel, herself. She had no false pride and could tell him things that Dizzy could not, appeal to him. And make him promise never to tell Dizzy she had done so.

The Prime Minister's study at 10 Downing Street overlooked the formal garden at the rear. Peel stood at the window with the elegant Lord Stanley. There were two desks. A male secretary sat at the smaller by the door.

Peel was drawn to Stanley. They were both men of wealth and high intelligence. Both still kept more than a trace of the Lancashire accent of their youth. When they were heated, it became quite pronounced. Apart from his ability, Stanley was very useful. Peel was reserved and found it difficult to unbend while the younger man had the knack of blending into any company. From one of the oldest aristocratic families, a son of the Earl of Derby, who sat in the Lords, Stanley had one of the best minds in the Commons. He was as much of a racing man as Bentinck, in his family's tradition. His grandfather had established the Derby stakes at Epsom. Like Bentinck, who was the King of the Turf, he mingled happily with the racing crowd, the touts and punters, but unlike Lord George who attended the House of Commons reluctantly as a duty, Stanley was also a born politician, fearless in debate, an effective, incisive speaker.

"Colonial Secretary?" Stanley repeated.

Peel smiled. "I'd have offered you the Foreign Office,

but the Queen, or rather, Prince Albert insists on Lord Aberdeen."

"I am honored, of course," Stanley said. "But I do have reservations."

"Reservations?" Peel frowned. "What is this? Others have said the same—young Gladstone."

"He may be hesitating for the same reason as myself."

Peel had stiffened perceptibly. He had not been prepared for this reaction from men who had sworn they would back him in any capacity. He was the undisputed leader and took obedience for granted. "What reason?" he demanded. "Our first duty is to our party and our country."

"Sir Robert, I will not serve in a government which contains that scoundrel, Disraeli." Stanley replied firmly. "He is an unprincipled adventurer, who only ran to us because the Radicals would not have him."

Peel considered him. "Does Gladstone feel the same?"

"For some reason, he admires Disraeli's talents—but disapproves chiefly of his moral character."

"I see," Peel said quietly. "Well, let us not decide anything in haste. We'll speak again later."

When Stanley had bowed and gone, Peel stood for a long moment looking out on to the garden which had been freshened by a shower of September rain. He turned to his desk and sat heavily. His secretary was watching him. "It is very difficult," Peel sighed. "I had a letter from Disraeli, surprisingly humble. And another, in secret, from Mrs. Dizzy, begging me not to destroy her husband's hopes."

"What presumption!" the secretary remarked.

Peel nodded absently. Many other claims had been made on him, with much less justification. He sighed again. "He really ought to be given some recognition."

Disraeli was writing at his desk and looked up as Mary Anne hurried in, excited, bringing a letter. "This has just come by messenger from Sir Robert," she told him. "I nearly opened it myself."

He broke the seal and unfolded the paper eagerly. He began to read aloud. "My dear Sir, I must in the first place observe. . . ." He stopped and read on silently, the anticipation draining from him. Mary Anne bit her lip, realizing at once what the letter must say.

He began to read it out again, very quietly. "I should have been very happy had it been in my power to avail myself of your offer of service; and your letter is one of the many I receive which too forcibly impress upon me how painful and invidious is the duty which I have been compelled to undertake. I am only supported in it by the consciousness that my desire has been to do justice." He stopped again and closed his eyes.

Mary Anne took the letter from him and laid it aside. She could read it all later. She held him, comforting.

The day was dull and overcast, the sky leaden over the tournament field. The bright colors of the pavilion stood out more sharply by contrast. Two fully armored knights wheeled their chargers into position in front of the striped tents at either end of the lists and began the ponderous gallop toward each other, levelling their heavy tilting lances.

The spectators, ladies in feathered bonnets and three-tiered dresses, gentlemen in tall hats, tailcoats and pantaloons, applauded encouragingly. Many of the gentlemen carried rolled umbrellas against the rain which had threatened since early morning. Among them, just in front of the pavilion, Disraeli and Mary Anne stood with Lord Lyndhurst and his young wife. They had been on honeymoon and missed the famous Eglinton Tournament of three years before, that brave attempt to recreate the spectacle and fashions and high, romantic code of the late Middle Ages. The Eglinton Tournament had been turned into a fiasco by drenching rain. Since then, there had been others. Although the sport had not caught on as the organizers had hoped, it was an unusual and pretty way to spend an afternoon.

The two knights thundered toward each other. Their

lances points smashed into each other's shields and one knight was violently unhorsed, crashing to the ground as his mount lurched and staggered. There was a gasp of alarm from the spectators, followed by cheers and applause as he tried to struggle to his feet, slipping and falling back on the soft ground. His squire ran to help him.

"Well hit!" Lyndhurst shouted and laughed. "You approve of this mock medievalism, Dizzy?"

Disraeli's lips curved very slightly. "We lament the passing of chivalry. Why not try to revive the ideal?"

"If only it doesn't rain," Mary Anne said, glancing at the sky. Lady Lyndhurst agreed. The clouds were darkening.

The victorious knight cantered past, receiving the applause of the crowd, acknowledging with a wave a particular group of young men who pressed forward to cheer him. Among them, Disraeli recognized George Smythe, the dashingly handsome son of Lord Strangford. They had met a few months before, when Disraeli took Mary Anne on a return trip to Paris. Smythe had been a boy when they last met, brilliant, excitable and erratic. Now he was an MP at twenty-six, and Disraeli was struck by his similarity to himself at that age.

The whole stay in Paris had been an enormous success. After being passed over, Disraeli had hidden his disappointment, realizing that many were just waiting for him to show it by turning against his party leaders. He refused to be so petty. Even when some of the country members had revolted against Peel's government, after he announced his decision to revise the Corn Laws that protected farmers against the importation of grain from abroad, Disraeli was careful to defend Peel and voted with the government. He also defended Gladstone when he was under attack as Vice-President of the Board of Trade, for lowering the tariffs on foreign corn. Both men, the entire government, had been voted in on their pledge to protect agriculture by maintaining the Corn Laws, which the Liberals wished to drop in favor of free trade.

Disraeli did not believe either would go back on his given word and the party's promise to the electors. His defense of them was masterly and added to his reputation. The Chief Whip asked him to stand by to answer any further attacks from the Opposition. He was being called on to do a cabinet member's work without the position. Peel thought he was tamed and contented, but he was mistaken.

In Paris, Mary Anne was thrilled to see her Dizzy received as a leading statesman. It made up in part for the grudging acceptance he was used to at home. They were invited everywhere, to receptions and dinners. The Court was in mourning, but the old King Louis Philippe invited Disraeli to a private audience, then to dinner at the Tuileries and, afterward, took him and the Queen of Sardinia on a personally conducted tour of the palace. Smythe, too, had seen the honor paid to Disraeli by fashionable, literary and diplomatic Paris. He thought of himself as first in a band of other young MPs, who were looking for a spokesman for their own brand of Conservatism, romantic and idealistic. Dizzy was the natural choice.

At the tournament, a light rain had begun at last. In the lull, while two other combatants wheeled into position, Lord Stanley strolled round the perimeter and came on Lord George Bentinck who sat glumly on a shooting stick. "Enjoying the pageant, Bentinck?" he inquired.

Bentinck turned up the collar of his huge, white greatcoat. "Not particularly," he growled. "Do they seriously think the country's going to give up football and cricket and take to wearing coal scuttles on their heads and bashing each other with sticks?"

"I'm told that Bendizzy was tempted to enter the lists," Stanley chuckled. "Can you see him as a knight in shining armor?"

"What device would he wear on his shield?" Bentinck wondered. "Three golden balls?"

The unhorsed knight had been carried off and the two new combatants were in position. Watching from outside the pavilion, Lyndhurst cursed the rain. "It's amusing enough, I suppose," he commented. "But it has no real value."

"Not in practical terms, perhaps," Disraeli agreed. "Not in terms of the price of bread or a pound of sausages. Yet it reminds us of the principle that property has its duties as well as its rights. The protection of the weak by the strong."

"I might have known you'd take the poetical view," Lyndhurst grunted. "It certainly appeals to our friends, Young England."

The two new knights charged and collided violently, unseating each other, so that they hit the turf in a smash of suffering flesh and buckled metal, nearly side by side. For a second or two, they lay as if stunned, while the spectators held their breaths. The rules were that the unhorsed must make every effort to rise unaided. If both combatants were unseated, the first to rise would be the winner. There were cheers and applause as both knights started the struggle to get to their feet, clutching at each other for leverage, slipping and sprawling again in the mud churned up by the horses' hooves.

"Oh, thank Heavens," Mary Anne exclaimed, "I thought they'd both had their brains knocked out!"

"Young England?" Lady Lyndhurst asked her husband.

"A nickname for three or four very young, well-born MPs, my dear," he told her, nodding toward the noisy group who cheered on the struggling knights. "They were all together at Cambridge."

"Conservatives?"

"Unfortunately," he said drily. "They preach a romantic vision of the Monarch ruling through an enlightened aristocracy, that kind of thing. Nonsense."

"Not necessarily," Disraeli mumured. "Not if it could be achieved."

Lyndhurst knew that he was attracted to the vision they had put forward, and considered it a dangerous sidetrack for Disraeli to be drawn into. "It can't be," he said shortly. "It's as impractical as this gallimaufry today. All part of the same—Blast!" He broke off as the rain suddenly came down in earnest. The ladies round them squealed and he took his wife's arm, joining in the rush for the pavilion.

By the time Disraeli and Mary Anne reached it, the entrance to the pavilion was crowded and he drew her in under the protection of a striped awning at the side. They had to stand well back because of the slant of the rain. In the confusion they had become separated from the Lyndhursts. As he looked round, he saw that Smythe and the group of young men were beside them, also trying to find shelter.

"May we?" Smythe smiled.

Disraeli nodded. "Please. My dear, you remember George Smythe?"

Mary Anne was laughing, shaking out the skirt of her dress. "Of course," she said, as Smythe bowed. "Isn't it a dreadful day? What a pity the tournament has been spoiled."

"It is, indeed, Ma'am," Smythe agreed.

"You might almost say it was a 'wash-out,'" Mary Anne added.

The young man with him laughed. "May I present my colleagues, Lord John Manners and Alexander Baillie Cochrane?"

Both men bowed to Mary Anne. Cochrane was reserved and hung back, but Manners stepped forward to shake hands with Disraeli. He was the youngest of the three, taller than the rather fine-boned Smythe, intelligent, thoughtful. "I have looked forward to seeing you, Sir," he said.

"I have told Johnnie that we have spoken and that you agree with us," Smythe put in.

"To an extent," Disraeli acknowledged, cautiously. He moved Mary Anne back as the rain increased. "I'm not entirely sure that our views are the same."

"Basically, we believe like you that Conservatism should be progressive and dynamic," Smythe told him,

184

earnestly. "We are against the misuse of power and wealth, *for* the Monarchy, the rule of law and the rights of Labor."

"I see nothing to disagree with in that," Disraeli said. Mary Anne smiled and nodded. She had heard him say much the same, many times.

"We are convinced," Manners stressed, "that a ginger group, speaking and voting according to its beliefs, could help to shock our party out of its fear of progress. And to return to its basic principles, as you have often called for."

Disraeli's expression was unreadable. "That would depend on the number involved."

Smythe smiled. "As well as us, there'd be at least forty of the country members, if you could get them sufficiently worked up."

"You want my husband to join you?" Mary Anne asked.

"No, Madam," Smythe said seriously. "We want him to lead us."

Although not wholly unexpected, the proposal both surprised and flattered Disraeli. He knew Cochrane was against him and Manners undecided. Only Smythe was a true disciple. Yet he must have won over the other two. How serious and dedicated they are, he thought, and how young, to imagine that much of anything can be achieved by a splinter group of four. He looked away, out at the rain-drenched, abandoned tournament field. He smiled very faintly. A knight in full armor was squelching past, his chainmail feet slipping in the mud. Over the bedraggled plumes of his helmet he was holding an open umbrella.

Disraeli walked slowly down a corridor in the Commons with Lyndhurst.

"So you've really taken up Young England?" Lyndhurst asked.

"I sympathize with their aims," Disraeli admitted. "Like them I believe in acting according to my con-

185

science. So far it has not clashed with our Government's policies."

Lyndhurst paused. "You think it might."

"That depends on Peel. He is becoming more arrogant with power."

"True enough," Lyndhurst nodded.

"Yet some of his views are against the very principles which he represents as leader of our Party."

"He certainly can't stand being argued with." Lyndhurst lowered his voice. "I must warn you he is not very pleased with the attitude of your new friends."

"He has tried to crush them," Disraeli said. "Which is why I have promised to criticize the Government on their behalf, whenever I feel it is justified."

Lyndhurst felt even more troubled. "The danger is that many will think you are driven by resentment. It could badly damage your career."

"I have been silent too long. I shall support Peel when I agree with him and attack him when I do not," Disraeli told him firmly.

"It will be David against Goliath. Be careful," Lyndhust warned.

"If I were careful, how could I tilt against windmills?" Disraeli said with a slight smile.

Disraeli had risen in his seat behind Peel. Next to him were Smythe, Manners, Cochrane and other noticeably young Members of Parliament. They were tense with excitement, watching him.

"On the few occasions when I have not fully agreed myself with the policies of the Government, I have merely refrained from speaking and from voting." There was a stir of interest, a new electricity in the House. Peel looked round at Disraeli and nodded indulgently, with a touch of disdain. Disraeli glanced at him and went on. "I shall abstain from voting on this futile Irish Arms Bill. But I must speak. There are some measures which to introduce is disgraceful and to oppose is degrading!"

The tension increased and members muttered as they realized he was criticizing his own party's motion. There were some startled shouts of "Hear, Hear" from the Opposition benches.

Disraeli's voice increased in power. "The real answer to the Irish Question is not the use of force, but by doing justice to Ireland, by seeking out the causes of the past great misgovernment—to put an end to a state of things that is the bane of England and earns us the condemnation of all Europe!"

Sudden wild applause came from the Opposition and cries of Bravo! Bravo! O'Connell rose to his feet, applauding with the rest. Peel sat hunched in his seat, furious. The young MPs next to Disraeli applauded enthusiastically, but the rest of the Conservative benches maintained an icy, angry silence.

In the main room of the exclusive Carlton Club, with its busts and portraits of Tory statesmen, members were standing talking in excited groups. Peel strode in with Lord Stanley, Gladstone and others. He was seething with rage. "It is outrageous! That those puppies should attack their own Government!"

"They must be brought to heel," Stanley insisted. "The younger men, Young England, can be. Disraeli is the only dangerous one. He's put them up to it."

"He should be driven from the Party," Gladstone said.

"And from this club! He should never have been allowed into the Carlton in the first place," Stanley urged.

Calming himself with an effort, Peel cautioned, "We must be careful not to make too much of it. It will make him seem more important than he is."

Just then, Lord George Bentinck came past them with a group of country members. They, too, were all still angry.

"I don't know how you kept your temper, Prime Minister." Bentinck growled.

Peel shrugged as if to say the matter was of no significance whatsoever. "That scoundrel in fancy dress swore to support this party!" Bentinck went on. "The one thing

187

I can't stand is someone who breaks his word!" The other country members agreed. Peel bowed to them slightly, as they moved on.

"That's the answer to Disraeli. Good honest Bentinck," Stanley said with a smile.

Gladstone qualified it. "He takes more interest in his estates and racehorses than in politics."

Peel corrected him, tetchily. "Yes, but the other country members respect him, follow his opinions. They're the backbone of the party."

"Now that he's antagonized them," said Stanley, "I imagine that is the end of the Jew d'esprit."

Dizzy found it depressing now to visit Count D'Orsay and Lady Blessington. Gore House, the scene of so much gaiety and splendor, had become their prison. They had been trapped inside it for nearly two years, unable to go beyond the garden walls because of the small army of writ-servers, debt-collectors and bailiffs who prowled outside. Visitors were only admitted after being carefully scrutinized and identified through the gates.

Strangely, the reason was the long-awaited settlement of Lord Blessington's will. D'Orsay and his wife's lawyers had reached agreement on what he was to be paid, over forty thousand pounds. A great sum, but he had already raised and spent more than twice that on his expectations. There was nothing more to come. When news of the amount of the settlement was leaked, his angry creditors closed in at once and he had to take sanctuary in Marguerite's house. All they had to live on was her annual allowance, but even that was uncertain. D'Orsay might have asked help from the authorities in France, but he was considered suspect because he had befriended the exiled pretender to the throne, Prince Louis Napoleon.

Lady Blessington had just finished reading Disraeli's latest novel, *Coningsby,* the first in a series of three, each showing a different aspect of contemporary life. *Coningsby,* the first, had as its background the character and origin of the political parties. The second would show the condition of the people, and the third the meaning and value of religion. From his earlier writing, no one had been prepared for the penetration and brilliance of *Coningsby* and it created a sensation. Three editions were already sold out and the first 50,000 copies to reach America had gone at once. "I am proud of you," Lady Blessington told him. "More than Mary Anne, more than your family, I am proud of you."

Disraeli was touched and kissed her hand.

"A masterpiece, Dis," D'Orsay agreed, with complete sincerity. "You have not only written a wonderful book, but created a whole new genre—the political novel."

"Thank you, Alfred," Disraeli said. It was still important to him to know they had been impressed. He smiled. "Even the critics have not been too unkind, for once."

Lady Blessington snorted. "They would have lost their own reputations, if they had been."

"One hears of nothing else," D'Orsay said. "It is all *Coningsby* and Disraeli. Everyone adores it."

"Not quite everyone," Disraeli conceded.

"Ah, no, perhaps not. It is not likely to recommend itself to Sir Robert."

Assisted by Young England, Disraeli had continued to critize Peel's government, whenever he thought it justified. He had many targets. In power, Peel had shown a staggering disregard for earlier promises and for the opinions of his supporters. He counted on his own authority and popularity to make them follow him, whatever he decided. He was irritated and angered by Disraeli's stings, although he made a pretense of amused stoicism when he listened to him, like a Headmaster whose omniscience has been challenged by a Fourth Form boy. To lessen the effectiveness of the criticism, behind the scenes attempts were made to drive Disraeli into open opposition. He did not fall into the traps.

At the start of the new session, the Liberals had censured the government over Ireland. When Disraeli rose to speak, members crowded in as usual. Instead of the blistering attack they expected, they heard him deliver a masterly defense of Peel's Irish policy. That was not the only surprise. They were hearing a new voice in the

Commons. The members hushed as they realized they were listening not merely to an adroit politician, but to a statesman. Lucid, profound, summing up the problems of Ireland in a way that had never been heard before— " ... Thus you have a starving population, an absentee aristocracy and an alien Church, and in addition the weakest executive in the world. That is the Irish question"—Dizzy held them spellbound and was given an ovation at the end. Daniel O'Connell rose and bowed to him. Peel, himself, had to pay tribute.

Now the uneasy truce was at an end. *Coningsby* was the manifesto of Young England, its heroes based on Smythe, Manners and Cochrane, with an enlightened Jewish financier, Sidonia, a combination of Disraeli himself and his friend, Lionel de Rothschild. In it, he gave his own view of contemporary politics and mercilessly dissected the type of hollow Conservatism which Peel represented.

"No, I do not imagine he cares for it," Lady Blessington said. "What was that you heard, Alfred?"

"Oh, I don't like to repeat stories," D'Orsay drawled. Disraeli was instantly alert. D'Orsay smiled to him and shrugged. "It may not signify. Your priggish friend, Mr. Gladstone, now has a seat in the Cabinet, I believe."

Disraeli nodded. The President of the Board of Trade had to be replaced and Gladstone was promoted. A natural choice, particularly as he had proved to have a genius for financial affairs and had become one of Peel's most ardent disciples.

"It seems," D'Orsay went on, "that Lord George Bentinck was overheard in the Carlton telling your Mr. Gladstone that he believed you would soon come out in your true colors and join the Radicals. Gladstone said it sounded as if Bentinck hoped it would happen. Bentinck replied, he did not hope for it, but would not be surprised."

Disraeli pursed his lips. It was a confirmation. He had hoped for the support of a section of the country members. It had not come. They all took their lead from Bentinck. He had never actually met the forthright, racing lord, but had been told that Bentinck despised him for doubting the word of their leader. Nothing would ever induce him to back an "oriental adventurer."

"Are you, Dizzy?" Lady Blessington asked. "Are you a secret Rad, like Bentinck tells everyone?"

"No."

"What are you?"

Disraeli hesitated. He knew that what he said would be repeated in the right places. "I am still at heart an independent. I have never been a true follower of either of the two aristocratic parties. My opinions are the result of what I have read and thought. My sympathies and feelings have always been with the people. And when I was forced to join a party, I joined the one with which I believe the people sympathize. I still hold very much the same opinions as always."

"What are they?"

"They are like a religion. Sensible men are all of the same religion."

"And what is that?"

Disraeli smiled. "Sensible men never tell."

D'Orsay and Lady Blessington laughed. "Your rapier work is very fast," D'Orsay said admiringly. "By the bye, I am told that O'Connell now bows to you when you pass."

"Yes. I give him a sort of noncommittal nod back, and that seems to satisfy him."

"All the enmity has gone?"

"The Great Dan never deserts an enemy," Disraeli murmured. "No, I really think the only way to deal with him is to hang him, as Sydney Smith suggested. Then build a statue to him under the gallows."

Peel had had enough. He took the first opportunity, when Disraeli had mockingly adivsed the younger members not to be frightened of him when he seemed to be angry, that he was only bullying them into voting for him. "In a popular assembly it is sometimes expedient to act the part of the choleric gentleman."

Peel rose to smash him, with all the power and sarcasm

191

of thirty years experience. In his strong, hard voice, he destroyed the argument of the motion which Disraeli had supported, then the facts put forward by Disraeli, then at last came to Disraeli himself, and the accusation that he had spoken emotionally only for effect. The House was rapt as his scorn poured out. "It is certainly very possible to show great vehemence, and yet not to be in a great passion. On the other hand, it is possible to be exceedingly cold, indifferent and composed in your manner, and yet to cherish very acrimonious feelings." There was laughter from both sides, directed against Disraeli, who sat, expressionless. "The honorable gentleman undertakes to assure the House that my vehemence was all pretended, and warmth all simulated. I on the contrary will do him entire justice; I do believe that his bitterness was not simulated, but that it was entirely sincere." There was loud laughter and applause. Peel bowed ironically to Disraeli. "The honorable gentleman has a perfect right to support a hostile motion ... but let him not say he does it in a friendly spirit.

Give me the avowed, the erect, the manly foe;
Bold I can meet, perhaps may turn, the blow;
But of all plagues, good Heaven, Thy wrath can send,
Save, save, O save me, from the candid friend!"

When Peel sat to cheers and applause, Manners and Smythe, who sat with Disraeli, were worried. The ridicule had been extremely effective and they waited for him to leap up in answer. He was motionless and pale, his arms folded, his hat tilted forward. He gave no reaction to the jubilant laughter from the Opposition and the applause from his own side. Many thought that Peel had squashed him and that he did not have the courage to reply. As so often in the past, they were wrong.

Disraeli had realized that Peel had just played into his hands. He glanced along the Front Bench. Gladstone and Graham, the Home Secretary, were applauding their chief vigorously, but Lord Stanley was looking around and turned away. He had realized, too. The well-known lines

Peel had quoted were by George Canning, the former Tory Prime Minister, his close friend. Canning had been broken and driven to his death by Peel siding against him, when he tried to bring in Catholic emancipation. A few years later, Peel had brought it in himself. It had been the most dubious act of his life.

Disraeli waited and prepared his reply carefully. It was not till ten days later that he rose, and by that time most of the members had realized or been told the significance of the lines of poetry Peel had used against him. He began by accusing the Prime Minister of blocking discussion within his own party and of turning his followers from Conservatives into old-fashioned Whigs. He, himself, he protested, had been elected to support a Tory Ministry, which the government no long was. The speech was light and bantering and drew louder and louder laughter and cheers. With the laughter, there was anticipation as Disraeli's wit became more cutting and he was clearly closing in for the kill. "I do not think it is the majority that should cross the House, but only the Ministry . . . I know there are some who think that he is looking out for new allies. I never believed anything of the kind. I don't believe he is looking to any coalition, although many of my constituents do. The right honorable gentleman caught the Whigs bathing, and walked away with the clothes. He has left them in the full enjoyment of their liberal position, and he is himself a strict conservative of their garments." He had to stop because of the volume of the cheers and laughter. When he went on, as cool and deliberate as ever, Peel could not hide his nervousness. The house had reached a peak of excitement and was now puzzled as Disraeli begged pardon contritely for having made Peel reprove him, perhaps he had deserved it. Then he advised the Prime Minister not to punish his supporters with satire, but to stick to quotation. "He is sure to be successful, partly and principally because his quotations are so happy." The House was deathly silent. "The right honorable gentleman knows what the introduction of a great name does in debate— how important is its effect, and occasionally how electrical.

He never refers to any author who is not great, and sometimes who is not loved." He paused. "Canning, for example" he suggested, as if it had just occurred to him. At the mention of the name at last, the faintest rustle ran through the chamber like a sigh as the members on both sides tensed. Disraeli nodded. "That is a name never to be mentioned, I am sure, in the House of Commons without emotion. We all admire his genius. We all, at least most of us, deplore his untimely end; and we all sympathize with him in his fierce struggle with supreme prejudice and sublime mediocrity—with inveterate foes and . . . with candid friends." As he glanced very briefly at Peel, the excitement could no longer be held in and wild cheering broke out, both on the other side and behind Disraeli. Smythe and others of Young England were on their feet. Disraeli quelled the noise with a lift of his hand, although laughter and scattered applause continued. "The right honorable gentleman may be sure that a quotaton from such an authority will always tell. Some lines, for example, upon friendship, written by Mr. Canning, and quoted by the right honorable gentleman!" His voice was clear, precise and deadly. "The theme, the poet, the speaker—what a felicitous combination!" Peel was stunned, staring about him at the tumultuous reaction of the House. To an extent his haughtiness had antagonized everyone except his most devoted followers. He winced as Disraeli's voice cut through the cheering and applause again. "Its effect in debate must be overwhelming. And I am sure, if it were addressed to me, all that would remain would be for me thus publicly to congratulate the right honorable gentleman, not only on his ready memory, but on his courageous conscience."

When Disraeli sat down, he was given an ovation. Laughter, cheers and applause mingled in a continuous roar. Nothing could be remembered like it. Many members rose to cheer. Others repeated to one another, "The theme, the poet, the speaker . . ." Disraeli had folded his arms and only nodded slightly to people who were trying to catch his attention, waving hats and papers. The Home Secretary was trying to follow him, shouting that the government was glad to have him now in open rebellion instead of secret mutiny.

Peel appeared to have been stupefied. He was as much shattered by the reaction of the House as by the unanswerable sarcasm of the speech. He got up later to try to reply, but instead of his usual incisiveness, he floundered and hesitated, assuring Disraeli that his feelings were not hurt, that he would never attack him again, hoping he had got his rancor out of his system. As he came to a stop at last, he cursed the day he had listened to Stanley and written that letter turning down the Jew's offer of service.

On the Conservative back benches, Bentinck glared angrily at some of the country members who were still chuckling.

The battle was on. Disraeli could not stop now. There was no possibility of a reconciliation with Peel after that speech, and none was offered. He did not go any more to the Carlton Club. He might even have been assaulted. He knew that he had fully committed himself and might well have ruined his career. Through Lyndhurst, he had heard that the Queen and Prince Albert considered him a dangerous troublemaker. Peel had an apparently unshakable grip on the entire party, as well as the respect of the Throne and a majority of over seventy in Parliament. He was a Goliath, indeed.

George Smythe, Lord John Manners and the few others who were nominally with Young England gloried in the stand Disraeli had taken. But he was nearly forty, while they were still in their twenties and had no need to think seriously yet about their futures. And he could not fully trust them, for all their enthusiasm. Cochrane had already withdrawn. Smythe's father, Lord Strangford, had once admired Disraeli, but had now turned against him. Manners' father, the Duke of Rutland, was alarmed by the association. Both were putting pressure on their sons to apologize to Peel and toe the party line. Disraeli wished he could agree with Mary Anne, who adored both young men for their hero-worship of him and was convinced they could never desert him. He was comforted by her love and her enormous pride in him. And also by his father's.

Disraeli decided not to waste any time before continuing the attack. He must not lose the momentum and, somehow, he had to win some support. The most likely source was still the country members, although nothing that was said or done seemed to affect their dogged allegiance to Peel. Yet he knew they were worried by the falling price of wheat, which was adding to the hardship in agricultural districts. Two weeks later he saw his chance, when one of them questioned the government's proposal for a further reduction of the customs duties on imports.

Both sides of the House had been watching Disraeli, wondering if he would return to the attack. They doubted if the effect of his last speech could ever be repeated. It had been so masterly they had responded almost in spite of themselves and, afterward, had felt uneasily that their reaction had been unfair to Peel. Yet when Disraeli caught the Speaker's eye and rose, there was the same immediate sensation of suspense. The members of the government, seated on the Front Bench around Peel, shifted uncomfortably. The Prime Minister was determined not to be caught out as he had been before. He stretched out his legs and crossed his ankles. Clasping his hands loosely in his lap, he lowered his head and closed his eyes.

Disraeli stood poised, waiting until all sounds had died away. He wore a sky-blue frock coat, waspwaisted, with peaked shoulders. The long points of the bow of his primrose stock hung down over the chains spanning his embroidered waistcoat. He waited with his thumbs in the pockets of his waistcoat, then tucked them in the arm-holes. The applause and laughter began almost at once, mostly from the Liberal Opposition, although some Conservatives on the benches behind Peel laughed, too, but discreetly, afraid of him. In the same dry, dispassionate style they remembered, Disraeli picked out the holes in the arguments of Lord John Russell and Cobden, leading Liberals who wanted an end to protection from the farmers. As slowly as before, he turned to Peel who was moving closer and closer to agreement with the Liberals. "There is no doubt a difference in the right honorable gentleman's demeanor as leader of the Opposition and as Minister of the Crown. But that's the old story. You must not contrast too strongly the hours of courtship with the years of possession." He paused as the laughter swelled. "It's very true that the right honorable gentleman's conduct is different. I remember him making his protection speeches. They were the best speeches I ever heard." A section of the Conservatives, led by Bentinck, clapped loudly, deriding him, and he bowed slightly in their direction. "It was a great thing to hear the right honorable gentleman say, 'I would rather be the leader of the gentlemen of England than possess the confidence of Sovereigns.' That was a grand thing. We don't hear much of 'the gentlemen of England' now!" As he rapped out the last words, there came great cheering, laughter and applause from the Opposition. A smattering of the Conservatives behind Disraeli also applauded and called quietly, "Hear, hear," their heads bent. Again the cheers and laughter mounted to a crescendo as Disraeli repeated the amazing triumph of his first open attack on Peel. When he was reaching the close, the laughter faded as he raised his right hand. It turned slowly toward Peel. "For myself, I care not what may be the result. Dissolve, if you please, the Parliament you have betrayed, and appeal to the people who, I believe, mistrust you. For me there remains this at least—the opportunity of expressing thus publicly my belief that a Conservative Government is an organized hypocrisy!"

The grip he had on the House was incredible. No one in living memory had developed such a power over its sympathies and passions. The tumult when he finished shocked Peel out of his pretended unconcern and he stared about him. Beside him, Gladstone was incensed and glared at the cheering Opposition. On his other side,

Lord Stanley was disturbed and glanced round at the benches behind them. More of the Conservatives, larger numbers of the country members, were quietly but steadily applauding.

chapter eight

Sir Robert Peel paced the carpet in his study at 10 Downing Street. He was dangerously angry. His secretary kept his head down, pretending to write. Members of the Cabinet, Lord Stanley, Graham and Gladstone, watched Peel as he read out extracts from a report of Disraeli's latest speech from a copy of *The Times*.

" 'I support Conservative principles. I merely wish to be informed what those principles aim to conserve . . .' " He threw the paper down on his desk. "He is rousing the country!"

"He has certainly ceased to be merely a nuisance," Stanley said. Privately, Stanley thought it a great pity that Sir Robert did not answer the Jewish mountebank's arguments with others equally strong. Instead of leaving it to the Whigs or taking refuge in disdainful silences. The party needed reassurance.

Peel knew of his subordinate's reservations, but had no time for niceties of morality when more urgent matters were in hand. "He is not the keeper of my conscience!"

he snapped. "I decide what is right for the country—
and the party!" Graham nodded submissively, but Stanley
and Gladstone were uneasy. They did not follow Peel
blindly, like Graham, because of his prestige, nor out of
self-interest like others, because of his power. They were
both scrupulously honest men and could only follow
someone in whose integrity they fully believed. Peel
rapped the paper on his desk with his knuckles. "He must
be disowned by us all—discredited!"

"At least, he is isolated," Gladstone put in. "Manners
and Smythe are ready to break from him."

"Good," Peel said and sat behind his desk. "I don't
want anyone else on our side standing up with him to
defend the Corn Laws."

There was a long moment of silence. During it, Gladstone's uneasiness was resolved. In his election speech, he
had declared that the Anti-Corn Law League was nothing
but a gigantic fraud. He stood four-square for protection.
But his work at the Board of Trade and Peel's influence
had begun to change his mind. Peel had confided his own
conversion to Free Trade in him and Gladstone was
forced to wrestle with his conscience. It now dictated to
him that the only honorable course for him was to back
his leader and not to keep the promises made to those
who had voted for him.

Stanley's uneasiness was of another kind. "Protection
of the farmers and trade was the main plank on which
our Government was elected," he objected. "I was prepared to agree to a suspension of the Corn Laws, if that
was all that was intended. But if that is only a secret
prelude to repeal . . . I have tried to school myself into
the belief that, under certain circumstances, the interests
of the country might require even a sacrifice of personal
and public honor." He hesitated. "But I have failed to
bring myself to so humiliating a conclusion."

Peel glowered at him without replying. If Stanley resigned, it could have a much more serious effect than
Disraeli's pinpricks. If only he could see how foolish it
was, how shortsighted, to be bound by narrow concep-
tions of honor, when England had become the workshop

of the world and they had the God-given opportunity to free the import of raw materials at last and make her the center of the world's trade.

Stanley's resignation and the unforeseen reluctance of most members of the Cabinet to the repeal of the Corn Laws, except Gladstone and Graham, forced Peel to resign. The Queen and Prince Albert were turned completely against Disraeli and displeased with Lord Stanley for his desertion of "dear Sir Robert," in whom they now had total trust. Lord John Russell, however, was unable to form a Liberal Government with such a large majority against him in Parliament and, when the flurry was over, Peel returned as Prime Minister. He was in a stronger position than ever before, since now his colleagues knew they had to obey him or resign from office like Stanley. He gave Stanley's post as Colonial Secretary to his favorite, Gladstone.

It created difficulties for Gladstone. As a Cabinet Minister he had to resign his seat and offer himself for reelection, but his constituents refused to have him. They considered his broken promises more important than his conscience. He tried for eight different seats before giving up. He remained Colonial Secretary but was no longer able to speak in the House of Commons, and so Peel was deprived of both Stanley and him, the only two who could even make a show of answering Disraeli's slashing offensive, which began again at once.

Disraeli and Mary Anne had been on another visit to Paris and found a letter waiting for him when they returned. It was from George Smythe, to say that Peel had arranged for him to become Under-Secretary for Foreign Affairs and that he had accepted. "I am sorry to pain you—as I know I shall by thus becoming a Peelite—why I do so there are many reasons—but my object in writing this letter is only . . . to assure you that whatever be your feelings toward me, I shall ever feel to you as to a man of genius who succored and solaced and strengthened me, when I was deserted even by myself." Mary Anne was horrified, but Disraeli understood. Smythe had given in to the threat of being disowned by his father. He could not help seeing the irony of being deserted by Coningsby himself. He could no longer count on anything but well-wishes from John Manners, either, and he was alone. As he always knew he would be.

Many people doubted his sincerity in fighting for protection, to keep the Corn Laws. The simple answer was that he had been brought up to believe in their necessity, knew for himself the crippling poverty of the agricultural districts and had been elected by just such a community, whose very existence depended on protection. It was not that he totally disbelieved in Free Trade. He saw that an element of that in certain commodities was necessary for national prosperity, yet he also saw that the idea of removing all import duties, unless the rest of the world did the same, was filled with danger. It would lead to a scramble to produce more, to more factories and workshops and factory-hands, and to more machinery and lower wages to enable the goods to be sold at competitive prices abroad. The second in his trilogy of novels had appeared, *Sybil or The Two Nations,* whose setting was the condition of the people. The two nations were the rich and the poor. Unlike Peel or Stanley or Gladstone or Bentinck or Russell who knew only the first, he had an intimate knowledge of both. The descriptions of life in the teeming industrial towns, which he had read in parliamentary committee reports of investigations during his long hours in the library of the Commons, had appalled him. He visited the industrial and mill towns of the Midlands and North, the day and night factories, the cotton mills, the ironworks, and saw the conditions of life for the poorer workers in their overcrowded, evil-smelling, filthy rookeries, the ignorance, the vice, the sheer brutality of every aspect of their existence. With many of those he met he could scarcely communicate, not because they were unintelligent, but because of their almost total lack of education. Their vocabulary was limited to the most basic words, to slang and casual obscenities. They had no thoughts beyond those connected with work, food, family, sex and the struggle for survival, no enjoyment except full stomachs—a rarity—and drunkenness—habitual. They accepted disease, child mortality and death by the age of thirty as normal. Religion was meaningless to them and there was not one single thing to stimulate them or give them hope or lift their thoughts even for a moment out of the brutishness and ever-worsening conditions of their life.

He had taken Mary Anne to Bradenham, which was like escaping from a nightmare. As he worked on his book throughout the autumn months, he had realized that the Queen ruled over not one nation, but two. And those two, for all practical purposes, were mutually incompatible. Unless something was done by those who could, it would lead sooner or later to divisions within the country that would be unbridgeable. He toned down the descriptions in his novel to make them acceptable, writing it as another political romance, with a hero who is equally at home in Westminster and Mayfair or rural and industrial communities. Its heroine, Sybil, was the daughter of one of the Chartist leaders. Its impact throughout the country was tremendous, repeating the success of *Coningsby*.

Some critics accused him of exaggeration in the passages showing the lives of operatives, miners and iron-workers. Other readers knew that the whole truth was far more shocking, and shaming. His theme was a plea to halt the soulless industrialization of England before it was too late, before all the traditional virtues were lost, to create conditions in which the labor forces would live and work like human beings. The danger he saw in the repeal of the Corn Laws was that more and more people would be lured from the land into the factories and the hell's kitchens that surrounded them, that a few, and the most unscrupulous, would become rich, and the majority, and the least able to defend themselves, would sink into ever greater poverty and squalor.

His attacks on Peel's maneuvers to end protection went on into their third year.

Disraeli came very quietly into the drawing-room at Grosvenor Gate to find Mary Anne waiting up for him.

There was a light supper for two laid on a small table. "I thought you would be in bed, my darling," he said, touched.

"Not without hearing how it went," she told him. "And not without you."

He smiled and kissed her. He made a pretense of being impressed by the cold chops and salad and sat at the table. "Splendid, my dear. A feast!"

"So? Did your speech go well?"

"The House was crowded. They began by not wanting to listen and ended by cheering. Even some behind me. For several minutes."

Mary Anne was delighted, but could see that he was depressed. "I was afraid you'd go to the Carlton Club after."

He shook his head. He was less welcome there than ever. She brought his red Morocco slippers from the fireside and knelt by him to take off his shoes. He reached down to stop her. "No, no," he said gently.

"Shh, sit still or I shall be cross," she commanded.

Disraeli leaned back and watched her fondly as she put on his slippers. Then she sat on her heels, looking up at him. "Now tell me what is wrong," she ordered. "You said your speech was a great success."

His hands cupped her face, his thumbs easing away the lines of worry between her eyebrows. "But no one would follow my lead. I have attacked this government over and over again. Peel only grows stronger and stronger—even though he has gone back on all his promises."

"Surely others must see that?"

"Of course. The forty or fifty country members in our party. In any vote, they could put an irresistible pressure on Peel, but they are unwilling to believe he has sold them."

She frowned again. "Sold them? Why do they not protest?"

He shrugged. "Because it would mean admitting that I am right. Lord Stanley resigned from the Government but will not support me openly. He will not even speak to me."

"What about Young England?"

"That is over," he sighed. "Today Lyndhurst told me that even the Queen and Prince Albert back Peel. They find my speeches offensive—almost treason."

She straightened. "Then they are wrong! If I ever see them, I shall tell them so," she announced.

Disraeli smiled. "Thank you, my dear. If only you could convince the ordinary members of my own party."

"What do they matter?" she exclaimed. "Look how the young folk cluster round you, and the people in the street. They know what you stand for."

"They do not vote in the House of Commons," he reminded her.

"Even there change must come," she said. "Sooner or later they must accept new ideas."

"But how long will it take? I am completely alone. The voice that cries in the wilderness."

"You must still fight for what you believe in," she insisted. "Even if the Queen is against you—even if you are rejected by all Parliament!"

Seeing her gazing up at him, seeing her faith and confidence, Disraeli drew her to him, "You are the noblest spirit I have ever known," he whispered. "The most sympathetic, the most understanding, the most severe of critics—the perfect wife." He saw that her eyes were wet with tears and he kissed them.

The atmosphere in the House of Commons was feverish. Disraeli was again standing at his place just behind and along from Peel. The spaces on either side of him were empty, although the House was packed. The members on both sides listened to him with rapt attention. Again he had made them laugh and cheer and had silenced them with that abrupt motion of his hand. Up in the visitors' gallery, Gladstone found himself holding his breath, seeing something demonic in that slim, black-haired figure in bottle green velvet, the glint of the ruby ring given to him by Mary Anne on the pale, uplifted hand.

Peel sat with his arms crossed, his hat tilted forward, taut with resentment and outrage, as the voice he had come to dread rang out over him. "While we are admitting the principles of relaxed commerce," Disraeli said, "there is extreme danger of our admitting the principles of relaxed politics. I advise, therefore—whatever may be our opinions about Free Trade—that we all oppose the introduction of free politics." The laughter which came was from both sides. "Let men stand by the principle by which they rise, right or wrong. I make no exception. Do not, because you see a great personage giving up his opinions—do not cheer him on, do not give so ready a reward to political turncoats." The applause which began, when his hand lowered until it was pointing towards the Front Bench, stopped as it slowly turned back to lie over his heart. "Above all," his voice was lower, fuller, serious, "maintain the dividing line between parties, for it is only by maintaining the independence of party that you can maintain the integrity of public men, and the power and influence of Parliament itself."

As he finished, the feelings which had been held in with such difficulty broke out in a storm of applause and cheering from both sides. He stood for several minutes, his eyes moving slowly from end to end of the House, while the wild sound increased around him, then gradually faded as he sat. There was silence for a long moment as everyone waited for Peel to reply. Several Ministers on the Front Bench were watching Peel. He glanced along at them and shook his head as if to say, "It is not worth answering," then his head rose at a stir of shock and incredulity. The members of the Opposition were gazing beyond him at the Government back bench. Peel swivelled and looked round.

Reluctant, painfully self-conscious, Lord George Bentinck had risen. He was wearing his huge, white greatcoat and the pink collar of his hunting coat could just be seen underneath. He bowed to the Speaker and excited whispers ran round the chamber. "Sir—" he began, and paused to clear his throat. "When the honorable gentleman who has just spoken predicted and denounced in the last session the eventual defection of the Prime Minister, there was no member of the Conservative Party who more violently condemned the attack as unfounded, or more readily opposed the motions of the attacker. Now . . . I must rise to support him." The sensation was as if a mortar bomb had exploded. Bentinck's voice was hard and strained. "The trust I held sacred has been betrayed. To abolish the Corn Laws to which we are pledged is dishonorable to Parliament as well as to the Government!"

While he paused to collect his thoughts, there was utter silence. The members were stunned. Then, in the silence, the country members began to applaud. The sound was hard, rhythmical, determined. Disraeli gazed up at Bentinck with the beginning of a wild hope.

It was late evening in the Carlton Club. Disraeli, coming in, saw Bentinck standing by the open fire, still in his greatcoat and hunting clothes. With his flushed face and his light brown hair dishevelled over his broad forehead, he looked as if he had just returned from the chase. He was a handsome man, tall, athletic and direct. His booted feet apart, his shoulders braced, the whole bearing told that he had been trained as a soldier. The Members near Bentinck moved away as Disraeli came towards him and paused. Bentinck was embarrassed. He had never liked Disraeli and was unsure of him. Disraeli bowed slightly and Bentinck replied with a stiff nod as though it was forced from him.

"I must thank you, Lord George, for rising to support me," Disraeli said quietly.

Bentinck hesitated, and coughed. "D'you see? I own race horses. I understand more about pedigrees than politics," he explained. "I keep horses in three counties and they tell me I shall save fifteen hundred a year by Free Trade. I don't care about that. What I cannot bear is being sold."

Disraeli nodded. "I understand."

"Hang it, I trusted Peel completely!" Bentinck said harshly. "And just as you said, he is all set to go back on his solemn word—and that's unforgiveable!"

"The effect of your speech was remarkable."

Bentinck scratched his chin. "Eighteen years in Parliament, it's the first time I've opened my mouth. I'm a plain man and left the talking to others. But when they turn dishonest, it's time for the rest of us to speak out."

"Will you do so again?"

"Let them try to stop me," Bentinck growled. "But I wish I had more skill in debate, to be more help to you. All I have to spur me on is anger."

"It's a good weapon," Disraeli smiled, "in a good cause."

Sir James Graham had predicted to Peel and Gladstone that Bentinck's intervention would be a flash in the pan. They soon found that he, who once never spoke, now could not be stopped. Backed by him and the country members who followed him, Disraeli gained new power and new respectability. A few days later, Bentinck was on his feet in full spate, vehement and commanding. He stood beside Disraeli. Many of the Conservative members behind them cheered and applauded.

"I say again—this Government's deliberate dishonesty!" He gestured to Peel directly, scorning to use any of Disraeli's finesse. "May I remind the Right Honorable Baronet that, in the past, when someone of eminence in his party changed his opinions he denounced him as base and dishonest and brought him down? Yet now he tells us that he has changed *his* opinion. Does he not stand convicted by his own verdict?"

As the speech rolled on, rivalling Disraeli's in length, but more violent and direct because he did not have the same polish or self-control, Bentinck's anger was the final proof to Peel that he now had to face a full-scale revolt inside his own party.

Disraeli acknowledged that, although he had often brought the country members to their feet cheering, they would never have followed him. Bentinck was their man and his absolute honesty and sincerity gave the revolt the respectability it needed. As a realist, Disraeli knew that his powers were far greater than his new ally's, but he very quickly came to appreciate him for what he was. As well as the honesty and sincerity, Bentinck had courage and utter determination, once his course was decided. He was genuinely humble about his abilities and had never wanted to take a prominent role in Parliament, which he had always seen more as a sort of club to which he belonged. He was sketchily educated and not widely read. He tried to work through Disraeli's novels to understand him better, but got stuck. In tandem with Dizzy, he felt like a cart-horse yoked to a show-jumper. Up to this moment of his life, his sole ambition had been to win the Derby, the only classic race that horses from his famous stables had not won. He often felt ashamed of his ignorance of basic parliamentary procedures, when speaking to Disraeli, and found himself in the perplexing situation of having to trust someone of whom he was deeply unsure.

Yet as the weeks went on, he could find no fault in his strange partner's conduct or actions and started, reluctantly, even to enjoy their meetings to plan tactics. Disraeli was obviously making an effort to narrow the gap of interests between them. He read the racing news and studied form. He took a half share with Bentinck in Kitty, a thoroughbred filly, and came to inspect her at the stables. Bentinck cherished the memory of the dandy in a russet velvet frockcoat, yellow waistcoat and fawn trousers, with little pink bows on his glossy pumps, picking his way over the cobbles and between the scattered heaps of wet, sour-smelling straw to reach Kitty's stall, of him talking to John Kent, the trainer, of Bucephalus and Pegasus and "fiery-footed steeds." At least, the fellow could ride.

On his part, Disraeli realized how much he needed Bentinck and did not grudge him his place at the head of the Protectionist Party, as they came to be called. As the younger son of the Duke of Portland, wealthy and noble, he commanded respect. His personal qualities added to that made him a natural leader, whom men followed

209

without question. Disraeli was perfectly content to be his lieutenant, to brief him and advise him. But Bentinck would not accept leadership. "I am the last of the rank and file," he said, and treated Disraeli as his equal.

They worked more and more closely together and Disraeli was impressed by Bentinck's determination to learn. He spent whole days, weeks, in the library of the House, studying the arguments and speeches of previous years, reports, lists of trade and agricultural figures. He knew that his opponents could attack him through the gaps in his knowledge and he became obsessed by practical details, absorbing and memorizing them at a rate that astounded Disraeli. Soon no one could catch him out in any of the subjects that surrounded the main debate. "You have a genius for mathematics," Disraeli said, admiringly. "How did you develop it?" "From years of calculating the odds at race meetings," Bentinck told him. "Come a nasty cropper, if you can't remember and add up." It was the very first time that Bentinck heard Disraeli laugh.

Peel decided not to wait any longer, so as to catch them before they were prepared. By an adroit maneuver, he took the impetus out of the revolt by having a rumor spread that he planned to offer so much compensation to the farmers that they would gladly agree to a change in the Corn Laws. On the night he rose to speak, the House was at a high pitch, eager to hear his proposals. Instead of launching straight into them, he showed his old mastery of tactics and spoke first of all on the other customs duties to be altered, on candles and soap, boots and shoe leather, brandy and sugar. He defused the excitement in the House by going into interminable, petty details and, only two hours later, casually mentioned that the Corn Laws were to be totally repealed, by stages over the next three years. The promised compensation was as good as nonexistent. The country members knew they had been deliberately cheated and many who had only felt anxious before now became angry.

Disraeli and Bentinck had to act swiftly. Disraeli saw that their best, and only, plan would be to delay the first reading of the Bill to abolish the Corn Laws for as long

210

as possible. By-elections were coming and through them they could heighten the indignation of the country. Speaking themselves and organizing their supporters to speak, they prolonged the first debate for an incredible three weeks. Sittings often lasted till four or five in the morning. Mary Anne would come in her carriage to the rear door of the Commons and wait until Dizzy could slip out for a snatched supper from the hamper she brought. Bentinck often would not join them. When he was to speak, it was such a strain that he could eat nothing all day, except one slice of dry toast. Disraeli's main speech, perhaps because of his new responsibility, was impressively serious. Bentinck was the revelation. When he rose to sum up their case on the last night, everyone expected a repetition of the violent tirades for which he was now famed. It was long past midnight. He spoke quietly and diffidently, almost without notes, refuting the abolitionist arguments with an unending list of facts and figures. He astonished the House with his feat of memory and the minuteness of his reasoning. As he went on, hour after meticulous hour, the astonishment turned to boredom and, finally, as his case became unanswerable, to sheer admiration. But the Liberals voted with the Government's supporters for repeal and the first reading was carried in Peel's favor.

During the second reading, suspense mounted and passions grew wilder. Throughout the country, families were split and lifelong friendships ended. Several MPs resigned rather than vote, as Peel ordered, against their pledge to their constituents. He, himself, seemed to be losing his imperturability and control of the House. At times, he was seen to be nearly in tears. Once, when he mentioned the word "honor" in speaking and was jeered by members on both sides, he could scarcely go on. And once, after another of Disraeli's philippics, he remained seated on the Front Bench after everyone else had gone, staring into space, and was only roused from his thoughts when the clerk came to lock up.

Emotions became so heated that Colonel Peel, the Prime Minister's brother, sought Disraeli out after one stormy evening and challenged him to a duel with pistols, on his brother's behalf. Friends urged Disraeli to refuse the challenge, but he had been called a liar in public and, with everyone's eyes on him, could not let it pass. He agreed to meet him at dawn the next morning in the park at Wormwood Scrubbs. Peel's second was a naval captain and Disraeli's was Bentinck. The seconds got together late at night at White's Club and Bentinck extracted a full apology from Colonel Peel. The attempt to show up Disraeli either as a liar or a coward had failed.

The date for the third and last reading of the Bill came and the final result was still far from certain. In fact, nothing was certain. A section of the younger Irish MPs had shown a willingness to side with the Protectionists, in return for their vote against a Bill for the use of more repressive measures in Ireland. At the same time, Disraeli and Bentinck had to use all their skill and persuasion to hold their supporters together. A supreme effort had to be made and Disraeli rose to deliver the most important speech of his life. He spoke for three hours and there was no doubt in anyone's mind that they were hearing the greatest orator for generations. The blend of reason, scorn, humor, fact and philosophy was without equal, and when he reached his long, closing denunciation of Peel and his followers, the reaction of the House was louder and longer than any in the longest memory. Nearly every sentence was punctuated by cheers and ringing laughter.

He stood, relaxed and sardonic, holding his handkerchief in his left hand. He passed it to his right to make a small, circular gesture. "Why, what a compliment to a Minister—not only to vote for him, but to vote for him against your opinions." There was a shout of laughter, and he hesitated in raising the handkerchief to his lips. "And in favor of opinions which he had always drilled you to distrust." As the laughter swelled again, mixed with cheers, he dabbed his mouth, transferred the handkerchief and put it back in his hip pocket. He rested his hands on his hips, looking round. "That was a scene, I believe, unprecedented in the House of Commons. Indeed, I recollect nothing equal to it, unless it be the conversion of the Saxons by Charlemagne, which is the only historical incident that bears any parallel to this illustrious occasion. Ranged on the banks of the Rhine, the Saxons determined to resist any further movement on the part of the great Caesar; but when the Emperor appeared, instead of conquering he converted them. How were they converted? In battalions, and baptized in platoons. It was utterly impossible to bring these individuals from a state of reprobation to a state of grace with a celerity sufficiently quick."

The laughter which had continued almost without a stop became such loud cheering that he had to pause again. He gestured toward the Prime Minister sitting below him on his right. "I must say, in vindication of the right honorable gentleman, that a great injustice has been done to him throughout these debates. He has been accused of long-meditated deception, of always having intended to abandon the opinions by which he rose to power. Sir, I entirely acquit the right honorable gentleman of any such intention. I do it for this reason. I find that between thirty and forty years, the right honorable gentleman has traded on the ideas and intelligence of others. His life has been a great appropriation clause. He is a burglar of others' intellect. There is no statesman who has committed political petty larceny on so great a scale. . . ." He went on to deride Peel's adoption of every new, popular theory and his recent conversion to Free Trade. "Will he go to the country with it? I won't believe it. I have such confidence in the common sense, the common spirit of our countrymen, that I believe they will not long endure this huckstering tyranny of the Treasury bench! These political peddlers that bought their party in the cheapest market, and sold us in the dearest." In the cheers, he glanced at the solid block of Peel's supporters who sat alone in silence. He turned to the Speaker and his voice was deep and solemn. "I know, sir, that there are many who believe that the time has gone by, when one can appeal to those high and honest impulses that were once the mainstay and the main element of the English character. I know that the public mind is polluted with

213

economic fancies—a depraved desire that the rich may become richer without the interference of industry and toil. I know, sir, that all confidence in public men is lost. But, sir, I have faith in the primitive and enduring elements of the English character. It may be vain now to tell them that there will be an awakening of bitterness. It may be idle now to warn them. But the dark and inevitable hour will arrive. Then when their spirits are softened by misfortune, they will remember those principles that made England great—and which, in our belief, will only keep England great. Then too, sir, perchance they may remember—not with unkindness—those who, betrayed and deserted, were neither ashamed nor afraid to struggle for the 'good old cause'—the cause with which are associated principles the most popular, sentiments the most entirely national, the cause of labor, the cause of the people, the cause of England!"

He sat to a storm of cheers, lasting for many minutes. It was eight years since his maiden speech had ended with the words, "Aye, sir, I sit down now, but the time will come when you *will* hear me."

Lord John Russell and other speakers who tried to follow him could not make themselves heard. Every time there seemed to be a lull, the cheering for Disraeli broke out again. At last, Peel rose to answer him. He was visibly shaken and looked as if he might break down, but he was infuriated and retaliated by saying that of all the difficulties and sacrifices he had foreseen in his decision to sweep away the Corn Laws "the smallest were the continued venomous attacks of the member for Shrewsbury." In his attempt to justify himself, he wondered why, if Disraeli had always had this opinion of him, "he had been ready to unite his fortunes with mine in office?"

The suggestion was that Disraeli had not begun to attack out of any conviction, but merely because he had once asked for a position and been refused. Disraeli had to deny it. He was exhausted and unprepared and his reply at first was rambling and imprecise, saying that someone highly placed had hinted that he might be given a post. Gaining confidence, he said, "It is totally foreign to my nature to make an application for any place." Carried away by the applause of his supporters, he added, "I never asked a favor of the Government. I never directly or indirectly solicited office." He saw Peel's cool, assessing look and remembered the letter he had written to him. He faltered. "Whatever occurred in 1841 between the right honorable gentleman and myself . . . I dare say it may have arisen from a misconception." He resumed his seat, reliving the long-ago disappointment, when he had not even been given an under-secretaryship in spite of Lyndhurst's urging. He could say honestly that it had not unduly influenced his actions. Yet he realized he had blundered badly and that his future was now in the palm of his most inveterate enemy.

Peel searched late into the night for Disraeli's letter, which was not in any special box or file, as his secretary had thought it of little importance. He did not find it until some days later. By that time, he had second thoughts about the fairness of using it. What politician had not said things, damning things, in the heat of the moment? In any case, it was too late.

As the final votes were counted and the tellers conferred, members stretched their legs in the lobby and corridors of the House. Sir James Graham paused near Daniel O'Connell and heard him make a reference to Disraeli's last speech. Graham asked him what he thought of it.

O'Connell was older, heavier, an old bull whose fighting days were nearly over. "I should have said that it was one of the ablest speeches I ever heard in the House of Commons," he decided, "but for the invective."

"Ah, yes," Graham said, and shook his head disapprovingly.

"But for the invective," O'Connell repeated. "And that made it incomparable."

In a quieter corridor off the lobby, Disraeli paced with Bentinck as they waited tensely for the result of the vote to be announced. It was so crucial, he could not bear to keep thinking of it and was glad to let his mind wander . . . Mary Anne would be waiting up, until she heard. He thought of Sarah and his father at Bradenham. The flowers of this mild Easter would be out and green buds on all the beech hedges. Sarah would not sleep tonight, either. And his mother, so ill she could not live long. He paused. How callous, he thought. In the paper that morning, he had read the small announcement of the death of Lady Henrietta Sykes, widow of Sir Francis, at Little Missenden, only a few miles from Bradenham. He had been so intent on the day's vote, he had spared it no more than a passing thought. Henrietta. . . . And Sykes had been dead for three years. Clara Bolton for seven. All the leading actors in what had once been the central drama of his life, all dead, tragically early.

He sighed and raised his head, to see Bentinck watching him. "Have we done it?" Bentinck asked.

Disraeli shrugged.

"At least, we gave him a fight," Bentinck muttered.

"Thanks to you," Disraeli said. "For one who claims to be no speaker, you have developed a powerful command of the House."

"I only tried not to let you down," Bentinck said stiffly. "Besides, I find I quite enjoy it—now I've got started." He hesitated, not quite looking at Disraeli. "Whatever happens . . . I'm glad we fought together. I only wish I'd got to know you properly years ago."

His voice was gruff. Disraeli was touched, understanding how hard it had been for Bentinck to make himself say this. They smiled slightly to each other.

The moment was broken and their tension returned, as Lord Edward Stanley came to them. Like Gladstone, he had been listening from the gallery. He bowed abruptly to Bentinck, virtually ignoring Disraeli. "The result has to be confirmed, but I've heard the total," he told them gravely. "Peel has won—and the Corn Laws have been abolished, by a majority of ninety-eight."

Bentinck could no longer hide the strain and slumped, tiredly. "All our work," he grunted, bitterly disappointed. "All that effort for nothing."

"No. Work out the figures," Disraeli said quietly. Bentinck and Stanley looked at him, surprised as they saw his excitement. "All the Liberals, Radicals and Irish are committed to repeal and would go with the Government."

"Yes," Bentinck nodded.

Disraeli nodded back. "But with a majority of ninety-eight, that means that Peel only got one hundred and twelve Conservative votes! Over two hundred must have voted for us."

In the short, electric pause as they realized, Stanley gasped.

Bentinck drew himself up. "By Heaven, you're right . . ." he breathed. His face flushed and he held out his hand to Disraeli. "Peel may have won the vote—but he has lost the Party!"

The entrance hall to the drawing-room at Grosvenor Gate was hung with rose-colored silk, draped and domed to give the impression of a Persian tent. Lord George Bentinck blinked as he came through it with Disraeli into the blue drawing-room beyond. Mary Anne rose as they came in. She had given her cheeks just the lightest brushing of rouge powder and wore a dress of flower-printed silk with half sleeves and a lace collar. Her figure was still slim and youthful and she prided herself on not needing stays. She must be well over fifty, Bentinck thought, but she looks pretty trim for all that. The first few times he had met her, he thought her very distant and stand-offish. Then one day when he was waiting for Disraeli, she had confessed that she never knew what to say to him, because he frightened the life out of her. Bentinck had confessed that he felt the same about her and she had laughed and turned into the most amusing chatterbox he had ever come across.

Today she was excited and as they bowed and Disraeli kissed her hand, she demanded, "Well, what happened?"

"With most of the party against him, Peel has resigned," Disraeli told her.

She clapped her hands. "Then you have triumphed!"

"A bitter triumph, ma'am," Bentinck said.

"The party is now divided in two," Disraeli explained, "split between the official Conservatives and those who have gone with Peel. Most of the former leaders have stayed with him."

"Then who is Prime Minister?" Mary Anne asked.

"Russell," Bentinck answered. "The split has let the Liberals back into power. Of course, they're in a minority, so there's bound to be a general election."

"Who will lead the Conservatives?" she asked.

"Stanley—in the House of Lords," Disraeli told her.

She glanced from him to Bentinck, who was taut. "And in the Commons?"

"We've had enough of leaders," Bentinck grunted.

Mary Anne caught Disraeli's look and understood. "Will you excuse me?" she smiled. "I have things to attend to."

Bentinck bowed again as she went out. He was aware of Disraeli watching him.

"We need a focus," Disraeli said quietly. "We must have a leader."

"We both know who it should be," Bentinck declared. "You're the only—"

"Not me," Disraeli broke in. "The others are still not sure of me. While they trust you completely."

Bentinck grimaced. "I'm almost uneducated," he objected roughly. "Never even had a taste for political life till these last months. How could someone like you consent to serve under me?"

Disraeli paused. His voice was quieter. "Quite simply. At the risk of embarrassing you—because I admire you profoundly and sincerely. I am also grateful to you for forcing Lord Stanley to acknowledge me."

Bentinck snorted. "I just told him. He could whistle for me, if he didn't take you. And he's no fool. He knows we need you to work out our strategy." He broke away, agitated. "Hang it, I'm an outdoors man! It'll mean a total change in my way of life. These past months have been bad enough. I'll have to spend all my time at the

House. I've still so much to learn—procedures, business. I'll have to rely on you for everything."

"I shall be proud to work with you," Disraeli said sincerely.

Bentinck looked at him, embarrassed. "And I with you." It was something he had never thought he would hear himself say. Disraeli bowed. He was dressed at his most flamboyant, in a sky-blue coat, purple pantaloons with gold stripes down the sides, his ringed fingers almost hidden by his lace ruffles, the loops of gold chains winking across his embroidered cream silk waistcoat. As Bentinck gazed at him, he could not contain himself any longer. "Why d'you wear all those gold chains?" he growled. "Are you practicing to be a Lord Mayor or something?" Disraeli was taken by surprise and laughed. "Hang it!" Bentinck exclaimed. "For years I couldn't stand the sight of you because of your rings and perfume and fancy way of dressing. D'you have to be such a cursed dandy?"

Disraeli's back had stiffened. He restrained himself. Bentinck was not one of those clod-hopping yahoos who derided everything that did not conform to their own dull nonexistence. He would understand. "A dandy is not a mere clothes horse," he explained. "To be a true dandy is to be self-disciplined, detached, spiritual. It is at the same time a gesture of individuality and a mask behind which the slights and sneers of the world cannot reach."

Bentinck had never thought of Disraeli's manner of dressing as being anything other than natural flashiness, another way of showing off, of proving how different he was from the normal, ungifted run of creation. "Well, maybe you needed something to hide behind once," he muttered, then broke out exasperatedly, "But hang it, that's why a lot of the others still distrust you! They want their leading statesmen to look the part—not like Italian dancing masters!"

Disraeli's lip curled. He was about to make a retort, when all at once he was struck by the image, and smiled. Bentinck chuckled and they both began to laugh quite openly together, as friends.

Lord John Russell was tired, more tired than he could remember. He stiffened his neck and moved his spine a few inches slowly either way, the next best thing to a stretch, when one had to be careful not to show any sign of weakness. With so much to think of, policy discussions, the Irish famine, appointments and postings, as well as the daily government of the country, in the whole recess he had had no chance to relax. At the start of the new session, he was seated as Prime Minister on the Treasury Front Bench. Capable and intelligent, he was short and frail with a head that was large for his body and a sharp, high-pitched voice. He was in a precarious situation, with his party heavily outnumbered in the Commons, and he watched the benches across the floor of the House from him with satisfaction, seeing how the smaller number of Peelites kept aloof from the bulk of the Protectionist Conservatives. As long as that division remained, he was safe. He had tried to make his government more secure by offering posts to Peel and some of the former cabinet ministers, but they refused. The Peelites would not ally themselves formally with Russell's Liberals and would support them for one reason only, to prevent Bentinck and Disraeli or any combination of Protectionists from taking office. For many of them, revenge was more important than policy.

Beside Russell, also watching the benches opposite but with a more amused and calculating eye, sat the next most influential man in his cabinet, Viscount Palmerston, universally known as Pam. Genial, witty and forceful, a handsome, aging womanizer, with a superb house in Mayfair and an accomplished wife, many thought him better equipped to be a leader than Russell. Not so the Queen, who had heard with horror how he had been caught one night at Windsor trying to force his way into the bedroom of one of her younger ladies-in-waiting, who had only saved her honor by screaming for help.

Peel, looking older and heavier, sat on the Opposition Front Bench with Lord Lincoln and others of his chief supporters. Gladstone was missing, still trying to get himself re-elected. Behind them, both the Peelites and the

Protectionists waited for Bentinck and Disraeli to appear, and wondered what would happen. Tempers had cooled on the surface, but the passions of the last four years only needed a spark to roar into life. Peel had been a colossus. In power with the strongest Conservative majority for many years due to his immense prestige, at the head of a revitalized and vigorous party, created in his own image, but now, seeing him seated once again in Opposition everyone in the Chamber was reminded how he had been ignominiously brought down and the mighty Tory party shattered, possibly forever, by the persistent word-play of one man. Already, many among the Protectionists had begun to wonder how they had let themselves be mesmerized by Disraeli, a rank outsider, like a fairground magician in his rainbow clothes. Lord George Bentinck was sound, a leader they could accept, but how much was he under the influence of the dark enigma at his elbow? And how were they to submit to the adventurer's arrogance, if now he lorded it over them, a prancing, egotistical, dandified rooster, puffed up with pride because his crowing had made the house fall down?

Heads turned as Bentinck came in and waited at the bar of the House for Disraeli to join him. There was a rustle and mutter of astonishment as they advanced together to the Treasury table and bowed to the Speaker. The astonishment was at the total transformation of Disraeli. Apart from the white points of his collar and an inch of plain cuff, he was dressed from head to foot in black. He wore no jewelery and no chains. The only remaining touch of the dandy was in the length of the black bow of his silk stock. Above it, his narrow face framed by raven curls had the startling paleness of ivory. In his expression there was no longer any trace of the mocking, challenging smile. He was impenetrably composed and serious. On the Government front bench, Palmerston smiled to himself, admiringly appreciating a masterstroke by a theatrical talent as consummate as his own.

The surprise at Disraeli's appearance had been so complete, it had made everyone forget for the moment the question of where he would sit. Now both Peelites and Protectionists realized that a movement had taken place on their front bench and a gap had appeared in the space traditionally left for the leader of the Opposition. Bowing slightly to those on the left of the space, Bentinck took his seat in it. Looking neither to left nor right, Disraeli sat beside him. He settled his glossy tophat on his head, stretched out his legs and crossed his ankles. He looked coolly over the broad wooden table with its mace, despatch boxes and order papers at Russell and Palmerston. Only one man separated him on the Opposition front bench from Sir Robert Peel.

chapter nine

The general election could no longer be postponed and, through it, Disraeli achieved one of his dearest ambitions, to be one of the Members of Parliament for Buckinghamshire, the county in which his father lived, where he had fought three unsuccessful elections at Wycombe and where he was now a magistrate. His main support came from the farmers. He told them that independence was still the essence of his political position, that he considered the increasing centralization of government the most dangerous threat to liberty, and that his aim as ever was to raise the social conditions of the working classes, by shortening the hours of work and by improving the standard of public health and providing education. He was returned unopposed.

His mother did not live to see it. She died two months before the election. Disraeli wished it had caused him more real grief. They had never been close. All he felt was conventional sadness and sympathy for his father.

Throughout his life, she had remained at a distance, critical, sharp, with little of the tenderness he had seen and envied in other families. Isaac had been kind but self-absorbed during his childhood. Most of the affection and gentleness he had known came from Sarah. Sometimes, he wondered if the attraction he had always felt toward older women was an attempt to find a missing mother's love. It was certainly true that Henrietta had signed some of her letters, "Your Mother," and that he signed himself at times, in notes to Mary Anne, "Your Child." But that was mere fancy. He preferred maturity in women, although ideally it should be allied to beauty, a pleasing figure and a warm heart.

The election brought little change to the state of the parties. Russell's Liberals were still in a minority, only able to govern with the support of the Peelites. Lord John Manners was still out of Parliament, but Gladstone had got back in, as junior MP for the University of Oxford. Sometimes now, it was he who sat stiffly between Disraeli and Peel on the Opposition front bench.

The racing season had been good for Lord George Bentinck. His horses ran well and his wins were popular. He was his usual expansive, noticeable self at the tracks and, as King of the Turf, he was always greeted with a cheer.

At dinner, after the third day of Goodwood, relaxing with his friends and rivals, he asked, "Will any of you give me ten thousand pounds for my stables?" Everyone laughed, then fell into incredulous silence when he repeated the offer. He had thought long and painfully before making up his mind. Everything had to go, trainers and staff, champions, mares in foal, colts in training, lock, stock and barrel. He had accepted the leadership of the main section of the divided Conservative party in the Commons. He would gladly have let Disraeli lead, but out of two hundred not ten men could be found who trusted him. So to keep what was left of the party together, Bentinck sold his stables and made a sacrifice that won the respect even of his enemies.

Up in the gallery of the Commons, Mary Anne sat wrapped in a fur-trimmed pelisse. It was a bitterly cold December day but, after the carriage ride to Westminster, the chamber was warmer than she expected. She pulled the wrap open and leaned forward, peering down at the packed House. Every seat was filled on both sides, even the gangways and the cross-benches. She recognized the Terrible Twins, Russell and Palmerston, on the front bench to the right of the Speaker in his high, thronelike chair. In front of the Speaker were the clerks, at the top end of the center table. With a thrill of pride, she caught sight of Dizzy, slim and handsome, seated next to Bentinck on the other front bench. William Gladstone was next to him, then another man whom she could not place. They were between Dizzy and Peel. She sat back and smiled to the charming Catherine Gladstone who was on her left. Although their husbands were nominally in different camps, the two women had kept up their friendship and Gladstone himself still called at Grosvenor Gate from time to time. A dark-haired, serenely beautiful woman in her early thirties was sitting on Mary Anne's right. She was poised, not looking down into the chamber, but gazing at the entrance and the bar of the House. Her hands were folded in her lap and only the whiteness of her knuckles showed the strain she hid so well. She was Baroness Charlotte de Rothschild.

The atmosphere of tension in the House affected everyone. The air was filled with a constant murmur, but no one spoke above a whisper. Bentinck had a short sharp fit of coughing which sounded unnaturally loud, but shook his head when Disraeli offered to pour him a glass of water from the carafe on the table. Pale and sweating, he had been in bed for the last week with a bad attack of influenza and had made himself get up, against his doctor's advice. It was a day on which he did not want anyone to think he might be using illness as an excuse to stay away. For the past year, Dizzy had backed him with unswerving loyalty. Today, Bentinck had come to repay some of his debt.

Disraeli was withdrawn and serious. He had known for months that he would have to face a dilemma after the general election. One of his closest friends was the multi-millionaire banker, Lionel de Rothschild. Lionel and his brothers had inherited the financial empire of their father, Nathan, and with it his strictly orthodox religious views. They were so far above the ordinary run of men, both in wealth and capability, that the restrictions on British Jews, excluding them from politics and the professions, had no real relevance to them. Lionel was an educated patrician with all the family's business acumen. He entertained lavishly in his palatial villa at Gunnersbury Park near Chiswick, where the gardens, lakes and flowered walks were of an unrivalled perfection and where he had been known to seat five hundred at dinner. Unlike his renowned father, his business dealings were not always motivated by profit. He had raised the eight million pounds the government needed for relief supplies during the Irish famine and had refused to take any commission. Like Disraeli, he was intensely patriotic and, at the same time, proud of his race. There were only two points on which their views really differed. He was a pious believer in Judaism and he was a Liberal. Knowing his reserved, rather aloof nature, the political and financial worlds were shaken when he decided to challenge the last of the main disabilities of British Jews by standing for Parliament. It was a gesture that, perhaps, only he could make. It was true that Disraeli had already established himself in spite of the general prejudice, but he was an Anglican, fairly regular in his church attendance. Rothschild was uncompromisingly Jewish. He stood with Lord John Russell for the two seats in the City of London and both were returned with convincing majorities. His main hurdle had to come. The oath which had to be taken in public by every MP ended with the words, "on the true faith of a Christian" and unless the entire oath was sworn to, he could not take his seat.

The dilemma for Disraeli was that, on the one hand, he had his pride in his race and a passionate wish to see the civil restrictions on his fellow Jews removed and, on the other, he was trying desperately to be accepted by his party members, who were solidly united against the admission of practicing Jews to Parliament. They were not all simply prejudiced, although some were rabidly and unashamedly anti-semitic. A large number sincerely could not see how men who refused to acknowledge the divinity of Christ could be allowed to share in the legislative power of Parliament over the doctrines and structure of the Church of England. Many were like Lord Stanley who had no particular feeling one way or the other about the Jews, except for an inborn dislike, and saw no need for any improvement in their status. Bishops thundered that to admit unbelievers would destroy Christian England. To go openly against these views would put Disraeli's future career even more in doubt. Bentinck, Lyndhurst and other friends suggested to him that he would lose nothing by staying away on this day, especially as Rothschild was a political opponent. He had everything to gain by keeping silent. No one could guess what he would finally do. That he had decided to attend was the reason that Bentinck had risen from his sickbed. He had become aware of many things through knowing Dizzy. "I never saw anything like the prejudice against them," he told Manners as he left for Westminster. "For myself, I don't think it matters two straws whether they are in or out of Parliament—but I don't like letting Disraeli vote by himself against the rest of the party, if that's what he decides. Otherwise, I might have given in to the prejudices of the multitude. I feel like a condemned felon going to Botany Bay."

In the gallery, Charlotte de Rothschild's locked fingers jerked apart nervously. The Chamber was suddenly hushed. Mary Anne took her nearest hand and pressed it. They had just seen Lionel come into the Chamber and advance to the Sergeant-at-Arms, who waited at the bar. He was very erect and dignified, impeccably and somberly dressed, carrying his tall hat. Preceded by the Sergeant, he moved forward to the end of the Treasury table and bowed to the Speaker. Lord John Russell introduced his junior colleague for the City and the Clerk of the House

227

rose to administer the oath. He held a bible out to Rothschild and there was complete silence.

Disraeli heard Bentinck suck in his breath sharply beside him, as Rothschild put on his hat. "I desire to be sworn on the Old Testament," Rothschild said, firmly and clearly.

The House erupted around him in a storm of angry protests, fierce shouts of "Withdraw! This is an insult! This is a Christian Nation!" Gazing down at her husband, Charlotte was trembling and Mary Anne held her hand more tightly, making her control herself.

The Speaker was calling for order. As the noise died away, he announced, "Baron Lionel de Rothschild, you may withdraw."

Rothschild removed his hat and bowed again to the Speaker. He turned and walked back to the bar and the uproar began again. Many members were already on their feet, shouting for and against him, signaling to be heard. Sir Robert Inglis, Gladstone's senior colleague for Oxford, had the floor and stated his opposition frankly. "Sir, from the time that this has been a Christian nation and that this House has been a Christian legislature, no man —if I may use the word without offense—has ever presumed to take his seat here, unless prepared to take it under the solemn sanction of an oath in the name of our common Redeemer. I for one will never give my sanction to his admission!"

In the roar of agreement from his own side and shouts of protest from the Liberals, Disraeli rose and was indicated by the Speaker. "Another Hebrew!" Dizzy heard one of his party scream, as he bowed to the Speaker. He was deathly pale and motionless, waiting until the clamor faded. "Sir," he said quietly, "Baron de Rothschild has been freely and fairly elected to be a Member of Parliament. To deny him his seat as a Jew is to publish to the world that we are still influenced by the darkest superstitions of the darkest ages that ever existed in this country."

One of the Liberals shouted, "We take our oath as Christians!"

"Where is your Christianity, if you do not believe in their Judaism?" Disraeli answered. "They are a race who acknowledge the same God as the Christian people of this realm. They acknowledge the same divine revelation as yourselves. They are, humanly speaking, the authors of your religion." There were cries of shock and anger. "On every sacred day you read to the people the exploits of Jewish heroes, the proofs of Jewish devotion. The Christian Church has covered every kingdom with sacred buildings and over every altar . . . we find the tables of the Jewish law. Every Sunday—every Lord's day—if you wish to express feelings of praise and thanksgiving to the most High, or if you wish to find solace in grief, you find both in the words of the Jewish poets." The anger was growing and nearly every phrase was interrupted by protests. Behind him, he could hear voices calling, "Withdraw! Withdraw!" His voice rose. "Every man in the early ages of the Church by whose power, or zeal, or genius, the Christian faith was propagated, was a Jew!"

"Resign your seat and join them!" one of the country members shouted. There was a chorus of agreement.

"I cannot sit in this House with any misconception of my opinion on this subject!" Disraeli declared. "Whatever may be the consequence on the seat I hold."

There was the briefest pause, then another country member rose to cry, "We've heard enough! This is a Christian assembly!"

Again the chorus of agreement was cut off by the strength and passion in Disraeli's voice. "Yes!" he told them. "And it is as a Christian that I will not take upon me the awful responsibility of excluding from the legislature those of the religion in which my Lord and Savior was born!"

There was utter silence as he looked slowly round the government benches and turned to survey his own. The silence continued as he resumed his seat. For the first time in years when he finished speaking, there was no cheering or applause. He heard Bentinck breathe out beside him. Across from him, Russell murmured to a colleague, "It took great courage to say that."

In the gallery, Charlotte de Rothschild's back was very straight. Next to her, Mary Anne's eyes glistened as she gazed down proudly at Dizzy, seeing only him in the hushed and crowded chamber.

Lord John Russell's motion for the removal of the remaining political and civil restrictions on the Jews was carried by a large majority. Of the whole Protectionist section of the Conservative Party only Bentinck followed Disraeli into the lobby, to vote in its favor. But the Bill and another to change the form of oath were thrown out by the House of Lords.

After the debates, Bentinck had a visit from the Protectionist Whip, Major Beresford, a stuffily formal man who had come to tell him how seriously displeased the party was by his not only voting, but also speaking in favor of the Bills. Bentinck and Disraeli had an uneasy relationship with him, knowing that he was constantly running to Lord Stanley to have their instructions confirmed, and Lord George answered with surprising mildness that he refused to be criticized for standing up for religious toleration. Beresford repeated superciliously that the party disapproved of his attitude and Bentinck immediately resigned as leader in the Commons. The Protectionists having driven him to resign discovered to their dismay that they had no one with whom to replace him. He refused to reconsider and returned to the back benches with relief, even though Stanley begged him to change his mind. "Let them choose someone else," he said. "It is not merely what I have done or given up for them. During these two years, I have undermined my health and shortened my days." They both knew that Disraeli was the only one left who was fit to be leader and that he was the last man to whom the party would agree. "Which would not be the case," Bentinck told Stanley bluntly, "if you had played a generous part. If you had given him your approval, instead of this half-and-half, mincing, milkwarm acceptance."

Isaac Disraeli was eighty-two and nearing his end. His pride in Ben reached its peak when Sarah read him the text of his full speech on the Jewish disabilities. He realized how much his son had sacrificed, and also how important it had been to him to disclose his innermost beliefs, with no evasions, whatever the consequence. "For him, and us, that is the most important speech he has ever delivered," Isaac said. A month later, at the start of the New Year, Tita held him in his arms when he died, as he had held Byron. Isaac's death was peaceful after only a short illness. It came nine months after the death of his wife.

He was a conscientious man and his will shared out his assets proportionately among his children, with the largest share going to Ben as eldest son. He also provided for his servants. One problem was Tita, who had recently married the housekeeper at Bradenham. Disraeli arranged for him to be employed as a messenger for the Board of Control, run by Byron's old friend, Sir John Hobhouse.

Isaac had only leased the house and Sarah could not afford to keep it on just for herself. She had been left enough to live on and was moving to Hastings, to stay with friends. Disraeli and Mary Anne came to help her in the distressing task of sorting out all her father's effects.

"I had not realized he was so devoted to Mama," Sarah said. "After her death, he just slowly dwindled away."

They were in the library, where he had spent so much of his life. Mary Anne looked at the books with which the room was lined, filling every shelf, stacked on tables, windowsills and in piles on top of the manuscript cupboards. There were thousands of them. "Strange to think they are all that is left of him," she murmured.

They stood quietly for another moment, each remembering the kindly, humorous figure in his smoking cap and little, oval glasses, his pockets filled with slips of paper on which he had written quotations for his anthologies, remembering how when he was blind his fingers would still feel along the shelves to find his favorite volumes, recognizing them by touch. "This one, Sarah. Try page ninety to ninety-five."

For Sarah the worst thought was that soon all his possessions would be scattered and the very essence of him gone. She could have wept, but just then Ben touched her shoulder to show he shared her thought. "You'll have to decide which of them you want," she said. "But not now. You must not leave Lord Bentinck alone too long."

"Of course, not." Disraeli had been touched by Bentinck coming with him to see if there was any way he could help.

"He does not look well," Sarah added.

Disraeli agreed. He was concerned about Bentinck, who still drove himself too hard, debating, studying, sitting on committees. He was so conscious of the time he had to make up that he would scarcely pause to eat.

"It makes me angry to think how people laughed at him," Mary Anne declared. "They all thought he was unfit for his position."

"He proved them wrong," Disraeli said. "He is one of the ablest and finest men I have ever known. My prayer is that one day soon he will feel well enough to take on the leadership again."

He went to look for Bentinck and, when he pushed open the sitting-room door, saw him sitting where he had left him, in the armchair by the window. Bentinck was slumped, his chin resting on one hand, staring at the corner of yew hedge and sky outside. He seemed exhausted, pale and lined with fatigue.

As Disraeli closed the sitting-room door, Bentinck started and looked around. "Ah. Is your sister all right?"

"Very calm. They'll join us presently." Disraeli crossed to the butler's tray with its decanter and glasses. "A glass of sherry?"

Bentinck rose and shook his head. "Ah—no, thank you. It might send me to sleep. I have some memoranda to look at later."

"Let them wait," Disraeli said, pouring two glasses. "Sleep might do you good." He saw Bentinck lean on the arm of the chair. "Do sit down. You look worn out."

Bentinck pushed himself erect and took a deep breath. "I'm tired, that's all. After this session, I'll go home. Country walks, fresh air, that'll set me up again." He moved to stand with his back to the unlit fire. "But what are we to do? There's no real Government! The Liberals are only kept in power by the Peelites, who support automatically anything you and I oppose."

"They are vindictive. It will take time for their good sense to overcome their ill will."

"Where do you get your patience from?" Bentinck wondered.

"From my father," Disraeli told him, with a slight smile. "But it was a lesson I was a long time in learning." He brought Bentinck his glass of sherry and he accepted it without protest.

Bentinck paused. "I wish I'd got to know him better."

"He'd have liked you," Disraeli said. "I'm glad at least that he lived to see me a member for Buckingham, this country. He wanted me to have a home here, too."

"This one?"

"It's not for sale."

Bentinck sipped his sherry. "Was there one you liked?"

Disraeli nodded. "Hughenden Manor, not far from here. It would have been ideal. He left me ten thousand pounds to buy it."

"Why don't you?"

The subject embarrassed Disraeli. He had tried everything possible. He could not call on Mary Anne. She had by now given him thirteen thousand pounds to settle some of his oldest debts. His new financial adviser, Philip Rose, a local solicitor, had approached banks on his behalf without success. With the amount he already owed, Disraeli was not a good risk. He shrugged. "Ten thousand is less than a third of what it would cost."

Bentinck sipped again and studied his glass. He coughed. "I've been thinking about that. As one of the leaders of the landed gentlemen, you ought to have property yourself. I'll give you a loan of twenty-five thousand, free of interest, to complete the purchase."

233

It was so completely unexpected that Disraeli, for once, was shaken out of his poise. He stared at Bentinck. "How could—how could I accept? I could never repay it."

"What's money between friends?" Bentinck grunted. "Pay it back when and if you can."

Disraeli's mind stopped spinning. He was overcome by Bentinck's generosity. "I am . . . I don't . . ." he stammered. "What can I say?"

"Anything but thanks. Start thanking me and I'll change my mind," Bentinck said gruffly. "It's not only . . . I owe you a lot, too." The admission of sentiment made him feel awkward. He finished his glass, not looking at Disraeli. "I am acting politically," he stressed.

"So I see," Disraeli said gently.

It was a bright day and the valley was sheltered from the freshening wind, warmed by the early afternoon sun. Disraeli had taken Mary Anne for a walk to the old abbey at Wycombe, making a slight detour.

They came over the rise and started down the hillside. Across from them, they could see Hughenden Manor, a stately, white-walled house of three storeys, standing on a spur of the Chiltern Hills that reached down into the valley. They could not see the entrance which was on the north. All the principal rooms faced south, with a garden door opening on to a wide terrace, leading down to a superb lawn that was never without sun. Through the trees beyond they could just glimpse the roof of the vicarage and the square tower of the tiny church which served the tenants and workers of the estate that covered seven hundred and fifty acres. They walked on down.

Mary Anne thought they would follow the trout stream that ran through the valley, opening out at one point into a small lake, but Disraeli turned her toward the hill on which the house was built. All they could see now were the high, brick chimneys. "Are you sure Mr. Norris won't mind us crossing here?" Mary Anne asked, thinking he was leading her towards the plank bridge over the stream.

"No, no," Dizzy told her. "He's moved." The Norrises who owned Hughenden were old acquaintances. When they were boys, he and his brother Ralph had often visited them and flirted with their daughters. He paused now with Mary Anne on his arm, with a corner of the house just visible through a gap in the trees. "What do you think of it?"

Mary Anne hugged his arm. "It's so beautiful. I wish we could have bought it. And the woods and gardens are magnificent."

"Yes," he agreed. "When we have planted some more trees and chosen some peacocks for the terrace, it will be perfect."

Mary Anne gazed at him. "We . . . ?"

"I signed the papers this morning," he murmured. "It is now our country home."

For a second or two, Mary Anne was speechless, then she flung her arms round his neck. "Dizzy!" She kissed him and spun round with him, laughing. She broke free and ran up the slope toward the house, holding on her wide-brimmed straw bonnet with one hand. He laughed and ran after her.

A month later, Lord George Bentinck set out from Welbeck Abbey, his father's home in Nottinghamshire. He was going to stay for a few days at Thoresby with his friend, Lord Manvers, a comfortable walk of about six miles.

It was a crisp day in late autumn and he chose the path through the woods, where the trees were just beginning to shed their leaves. Parliament had recessed and already he felt much better, having decided to do no more work until the next session. He was pleased at the way things had gone lately. The party had floundered on without a leader in the Commons, run by a kind of loose committee. An impossible situation, and he had at last been able to convince Lord Stanley to show more confidence in Disraeli. Dizzy had done them proud. At Stanley's urging, he had resumed his place as their chief spokesman and ripped into the Liberal government at the end of the session with a series of speeches that had left the House stunned.

Bentinck chuckled as he strode along, swinging his stick. He could remember the faces of the country members round him when he had told them they were listening to their next leader. They had shaken their heads, but it was a fact. As sure as eggs are— He staggered and dropped his stick, as an unbearable pain stabbed through his chest. He clutched his breast, pressing on his heart in agony, gasping for air.

The path was narrow here, the trees closer together, and he felt trapped. He pushed through them, doubling over with the pain from his heart, and staggered out into the open space at the side. He looked round wildly, but there was no one in sight, no one who could help him. He tried to call out, but could make no sound except a dry sob. He dropped to his knees and gazed up in appeal for a moment at the empty, almost colorless sky, then toppled forward on to his face on the ground.

Servants were sent to look for him some hours later, when he had not arrived at Thoresby. By that time, the dead, brown leaves had already begun to pile up against his body, covering his face.

Bentinck's death threw the Protectionists into confusion. After his resignation they had asked Lord John Manners' elder brother, Lord Granby, to replace him as leader in the Commons. Though conscientious, he was unambitious and refused the position after a few weeks of hesitation. For the rest of the session the party had struggled on directed by the two Whips, advised by Lord Stanley. The result had been chaos, but at least Bentinck had been there and there was always the hope that, one day, he would resume the leadership. Now, even that hope was gone.

Throughout the world it had been a dramatic year, beginning with the discovery of gold in California. While tens of thousands dreamed of riches and struggled to find

236

passage to the New World, others struck at the repressive governments and old, absolute monarchies of Europe. There were riots in Berlin, Milan, Budapest, Vienna and Paris. The Austrian Emperor was forced to flee to Innsbruck. In Paris, King Louis Philippe was deposed and fled to England. In England, the news of republican successes abroad caused another great upsurge of Chartism. The City and the Government were alarmed by the call for a giant rally to be held in April on Kensington Common, after which the Chartists had announced they would march on Westminster. The defense of the capital was entrusted to the aged Duke of Wellington and two hundred thousand special constables were enrolled to confront the demonstrators, among them Gladstone and the exiled Bonaparte prince, Louis Napoleon. But the rally was a poorly attended fiasco, resulting only in another, even larger petition being sent to Parliament.

In its reactions to events abroad and crises at home, Russell's minority had shown itself to be weak and incompetent. Any really concerted effort by the Protectionists might have swept the government away, but without a leader it was not possible. Now they faced another year of indecision and disorganization and began to look about for someone to take Bentinck's place. It was soon apparent that they were ready to consider almost anyone —except Disraeli. At the same time, Bentinck's younger brother, Lord Henry, began to campaign on Disraeli's behalf, organizing a group to put pressure on Stanley and win over the less reactionary country members. Although he appeared uninvolved and reluctant even to be considered, the action was directed by Disraeli himself. While Bentinck lived, he would never have put himself forward, but with his friend's death, he realized that only prejudice stood between him and the next vital step in his career. He left Mary Anne to settle in at Hughenden and stayed in London to consult his new supporters and call on his most influential friends.

By slow degrees, the tide turned in his favor, as it became clear that there were no other candidates except

237

nonentities. Yet every inch of advance was blocked by the two Whips and, most immovably, by Lord Stanley. If the party rejected Bentinck merely because he voted for the Jews, Stanley asked, how on earth could they now accept Disraeli? Stanley was averse to the thought of having to work with him and avoided contact as much as possible. Given encouragement and a little authority, what tricks might the Hebrew conjurer play?

At last, Lord Stanley found a solution. Among the Protectionists was old J.C. Herries, who had started his career half a century before under William Pitt and had briefly been Chancellor of the Exchequer, almost the only one in the party who had held any important government office. Stanley wrote a long, involved letter to Disraeli, acknowledging that no one else in the party was his equal, praising his abilities which none of the others could match and repeating the obvious need for a recognized leader to take decisions in the Commons in any emergency. He went on, "But believing also that, from whatever cause, your formal establishment in the post of leader would not meet with a general and cheerful approval . . . I pay you the much higher compliment of thinking that you have both the clearness of perception and the manliness of character to be willing to waive a claim which your talents might authorize you to put forward and, satisfied with the real eminence of your position, to give a generous support to a Leader of abilities inferior to your own."

Dizzy read the letter at first with incredulity, then with anger at its unconscious insolence. The insult went so deep that his instinct was to leave the Protectionists and to quit politics. However, he decided to make one last move and composed a very careful reply. He thanked Lord Stanley for his frankness and agreed that the office of leader in the House of Commons should only be accepted by someone who had the confidence and warm regard of the party. If Stanley had still been a member of the Commons, he would have been happy to serve under him. "Honor and personal feelings attached me to George Bentinck and I would never have quitted him. But I am

238

now free from all personal ties, and am no longer disposed to sacrifice interesting pursuits, health and a happy hearth for a political career which can bring one little fame." However, he agreed that there were higher considerations which influenced all men in responsible positions. "But it is my opinion that I could do more to uphold the cause to which I am attached ... by acting alone and unshackled than if I fell into the party discipline, which you intimate." He closed with a suggestion that Stanley should try a water cure for his gout.

Stanley had told the Whips, "I have never seen, of late years, any reason to distrust him, and I think he'll run straight." When Disraeli's reply arrived, he knew he would have to think again. "Alone and unshackled," Disraeli had already split the Conservative Party. The courteously phrased reply was a veiled hint that, if necessary, he would do it a second time and leave Stanley at the head of a tiny Protectionist rump. It was not a challenge which Stanley could risk and he quickly called a meeting of the chief Tory peers.

Mary Anne was almost sick with excitement, waiting to hear what decision they reached. At first, she was almost as hurt as Dizzy when it was announced that they still could not bring themselves to appoint him. Instead, they proposed a committee of three, Herries, Lord Granby and Disraeli, all with equal power. In that way, Stanley's fears would be lessened, the doubters would be reconciled by not having the Adventurer in sole charge and they would have the advantages of his brilliance, while he could be effectively controlled by the other two. Because of the antagonism of so many in the party, Mary Anne accepted the result as the best that could be hoped for and was shaken when he told her that he had refused to join the Committee of Three. "You can't give up now!" she protested. "Have you really refused?"

"Officially," he explained. "Otherwise, I should have to consult the other two. Unofficially, I shall behave as if the Committee exists—but at the same time, ignore it. They will do anything to avoid giving me the position of leader formally. So I shall have to take it."

Stanley heard Lord Aberdeen's comment that the triumvirate reminded him irresistibly of another within living memory—Roger Ducos, the Abbé Sièyes and Napoleon Bonaparte. Privately, he agreed, but comforted himself with the thought that it would take three or four years, until Herries had retired and Granby moved to the House of Lords, before Disraeli could establish his claim to be leader. In fact, it took rather less. Within three weeks, the other two had shown themselves to be hopeless and were ignored. While Peel's chin sank more deeply into his collar and Gladstone fumed, Russell's government in debates and correspondence acknowledged Disraeli's undisputed position as leader of Her Majesty's Opposition in the House of Commons.

Old Lord Melbourne, almost senile now and spending half his days asleep, remembered his conversation with the foreign-looking, ringletted and romantic young man at Caroline Norton's, who had confessed so improbably that his ambition was to be Prime Minister. "By God . . ." he marvelled, "the fellow will do it yet!"

All this time, Disraeli was hard pressed for money. Unkind critics suggested that the real reason behind his sympathy for the Chartists was that one of their demands was for MPs to be paid a salary. A crisis was avoided when he managed to negotiate for a cheap, popular edition of his novels and for the republication of his father's *Curiosities of Literature*, which sold very well. As always, he sent a set to Gore House. Lady Blessington's letter of thanks was so sincere and touching that he felt a twinge of guilt for having called only occasionally on her and D'Orsay over the past twelve months. He decided he must visit them. D'Orsay's weird imprisonment in Gore House had gone on for eight years now, eight long years of being unable to set foot outside the gardens between sunrise and sunset, of holding off the siege of the debt-collectors and checking each arrival to make sure that he was not a process-server.

For twenty years he had championed the exile Prince Louis Napoleon, supporting him, keeping his cause alive while the prince himself was in prison. Since Louis Napoleon had been elected President of France, D'Orsay waited daily for the summons to Paris or the princely gift that would solve all his problems. No message came. The new President did not wish to be embarrassed by the memory of his raffish friends and the days when he had had to depend on the hospitality of Gore House, when only D'Orsay's belief in him had sustained his courage. D'Orsay would neither beg nor show his disappointment.

Disraeli thought of the Count and of Lady Blessington and the constant strain and overwork which was turning her into an old woman, heavy and lined. He resolved to call on them as soon as possible, but he was too late.

Faced with ruin from demanding creditors and the threat of prison for D'Orsay, Marguerite had decided the only answer was to arrange for the entire contents and the house itself to be put up for sale at once. D'Orsay must save himself and she would join him as soon as she was able. In the early hours of the morning, his valet made sure that the rear entrance to Gore House was not being watched, then D'Orsay and he stole out with one traveling trunk, drove without stopping to Folkestone and were across the Channel by Sunday night. Having engaged a leading auctioneer to conduct the sale, Lady Blessington followed him to Paris two weeks later. The very next day, Dizzy came to visit her, to be told that she had gone and all the treasures of Gore House were being catalogued. When he reached home, saddened and dismayed, her letter of goodbye was waiting for him. He wrote at once to Paris and was relieved to hear that Louis Napoleon had welcomed D'Orsay with kindness and remembered his debt of gratitude. But the next news he heard, only a month later, was that Lady Margaret Blessington had collapsed after the excitement of those painful weeks and the strain of the years before and had died of a stroke. And that D'Orsay was so affected by her death that he seemed to have lost his reason.

Death was clearing the stage of the major characters of Disraeli's early life—Henrietta, his parents, Lady Blessington, Melbourne, O'Connell. Bulwer, who had reversed his name and now called himself Sir Edward Bulwer Lytton, was broken in health and had fled abroad to escape Rosina's ceaseless persecution. One more leading actor was soon to make his exit.

Ever since the defeat of Peel, Disraeli had treated his former chief with scrupulous courtesy. They did not speak or communicate, but he always referred to Sir Robert in debate with great respect and the older man had been seen to applaud quietly during his most effective speeches. Once, to Gladstone's surprise, he even cheered Disraeli. It was at the end of the four days of heated debate over the Don Pacifico affair.

Lord John Russell was both blessed and cursed by having Palmerston as his Foreign Secretary. The victory over Napoleon forty years before had made England the dominant power in Europe. Forceful, farsighted and quick to reach decisions, Palmerston was ideally equipped to uphold the influence of Britain and to look after British interests, but he also had a passionate dislike of repressive government and saw it as his duty to interfere in the internal problems of other nations, even giving aid to revolutionary movements. At home, many people idolized him as the champion of the underdog, while politicians abroad thought of him with fear and mistrust. In Germany they had a rhyme.

If the Devil had a son,
He would be Lord Palmerston.

In the Don Pacifico affair, his virtues and defects were thrown into their sharpest relief. Pacifico was an obscure Maltese Jew living in Athens. When his home was ransacked by a mob, he saw no hope of being awarded damages by a Greek court and appealed to London as a British citizen. Palmerston's immediate answer was to send the Mediterranean fleet to the Piraeus, where the Admiral impounded all the merchantmen in the harbor until Don Pacifico was given justice. The Foreign Secretary's highhanded action outraged all Europe, including the Queen and Prince Albert, who had not been consulted, and Lord Stanley began a motion of censure against him in the Upper House. Disraeli, who admired Palmerston's determination to maintain the prestige of Britain, reluctantly had to lead the criticism in the Commons. Just as reluctantly, Russell had to defend his colleague and did so by drawing attention to Disraeli's lack of conviction in his attack. Urged on by Peel, Gladstone found himself in the rare position of having to defend Disraeli and the debate grew daily more violent, until Palmerston ended it and saved himself by the speech of his life, which he finished with the proud demand, "whether, as the Roman in the days of old held himself free from indignity, when he could say *Civis Romanus Sum*, so also a British subject, in whatever land he may be, shall feel confident that the watchful eye and the strong arm of England will protect him against injustice and wrong!"

It was past five in the morning when Disraeli got home after the last night of the debate. He had much to think about. Russell's government had won but could not last much longer, especially since Peel was obviously moving toward a reconciliation with the Protectionists. Dizzy went to bed and slept soundly, but Peel was too restless to sleep. The only way the Liberals could be defeated was if the old Conservative party was reunited and only Peel could convince his followers that the time had come to join forces with Stanley and Disraeli. Yet, if he did so, he would lose the last remnants of his own power. He attended to some business, then, feeling old and tired, went riding to clear his head. He always used the bit and spurs harshly and, on Constitution Hill, his horse threw him. He was carried home in agony, his spinal injuries so painful that the doctors who were called could not examine him properly. In the afternoon, Disraeli took Mary Anne out in their carriage and, while they drove round Regent's Park, two riders stopped to tell them the news. They were surprised to see that Disraeli looked distressed. Two days later, Dizzy and Mary Anne were at a great morning fête given by the Londonderrys in the rose gardens of their thatched cottage by the Thames. During it,

Lord Londonderry disappeared for a time. While the band played and his guests sipped ices, he galloped all the way to Whitehall and back. He found Disraeli in the conservatory with Lady Londonderry, who was making tea for the most important guests from a series of golden pots and kettles. Disraeli had explained how essential it was to win the cooperation of the Peelites and their leader, but Peel must live to set his followers in the right direction. "There's no hope," Londonderry told him. Peel was still lying on the couch on which he had been laid and from which he could not be moved. His wife was still not allowed to see him, in case her tears brought on the final crisis. In the afternoon, word came that the struggle was over and he was dead.

That evening in the Carlton Club, a group of the Peelites came together, stunned by the news. "At least, he died at peace with all mankind," Gladstone said. "Even with Disraeli."

"He killed him," Sir James Graham disagreed. "No one can deny Disraeli killed Bentinck. Now he has killed Peel."

Lord Stanely's young son, Edward, who had taken Bentinck's place as MP for King's Lynn, was listening and became incensed.

"I must protest, Sir!" he exclaimed. "It was purely a riding accident."

"Sir Robert had lost the will to live," Graham replied. "Disraeli broke his spirit."

Edward Stanley turned on his heel and left. It was in Gladstone's mind to agree with him. After all, Peel's last act in the House of Commons had been to cheer Disraeli and they had discussed the terms under which a new alliance between both sections of the party would be possible. Just then, one of the others broke in on his thoughts by spitting out Disraeli's name with contempt. "That mountebank has leapt to power on the backs of greater men," he continued. "Let no one think any of us will serve with or under him. Nor shall we rest until we have brought him down!" Listening to the chorus of agreement, Gladstone decided to remain silent. Time and circumstances had cooled his own indignation, but he had realized that, with Sir Robert dead, leadership of the Peelites must pass to Graham and himself. It would be suicidal to weaken the one link that kept their faction together, detestation of Disraeli.

Sarah had settled finally in a pleasant little house in Twickenham, close enough for frequent visits to Grosvenor Gate. She also loved to visit Hughenden, which Mary Anne had made so comfortable and attractive. Early in the new year of 1852, she came for a short stay but was disappointed when Ben was summoned almost at once to London. In the morning, she strolled with him down the long beech walk at the bottom of the garden, their shoes crunching in the thick frost that had turned the bare trees and bushes a glistening white. It was Ben's favorite walk in all weathers. Today he seemed lighthearted, flicking at the icicles that hung from the tips of the branches with his cane, telling her how he planned to increase the size of the estate. He had already made it more or less self-supporting by bringing in new tenants for the smallholdings and charging economic rents. He smiled describing Mary Anne's meticulous attention to the household accounts, which so irritated the local tradesmen. He also told her about the letters he kept receiving from a lady named Mrs. Brydges Willyams. She had first written after his speech on behalf of Lionel de Rothschild and he had paid little attention. Her letters became more frequent, after every speech of his that was reported in the papers, so flattering and yet so perceptive that at last he was sufficiently intrigued to ask a friend in Devonshire to make enquiries. All he knew about her was that she lived in Torquay. She proved to be a wealthy widow, living alone. Like him she was a member of the Church of England, although Jewish by birth. During the past summer, she had travelled to London to see the Great Exhibition and wrote to Disraeli inviting him to meet her one afternoon at the crystal fountain in the main hall. Her letter arrived too late for him to keep the appointment, even if he had wished to, but he wrote to apologize for his apparent rudeness and to thank her for her continuing, friendly remarks. Her next letter he took to his solicitor, Philip Rose, for it informed him that she wished to make him an executor of her will and one of its beneficiaries. On Rose's advice, he had begun a cautious correspondence, sending her copies of one or two of his novels and of his recent biography of Lord George Bentinck. She was so overcome that she had sent by return a present of fresh lobsters, sole and prawns to grace his table. Disraeli had, of course, to reply and the correspondence and interchange of gifts had gone on, becoming increasingly more intimate and friendly. And all this with someone whom he had never met.

Sarah smiled, yet she could tell that underneath the banter, his mind was occupied with more serious matters. "It must be difficult sometimes, working with Lord Stanley," she murmured.

Disraeli stopped short and laughed. He should have remembered his sister's uncanny ability to read his thoughts. Working with Stanley was more than difficult. It was nearly impossible. For every two steps Dizzy took forward, Stanley seemed to take at least one back. While Disraeli was daring, he was extraordinarily cautious. With Peel gone, Disraeli saw no earthly reason why the party members should not call themselves by their real name, Conservatives. Protection was as good as dead and could never be revived, as even the landowners and farmers now agreed. Yet Stanley kept insisting that they had a duty to bring back the Corn Laws. Disraeli still thought of him as "Stanley," although he had recently succeeded to the family earldom and was now Lord Derby.

While still "Stanley," he had proved the total difference in their temperaments a year before, when Disraeli had brilliantly stopped his whole party voting on an issue on which the Liberals were divided and Russell had been defeated by the split vote of his own side. He had resigned and the Queen asked Lord Stanley to form a government. The only man of experience he could call on was old Herries and the only one of real talent was Disraeli, to whom the Queen and Prince Albert objected, although they realized he could not be passed over. The other men whom Stanley approached were either afraid of the responsibility or asked for assurances that he would not attempt to revive protectionism and that they would not have to serve with the Jew adventurer. Stanley refused and told the Queen he could not find enough men capable of making up a cabinet. Disraeli asked him to reconsider. He even offered to stand down himself, if that would make others accept, but Stanley had lost his enthusiasm and was not prepared to take any risks. It was easier to say no and would give him more leisure to concentrate on his racehorses and his translation of Homer.

"I attempt to work with Lord Stanley—I beg his pardon—Lord Derby," Disraeli said. "It cannot be claimed to be more than an attempt."

The situation of the previous year had repeated itself. This time, the cause was Palmerston. There had been constant friction between him and his chief, Lord John Russell. Not only did Pam sometimes take action without consulting the Queen, he also neglected to inform his own cabinet colleagues. In two recent cases, he had shown a complete indifference to their opinions. In the first, he welcomed to England the defeated Hungarian revolutionary leader, Kossuth. The second was more serious. Just before Christmas, 1851, Prince Louis Napoleon carried out a masterly *coup d'état,* by which he made himself Emperor of France as Napoleon the Third. At once, Palmerston had announced his approval of the new emperor, in direct contradiction to the feelings of the Queen and the policy of his own government. Russell had his excuse at last and dismissed him. Palmerston could not wait to have his revenge. As soon as Parliament reassembled after the Christmas recess, he had moved an amendment to a Bill by which Russell proposed to establish a local militia force. Disraeli supported Palmerston and the Government was defeated. Russell was forced to resign. Lord Derby was a guest of the Duke of Beaufort at Badminton, at a shooting party. Disraeli sent him an urgent letter, begging him to accept office if the Queen summoned him and repeating his offer to stand down, if it would induce Palmerston to join Derby's cabinet and unite the party by becoming Leader of the House of Commons.

"Will he kiss hands this time?" Sarah asked.

Disraeli shrugged. Who could tell if Derby would have the courage to kiss Victoria's hands as her Prime Minister? "If he does not, it will be all up with us. We shall lose all credibility." However, Dizzy was far from confident when he left after lunch for London.

In the afternoon Sarah walked on the terrace with Mary Anne, but it was much colder and Sarah saw her shiver in spite of her fur wrap. Mary Anne behaved so youthfully and created such an illusion with her dyed hair and brightly painted cheeks that it was hard to remember she was now past sixty. Sarah regretted having suggested they take the air and asked if she would mind their going back inside. As they seated themselves gratefully in front of the fire in the drawing-room, Mary Anne said, "I wish Dizzy hadn't had to go back to town."

Sarah smiled. "Not this time, surely?"

Mary Anne warmed her hands. "We shall see. It is not just a question of whether Lord Derby accepts. I can't bear to see Dizzy disappointed again."

Sarah was shocked. "You mean, he might be left out altogether? It's not possible! Derby would insist on having Dizzy with him."

"Why? He has never really approved of him, never treated him with anything but the barest courtesy. They communicate almost entirely by letter. He will not accept Dizzy socially. We have never been invited to his home."

Sarah was biting her lip. Her throat had gone dry. She had not realized her brother was facing the most bitter rejection of his life. "So it is far from certain that he will be offered any Cabinet post at all?"

Mary Anne looked much older and very tired. "That is why I said, we shall see."

With his position as second only to Lord Derby in the party, he should have been given at least the Leadership of the House of Commons. Derby had welcomed with relief his suggestion that it should be offered to Palmerston and his promise to work loyally under him. "Don't let me be in your way," Disraeli had said. "It is everything for your government that Palmerston should be a member of it. He'll not give you trouble about principles, but he may about *position*. He would not like to serve under me—but he will find me a loyal lieutenant." Although he meant it, Dizzy had been hurt by Derby's reaction. Once he was sure of Disraeli's sincerity, he had immediately thought how much easier it would make his task if he could assure the Queen and the men he needed for his cabinet that the adventurer would have no post of importance.

Disraeli had a brief meeting with him before his interview at the palace and waited at Grosvenor Gate in a fever of uncertainty. Hours passed with no message from Derby, then he heard knocking at the door and voices and came out to see Derby himself hurrying up the stairs. He showed him into his study.

Derby looked disturbed and anxious. He was suffering again from gout. Though only in his early fifties, he had the slower movements of an older man. He was putting on weight and his side-whiskers were gray. His most striking feature was his high, domed forehead under which his eyes burned with a fierce, disciplined intelligence. He was of average height, faultlessly dressed, such an aristocrat in style and manner that the vowels of his flat, Lancashire accent always came as a surprise.

It was a difficult meeting for both of them. Disraeli waited courteously for him to begin, outwardly calm and attentive, showing none of the turmoil within. "Well, I've been to see Her Majesty," Derby said finally. "And kissed hands."

"Then let me be the first to congratulate you, Prime Minister."

Derby grimaced. "That may be a bit premature, Mr. Disraeli." Dizzy raised his eyebrows. "I went straight from the Queen to see Palmerston. And it's no go, I'm afraid."

Disraeli's dismay showed for a moment. "He would not accept our offer?"

Derby hesitated. "No."

"Did you—if you'll forgive me—did you tell him what I said?"

"Oh, yes. He owned it was generous—more than generous. He had no doubt of your getting on well together." Derby turned away. He appeared to have just noticed a small drawing of Hughenden that hung beside him in the blue-painted wall, but in reality he was embarrassed, an unusual experience for him. "No, he was most complimentary about you, in fact. You and Peel, he said, were the only ones who treated him like gentlemen in the Pacifico business." He paused again, wincing at the pain in his leg. "I thought everything was settled, d'you see? Then he brought up the question of Protection. He said he'd always been in favor of it, a moderate fixed duty. But it was too late for such things now. And he wanted my word that I would not attempt to interfere with Free Trade. I couldn't give it. I just couldn't." He looked at Disraeli at last, almost defiantly.

Dizzy felt like shaking him. To throw away his best chance for a principle that was not only dead but buried. Yet he saw that, within Derby's concept of honor, he had behaved in the only way he could. "So what now?" he asked quietly.

Derby scratched his right whisker. "I tell you, Mr. Disraeli, I don't know. I don't know what to do without him. None of the men available have ever held high office before. You, yourself—well, quite frankly, when I suggested your name to the Queen and Prince Albert, they were reluctant to have you in the Government."

"I understand they were very attached to Peel," Disraeli said evenly.

Derby nodded. "That is so. I told them you had had to make your reputation and win a position which no one else would provide for you. And that lately you had quite changed your tone. She swallowed that and finally said, if I had no alternative but to propose you as one of the

Secretaries of State, she would hold me responsible for you."

Disraeli's face was set. "I see."

All trace of expectancy had faded in Disraeli. Derby had every right to be blunt and forthright if he chose, and was not being intentionally insulting, but Dizzy saw no reason why he should endure it any longer. He had nothing to hope for and might at least end the meeting with dignity. "Then let me make your task easier, Prime Minister," he said. "I am more concerned for my country than for myself, more devoted to my Party than to my ambition. If, after fifteen years faithful service, that is still not acknowledged, it is far better for me to retire from the struggle and make way for someone more acceptable to the Crown and to Parliament."

Stanley was looking at him, almost as if seeing him for the first time. It had occurred to him that he had never thought of Disraeli as real, but as an actor with all his attitudes assumed and, at heart, insincere. There was no mistaking the sincerity now, and he remembered the earlier offer he had made to stand aside, the calm willingness to sacrifice himself for their party. How dear it must have cost him! Derby's cheeks flushed as he realized with shame that he had thought only of the usefulness of the gesture, not of the unselfish generosity of the man who made it. And he was suddenly very afraid of losing him. "There's no need for that. No need," he muttered. "I had thought of giving the position of Chancellor of the Exchequer to Lord Lyndhurst, but he is over eighty now. I—I would prefer to entrust it to you."

Disraeli felt the blood rush to his head. It was hard for him to grasp the words Derby had just spoken. Especially after he had resigned himself to disappointment and obscurity. "Next to you, that would be the key post in the Cabinet," he said blankly.

"Will you take it?" Derby asked.

Disraeli's expression was unreadable, yet behind it the turmoil had begun again as his mind leaped from possibility to possibility. After so long. All he had to do was say yes. Ideally, he would have wished for the Foreign Office, or the House Office. In either he knew his skills would be put to their best use. Yet to be Chancellor, responsible for all the finances of the Government. . . . "I know little about finance," he confessed.

"Neither did Canning," Derby said with a faint smile. "No one does to start off. They give you the figures. You'll soon learn." He paused. "And unlike some of the other Ministers, as Chancellor you won't come into contact with the Palace much. It will be best for them to get to know you slowly."

Disraeli did not show his own excitement openly until Mary Anne arrived. She cried and laughed and cried again, saying his name over and over. He took her in his arms and they danced round the drawing-room, until they collapsed breathless on the sofa and Dizzy drew her to him and she looked up at him with such fond pride that he had to kiss her again. "Oh, Dizzy, my own Dizzy—I always knew. Always," she breathed. In her happiness all the slights and disappointed hopes of so many years had been cancelled out.

Their first visitor after the news was given out was old Lord Lyndhurst, a little stooped but still spry in spite of his years. He chuckled as he wrung Disraeli's hand. "Everything comes to him who waits, my boy," he said. "And you've deserved it. No one more." Having been Chancellor himself several times he was able to offer much practical advice and ended, "Don't let them rush you into anything. As Leader of the House of Commons *and* Chancellor, you'll have enough power to stand up for what you believe in. But don't startle them. The party's the largest in the House, but if the others combine they can still defeat you. Don't try for anything too controversial at first. Let them become used to you. Tread carefully and you'll prove to the world that addition and subtraction are not the only qualifications for a Chancellor of the Exchequer." He was crossing the hall with Disraeli and stopped at a memory that made him smile.

"Do you remember that visit I paid to you and your family with poor Henrietta? There never were such happy times. Yet who among us then could have imagined this day—except yourself?"

"One other," Disraeli said. "My sister."

"Ah, yes." Lyndhurst nodded, remembering Sarah. "She must be very proud."

Sarah's pride and excitement matched Mary Anne's. Over the years, Mary Anne had replaced her as Disraeli's closest confidante, but she bore no resentment. She loved Mary Anne for her happy heart and her devotion to her brother. There was still a very special bond between Ben and herself and she was content with that.

The reactions to Disraeli's appointment in political circles varied from humorous to outraged, although here and there he was fiercely championed, especially by Derby's son, Lord Edward Stanley, who had fallen out with his father and responded to the new Chancellor's more progressive ideas. The pattern was repeated throughout the country. Disraeli took little notice. He was far too busy helping Derby to choose the rest of the Cabinet. It was a strange situation. Although most of the hundred or so who had split off with Peel had now drifted back to the main party, among the thirty to forty staunch Peelites were all the best men and, like Graham and Gladstone, they could not accept office, not since it meant becoming Disraelites. Derby had very scant knowledge of the rank and file members of his party in the Commons, so had to take Disraeli's word for their capabilities. Among those he agreed to were Lord John Manners and, with great unwillingness, his own son, Edward, who became Under Secretary for Foreign Affairs. Each day Derby realized more fully how lucky he was to have Disraeli's support and they were soon on much better terms; if not intimate, at least frank and businesslike. Without him, he knew he would probably have given up. He often wondered what he had let himself in for and how he could try to run the country with a minority government and a gaggle of untried men. It was brought home strikingly to him one afternoon during a speech in the House of Lords, when the Duke of Wellington, now in his eighties and grown deaf, leaned over and asked for the names of the new ministers. As Derby repeated the obscure names, the old Duke kept demanding loudly, "Who? Who?" his piercing voice interrupting the unfortunate speaker. In a very short time, Derby's government was known as the "Who? Who?" Ministry.

None of the gibes, jokes, sneers and criticism could disturb Disraeli's vast and secret enjoyment of his new position. It was almost unique for someone with no previous experience of office to be made, at one stroke, a member of Cabinet and Leader of the House of Commons. It had only ever happened to one other man, one of his heroes, the great William Pitt. Disraeli felt that, at last, he had won a place in history. He knew the government could not last long but, however long, it was worth it. While affecting to be above such trivialities, it gave him enormous pleasure and excitement to take over the Chancellor's residence at 11 Downing Street, next door to the Prime Minister at Number 10, although it cost him nearly eight hundred pounds to buy the personal furniture of the last occupant, as was the custom. Yet even that was worth it. Best of all, for the traditional payment, the black silk official robe, thickly embroidered with gold, was handed over to him by Sir Charles Wood, the outgoing Chancellor. The robe was an object of special reverence to Disraeli, for it had once belonged to Pitt. To feel it on his shoulders and to smooth down the gold-encrusted lapels gave him a momentary sensation of power that was indescribable. "I fear you will find it very heavy," Wood said. "Not at all," Disraeli murmured, "I find it uncommonly light."

He needed the robe for his first appearance at Windsor Castle, for a ceremony that was without parallel. In the whole Cabinet, only Derby and two others had been Ministers before. Not one of the other seventeen was even a Privy Councillor. They had to be sworn in and receive their seals of office from the Queen without delay.

In the Audience Room used as a temporary Council

Chamber, Disraeli bowed with the others as Queen Victoria entered, followed by Prince Albert, who remained behind her throughout, to her right. With motherhood she had become stouter. Her hair was drawn back in two glossy wings from a center parting. She wore a hooped dress of small brown and white checks and banded with darker panels, with long sleeves, modestly highnecked to cover her shoulders, as Albert preferred. She could no longer be called pretty. She was very short, her public expression prim, even severe. Her cheeks were pouched, her nose drooping, her chin receding, yet she radiated an awesome dignity. The aura of majesty which surrounded her made some of the men facing her tremble. Disraeli bore himself proudly but dutifully, a High Renaissance figure in his gold-faced, black gown. Although she was eager to see him, her hooded eyes gave no sign of it when they passed over him. Attended by Lord Derby, robed Privy Councillors and court officials in uniform, she took her place at the end of the long table on which lay a row of official seals in their leather cases. At the same moment, all seventeen men facing her knelt to be sworn in, then advanced one by one to take the oath of office. As each was called, the seal nearest the Queen was handed to her and the row on the table pushed up.

At last, it was Disraeli's turn. He advanced and bowed low. Victoria nodded distantly, looking straight through him. He knelt before her and she gave him her hand to kiss, gazing icily over his head, making it perfectly clear that she disapproved of him and resented the fact that like everyone else she had been forced to accept him. Behind his attitude of reverent correctness and composure, it was impossible to read his feelings. His own eyes were fixed on the seal of the Chancellor of the Exchequer as she handed it down to him and, for a second, they both held it, his fingers slim and graceful, hers short and stubby. He rose and bowed again, backing from her presence.

chapter ten

In August of 1852, Dizzy was saddened to hear of the lonely death of D'Orsay in Paris. He did not have much leisure to mourn for him. He had never thought the government in which he was Chancellor of the Exchequer would have a long life. At any moment, if the Peelites voted with the Liberals and Radicals, it could be brought down, but as long as the government stuck to sound Conservative measures, he expected Gladstone, Graham and the rest to back it. He had underestimated their thirst for revenge and the extent of Gladstone's jealousy.

Gladstone had been groomed by Peel as a future Chancellor, himself, and the sight of the Hebrew mountebank in the office that should be his was unbearable. He would never admit, not even to himself, that what he felt was jealousy. He denied any personal enmity, sometimes walking home with him after a debate to call on Mary Anne, apparently friendly. Yet when he was alone with his wife, Catherine, more often than not they could not bring themselves even to speak Disraeli's name, "that Jew." Try as he might, however, Gladstone could find no political grounds to oppose him and fell back on his conscience which would not allow him to support someone so obviously morally suspect and unaware of the true nature of revealed religion.

Disraeli took his position very seriously and won the respect of his department by his willingness to learn and the exhausting hours he worked. Nine months after coming to office he had to present his main Budget. It was very important. By it, his Government would stand or fall. After weeks of preparation he managed to produce sensible housekeeping figures, of which Derby approved, in spite of being given little help by others of their colleagues. Mary Anne was anxious when he left for the House, as he had not yet recovered from a serious bout of influenza. His speech lasted five hours and by the end he was exhausted, both by the effort and by knowing he faced a highly critical audience. In spite of two Liberal members who giggled and chattered throughout, hoping to distract him, his speech was well received and he was loudly cheered for his measures to help the farming community which had lost by the abolition of protection and for his proposals to equalize taxation.

Derby thought he had carried it off brilliantly and congratulated him. Even the Queen was impressed and sent her congratulations through Prince Albert. It was a false calm. Gladstone had been ready to denounce his proposals, whatever they were, merely because he made them. When the Opposition did not begin the attack, he whipped the Peelites up into a rage of indignation that the man who brought down Peel should have introduced what was virtually a Free Trade Budget, and the storm broke. All Disraeli's old opponents joined in the cry to bring him down and the debate raged round him for seven days, his figures questioned, his proposals ridiculed. Bulwer Lytton and Manners were among the few who defended him. Throughout, he sat impassively, letting the jeers and criticism wash over him, only raising an eyebrow when he heard that Gladstone had complained that his proposals were "'unconservative." At the close of it all on the last night, he rose to reply, cheered on by his own party who now realized that the Peelites had joined with the Liberals against them. Although excited himself by the atmosphere, as usual he kept himself in control, lashing his critics with cool irony. His words produced violent reactions which were echoed by a December thunderstorm which roared outside, the flashes of lightning seen and crashes of thunder heard in the lamplit Chamber. The effect was incredibly dramatic and passions rose higher and higher. After nearly three hours of speaking, he declared, "I have been told to withdraw my Budget, as others have done. Sir, I will not submit to the degradation of others." There was a din of cheers and counter-cheers. "Yes! I know what I have to face," he called. "I have to face a Coalition!" Many Conservatives rose to their feet cheering him as he glanced at the two benches opposite, the one above the gangway with the Liberal leaders and the one below it where the Peelites now sat. "The combination may be successful. A Coalition has before this been successful." He raised his right hand in the gesture that now as always silenced the House. "But Coalitions have always found this, that their triumph has been brief. This, too, I know—that England does not love Coalitions!" He brought his hand slowly down on to the table in emphasis. "I appeal from the Coalition to the public opinion which governs this country—that public opinion whose irresistible influence can control even the decrees of Parliaments!"

It was one o'clock when he sat down, ending the debate. He crossed his legs. He picked up his tophat from beside him, put it on and leaned back, folding his arms, seemingly unaware of the clamor on both sides. Opposite him, vigorous and handsome, Gladstone sprang to his feet and demanded to be heard.

Along from Disraeli, two of his younger aides, the serious Lord Edward Stanley and the dashing Lord Henry Lennox, were applauding wildly. Seeing Gladstone ges-

ture to the Speaker, they looked puzzledly at each other.
"What does he want?" Lennox wondered.

"He's trying to speak."

"How can he?" Lennox protested. "The debate's over."

Traditionally, the debate finished with the reply of the Leader of the House. It was unthinkable for a private member to attempt to follow him. The conservative cheers turned to booing and shouts of "Sit down! You've had your chance! Vote! Vote!," while the Opposition's protests became cheers of encouragement. "Mr. Speaker —Sir!" Gladstone demanded. "The right honorable Chancellor of the Exchequer—I will be heard!"

His words were virtually drowned out. Disraeli could have silenced his supporters, but he had been angered by the obvious vindictiveness of the Peelites who had come into the open as enemies. In the Peers' Gallery, Lord Derby sat watching tensely with Lyndhurst.

Little of what Gladstone said at first was heard, but finally his harsh voice could not be stopped. He was a powerful speaker, his tone lofty and magisterial. "I must tell the right honorable Chancellor of the Exchequer that whatever he has learned—and he has learned much—he has not yet learned the limits of discretion, of moderation, that ought to restrain the conduct and language of every member of this House, the disregard of which is an offense in the meanest among us—but is of tenfold weight when it is committed by the Leader of the House of Commons."

Both sides had quieted to hear him. There was an audible gasp and everyone looked at Disraeli to judge the effect of the reprimand on him. He was completely still and expressionless. Gladstone went on more strongly. "Before I proceed to a detailed criticism of his financial schemes, I must say that this Budget is the most subversive in its tendencies and ultimate effects of any I have ever known!" As he paused for effect, he glanced across at Disraeli and hesitated, seeing him undo the button of his coat, pat his waistcoat pockets and bring out his quizzing glass. He stared as Disraeli swivelled slowly to peer up at the clock above the Speaker's chair, then dropped the quizzing glass back into his pocket, yawned elaborately and pulled his hat down over his eyes. His head drooped. There was a swell of laughter and applause. In the gallery Derby was smiling. "Gladstone's so dull," he chuckled. "So dull after Dizzy." He, too, lowered his head on to his arm and appeared to go to sleep. But Gladstone was not to be silenced. Nothing could stop him when he was moved to speak and the debate began again with all its passion and anger. The division was not taken until four in the morning.

When Dizzy at last reached home, tired and serious, Mary Anne was waiting up for him as always. He told her quietly that his Budget had been defeated and Derby's Government forced to resign. It was not that the measures he proposed were wrong, but simply that it was *his* Budget. After nearly fifteen years in Parliament, his first taste of office had lasted less than ten months and it was hard to bear.

In the Coalition Government of Liberals and Peelites which took over from them, under Lord Aberdeen, Gladstone was given Disraeli's place as Chancellor of the Exchequer. There had been no apologies nor exchange of courtesies between them. They remained at a polite distance, but Gladstone refused to make the customary payment to the outgoing Chancellor for the furniture and effects in 11 Downing Street. In turn, Disraeli refused to part with the robe which was traditionally handed over. Gladstone had to give in over the payment, but Disraeli could not bear to see Pitt's robe worn by Gladstone whom he thought of as a canting hypocrite and simply ignored all demands for it.

He discovered that being even an ex-Minister had some rewards. He was now genuinely a national figure and, as a result, his creditors were much more reasonable. Neither Mary Anne nor he had been well for some time, so as soon as decent weather came in the new year, he decided they should take a short holiday in Torquay.

He had chosen the little resort on the Devon coast not only for its mild climate and scenic attractions, but because it was there that his intriguing admirer lived, the widow, Mrs. Brydges Willyams. Their exchange of letters and small presents had continued, until he could no longer resist the desire to meet her in person. He took rooms for a week with Mary Anne in the Royal Hotel and, on the afternoon of their first day, they drove up to her villa, Mount Braddon. The house was pleasantly old-fashioned, with a superb view over Tor Bay. The lady herself, who was almost overcome at having her hero actually under her roof, turned out to be extremely stout and exceedingly plain and the reason for her refusing all invitations to visit Hughenden became obvious. At her age, the journey could well have proved too much of a strain. She was over eighty.

Dizzy's charm and Mary Anne's artlessness soon broke the ice and, within half an hour, they were all relaxed and chatting as intimately as the letters which had passed between them. In spite of her age, her mind was very clear and active. With no children, living on her own, she had become an avid reader and delighted in discussing books and politics with her "dear Dis." Mary Anne and she talked happily about gardens, which they both loved, and Dizzy's career, which obsessed them both, and his health, about which they both fussed to his amusement. Locally, she was considered strange, eccentric even, and she had little company. She had been a widow for over thirty years and these were the first really happy days she had known in all that time. She took to Mary Anne at once for her warm heart and open manner, but actually to see and speak so easily and frankly with Dizzy whom she thought of as the greatest living Englishman, was like a romantic dream.

It was a romance, for once Disraeli had recovered from the surprise of her age and odd appearance, he treated her with the same gallantry as he did Mary Anne. He always responded to beauty, but he also responded to inner qualities which the rest of the world sometimes did not suspect. To him, it seemed very fitting that Mrs. Brydges Willyam's first name was Sarah and she very quickly took her place among his closest confidantes,

262

Mary Anne, Sa and Lady Londonderry. He had seen beyond the swollen, wrinkled exterior to the astute and inquiring mind and the hesitant affection which lay hidden. It was with some embarrassment on their last day that he received a memorandum from her, outlining the provisions of her will, of which he was to be one of the executors. "I think it right to point out," she said, "that my executors will also be my residual legatees and that the interest they will take, although not a considerable one, will at all events be substantial."

It troubled his conscience now to remember that he had been induced to write to her originally because of her suggestion of leaving him something in her will, and had continued the correspondence after discovering that she was fairly wealthy. Now she was asking him to take this memorandum to his solicitor, Philip Rose, so that Rose could act for her. "I think, perhaps, a local solicitor might give you more impartial advice," he suggested.

"Very well, if that is what you wish," she answered. "But pray take this to Mr. Rose, for I shall in no wise change my mind."

"Surely there is some member of your family?" he protested.

"No one. I have outlived them all. You are the nearest to me in blood of anyone I know." It was a particular pleasure of hers to fancy, since they were both remotely descended from one of the leading Jewish families, the Laras, that they were related. It added to the bond between them, that the man who had become the living champion of their race should also be a kinsman. "So we shall say no more about it."

The Sheldonian Theater, Oxford, was packed with graduates in their academic gowns. On the platform, the dignitaries of the University were spaced out, wearing their gowns and colorful hoods. It was a historic occasion, the installation of Lord Derby as the new Chancellor of the University, distinguished by the presence of Bishop Wilberforce, Judge Haliburton, Grote, Aytoun and Macaulay among others. Bulwer Lytton had just been capped. The

263

students in the Undergraduates' Gallery applauded enthusiastically as Gladstone, tall and handsome, was capped in his turn by the urbane Lord Derby.

Up in the Ladies' Gallery, Mary Anne sat next to Catherine Gladstone, who was thrilled by her husband's reception, knowing how much it meant to him. As they clapped, Mary Anne leant toward her and whispered, "You must be very proud of your husband."

Catherine smiled. As the applause died away and Gladstone took his seat, she glanced at Mary Anne whom she sensed was nervous. "Oh, yes," she said, "but then, William is an Oxford man, which is one of the reasons he is so popular here."

Mary Anne smiled and was grateful, knowing it was said to comfort her in advance for a less enthusiastic welcome, even antagonism for Disraeli, who, like the others, was to be granted an honorary degree. She knew that Derby, himself, was nevous. Let them at least be polite, only polite, she prayed silently.

There was a complete hush as Disraeli's name was announced and he walked down the aisle in his gown toward Derby. He was pale and composed, expressionless. A murmur began among the undergraduates: "There he is . . . There's Dizzy. . . ."

Mary Anne was unable to hide her agitation any longer. Catherine watched her compassionately as she sat forward, twisting her handkerchief, tensing as subdued applause began.

The applause grew and swelled as Disraeli moved steadily toward the Chancellor. Prepared for the worst, he did not hear it, nor the first isolated shouts of "Bravo! Bravo! Dizzy!!" But soon the shouts were taken up and the applause grew to a deafening volume. Nothing like it had been heard that afternoon, nor in anyone's memory. Those in the University who had criticized his recommendation for an honorary DCL were astounded. Derby was smiling broadly. As Disraeli reached him and bowed, the acclamation reached a crescendo. It cut off, when Derby turned to the amphitheater.

He called the traditional questions. *"Placet-ne vobis, Domini?"*

In answer, the undergraduates roared their approval, *"Maxime placet! Immense placet!!"* There was a storm of applause and cheering.

In the Ladies' Gallery, Mary Anne was trembling, her handkerchief shredded in her lap. She bit her lip as Catherine Gladstone touched her hand, smiling.

When it was over and he was capped, Disraeli walked slowly to his seat. Only an increased tightening in his mouth and the faintest flush on his pale cheeks showed how deeply he had been moved. He hesitated before he sat down, as if to acknowledge the delirious cheering of the students. Instead, he raised his eyeglass and looked up at the Ladies' Gallery. Finding Mary Anne, he threw a kiss up to her from the tips of his fingers, and the cheering became an affectionate ovation.

It was a day worth living for, and one he would never forget.

It was as well that Disraeli had such days of unexpected triumph to remember. They were followed by more grinding years in opposition, struggling to hold his party together against disillusionment and factions and the unending, petty revolts against his authority. As he had prophesied, the Coalition Government soon began to split apart with such contrasting personalities as Russell, Palmerstone and Gladstone in the cabinet, but it clung to power.

In some ways, he was glad not to be so hard-pressed by work. Mary Anne and he had genuinely grown to love Hughenden and their estate. It was not only a peaceful haven. He took his position in the county and his duties as a magistrate very seriously. He built up excellent relations with his new tenants and studied agricultural advances in an attempt to make the estate self-sufficient, for he could not afford to maintain it as a pleasure-garden. Together they planned more improvements to the house and grounds. He already had his peacocks. Now he acquired two swans for the little lake and named them Hero and Leander, though Mary Anne could never understand why. Although as vivacious as ever, now in her sixties she was aging quite quickly. When they went for their walks through the woods, more often than not she now drove in a tiny pony cart, while he walked beside her. His most cherished relaxation was to sit and talk to his woodmen as they worked, planting, pruning, husbanding the trees, simple, uneducated men. He learned country lore from them and always felt refreshed by their quiet humor and the unsophisticated directness of their thinking. They dealt in fundamentals and for an hour or two he felt his life slow to the same pace as theirs, not ordered by the hurrying clock at Westminster but by the primeval pulse of the seasons.

He had fulfilled another of his ambitions. He had founded a newspaper, *The Press*.

This new venture into journalism was a result of the bias of existing newspapers, most of which were Liberal in policy. The others were reactionary Tory. He convinced some of his wealthier supporters that there was a need for a weekly paper to promote the kind of progressive conservatism in which they believed. He named it *The Press*. Its circulation was only a few thousand but, with contributors like himself and Bulwer Lytton who by now had become a close political colleague, its influence was considerable. Although they wrote under pseudonyms to give *The Press* an illusion of impartiality, their control of it was an open secret. The journal was successful, yet it helped to revive the persistent criticism of Disraeli's ambition. It existed not to promote the party, his enemies sneered, but himself. And it led to a coolness between himself and Derby, which lasted for some time. *The Press* hardly ever mentioned the 14th Earl.

Perhaps the main difficulty Disraeli had to face was having Lord Derby at the head of the party. While Disraeli rallied and maneuvered his troops in the Commons, Derby was content to sit quietly in the Lords, watching the conflict from a distance. When vital deci-

266

sions were to be taken, he would often be inaccessible at his country seat, Knowsley, polishing his graceful translations of Homer. It was deliberate. While Disraeli maintained the function of an Opposition was to oppose, Derby had no wish to be involved in political skirmishing which might bring down the Government and find himself again trying to lead the country with a minority in Parliament. He would far rather watch his horses come in among the front runners at Newmarket or Doncaster races.

The years revolved, the wearying repetition of party upheavals and squabbles, of schemes and excitements which came to nothing, punctuated only by visits to Sarah at Twickenham, Mrs. Brydges Willyams at Torquay and longer periods of rest and relaxation at Hughenden. Mary Anne's health was giving cause for concern. There were weeks when she was not able to keep any food down and lost weight alarmingly, although the doctors could not diagnose what was wrong. She made light of it, yet it was worrying. Dizzy also suffered from bouts of exhaustion. He could not hide from himself that he was growing older, the lines of his carefully schooled expression becoming deeper, his hair thinning. Mary Anne always cut his hair herself and whenever she saw a gray one, plucked it out. The days for such an easy remedy were over. Now, the sweep of waves at each temple had to be regularly touched up with black dye and the negligent curls on top combed carefully into place.

They returned to Paris, their first visit for many years, and were received graciously by Napoleon the Third whom they had known at Gore House in his days of exile. At dinner in the Tuileries, they sat on either side of him and his beautiful Empress, Eugenie, dazzlingly gowned, with a necklace of huge emeralds and diamonds round her exquisite throat. The pomp and glitter made a piquant contrast to the circumstances in which they remembered him.

The reason for their stay was a secret hint that had come from Disraeli's informants in Paris, among them a young man named Earle, who passed on confidential reports to him from the British Embassy. Through Palmerston's insularity and Liberal criticism of the Emperor's policies, the alliance between Britain and France was breaking up. Napoleon anxiously wanted to preserve the friendship between the two nations as a prop to his own power and prestige in Europe. Disraeli had come to reassure him that the Conservatives at least still backed the alliance. In return, he hoped to win his support by convincing him that England would soon have a Conservative government. Napoleon was skeptical, seeing no possibility of Palmerston being turned out. "Lord Derby does not have the men," he said. "Palmerston has the men, but no party," Disraeli told him.

Not long after came news of a mutiny among the native troops in India. The first reports were considered impossibly exaggerated, yet soon their truth could not be doubted nor the extent of the uprising minimized. Despatches told of pillage and massacre, residences besieged, whole provinces in arms. Disaffected princes like the brutal Nana Sahib emerged to lead the revolt. Disraeli was one of the few who took it seriously from the beginning. Control of the huge subcontinent was nearly lost and only regained after heroic efforts by the defenders and savage fighting by the outnumbered relieving forces.

Palmerston's propularity remained undiminished. He would deal with India as he had dealt with the Crimea and the Chinese pirates. He seemed sure of his position for as long as he chose, and his arrogance in power showed he had no intention of standing aside. His relations with the Queen had vastly improved. Earlier in the year, in her weakened condition before the birth of her latest child, Princess Beatrice, she had been grateful to have someone so strongly dependable at the helm, especially as he had now agreed to recognize Albert's unique value officially by helping to create him *Prince Consort*. Palmerston basked in the belated favor of the Throne and willingly underwrote the plans for the marriage of the Queen's eldest daughter Victoria, the Princess Royal, to

Frederick Wilhelm, Crown Prince of Prussia. He was riding high and no one could have predicted that he would be toppled by bombs thrown hundreds of miles away across the English Channel.

On the evening of 14 January, 1858, as Napoleon and the Empress Eugenie drove in a procession to the opera through cheering crowds, bombs were thrown at their carriage by Carbonari, members of a secret political society dedicated to the unification of Italy. Many onlookers were killed or injured, although Napoleon escaped with only a cut on his cheek from flying splinters. Police and escort hurried to their overturned carriage, horrified to see Eugenie's pallor and her dress spattered with the Emperor's blood. "Don't worry about us," she told them. "Such things are our profession. Take care of the wounded."

Duke Ernest of Saxe-Coburg-Gotha, Albert's elder brother, was in the carriage in front of them and also escaped unhurt. Impressed with their courage, but pale and shaken, he arrived the following evening at Buckingham Palace for Vicky's wedding and gave the first eye-witness account. One of the most troubling aspects of the affair was that the conspirators were led by Felice Orsini, a revolutionary patriot, who was accustomed to take refuge in England where he had written two books about his life and experiences, which were widely admired. The French police had discovered that the attempt had been planned in London and the bombs used made in Birmingham. Feeling in France became violently anti-British. Senior officers in the French army threatened retaliation and the French Foreign Minister sent an icy despatch, asking how long England was prepared to shelter assassins. In Britain, sympathy for Napoleon and his beautiful Empress turned overnight to resentment and anger. The situation was potentially dangerous. To appease the French, Palmerston brought in a Bill to make conspiracy to murder a felony, punishable by life imprisonment, and counted on his personal prestige to get it passed without difficulty. But he had seriously underestimated the extent to which national pride had been outraged. The Bill was taken as a surrender to demands from across the Channel. An amendment was proposed on which he was defeated, with many of his own party voting against him, and he was forced to resign.

Knowing that the Queen had sent again for Derby, Disraeli waited at Grosvenor Gate. Although schooled by now to disappointment, he could not prevent a stir of nervous excitement. Mary Anne and Sarah were with him. As if he did not have enough on his mind, he was concerned about them both. Mary Anne, brightly rouged and animated, had clearly not recovered yet from her most recent spell of illness, though she tried to conceal it for his sake. Sarah also was drawn and loss of weight had aged her. She should have been resting, but had hurried to town to be with her brother during this crisis. She refused to discuss her health. "Will Lord Derby kiss hands this time?" she asked.

"He has still not decided," Disraeli told her flatly.

"But he must!"

"He's turned it down before," Mary Anne reminded her.

"He could not do so again, surely," Sarah asked. "It would be as good as proclaiming he did not consider his own party fit to govern."

She looked at her brother, but he was silent. No one could foretell with certainty what Derby would do. Most probably he would ask for time to consider. Disraeli knew that everything was over if they shirked their responsibility this time. When word came at last from Derby, he hurried to his house in St. James's Square.

Even though they had worked closely for a number of years, they still did not feel at ease socially. Disraeli had only once been invited to Knowsley. Derby had excused himself from invitations to Hughenden, although his son Edward was a frequent visitor. It added to the stiffness of their meeting. Derby was in his study. "Thank you for coming so promptly," he said. "The news is that her Majesty is determined I should try to form a Government."

"Then I sincerely hope you will do so, Lord Derby," Disraeli said evenly.

Derby grunted in exasperation. "What's the point? The Liberals and Radicals will still have a majority of two to one over us in the Commons."

"The point is that our party has only been in power for nine months out of the last twelve years. It has been no easy task to hold it together."

"Yes, I know," Derby admitted. "And you have done it almost single-handed. Hang it, without you, they'd have made mincemeat of us!"

Disraeli shrugged. "It is merely a question of tactics. He paused. "I cannot guarantee to hold them together much longer. They need more than promises. If we do not accept office when it is offered, we may as well admit that the Conservatives are finished as a political force."

"You're right, of course." Derby was troubled, and his leg hurt. He had decided to receive Disraeli standing, to keep the affair businesslike. It had been a mistake. He felt awkward. "Nothing will have changed, you realize? We'll only have another few months before the others unite against us."

"Much may be done in that time," Disraeli said smoothly. "Tactics will become more important."

Derby had to move to relieve the ache in his leg. He limped to his desk, which he leaned on with one hand. "Yes, but don't you see," he began. "I . . . I have a duty to the country. If I can't get together a strong, reliable cabinet, then it would be immoral of me to take office. That's all that stopped me last time."

It was as close to an apology for the past as he would ever come. Disraeli's voice was sympathetic. "But now you will be able to field a much more capable team. Salisbury will serve, and Parkington. And there are younger men coming up—Manners and your own son, Edward Stanley."

"And you," Derby said quickly. "I'd want you to be Leader of the House and Chancellor of the Exchequer again—they'll be our key posts. No one else but you can fill them." He moved round to sit at his desk. When

Disraeli still did not reply, he looked round, questioning.

"I am not sure," Disraeli said simply.

"Not sure . . . ? Hang it, there's no question!" He was surprised. Disraeli for once seemed embarrassed.

It was not embarrassment, but something far deeper and more difficult. Disraeli shook his head. "I have no doubt as to my capabilities, Lord Derby. False modesty would be out of character." He hesitated. "Yet I am aware that I am still not fully trusted by many in our own party. I am an unfortunate necessity—to marshal the attack in debate. But many who might join us will not, because of me. And since you wish to choose the most able team—"

"I lead in the House of Lords, you in the Commons," Derby broke in. "That is the way it will be. Without that, I won't go ahead and anyone who's too stiffnecked to serve under you is no use to me."

Disraeli had made the offer to stand aside before and had felt bound to make it again. He was profoundly relieved it had not been accepted. "I am—I won't say flattered. I thank you." He paused. "Do I then take it you do plan to form a Government?"

Derby realized that, somehow, he had taken the mental step to commit himself. "I seem to have talked myself into it. Or been talked, I'm not sure which." He smiled briefly and sat at last, swivelling his chair to rest his foot on a small, brocaded stool. "We'd better draw up a list of names."

"There is one thing," Disraeli suggested. "We'd be in a much stronger position if we could patch up the split in our own party, once and for all."

"Agreed. In fact, I've thought of offering the post of Secretary for War to Sir Robert's brother, General Peel. I'm sure he'll accept."

Disraeli nodded in agreement. How ironic, he thought. All those years ago, Peel's brother had challenged him to a duel. Now they were to be colleagues. It was surely a sign. "I was thinking in particular of William Gladstone," he said. "He is by far the most capable of them, and as much a Tory as either of us."

Derby stared at him. "Gladstone? But surely you realize that he, of all people, would never agree to serve under you?"

Disraeli spread his hands. "We meet socially quite often. Our wives are friendly. I would feel no loss of pride in approaching him—and it would be worth any sacrifice to have him with us again."

As Disraeli pointed out, Derby had less trouble in selecting a Cabinet on this occasion, although there were still problems. An unexpected setback came over Bulwer Lytton, who was offered the Colonial Office. Lytton had grown proud and tetchy and, feeling he should be above the degrading process of elections, wanted a peerage in return. Derby had no use for him in the Lords. He was needed principally to back Disraeli in the Commons. At Disraeli's insistence, young Edward Stanley was appointed Colonial Secretary in his place, and soon justified the choice, somewhat to his father's surprise. Another difficulty was over the India Bill and the choice of a new Governor-General, who would one day soon become Viceroy. One solution that presented itself was to offer it to Disraeli, himself. It would be a signal honor for him. He would fill the post admirably and, as a bonus, it would remove him from his controversial position in Parliament. Yet there he was indispensable. Another difficulty was to replace the President of the Board of Control, who had swiftly proved himself unsuitable. With Derby's permission, Disraeli decided to make his approach to Gladstone.

On a warm, spring day in early May, the Gladstones came to tea at Grosvenor Gate. Catherine had not seen Mary Anne for several months and was shocked by the change in her appearance. From being too thin, she had quite quickly put on a considerable amount of weight, which she tried to conceal by wearing a bright red, frogged military tunic over her striped skirt. With her made-up face, her eyebrows heavily blackened and an obviously artificial wig, she really looked rather bizarre. However, she was still merry and girlish in her manner and one almost forgot her appearance after a while.

Disraeli appeared not to notice that it was in any way unusual. Catherine exerted herself to seem relaxed and charmed. She admired William's composure, his knack of being politely detached.

"You made hats?" Gladstone asked, puzzled.

Mary Anne smiled. "Yes, mother and I were dreadfully poor. I was an apprentice milliner—to eke out my allowance. But it didn't last." She sighed. "I was the belle of Clifton. All the gentlemen in the West Country paid court to me. And I married my first husband when I was seventeen."

"You make it sound as though you'd had half a dozen, my dear," Disraeli murmured. They laughed.

"I think it sounds very romantic," Catherine said.

Mary Anne tapped her hand. "So did I at the time. But I didn't know the meaning of the word until I met Dizzy." She looked at him fondly. "D'you know, he used to be a dreadful ladies' man, but since the day of our engagement, he has not looked at another."

Disraeli bowed where he sat. "It is fruitless to try to improve on perfection."

"Hear, hear," Gladstone echoed.

Mary Anne smiled at him. She was pleased to see that he was relaxing. He had been excessively correct and prudish as a young man. In middle age he was in danger of becoming severe, but he had a really delightful smile when he chose to show it. She turned to Catherine.

"More tea, Mrs. Gladstone?"

"No, thank you. That was lovely."

"Mr. Gladstone?"

"Thank you, no." Gladstone knew from the glance Catherine had given him that she felt it was time to leave. He was relieved the visit had passed off so well. In fact, it had been unexpectedly pleasant. Thanks, of course, to their hostess. He could never forget her kindness to him, when he was a fledgling MP. For her sake, he was prepared to socialize with Disraeli even, at intervals. Although he doubted that he could ever stifle his natural antipathy completely. It disconcerted him the way the man sat so motionless, sphinxlike, as if assessing him.

A few more minutes. "I believe we were all married in the same year."

"I believe so," Disraeli agreed. How could one ever tell what was really in Gladstone's mind, he wondered. They had so little in common ground apart from politics, and he had promised Mary Anne that no shop would be talked.

"Just before the Queen and the Prince Consort," Catherine said.

"Yes," Mary Anne smiled. "How recent it all seems. And yet, I was looking in one of my scrapbooks today and realized that it was nearly twenty years ago."

"You keep a scrapbook?" Gladstone asked.

Mary Anne laughed. "A dozen!"

Catherine was intrigued. "What do you put in them?"

Mary Anne seemed surprised by the question. "Why, anything from the newspapers or magazines which mentions Dizzy."

"Of course."

Disraeli noticed Catherine's faint frown of disapproval. "Mary Anne is my most faithful archivist," he said drily. Gladstone nodded, smiling.

On a stool by Mary Anne was a pile of newspapers and periodicals. From among them she pulled out a velvet-covered scrapbook and opened it. "Look—here is a report of his latest speech in *The Times,* and comments in the *Quarterly Review.* And—" She turned a page and hesitated. "Oh, no, not that. Well, why not?"

Catherine leaned forward. "What is it?"

"A cartoon from *Punch.*" She held up the scrapbook so they could see it. It showed Disraeli and Gladstone in tights, as two circus acrobats.

"The Balancing Brothers of Westminster," Catherine read. "But it's. . . ."

"Yes, isn't it clever?" Mary Anne laughed.

"The artist was kinder to you than to me," Disraeli murmured to Gladstone.

Gladstone's mouth turned down. "I do not find such drawings amusing."

Mary Anne considered the cartoon. "I suppose

it means that whenever Dizzy proposes something you propose the opposite—and vice versa—just out of habit. But it could mean that your talents are so well balanced that, together, you could achieve something outstanding."

"Well, that is another matter," said Gladstone, coughing with embarrassment. He wondered momentarily if she had brought this up accidentally or if it were not contrived.

"Perhaps we could leave the ladies alone for a few moments," Disraeli suggested. "If they don't mind."

"Not at all," said Mary Anne, smiling to him.

Catherine glanced at her husband. "If you wish."

Disraeli rose. "In that case, we shall be in the study." Gladstone rose with him. They bowed to the ladies and left.

Mary Anne sat back and nodded confidentially to Catherine. "We are very fortunate in having such remarkable husbands."

"Yes," Catherine agreed. "William is always saying how clever Mr. Disraeli is."

Mary Anne was pleased. It was so long since they had had one of their intimate chats. Of course, Catherine was a mature woman and no longer the impulsive and inexperienced girl she had been at her marriage. She had even grown to resemble William slightly, with that severe look which she had had when they arrived for tea. It had completely vanished now the men had gone, yet there was a hint of anxiety. She was silly to worry about Dizzy and William. There was no need for their ambitions to clash. "Do you know what Dizzy admires most about William? It is his moral courage. Of course, Dizzy has none at all?"

"That can't be true," Catherine protested.

"Yes, it is," Mary Anne assured her. "When he has his shower, he can never pull the string for the cold water. I always have to do it for him."

In spite of herself, Catherine laughed at the picture it suggested. It was oddly comforting, too, to hear that he had his weaknesses.

"You must visit us at Hughenden some day," Mary Anne insisted.

"That would be delightful. And you must come to Hawarden."

"I long to," Mary Ann assured her. "I hear it's very beautiful."

"I think so." Catherine smiled. "And more so each year. William has cleared another acre in the park."

"Cleared it?"

"Of trees," Catherine explained. William was touch-ingly proud of his skill with an axe. "His relaxation is tree-felling, opening up new areas."

The idea of it seemed extraordinary to Mary Anne. "How different from Dizzy . . ." she said. "His passion is to plant trees and watch them grow into forests. None of our visitors can leave until they've planted one, as a memorial. Our woodmen have strict instructions never to cut any down."

Catherine's reaction was just as astonished as Mary Anne's had been. There was a pause. They smiled at each other. It had been lighthearted conversation but, simul-taneously, they both realized the unbridgeable gulf be-tween their husbands.

Disraeli and Gladstone sat facing each other on either side of the picture window, looking out toward Hyde Park. Dizzy was deliberately relaxed and open. They had briefly discussed the surprising defeat of the last govern-ment and the difficulties that now faced Derby. Gladstone would not be drawn out. He was more accustomed to Disraeli's reserve than to this apparently frank, confiden-tial manner. It put him on his guard. He coughed and raised one hand, moving his fingers near his mouth.

Disraeli noticed the gesture, and stubbed out his cigar. "You should treat a cigar like a mistress," he confided. "Put it away before you are sick of it."

Gladstone's lips tightened, not in a smile. He realized it was meant humorously, but he found it coarse.

"Well," Disraeli continued, "that is the position as we

both know it. The differences that divided us no longer exist."

Gladstone demurred. "The issues have changed."

"Totally! And frankly, I wanted to talk to you, because we need you. What can you achieve, standing apart both from the Government and the Opposition? In my opinion, it is of the utmost importance to the country for you to assume a leading role in the conduct of affairs. You owe it also to yourself." When Gladstone made no response, he went on. "After all, it would be no great step—you have supported us pretty steadily for the last three years."

Gladstone had known all along that this was the probable reason for the meeting. A few weeks before, he had been approached privately by Derby. To have overtures made also by Disraeli must mean they were sincere—or perhaps in greater difficulties than they would admit. He must be wary. "There is a small but active section in your party," he began cautiously.

"*Our* party," Disraeli corrected.

Gladstone allowed the correction to stand. "A section who regard me as representing dangerous ideas. I should, unfortunately, be a source of discord in your own following."

Disraeli was relieved that at least he was prepared to discuss. "You wish for reform," he said. "So do I, and always have done. That same section has always distrusted me because of it."

"Perhaps." But distrust of Disraeli was not based on his known Radical leanings.

Disraeli pressed him. "Together, we could prove that social progress is not the sole preserve of the Liberals."

Gladstone pursed his mouth. "You could never convince the Tory landowners."

Disraeli realized that there was little hope of making any of his points, unless the air was cleared. Naturally, Gladstone was on his guard, but it meant that he was keeping his mind rigidly closed, too. "Mr. Gladstone," he said slowly. "I am afraid that, in truth, it is the relations between us that form the great difficulty."

Gladstone stiffened. He had hoped to avoid any suggestion of a personal element in their discussion. "Between us?" he repeated. "I have never in my life taken a decision which has been influenced by them."

On his part, Disraeli had hoped to be answered with the same frankness that he had shown. He could see that Gladstone was not responding, but still tried. "I am relieved to hear it. I promise you that, if you join Lord Derby's Cabinet, you will find warm personal friends and admirers. You may consider me as neither but, I assure you, you would be mistaken."

Gladstone cleared his throat. "The—uh—the reconstruction of a Party cannot be carried out by one man rejoining it. I must consider the conditions that would make cooperation possible—what changes would be needed in the Government to make it worth a trial."

He was hedging, but the arrogance behind his words chilled Disraeli. He decided to make one last emotive try. "What I said just now was not mere empty words—and I shall prove it. For all our sakes, I am prepared to make any sacrifice to induce you to take office." Gladstone was motionless, waiting, held by Disraeli's eyes. "I have asked Sir James Graham to accept my post as Leader of the House, to allow both of us to serve under him. If he will not, we shall let our fellow members decide which of us is to lead. In either case, I shall consider you as sharing equally in any position I may hold."

Gladstone gazed at him. If this was true, it was a tremendous, an unparalleled gesture. No one could reject such a generous offer—if it were sincere. If only anyone but this man had made it. . . . "I—I need time to reflect," he said finally.

Disraeli's voice was more urgent. "The situation is critical. To stand aside now is, on your part, a great responsibility. Don't you think the time has come when you might deign to be magnanimous?"

Gladstone felt pressured, torn between wanting to respond and, at the same time, to escape. If they worked together in tandem, would he be able to resist the erosion of his independence and of his most fundamental beliefs?

His throat was dry. He folded his hands and sat upright. "There is a Power beyond us that disposes of what we are and do, and I find the limits of choice in public life to be very narrow."

Nothing more could be said.

chapter eleven

Lord Derby had been out of town. When he returned, he came straight to Grosvenor Gate. He was not surprised by Gladstone's attitude. Naturally, Disraeli had to try, but he could have told him the outcome beforehand. "Sanctimonious humbug!" he snorted. "What else did you expect?"

"I hoped he would respond."

"He may wrap himself in a cloak of morality, but he is really driven by only two things—personal ambition, and envy of you!"

Disraeli was saddened and disturbed. He did not care for Gladstone as a man. He found the personality unappealing, yet he had always taken him at face value, as beyond petty rivalry. Yes, in one sense they were rivals, for parliamentary honors, but he had always imagined them as one day working together.

"What will he do now?" Mary Anne asked.

"Play his own game," Derby said. "Sit on the fence, waiting to see which way to jump." He would have been useful, but they didn't have him. And he had to admit, if it came to a choice between him and Disraeli. . . . "Well, that's enough of him. I must get back to Downing Street." He tapped Disraeli on the shoulder. "And you must get ready. Now remember, don't commit us to anything, and don't try to be witty."

"Most definitely not," Disraeli promised.

"They still distrust you. This time you must win their approval."

Mary Anne was anxious. "Whose? Whose approval?"

"It has been decided that I shall be the one to report Cabinet business," Disraeli told her. "I have to go to Windsor for an audience with the Queen and the Prince."

"But that's wonderful! It's what you've prayed for—a chance to win them over."

Disraeli smiled faintly. "That remains to be seen."

"Of course you will!" Mary Anne said positively. "I forbid you to be nervous."

Derby smiled at her, admiringly. He liked them both more and more.

Disraeli scratched his chin. "Easier said, my dear. To face the Queen and Prince Albert is like looking down the muzzle of a double-barreled shotgun."

The eyes of the Queen and the Prince Consort were both light blue and remarkably similar. They were also very direct. Disraeli felt them bore into him.

He was standing, facing them in the small Audience Room at Windsor Castle. Protocol insisted that they remain standing. This was the longest interview Disraeli had had with them so far, although he had had conversations with the Prince, who had proved to be enlightened and receptive. He kept his gaze mainly on Prince Albert, tall, handsome and serious, though he was acutely conscious of the dumpy figure of the Queen, radiating dignity and disapproval as she watched him. He had been explaining his Government's India Bill to answer the recent crisis.

Victoria spoke, her voice high and clear, almost girlish. "You spoke of a change in policy, Mr. Disraeli. What do you propose?"

Disraeli bowed. "Little can be done, Your Majesty, while the entire subcontinent remains in the corrupt control of a commercial company. We propose to take the power and rule of India from the East India Company and transfer it to the Crown." Victoria could not hide her flush of pleasure. It was the very solution she had asked for, demanded, but had been denied by short-sighted, previous Ministers. He was encouraged and went on. "To appoint a Viceroy, and to issue a Proclamation to the native princes and population that the Queen of England guarantees their laws, their customs and their religion."

"That could do much," Albert said, impressed.

Disraeli bowed. "More than all our fleets and armies, sir."

"I look forward to seeing your detailed proposals." Albert paused. He knew instinctively that Victoria was having difficulty in hiding her excitement. To be truly Queen of India had always been one of her deepest wishes. The measures suggested by the new administration sounded excellent. All would depend on whether they were strong enough to carry them. "What is the feeling of the House toward your Government?"

"Not kind, sir," Disraeli admitted. "But for the moment, the Opposition is content to let us pull their chestnuts out of the fire." The Liberals had saddled them with the problem of clearing up after the Mutiny, and agitation for Reform among others. Albert allowed himself a slight smile. Disraeli was again heartened. He seemed to have been able to strike just the right note. "And of course," he added, "after so many years in temporary quarters, it is an inexpressible pleasure to be in the new House of Commons, which is so admirably adapted to our needs."

Victoria looked at Albert, delighted. He smiled more openly. "I, as you may know, was Chairman of the Reconstruction Committee."

Disraeli allowed himself to be reminded. "Ah—of course. That explains—if I may be permitted?—the brilliant use of space and the perfect blend of comfort with harmonious proportions." Albert inclined his head to acknowledge the compliment. Victoria's glance, when it returned to Disraeli, was less steely. That came off well, he thought. It was fortunate they had not heard his comment when he first entered the new buildings, that the low standard of architecture in England was due to the fact that no architect had ever been shot, like Admiral Byng, *pour encourager les autres.* One more? he wondered. "Which reminds me—it is my hope that under our Government, we shall at last see a start made on the construction of your Royal Highness's scientific institution at South Kensington."

"I should find that very welcome," Albert admitted.

Disraeli bowed. Set a sprat . . .

Victoria was unable to contain her impatience to confer with Albert. "We must not detain you any longer, Mr. Disraeli," she said firmly.

Disraeli bowed again. "Your most faithful servant, Ma'am." He retreated to the door, bowed again, waiting until it was acknowledged by Albert, and left.

Victoria's shoulders relaxed. She took a step or two after him and turned, smiling. The smile quite transformed her plain, rather sallow face. "What an extraordinary man . . ." she laughed. He had been perfectly well behaved and quite charmingly complimentary to Albert. So patently sincere, too. She was glad now that he and his odd wife had been invited to the Court Ball for Vicky's wedding. She should have spoken to them. "He really is quite handsome, don't you think, Albert? Although so livid, so very Jewish."

Albert was assessing the practical side of what Disraeli had said. Conservative policy interpreted by this man should be interesting. He nodded, vaguely hearing what she was saying. "I cannot understand why I once had such an unfavorable opinion of him," he mused. "Our views are really surprisingly similar. *Wie unerwartet.* . . . How unexpected." He held open the connecting door to the study they shared and smiled to Victoria as she passed him. She paused and kissed his cheek. He looked really animated, she thought. Yes, she must reconsider her opinion of Mr. Disraeli. Dizzy.

The principal measures to which Derby's administration were committed were Disraeli's concern. First, however, he acted swiftly to put an end to the tension between France and England. Strictly speaking, it was not his responsibility, but the personal relationship he had reestablished with the Emperor Napoleon and his contacts in Paris enabled him to prepare the way for an exchange of notes between the Foreign Ministries. The pride of both sides was satisfied and the crisis ended. The young man in the British Embassy who had secretly been so useful to him, Ralph Earle, was invited to become his private secretary. It was what Earle had been angling for. He was only twenty-three, clever, ambitious and unscrupulous. Disraeli's former aide, Henry Lennox, was jealous of him and distrusted him, with reason, but he was immensely useful in handling confidential affairs. Looking to the future, Disraeli also cultivated several other, promising, younger men, among them the scholarly Stafford Northcote and the brilliant, volatile Robert Cecil, younger son of his old friend, Lord Salisbury. By Derby's agreement to move Edward Stanley to the Board of Control, he was able to offer Bulwer Lytton the Colonial Office again. Lytton had learned his lesson not to try bargaining for honors and accepted gladly.

He needed his mastery of tactics to steer the various stages of the India Bill through a hostile Parliament, but finally it was done and laid down the lines on which India was to be governed for the next sixty years. Many times, he came close to defeat, yet survived, exploiting the enmity between Palmerston and Russell, between the reactionary and progressive elements of the Liberal party, and appealing to the sense of fairness and justice which he always believed lay at the heart of British character. His arguments reached out to the people beyond the walls of Westminster. The Opposition collapsed in anarchy and, when the Bill was passed, crowds cheered him in the streets as he drove back to Downing Street. Telegrams had just been introduced and he delighted in sending them off, to Sarah, to Mrs. Brydges Willyams, to announce his successes. He had taken care to consult Prince Albert and been invited to spend a few days at Windsor. Unfortunately, the honor did not extend to Mary Anne. Nationally, and abroad, his prestige was growing. Foreign statesmen who had written him off were eager again to correspond with him.

For twelve months, by exploiting his opponents' disagreements and weaknesses, Disraeli had been able to carry all his Government's Bills in the House, despite the overwhelming majority against him. Both Derby and he knew it could not go on. Eventually, the Opposition would unite against them. Both knew they were committed to introducing a Bill to extend the franchise. An increase in the number of people allowed to vote was inevitable and just. The great Reform Act of 1832, masterminded by Lord John Russell, had been a notable step forward but, in the decades since then, agitation for further reforms had increased. While the Liberals had constantly promised new reforms, they had never carried them out. The specter of an enfranchised laboring class, the vast, politically unstable mass created by the Industrial Revolution, terrified them, as it did many on the Tory side. The 1832 Reform Act had transferred power from the aristocracy to the middle classes. By setting up property qualifications and cancelling the time-honored electoral rights of the poor, it virtually disqualified the majority of the working class from voting. Quite simply, as Disareli explained it to doubtful members of the Cabinet, he believed that all sections of the country should be represented in the House and no one class given an advantage over the others. Derby completely agreed. They must remedy the failure of the Act of 1832 to meet the needs of the day.

At once, the Liberals began to object that the Conservatives had no business to meddle in reform, which was their sole province. Russell and Palmerston made their peace and began to rally their supporters. At the same time, there were rebels and many who were uncertain on the Conservative side. Again, Disraeli was invited to Windsor and spent nearly three days in consultation with the Prince, whose lucid, caring mind was of incalculable value in preparing the complicated provisions of the Bill and in searching out anomalies. The two men developed a genuine respect for each other.

As the day for the introduction of the Bill drew nearer, Disraeli spent as much time as possible using his powers of persuasion on the rank and file members of the party. One night, as he, Lord Salisbury and a nervous Bulwer Lytton came into the Carlton Club, they found a group of younger MPs in hot argument. Derby's son, Stanley, was Disraeli's firmest supporter and, indeed, had only accepted a Cabinet post to help eventually in the work of reform. The leader of those in disagreement was clearly Salisbury's son, Robert Cecil. Seeing Disraeli, he swung to face him, an intense, striking man of twenty-seven, tall and broad-shouldered. "Mr. Disraeli, you cannot expect us to back this bill!" he protested.

"But I do, Robert," Disraeli said gently.

"To give the right to vote to the lower paid, the uneducated, can only benefit the Liberals!" One or two of the others muttered in agreement.

"I should hope that to cure injustices would be the aim of every responsible Government."

"Reform is a dangerous experiment!" Cecil asserted. "Dangerous for the country *and* the Government."

"Robert. . . ." Salisbury interrupted.

"No, Father, I must speak. It is only what many others are thinking."

"Hear, hear," the heavy-set man behind him said quietly.

Apart from Cecil, none of them was able to look directly at Disraeli. Disraeli had known him since he was a boy and liked him. Hot-headed and wrong he might be, yet he had courage. He smiled faintly. "Political thought must develop, even in the Conservative party."

Cecil was stung by his apparently indulgent attitude. "Well, I tell you frankly, sir, I cannot support you." He turned away curtly, followed by others of his group.

"I apologize for my son," Salisbury said, embarrassed.

Disraeli shook his head. "There's no need." The boy was impetuous, but he had been the same himself and must have caused a deal of annoyance to his elders.

"I, of course, shall back you," Salisbury promised. He bowed and left.

Stanley had followed Robert Cecil and said to him quietly, "It's not hopeless. The Radicals should back us."

"Precisely," Cecil agreed drily. "Disraeli is selling us out."

Lord John Manners was beside them. "Well, I am with him," he said. "The right to vote must be extended."

"It must," Stanley emphasized. "Besides, it is a way to beat the continuous majority of the Whigs in Parliament." He moved back with Manners to join Disraeli who was speaking to other worried members.

Cecil looked at Henry Lennox, who had taken no part in the discussion. "I don't know," Lennox admitted. "I can't vote against my own party. But——" He shrugged.

Beyond him, Cecil noticed Gladstone, seated in a high-backed, leather chair, listening. "Have you heard, Mr. Gladstone? What do you say?" The others turned with him.

Gladstone sat very still, his legs crossed, his elbows on the arms of the chair and his fingertips together in front of his chest. His preying mantis position, Disraeli called it. He had been listening now for some weeks, to voices on both sides, and assessing. "The right to vote should only be granted to those who can prove they have earned it," he stated categorically. "I have never believed in the sincerity of this Bill. Its attempt to curry favor with the lower elements is the act of an unprincipled adventurer, desperate to cling to power at any price. You should appeal to the honor of your Party Leader."

"It's no use," Cecil complained. "Lord Derby is only interested in his race horses. He leaves everything to Disraeli. That's what it's come to. We are governed by a Jew and a Jockey!"

Disraeli saw his Reform Bill defeated. He had known there was little hope of saving it, as soon as the reunion of Whigs, Liberals, Peelites and Radicals became certain. Then two members of Derby's Cabinet resigned. Between those who thought the Bill went too far and those who insisted it did not go far enough, it was doomed, although Disraeli defended it skillfully and Lytton, forcing himself to rise, made one of his greatest speeches. Deaf, stammering, almost grotesque in delivery, he nevertheless reached the heights of eloquence. To many people's surprise, Gladstone also spoke and voted for it. None of them could change the final result. Disraeli sat on the Government front bench between Bulwer Lytton and Stanley and listened impassively, as the Opposition howled exultantly to him to resign.

Behind him, Robert Cecil glanced round angrily at Lennox. "He's smashed his own Government with this Bill!"

Lennox was agitated and disappointed. He had really wanted Dizzy to bring it off. "All the Liberals had to do was promise the Rads more sweeping reforms, if they voted against it."

"And once again, Derby will have to quit," Cecil said bitterly, "because of that mountebank!"

Disraeli looked down to the cross-benches and saw Gladstone sitting quietly, listening to the clamor. Perhaps if he joined them now and brought his followers with him...?

Appealed to by Derby, Gladstone still would not commit himself. Instead of resigning, they went to the country, but, although the Conservatives won a larger number of seats, it was not enough to give them an overall majority. Palmerston and Russell made a pact to serve under whichever of them was sent for by the Queen. Once again, the choice was Palmerston.

When Sarah came to visit Ben and Mary Anne at Hughenden in September, she was relieved to find him not downcast. "This time, we lasted nearly a year and a half. It is an improvement," he told her. They sat on the

289

terrace in the late afternoon, with the sun gilding the stone urns, listening to the raucous call of the peacocks as they strutted on the lawn.

Mary Anne was lying down before dinner and Sarah had been glad of the opportunity to talk alone with Ben. She was anxious, knowing that the expenses of his time in office must have put a considerable strain on his finances. Entertaining colleagues and visiting dignitaries alone must have been runious. Apart from the £30,000 he owed the Bentincks, he must have more than double that amount in other debts. "How are you managing?" she wondered.

"It's better not to ask," he sighed, then chuckled. "However, there is one ray of light. Now that I have served twice in the Cabinet, I am entitled to a pension."

"A pension?"

"Oh, yes," he assured her. "Two thousand pounds a year. I affect to be reluctant to accept it. But truly, without it, I cannot imagine how we could survive." He saw her frown of concern. "Now, now, Sa, you mustn't worry. All my life, things have always turned up, when they were most wanted."

She smiled. "Yes, I suppose they have."

"My debts are my oldest companions. I could not give them up now." He looked at her, as she laughed quietly, sitting back in her cane chair, pale, features fined down so much that she was almost gaunt. He looked at her hands that lay quietly in her lap, blue-veined, nearly translucent, and realized how wasted and thin she had grown. "And you, my dear," he probed gently. "How are you? You must take care of yourself, for all our sakes."

"Oh, I am fine," she smiled. "I have become a little delicate, that's all. I have no appetite. I shall mollycoddle myself for a week or two, then eat again and grow fat and contented."

They laughed and talked of the days when Ben had come here to Hughenden to flirt with the daughters of the house, of their parents and the old life at Bradenham. Much as he loved and confided in Mary Anne, there was

290

a bond of shared memories and dreams between himself and Sarah that nothing could replace.

Mary Anne and he meant to spend Christmas on the estate with their local friends and tenants, but an urgent message brought them hurrying to town. Sarah had collapsed and was not expected to live. From Grosvenor Gate, they travelled to Twickenham every day, every day watching her sink a little more. The wasting disease could not be slowed nor halted. Sarah's birthday was just before the end of the year. He was trying to think of a present which might please, even stimulate her, when word came that she was slipping away. He raced to her small, neat house in Twickenham, but was too late to speak to her for a last time. She was only fifty-six.

The drawing-room at Hughenden was a charming, light room, looking out on to the terrace. It had flock wallpaper, chairs and footstools covered in turkey work, comfortable settees and inlaid, Georgian cabinets. Disraeli came in quickly, looking for Mary Anne. He found her lying on one of the settees in a nest of cushions. She was weak and drawn, but wearing a gaily covered wrap round her shoulders over a girlish, pink dress, her hair covered by a lace cap. Letters, accounts and bills were scattered on a low table beside her and she was reading a copy of the *Quarterly Review.* "My dearest," he protested, "the doctor expressly said you were to stay in bed."

"I only lie there fretting," she told him. "Besides, Lord Stanley is coming to dinner and I have to cut your hair before he arrives."

"Please, my fair Delilah, spare me that martyrdom." She was too upset to respond. "Is something wrong?"

"I have been reading this article of Robert Cecil's in the *Quarterly Review,*" she said with a tremor in her voice.

"Ah. . . ." He wished he could have kept that from her.

"Is that all you can say? The son of one of your oldest friends could write such things—" She began to read.

" 'Mr. Disraeli's policy has long misguided and discredited the Conservative Party in the House of Commons. His tactics are so various, so flexible, so shameless—the net by which. . . .' " Disraeli stopped her by taking the magazine gently from her. "He is only trying to make his name, as all young politicians do, by attacking their elders."

She was close to tears. "What makes me so angry is that it appeared in the *Review,* the leading Conservative journal! It is clear proof that your own Party still does not trust you."

"Yes, well, I have dealt with it," he told her, soothingly.

"How?"

"I wrote an open letter to our leading men, saying that, since they obviously all agree with this attack on me, I intend to resign as soon as possible."

"Did they accept?" Mary Anne asked, worried.

"Of course, not." He smiled. "The mere threat was enough. They have all begged me to reconsider, which, of course, I shall."

Mary Anne stared at him. "It's a game to you. It's all a great game. . . ."

"Not entirely."

"No, it is not! After twenty-three years of struggle, twenty-three years of service, what do you have? Nothing but bills and debts and demands for payment." As she spoke, she touched the bills and letters on the table.

"Don't worry, Mary Anne. They'll all be met."

"But how? By borrowing more and more money! How will it end?" She had borne it patiently for so long. Now, in her illness, fear of the future almost overwhelmed her.

"You mustn't distress yourself, my dearest. Whatever happens, you know that you will not suffer," he promised.

She gazed at him, her eyes huge. "I am not thinking of myself! Don't you understand? I shall not always be here and my income dies with me. What will you do when I am gone?"

Disraeli knelt beside her, moved. "I cannot imagine such an empty world," he whispered. She attempted to speak but he laid a finger on her lips.

"No, Mary Anne, I will not think of it. I would sooner be with you in a hovel than with a duchess in a tower of gold."

She smiled tremulously and kissed his hand. As always, he calmed her. "Now," he went on, "shall I tell you why I came looking for you? The news I have that will make the wife of every Member of Parliament envious of you?"

"Envious?"

"Mad with envy." He smiled.

"Don't tease, dearest. What news?" She could see now that he was excited.

"That you and I have been invited to spend a weekend at Windsor Castle with the Queen and the Prince Consort."

She gasped. "But wives are never asked!"

"That is what makes it so special. Are you pleased?"

She nodded, unable to speak for a moment. Then her own excitement was swamped by apprehension. "I don't know whether I'm thrilled or terrified. . . . Is it true? I always say and do the wrong thing. I shan't know how to behave." She had only seen the little Queen and the Prince at a distance, so regal, so ringed with protocol at balls and garden parties. Face to face. . . . She bit her lip.

Dizzy laughed. "Just be yourself, Mary Anne. They are bound to adore you." He kissed her forehead.

The great round tower of Windsor Castle, with its battlements, stood somber against a darkling sky. But in the dining-room all was light and color. Goldplate, glittering candelabra, footmen in scarlet livery, a select number of guests, gave the room life and brilliance. The ladies were in full evening dress, the gentlemen in all the panoply of uniform or court dress, many of them wearing the royal blue Windsor uniform designed by Albert, himself.

Strained, tired and prematurely aging, Albert sat in

the center of the long table with the elderly Duchess of Cambridge on his right. Queen Victoria was seated opposite him. On her right was General von Bonin, leader of a visiting Prussian delegation. Along from them were other high-ranking Prussian officers, the Foreign Secretary, Lord John Russell, and Victoria's eldest, unmarried daughter, Princess Alice, a serious, intelligent girl of eighteen. The remaining guests were ladies and gentlemen of the Court and the Duchess of Cambridge's Household. The Disraelis sat facing each other near one end, among the less important guests. Mary Anne sat between a rather solemn, young Prussian and the Speaker of the House of Commons, Disraeli between a short-sighted, old lady who ignored him and a very nervous, young lady-in-waiting. Outside, an orchestra played selections from *Ernani* by Verdi.

It was near the end of the meal. Conversation was muted, rather solemn. Albert had tried to stimulate conversation during the first courses, but was too tired to keep it up. Taking her cue from him, Victoria had also carried on a flow of talk, hampered by protocol which insisted that only one or other of the royal couple could begin any new topic. Alice spoke quietly to Lord John. Disraeli found a safe subject in which to engage the lady-in-waiting, Tennyson's *The Idylls of the King* which had just appeared in installments and to which she was devoted. She also confessed shyly that she had cried, reading *Henrietta Temple*. Disraeli was gratified. Even more so when he heard that Her Majesty had borrowed it. He was relieved that, in the collected edition of his novels a few years before, he had revised some of the more lurid passages.

So far the weekend had been an anticlimax. Mary Anne had been so excited in anticipation she had hardly been able to sleep for the last three days. They had arrived, that cold January afternoon, and been greeted at the head of the stairs by Princess Alice and the Chamberlain. After being shown to their room, they had a brief, formal meeting with their hosts, who had to leave almost immediately for an audience with the Prussians. A long, uneventful drawing-room had followed with all the guests formally presented to HRH The Duchess of Cambridge and to one another, and they exchanged another few words with the Queen and the Prince Consort as they circulated. By the end of it, Mary Anne's legs were aching and she was longing to sit down, but it was not permitted. She had really looked very fetching in a rose afternoon gown. The bell-shaped crinoline style suited her, now that she had regained her youthfully narrow waist. Tonight she was in pale jonquil and, on Dizzy's suggestion, knowing the Prince's prudishness in matters of dress, had her bust and shoulders covered with lace. As he murmured to the lady-in-waiting that, regretfully, he had been rather too busy for a number of years to write any fiction, he heard Mary Anne chatting on busily and brightly to the Speaker. She laughed at something he said, but turned it into a gurgle. She, alone, at their end of the table showed any sign of animation.

Victoria was talking to Von Bonin. She and Albert had recently returned from a visit to Berlin, to see Vicky and her husband, the Prussian Crown Prince. They had just presented her with her first grandson and, although she thought privately that Vicky might decently have waited another few years, she was delighted. "Yes, I am very pleased with my little grandson, Wilhelm," she said smiling. Poor baby, his little left arm had been damaged at birth and might always be affected. If only they had let her send over an English doctor, as she had wished. "I have told my daughter that she must not bring him up too much in the English manner, or the German people may resent it." It was the right thing to say. Von Bonin looked pleased. Those Prussians, whatever Albert maintained, could be almost insufferably self-satisfied. She heard Mary Anne laugh and glanced down the table, involuntarily. What an odd woman! She had really invited her out of curiosity, having heard so much about her. She could quite see what her informants had meant. All that rouge and lipsalve and powder. And surely that was a wig? She caught Albert's eye and agreed silently. It was time for the ladies to retire.

The ladies assembled in the blue drawing-room, waiting for the Queen and the gentlemen to rejoin them. It would not be long, as the Prince did not approve of too much drinking. Over the years, the interval had grown less and less. In contrast to the impression of ease introduced by dinner, they were much more stiff and self-conscious, formed into groups. Mary Anne stood alone, rather pointedly excluded by the ladies of the Court. Knowing she was an outsider, it did not trouble her. The room, the paintings on the damask walls by Reynolds and Canaletto, the marble busts, were enough to interest her. It was enough just to be here, yet she longed for the moment Dizzy would come through the door.

Princess Alice looked round from the group which she was with and saw her standing alone. In spite of her slight smile and apparent absorption in some views of Venice, it was clear that she felt quite lost. Alice had a twinge of compassion and made straight for her. Mary Anne smiled gratefully and bobbed a curtsey.

The ladies waiting for the Queen and her aunt, the Duchess of Cambridge, glanced at one another, hearing Alice laugh as she stood talking to Mary Anne. Since the Princess had joined her, no one else had been invited to enter the conversation. It was their turn to feel excluded.

There was a momentary tension as the door was opened. Victoria came in with the Duchess. The ladies curtsied, those nearest her expecting her to pause and speak, but she had spotted Mary Anne with Alice and marched across to them. Mary Anne and Alice curtsied. "It appears my daughter has monopolized you all evening, Mrs. Disraeli," she said.

"Her Royal Highness has been most kind, Ma'am," Mary Anne smiled.

Victoria nodded. Yes, Alice was thoughtful. "And what have you been discussing?"

"Education, Mama," Alice said. Victoria's eyes opened slightly in surprise. "I can scarcely believe it, but Mr. Disraeli left school at fifteen. He was never at University."

Victoria looked at Mary Anne. "Surely I heard he received a degree at Oxford."

"An honorary one, Ma'am."

"What was it?"

Mary Anne had dreaded the question. "A—well a DCTL, I think."

Victoria and Alice were puzzled. "Do you mean a DCL, Mrs. Disraeli?" Alice asked. "Doctor of Civil Law."

Mary Anne smiled. "Something of the sort. They're all one to me."

Victoria found herself smiling, too. She was charmed by Mary Anne's naturalness.

"If it were permitted for young ladies," Alice confessed, "I should have liked to go to University."

As Victoria frowned, Mary Anne said, "Really, Your Royal Highness?"

"There's nothing I'd have liked more."

"That's a very modern idea," Mary Anne said. "But perhaps, my dear, you don't know what it is to have an affectionate husband."

The people round them listening were shocked and waited for the Queen to show her disapproval. Even Alice held her breath. Instead of turning one of her chilling stares on Mary Anne, however, Victoria nodded. "How very true. . . ." The Disraelis were clearly as devoted a couple as herself and Albert. "And were you present at the degree ceremony, Mrs. Disraeli?"

"I wouldn't have missed it!" Mary Anne told her. She had been quite relaxed, talking to Alice, and completely forgot all her fears talking to the Queen. "Dizzy was quite apprehensive. But they cheered him louder than anyone—and Bulwer Lytton and Macaulay and Mr. Gladstone were all there. And they were waiting all evening in the rain to cheer him again, after the dinner—the Gaudy, or whatever they call it."

"Is that so?" Victoria commented, intrigued. Albert used to compare Mr. Disraeli very unfavorably with Mr. Gladstone, but lately had begun to revise his opinion. "I don't expect your husband is quite so busy nowadays."

"If only that were true," Mary Anne sighed. "He never seems able to stop. But then, you'd understand that, Ma'am."

"Only too well," Victoria confirmed. There were whole weeks when she scarcely saw Albert. He was always working at State business, eighteen hours a day, driving himself on in spite of insomnia and a weak chest. She remembered hearing that Mrs. Disraeli had been seriously ill, herself. "Would you care to sit down, Mrs. Disraeli?"

In the dining-room, Albert was speaking along the table to Disraeli, who was helping himself to a second glass of port. "So, like Lord John, you have no intention of retiring?"

"Politicians rarely retire, sir," Disraeli said. "Sometimes, indeed, they hang on until they have to be carried out."

The others laughed. "Frankly, you know," Russell chuckled, "I am surprised you did not accept the appointment as first Viceroy of India."

"The Government, no doubt, thought of it as an ideal way of removing me from the scene," Disraeli answered blandly. The laughter stilled as he went on. "I shall admit I was tempted. Sumptuous palaces, jewelled potentates, all the splendors of the East . . . and Mrs. Disraeli and I arriving for the Durbar under the palanquin on a gilded elephant—like a scene from one of my novels." The laughter broke out again. "But no," he said more seriously, "it would have meant saying goodbye forever to the House of Commons."

"That would have been a great loss," Russell conceded, "to both sides of the House."

Albert chose that moment of harmony to suggest that the time had come to remember the ladies. The gentlemen rose with him and some accepted the offer of a minute or two to relieve themselves. As they waited, Albert drew Disraeli aside. "We shall talk more fully tomorrow," he promised. "But—I know the present Government's views. I should like to hear yours, on this civil war in America."

"One thing is certain. It will be bitter—and more savage than any the world has yet seen," Disraeli said. "Though I imagine the Northern States will win."

"Inevitably, because of their industrial power," Albert agreed. "Afterward, however, they will be exhausted. We must help them to recover. Once America has emerged from her present difficulties, she may begin to play a significant part in world affairs."

Once again, Disraeli was impressed by how closely Albert's thinking matched his own. "I believe so, Sir," he professed. "Though not many see as far ahead."

"Unfortunately," Albert sighed. "I have one hope for the future—that the states of Europe may be united in peaceful alliance and linked in friendship with the new nation across the Atlantic. That, alone, would be a guarantee of peace and stability forever. Impossible to achieve, perhaps."

"Not if we work toward it, Sir," Disraeli said.

"You are not such a cynic as you would have us believe," Albert smiled. "Yes, it is so hard to make people realize that their duty is not only to today, but to the generations as yet unborn."

In the blue drawing-room, Victoria sat on a small settee with Mary Anne on one side and Alice on the other, in earnest conversation. The other ladies tried not to eavesdrop, but were consumed with curiosity to learn what they found so engrossing. It was beyond them how Her Majesty could take such an interest in that bedizened, comical, old woman. The bond they had discovered was a total dependence on and adoration of their husbands. "I am very worried about the Prince Consort's health," Victoria confided.

"You must get him to take care of himself," Mary Anne said.

"If only I could, Mrs. Disraeli," Victoria lamented. "But he deals with all the things I can't make head or tail of. Foreign affairs. It is so complicated, I leave it all to him. But he's so conscientious. If there is some problem, he cannot sleep until it is settled."

"Yes," Mary Anne sympathized. "Do you know, I have exactly the same trouble with Dizzy."

"Really?"

"Work, work, work," Mary Anne sighed. "It leaves him quite exhausted—especially now that he's begun to suffer from asthma."

"No!" Victoria exclaimed. "What does he take for it?" It was the kind of detail which fascinated her. She could not remember anyone so immediately sympathetic and understanding as Mrs. Disraeli. And to think her brilliant husband was a sufferer, too. . . . They whispered on, oblivious of everything until there was a stir among the ladies near them and Victoria looked up to see Albert coming toward her. Von Bonin and Lord John paused to pay their respects to the Duchess. While the other gentlemen hesitated, Disraeli followed Albert, noticing Mary Anne with the Queen.

Albert bowed. "I trust we have not been too long, my dear."

"Not at all," Victoria assured him. "We have been having such an interesting talk." She considered him. "You look more relaxed than I have seen you for weeks."

Albert made a slight inclination toward Disraeli. "That is because I have at last met a statesman with unbiased opinions." It was just loud enough for those in their immediate circle to hear.

Disraeli bowed. "It is difficult to remain prejudiced in the company of an enlightened prince," he said sincerely.

There was a murmur round them at the graceful repaying of the compliment. Victoria looked at Disraeli with a new appreciation. She must study him even more closely, she decided.

Albert was smiling. "Well, we have both been accused in our time of being alien," he murmured. "Hopefully, we have both now proved we have our country's interests at heart." He moved to circulate round the ladies. Disraeli hesitated, then stepped back, leaving Mary Anne with the Queen. Like everyone else, he was extremely curious to know what they were talking about, when they began whispering to each other again, almost at once.

A little later, one of the ladies was prevailed upon to play the piano. The Queen and Prince Consort were exceedingly fond of music, attending the Opera and Ballet and arranging for concerts at Windsor by all the leading artists. The lady played a Chopin Nocturne, her performance nicely judged, full of grace, just short of professional. Afterward, she accompanied one of the younger ladies-in-waiting, who sang one of the songs of Felix Mendelssohn. Both performances were greeted by reserved applause.

After the song, there was a dignified silence, which was broken by a giggle from the settee where Victoria sat between Alice and Mary Anne. On a chair at the side, seated by General von Bonin, Albert looked at them and smiled. Victoria had been so nervous and dispirited of late, it was a pleasure to see her enjoying herself.

On the settee, Victoria whispered, "And this was at dinner? What did the Duchess want Mr. Disraeli to do?"

"To attack the Government," Mary Anne told her. "She said, 'I can't imagine what you're waiting for.' "

"And what did Mr. Disraeli say?"

" 'At this moment, Madam, for the potatoes.' "

Victoria squeaked with laughter. When she smiled as broadly as that, she showed her gums. She covered her mouth quickly. The other guests were amazed, then pretended to have noticed nothing when she looked round imperiously. All at once, they began to talk among themselves. Albert smiled across to Disraeli, who was fairly ill-at-ease. The Queen was clearly captivated by Mary Anne, but Disraeli knew her and that she was quite capable of being carried away and going too far. He put his trust in Allah.

There was a strained pause on the settee, after the Queen's burst of laughter. Alice ended it by asking, "Do you attend many functions with your husband, Mrs. Disraeli?"

"Sadly, no," Mary Anne owned. "He's so busy."

"You must get him to take you to the exhibition at the British Museum," Alice said.

"Yes, it is very fine," Victoria agreed.

"So many beautiful things," Alice enthused. "There was a statue of Apollo which particularly impressed me—so pure, absolute perfection of form."

"Yes," Mary Anne nodded. "But you should see Dizzy in his bath."

Alice's eyes popped. For a second, Victoria was shocked, then she laughed delightedly. "Alice," she gurgled, "you should not be listening."

Alice smiled and lowered her head.

Again the room had fallen silent. "May we know why you are laughing?" Albert asked.

Victoria glanced at Disraeli and back to him. "I can't possibly tell you," she giggled. "It is a private conversation." Again she was aware of the silence and everyone watching. "Albert," she suggested, "why don't you play something?" He shook his head. She turned to Mary Anne. "He plays so beautifully, but there's been so little opportunity lately. I never hear him."

She sounded genuinely upset and Mary Anne was sorry for her. She turned to Albert and smiled. "Couldn't you, please, Your Royal Highness? It would be a great honor."

The Duchess of Cambridge put up her quizzing glass and looked disapprovingly at Mary Anne. Like most of the others, she was astonished when Albert hesitated, then rose. He bowed. "I am very rusty—however, if our guests insist. . . ." There was a ripple of applause as he moved to the piano.

Disraeli relaxed. He had been right. Mary Anne did not need subtlety to charm. She need only be herself. He saw the Queen whisper her thanks and pat Mary Anne's hand. They settled back as Albert began to play one of the simple, rather formal and melancholy pieces of his own composition. Disraeli watched Victoria who gazed at her husband fondly, evidently still deeply in love. He looked from her to Albert. Rapt, softened, in the world of his music, the stress which had aged him so much in the

302

last few years seemed to ease away. Thinking how well the weekend had gone so far, Disraeli allowed himself to feel content. He and this man were made to work together. He could afford to be patient. Prince Albert was only forty-two.

DISRAELI:
The Great Game

chapter one

In the yard of the small, square-towered church at Hughenden, a knot of tenants stood respectfully, watching as
Disraeli handed Mary Anne up into her pony-cart outside
the gate. Their attendance at morning service was a ritual,
during their periods of residence. Disraeli shook hands
with the vicar in his vestments, raised his hat to the
tenants and moved off, walking beside the pony-cart as
Mary Anne drove slowly up the path to the house.

It was a cold, gray day in December and Mary Anne
was wrapped in a fur rug, tucked tightly in around her
waist. But she had been so much better these past months
and felt well and cheerful. Though annoyed with Dizzy.
He had whispered something to her just before they
reached the door of the church and had refused to answer
her questions all through the service. Even when she
pinched him. Out of earshot of the churchyard, she insisted, "Now tell me! I don't understand. What do you
mean—you've settled all your debts?"

Disraeli smiled up to her. "Not all," he admitted. "A kind of settlement. They've been bought up."

"Bought up? Who by?"

"Andrew Montagu, a Yorkshire landowner."

It made no sense to Mary Anne. Why should this man buy up Dizzy's debts and how could it improve their situation, which was perilous? She frowned. "But why?"

Disraeli shrugged. The news had been too good to blurt out and he enjoyed teasing her. "Apparently, he wished to do something to help the party—to be precise, to help me. Rose put him in touch with Lionel de Rothschild, who mentioned my debts, my old friends. Against a mortgage on Hughenden, he has bought them all from the money-lenders and will charge me only a nominal three percent, instead of the ten or twelve I have been paying."

Mary Anne gasped and reined in. She held out her hand to him and he took it. "Dizzy!" She calculated quickly. "That means a saving of between four and five thousand pounds a year!"

He laughed up to her and kissed her hand. "For the first time in my life, my income will exceed my expenditure. I am solvent."

"That's wonderful, my darling," she breathed. "And you were always afraid you had no real friends. . . ." She urged the horse on. "We must get home and celebrate."

As they headed on up the path, they heard the sound of running feet. Ralph Earle, Disraeli's secretary, came in sight through the trees. When he reached them, he was breathless and agitated. "Sir—Mr. Disraeli!" He faltered. "A telegram. We have just had word." He pulled a crumpled telegram form from his pocket.

"Calm yourself, Ralph," Disraeli said. "What is it?"

Earle held out the telegram toward him. "Prince Albert's fever—its typhoid. They can't save him!"

Disraeli snatched the telegram form. It was from Derby, who had just been notified by Palmerston from Windsor Castle. For the last ten days, bulletins had announced that the Prince was indisposed by a mild attack of gastric fever. The doctors' examination had been cursory, hampered by protocol and the Prince's own fear of disease.

The latest examination, by a new doctor insisted on by Palmerston, revealed the truth, and that it was now too late for hope. By the time Disraeli reached London, the Prince Consort was dead.

With his youth and prudishness, Albert had at first amused, then antagonized the country. An untried, bookish, young man from Coburg in Germany, he had married Victoria when they were both only twenty. By his determination and his devotion to duty, he had gradually won respect and, finally, acceptance. Over the years, he had grown to be as loved as the girlish Queen and their respectable, highly moral way of life had set a new standard for public behavior. The royal family, whose antics had been scandalous in previous reigns, became the model for all family life. At the same time, Albert had revealed himself as possessing a political grasp of uncommon ability, impressing successive governments and foreign chancelleries, while his artistic and intellectual gifts won international renown. With the triumph of the Great Exhibition, which he conceived and brought to being, the British public took him unreservedly to their hearts. His sudden, needless death stunned the nation. Without exception, politicians who had worked with him felt the loss of a guiding spirit which could never be replaced. The effect on the Queen was incalculable.

At the recall of Parliament, tributes were paid to the Prince Consort's memory from both sides, for the most part solemn and formal. Disraeli felt the loss almost personally and his tribute silenced and moved the House. There was no applause when he ended. "He possessed a wisdom and energy such as few of our Kings have ever shown. The Prince Consort was the prime counsellor of a realm whose political constitution did not even recognize his political existence. Better known, perhaps, are his services to culture in England. Yet Prince Albert's contributions to the cause of the State were far more powerful and far more precious. He gave to it his thought, his time, his toil. He gave to it his life."

Disraeli was one of the first, apart from close family and her chief ministers, to be invited to an audience with the Queen. He attended her at Windsor, early in the new year. She had fled to Osborne, built by Albert on the Isle of Wight as their own family home, wishing never to see again the stone walls of the ancient castle in which her love had died. But the business of state had to continue and, weeping, reluctant, she had to return, to take up her duties. And she found she had so much to learn, so much she had been happy to leave to Albert. Her ministers were staggered to realize just how much he had done, the amount for which he had been responsible. Like Victoria, they felt guilt at having taken his ceaseless labor for granted. The memory of his final hours haunted her, the ragged breathing and wandering thoughts and his last kiss, the last gesture he made. She longed for death, herself, to be with him.

Disraeli was dressed all in black, as he faced her in the small Audience Room. Never more would she use the Blue Chamber in which Albert had died. It would be a shrine. He was glad he had been forewarned about her appearance. Her skin pallid, her cheeks sunken, haggard and hollow-eyed, she seemed so frail she could hardly stand. She was in deepest mourning, a black, highnecked dress with a white, widow's veil peaked above her forehead. Remembering her at their last meeting, smiling, her cheeks flushed with happiness, radiant in a white and gold ballgown, spangled with tiny, jewelled stars, he found the contrast infinitely touching.

She had dreaded the meeting, as she dreaded seeing any face from the days of her vanished happiness. Yet Disraeli's public tribute to Albert had been so just and true, so beautifully phrased, the only one of them all who really mourned Albert's unique spirit. She nodded, accepting his words of condolence, fighting her distress. "As you will undestand, Mr. Disraeli," she said haltingly, "I have the greatest difficulty in attending to business now that he is no longer at my side. I have often thought that I could not continue. But I am guided in all my decisions by the notes and memoranda he left—and by my knowledge of his thoughts and hopes."

"Your Majesty could have no surer guide," Disraeli

said quietly. "Not one of us would not willingly have bowed to his experience."

His voice was so sincere, so richly sympathetic that Victoria nearly broke down. She trembled and, for a swift, appalling moment, he was afraid she was going to collapse. She mastered herself. "You are the only—the only person who truly appreciated him," she faltered. She bit her lip and Disraeli bowed slowly, giving her time to recover. "I feel so alone . . . so helpless . . ." she sobbed, then caught her breath and stood upright. "In your position as leader of the Opposition in the House of Commons, I beg that you will not bring about any crisis. I feel that, in my present condition, I could not survive it."

Disraeli's mind was racing. He felt genuinely sympathetic, yet it was clear that she now considered him in an entirely new light, that he was in a highly favored situation. From outright disapproval, her opinion had changed to gratitude and trust. Certainly, no one in his party would dream of taking advantage of the upheaval caused by the Prince Consort's death, nor was any maneuver likely to succeed in the near future against Palmerston's majority. "To me, Your Majesty's wishes have always been sacred commands," he assured her. "I promise to take no strong action—unless it becomes an absolute necessity in the interests of the country."

"I knew I could depend on you, Mr. Disraeli. As on no other." She blinked tears away. "I must thank you again for your generous praise of my adored, my beloved husband."

Disraeli bowed. "In those conversations with which, of late years, the Prince honored me," he confessed, "I acquired a great deal, both in knowledge and in feeling, which will always influence my life."

Victoria caught her breath. "You alone—of everyone—seemed to realize his unequalled worth and character. And how immense the loss has been to myself, and to the country." Her mouth trembled. "I often look back to the brief but very happy visit which you and Mrs. Disraeli paid us here . . . at Windsor."

She could not go on. Disraeli understood that the only

way he could help her now was to leave. He thanked her silently, bowed and backed to the door. Opening it, he bowed again and stepped out.

When the door closed behind him, the tears which the Queen had been holding back with all her strength broke out. Her mouth opened in an unvoiced cry of pain. Her eyes closed and her head swung back and her body shook with anguish.

The ballroom of Baron Lionel de Rothschild's mansion at 148 Piccadilly was breathtaking in its opulence. The gigantic, six storey townhouse included a bewildering succession of drawing-rooms, private salons, family and public dining-rooms, billiard room, smoking-room, boudoirs and suites of bedrooms, corridors and passages, with an enormous, central staircase of glistening, white marble. An army of artists and craftsmen had been engaged on its furnishing and each room was filled with priceless treasures.

Mary Anne's idea of perfection was the ballroom, its huge, crystal chandeliers lighting up the gold, marble and crimson of its decoration and the vast, swathed, satin curtains. In a raised gallery at the far end, a full orchestra under a Viennese conductor played one of the latest Strauss waltzes. Her feet were tapping as she watched the dancers with her hostess, Baroness Charlotte de Rothschild, and Dizzy's old friend, Lady Chesterfield. She wore a ball dress of the palest lilac lace and satin, off the shoulders, the spreading skirts sewn with deep lilac satin bows. At nearly seventy, she no longer left her sloping shoulders bare, but covered them with a tiny lace shawl. Her face was brightly, defiantly made up, her eyes sparkled and she wore a yellow rose above the forehead of her ringletted, auburn wig. "It's the one thing that makes me feel envious!" she exclaimed. "I have always wanted to have a house with a ballroom."

"I am sure you would fill it every night," Anne Chesterfield smiled. Attractive and intelligent, she was almost the same age as Disraeli and had known him since before he was married. He had flirted both with her and her

312

younger sister, Selina, in his early days in London. It was through their father, Lord Forester, that he had won the nomination for Shrewsbury in 1841.

"Oh, I would!" Mary Anne assured her. "And if we ran out of guests, I'd get Dizzy to dance with me till dawn, all by ourselves."

They laughed with her and Lady Chesterfield glanced to the side, where Disraeli, Bulwer Lytton and Edward Stanley stood with the urbane, patrician Lionel de Rothschild.

Stanley was incredulous. "Gladstone has officially joined the Liberals?"

"According to my information," Rothschild said, "Palmerston has offered to make him Chancellor of the Exchequer again. It will be announced tomorrow."

"But is it certain?" Stanley insisted.

"The Rothschild information service is m-more reliable than a government despatch, Edward," Lytton murmured.

Stanley was still shaken. "Of course. Forgive me, Baron."

Rothschild smiled faintly and shrugged.

"He is the last person I'd have expected to desert his principles and his friends," Disraeli said quietly, troubled. The essence of the man was a rigid rectitude.

"I'm surprised it didn't happen sooner," Lytton told them.

"Why?"

"It's obvious. The Liberal leaders are old men, Russell and P-Pam. So one day soon he can hope to take their place. Whereas, with us, he w-would always be second to you."

"And yet you are still considered an adventurer," Stanley put in, bitterly, "while he is held up as the very model of an upright man. His political conversion has at least as much to do with ambition as with conviction."

Rothschild coughed. "I am sorry, gentlemen—however much I agree with you, it is not a subject we should discuss."

"Your pardon, Baron, I had forgotten," Lytton apologized. "You must allow me to observe, the fact that you are a Radical seems, at times, a mite incongruous." He took a swift glance round at the room and Rothschild smiled. Lytton bowed. "Well, if you'll excuse me, I must greet m-my hostess." Stanley and he moved on to bow to Charlotte.

Disraeli was lost in thought. Rothschild spoke quietly to him. "This will make things more difficult for you."

"H'm?" Disraeli put the problem aside. He shrugged. "It's bad enough having you on the opposite side of the House, Lionel."

"Thanks to you. You showed the way, I followed."

"You won through your own determination."

"Yes, but for ten, eleven years, while they refused to let me take my seat," Rothschild said, "you fought until I was allowed to take the Oath according to my own religion and conscience. We Jews have much to thank you for."

The waltz ended and the dancers bowed and curtsied. Their chatter and applause broke the moment. Among them, leading a lady to her seat, was a tall, striking man in his early forties. He was handsome and well built, but looked wasp-waisted in a white, foreign uniform with gold epaulettes.

"You haven't met my special guest," Rothschild said.

Disraeli had also spotted him. "The Prussian. He is the coming man, I hear."

"He has risen very quickly in their diplomatic service. Word is that before long he may be chief minister in Berlin." Disraeli was more than interested. The rise of militarism in Prussia, with its capital in Berlin, was a new and disturbing factor in Europe. "You may find him amusing," Rothschild went on. "His technique is to disarm by frankness."

"Indeed. . . ." It was a technique which Disraeli used on occasion, himself.

Rothschild led him forward and the Prussian turned, smiling. Disraeli assessed him quickly. Strong, sure of himself, projecting an impression of geniality, but the eyes were shrewd, missing nothing. Disarmingly and deceptively eager to be friendly. "Mr. Benjamin Disraeli," Rothschild said, "may I introduce Count Otto von Bismarck."

Bismarck clicked his heels and bowed. They shook hands. "I have heard a great deal about you, Mr. Disraeli. Most of it complimentary."

"Thank you," Disraeli replied. "What I have heard of you is all complimentary."

Bismarck laughed. His voice was curiously light for his size. "I am glad of a chance to meet you. Though I notice that your name is mentioned on the Continent with more respect than it is here." They moved aside into a pillared alcove. Rothschild remained at a slight distance, listening, ready to keep them from interruption.

"Are you staying long?" Disraeli asked.

"Only a few days, I'm afraid. I wished to see something of the other chancelleries of Europe."

"Very wise."

"But I find it difficult to talk to your British Foreign Office," Bismarck complained. "They seem to have no real interest in making contacts, exchanging views."

"They do not always have any," Disraeli murmured.

Bismarck chuckled. "You I think I could talk to. It is a pity you are not in power."

"An enormous pity." Disraeli smiled slightly. "Are you hoping the Rothschilds will open a branch of their bank in Berlin?"

Bismarck was surprised by the directness of the question. "It would be very desirable," he conceded. "But they seem strangely reluctant, although we have offered them honors and Court positions."

"They will accept only when you agree to emancipate their people."

"That may take time," Bismarck said carefully.

"I hear that you may soon be recalled to Berlin."

Again, Bismarck was surprised. "You are remarkably well informed, Mr. Disraeli. Yes, it is possible."

"And once you assume responsibility for Prussian affairs what will your aims be?"

Bismarck paused. "Frankly?"

"Preferably."

"I shall organize the army, without the help of Parliament. As soon as it is in a position to command respect, I shall subdue the minor states and give national unity to Germany."

"Under Prussian leadership."

Bismarck smiled. "Naturally. Of course, to do that, I must seize the first opportunity to declare war on Austria and to show France that we cannot be intimidated. Then Germany will be able to take her true place in Europe. That is what I came here to tell your Queen's Government."

It sounded fantastic, but had been stated so positively that Disraeli did not take it lightly. "Most impressive. Have you set a time limit for all this?"

"It shall be completed in the next ten years," Bismarck said simply. The music began again and he smiled. "Ah, excuse me. I have enjoyed our talk, but I have promised to dance with the Baroness von Rothschild."

He bowed and left. Disraeli watched him. As Rothschild came up, he said dryly, "Thank you. I had the two minutes allotted to those of little importance."

Rothschild laughed quietly. "Can you wonder the Foreign Office didn't listen to him?"

Disraeli watched Bismarck lead the beautiful Charlotte de Rothschild out on to the floor for a quadrille, smiling and charming. He was quite unperturbed that no one took him seriously. He had told the Foreign Ministers of Europe what he intended to do and no one had tried to dissuade him, because no one believed it possible. "They should have listened," Disraeli said. "Look out for that man. He means what he says."

The social and political world was convulsed by the marriage of Albert Edward, the Prince of Wales, to Princess Alexandra of Denmark. Many thought the wedding would be postponed, due to the Queen's extended mourning, but the match had been agreed by Albert and his sacred wishes could not be gainsaid. As the day of the wedding approached, the Queen retreated more into her self-imposed seclusion, partly because she could not bear

the thought of others rejoicing while her own happiness
had vanished forever and partly because she mistakenly
blamed the young Prince for his father's death. Discovery
of his son's first sexual escapade, while serving temporarily with the Army in Ireland, had broken the Prince
Consort's heart and, so she believed, lowered his will to
live during his last illness. Although the wedding was to
go ahead, she insisted on a minimum of official celebrations, but the people of England were not to be prevented
from showing their love for the boy she had turned
against and his young bride, the entrancing, open-hearted,
gentle Alexandra. From the moment he met her, when
she landed from her ship at the mouth of the Thames,
their journey together to London became one vast, triumphal procession. Victoria, however, had decided against
the wedding taking place in London, to avoid just such
scenes of popular enthusiasm. How could her people
make merry, when they remembered the loss of Albert?
The marriage would be solemnized in St. George's Chapel, Windsor.

The comparatively small size of the Chapel, attached
to the Castle, meant that the number of guests would be
severely restricted. After family and their connections and
foreign representatives, there were very few places remaining. Seating was strictly by precedence and many
people who expected invitations did not receive them.
Jockeying for invitations among the aristocracy became
frantic. Even old friends of the Queen, such as the Duke
and Duchess of Marlborough and the Duchess of Manchester, a former Mistress of the Robes, were not invited
and others only to a wedding breakfast after the ceremony. The rage and indignation of those who had been
passed over became unbounded, when it was learned that
only four tickets remained after the essential guests had
been reckoned and that two of the four had been sent on
the Queen's instructions to Disraeli and Mary Anne.

Victoria did not appear in the Chapel, but remained
half hidden in the tiny closet built for Catherine of Ara-
gon above the high altar. Pale and withdrawn, she sat in
her mourning and widow's veil, acknowledging only the

curtsey of the Princess Royal and the obeisance of the bridal couple.

After the wedding breakfast, which the Queen could not bring herself to attend, the special train carrying the guests back to London was so crowded that the Duchess of Westminster, wearing half a million pounds worth of jewellery, had to struggle for a place for herself and the aged Lady Palmerston in a third class compartment. Other guests were robbed. Disraeli sat all the way back on Mary Anne's lap, but they were amused and delighted at how splendidly everything had gone. Disraeli knew the Duchess of Manchester would not speak to him for the rest of the year and did not mind a bit. He could have asked for no more public sign of the Queen's favor than his presence with Mary Anne on this day of days. The only small cloud was information he had received from Victoria's uncle, King Leopold of the Belgians, with whom he had begun a frank and revealing correspondence, that Bismarck was displeased by the marriage. He had started his campaign of Prussian supremacy exactly as he had planned and, as a trial of force, intended to annex the German-speaking provinces of Denmark.

"It is a privilege to live in this age of rapid and brilliant events," he wrote to Mrs. Brydges Willyams. "What an error to consider it an utilitarian age! It is one of infinite romance. Thrones tumble down and crowns are offered, like a fairy tale, and the most powerful people in the world, male and female, a few years back, were adventurers, exiles and demireps."

His constant regret was that he was again an observer, for another seven years in the Opposition.

Yet his circumstances had changed. Materially, he was more secure than he had ever been. Not many months after he had written to Mrs. Brydges Willyams describing the royal wedding, he wrote to tell her how, in return for his championship of a permanent monument to the Prince Consort, the Albert Memorial, the Queen had sent him a specially bound copy of the Prince's speeches, inscribed, "From the beloved Prince's broken-hearted widow, VIC-

318

TORIA R." Letters and communications with the Queen became ever more frequent and ever more cordial. At the same time, he became a favorite with Bertie, the Prince of Wales, and his lovely wife, Alexandria, who had capitvated society with their gaiety and charm, seen as all the more striking by contrast with the Queen's unceasing mourning and refusal to show herself in public. His party, though not in power, was gaining in strength and, as he concentrated more and more on international affairs, which had always been his main interest, his international reputation increased, too.

For some months, Mary Anne and he were unable to use Hughenden. Their improved financial circumstances had made it possible for them to realize a dream. A team of builders and decorators, working to Mary Anne's design, changed the house back to how it might have been in Jacobean times. When finished, it was enchanting. Not a vast, stately mansion, it was a perfect home, of human proportions, warm and prettily picturesque and welcoming. Even so, it had cost more than they could afford, yet relief, as always, came when it was least expected. This time, it brought deep sorrow.

A local clergyman wrote to Disraeli that Mrs. Brydges Willyams was gravely ill. She had been ill before, but had recovered, apparently completely. She had a theory that no one needed to die before they were a hundred, provided they stayed clear of doctors and medicines. Disraeli was anxious, knowing she lived alone apart from a few servants. He hurried to Torquay, but was too late. She died just before he arrived. He had known, of course, that as one of the executors he had an interest in her "not inconsiderable" fortune. What he had not realized was that most of the other people mentioned in her will were already dead and that now he was principal legatee. His inheritance came to well over £30,000, more than enough to pay for all the improvements to Hughenden, which Mrs. Brydges Willyams had never been able to visit. Her last wish was to be buried in the little church there, near her only friends.

Abroad, the armies of Cavour from the north and

Garibaldi from the south met at the River Volturno and proclaimed the united Kingdom of Italy, under Victor Emmanuel. Napoleon the Third, who had plotted and fought with Cavour against Austria, established himself as the arbiter of Europe. Backed by the bayonettes of the French Army, he installed the Archduke Maximilian, a younger brother of Kaiser Franz Joseph of Austria, as puppet Emperor of the Catholic Empire of Mexico. As chief minister in Berlin, Bismarck reformed the army and made it the dominating power in Prussia, under King Wilhelm I. To demonstrate the efficiency of the new army and to intimidate the smaller states of Germany into accepting Prussian leadership, he launched a short, but bloody, war on Denmark, seizing the provinces of Schleswig and Holstein. In the United States of America, the Northern States battered the South into submission. Shortly after victory, the universally admired President Abraham Lincoln was assassinated.

Under Palmerston, England had gradually withdrawn from the center of world affairs by a policy of isolation. On the few occasions when intervention was threatened by the Foreign Secretary, Lord John Russell, over the Russian occupation of Poland and the Prussian annexation of Schleswig and Holstein, he found himself humiliatingly unable to act, because of reluctance to intervene among his colleagues and the weakening of British alliances on the Continent. Disraeli repudiated the Government's policies and gained much credit in the country by attacking the failure to support Denmark, which had appealed for military aid. Because of Princess Alexandra, popular sentiment was strongly on Disraeli's side. Secure in its majority, the Liberal Government ignored his criticism. In domestic affairs, he came more and more into open conflict with William Gladstone, who was making his reputation with a series of brilliant Budgets. The General Election of 1865 confirmed Palmerston and the Liberals in power.

In the early autumn, Disraeli and Mary Anne visited Raby, the home of the Duke of Cleveland. A huge, medieval castle, set in woods in which herds of red deer roamed, it delighted the romantic in Disraeli. He was also very taken with the Duchess, an unusually well-informed woman with a flow of droll conversation which kept him amused. Altogether, he was so charmed that they stayed a week. Other guests grumbled about the bad weather, but it gave him a perfect excuse not to follow the guns.

Among the younger guests, in whom he always took an interest, he found the Duchess's son by her former marriage to Lord Rosebery particularly promising and encouraged his ambitions toward a political career, although regretting that he inclined to the Liberals. He had high hopes for another of the younger men, Montagu Corry, son of an old colleague. Tall, good-looking and intelligent, Corry had been educated at Harrow and Cambridge and recently called to the Bar. Disraeli found him excessively serious. Corry froze into immobility and gravity whenever they exchanged even a few words and attempts to put him at his ease only made him more awkwardly stiff. After the first two days, Disraeli did his best to avoid him, but Corry made a point of seeking him out, appearing at Disraeli's elbow just when the conversation was most relaxed and drying it up with his staid, long-faced manner and solemnity. Mary Anne came to dread the sight of him, with his sober eyes and full beard, making him seem ten years older than his true age, twenty-six.

One wet afternoon, Disraeli had retired to his room to write some letters. Wishing to check a quotation from Cicero's speeches, he went down to the library. On the way, passing one of the salons, he heard the muffled sound of laughter, clapping and a rhythmical thumping. He pushed the door open and saw the girls of the house-party in a semi-circle, giggling and applauding. In the center of them was Montagu Corry, arms raised, fingers snapping, head wagging, while he danced with comical abandon, lifting his knees and high-stepping in the style of the Nigger Minstrels. As he danced, he sang with the appropriate accent,

321

Oh, de Camptown ladies sing this song,
Doo dah, doo dah,
De Camptown racetrack five miles long,
Oh, Doo dah day.
Gwine to run all night. . . .

As he sang, he revolved and found himself facing the door. Seeing Disraeli watching him, expressionless and unblinking, he was horrified and his face twisted into a ghastly smile of incredulity. He paused in mid step.

"Don't stop, Monty!" one of the Rosebery girls called.

He shook his head.

"Come on!" the others pleaded, laughing. "You're so funny. Don't stop!"

He had to give in to their insistence and they clapped as he turned and took up the song and dance again. "Gwine to run all night, gwine to run all day . . ." As he capered, he was agonizingly aware of the basilisk eyes watching his back.

That evening, he came face to face with Disraeli as the guests assembled for dinner. He could not bring himself to speak, he was so embarrassed. He was puzzled, when Disraeli nodded slowly, with the faintest trace of a smile, and murmured, "I think you must be my impresario."

Some months later, Disraeli was seated in his small study at Hughenden. It was comfortable and unpretentious, directly above the Garden Room, looking down on to the terraces and the valley. He had begun to suffer from twinges of arthritis and sat with his right leg resting on a stool, massaging the knee slowly as he read. His thoughts kept coming between him and the page. Much had happened. Shortly after the triumph of the General Election, Palmerston had died. He was eighty but so hale and vigorous, it had been completely unexpected. Right up to his death, he had been used to eating enormous, ten or twelve course meals, washed down with a matching quantity of wine and brandy. Only three years ago, he had nearly been cited in a divorce case, for adultery with a Mrs. Cane. The current joke held that she was certainly

Cain, but was he Abel? The consensus had it that he was. It only made him more popular.

Disraeli sincerely mourned him. They had always behaved to each other with caution and respect. Now things had changed. Russell had become Prime Minister. Since he sat in the House of Lords, Leadership of the Commons passed to Gladstone, who at once, backed by the Liberal majority, assumed the almost inevitable arrogance of power. He did not argue with the Opposition. He sought to crush it with oratory, flaying his former friends and colleagues, whose weakness and conservatism he had come to despise. Disraeli, however, had been building up a stronger team of younger men, who did not let themselves be browbeaten. Yet the main conflict was between the two leaders in the Commons. Disraeli recognized that Gladstone had developed an implacable enmity toward him which at last had come out into the open. The thought of sitting helplessly day after day for years to come, watching Gladstone exult in his power, was unsupportable. He shifted as Mary Anne looked in.

"That young man's here," she said flatly.

"What young man?"

"The one we met at the Duke of Cleveland's. Corby."

"Corry," Disraeli corrected. "Montagu Corry."

Mary Anne sniffed. "That's him. He's waiting in the hall."

"Well, I'd better have him up." He lowered his leg and started to push himself to his feet.

"No, I'll fetch him. You rest your knee," Mary Anne said. She turned back to the door and paused. "He's a very serious young man."

Disraeli agreed. "Yes. I think he is trying to impress me."

"What does he want?" she asked.

"He's hoping I'll find him some position, I imagine."

Mary Anne frowned. "Not here, surely? He'd make me very uncomfortable." She went out.

Disraeli laid down his book and composed himself, his expression remote and inscrutable, while he waited.

323

The door opened again and Corry came in. He had been trembling with nerves in the hall, but had managed to compose himself. He bowed. He was dressed very soberly in dark trousers and a charcoal frockcoat. "I hope I have not come at an inopportune moment, Sir?"

"Not at all, Mr. Corry," Disraeli said. "You wanted me to do something for you. What?"

Corry blinked at the bluntness of the question. "I—I am most anxious to get a start in political life, Sir. I ventured to hope you might know someone to whom my services might be acceptable—as a secretary, say."

Disraeli showed no flicker of reaction. "What have you been doing?"

"For the past three years, I have been in practice as a barrister." His heart sank as he saw Disraeli's mouth turn down.

"The Law..." Disraeli commented. "H'mm...I thought you had all the gravity of a county judge." He paused. "You also do a very funny dance."

The courage which had sustained Corry drained away. He remembered his extreme embarrassment, when he had been discovered amusing the girls. "Most regrettable," he muttered. "I—the ladies insisted. I realized at once, of course, that I had forfeited any hope of your good opinion." Convinced that his case was lost, he bowed again, preparing to take his leave.

"On the contrary," Disraeli said, stopping him. "Up till then, I had thought you devilish dull. But at that moment, I said to myself, and repeated it later to you, I think he must be my impresario."

Corry stared at him blankly. "Sir?"

Disraeli's eyebrows lifted. "Shall I make it more plain? Earle, my present secretary, has just entered Parliament in his own right. Now that he has personal responsibilities, I shall need a new Private Secretary. From all I have heard, you will do admirably."

It was nearly too much for Corry. His mind spun. "...I am overcome, Sir."

"Then you'd better sit down." He smiled as Corry collapsed abruptly into the nearest chair. Inquiries had

324

proved him to be scrupulously honest, highly intelligent, conscientious and capable of devotion. He would be a welcome change for Earle who possessed, of these qualities, only intelligence. "I take it you accept?"

"Why—yes," Corry muttered, then more loudly, "Yes!"

Disraeli's mouth twitched. "Good. I shall need someone I can trust, for I am about to go to war." Seeing Corry's puzzlement, he explained. "Since Lord Palmerston's death, Mr. Gladstone has assumed the Leadership of the Commons."

"A very forceful man," Corry said carefully.

Disraeli nodded. "Quite so. Like most converts, he has become a fanatic. And a dangerous one. I think he has had his own way too long."

When the parliamentary session resumed, the atmosphere of the House was disturbed and restive. With Palmerston gone, Russell was at last able to bring in some of the reforms he had blocked, but no one could estimate what effect they would have and most members were uncertain. The Radicals expected increased support from new voters in the industrial classes and continually backed the Liberals as the party most likely to enfranchise them. Yet the mild reforms suggested and introduced to the House by Gladstone were so hedged with qualifications that their result would be severely limited. The right to vote would be extended, but would still depend on the ownership of property.

Disraeli sat on the Opposition Front Bench, as Gladstone spoke. His old opponent was now fifty-six, his dark hair greying and receded. In compensation, he wore it long at the back. His expression had grown more intense, his features more deeply lined and severe.

Corry was listening in the Gallery, noticing how Gladstone was continually annoyed by mutters of protest from his own side and from the Radicals. "The limbo of abortive creations is peopled with the skeletons of Reform Bills!" his harsh voice declaimed. "Yet no one denies the crying need to extend the right to vote, at present only held by householders paying over ten pounds a year in rent. Her Majesty's Government proposes...." He paused, irritated, glancing across at Disraeli who, evidently bored, had taken out his white handkerchief and was tossing it slowly from one hand to the other. It was infernally distracting. He resumed. "We proposed to lower the qualifications from ten pounds in the boroughs to seven pounds, and in the countries from fifty pounds to ..." He glared round at protests from behind him and a scream from the Radicals.

"No qualifications! Traitor!" the Radicals shouted.

Gladstone ignored and overrode them. "From fifty pounds to fourteen. By a reliable system of computation, a further four hundred thousand new electors...." His voice grated on.

That evening a number of leading Conservatives met in the Carlton Club, among them Lord Stanley, Henry Lennox, Lord John Manners and Robert Cecil. They were worried, some of them dispirited.

"There is nothing Dizzy can do," Lennox said.

"We must trust him," Manners insisted.

"He is a master of parliamentary tactics," Cecil admitted. "But this new Bill of Gladstone's gives us no opportunity to fight!"

Stanley was troubled. "Well, at least it is a step forward," he said reluctantly. "We can support it, although it will keep the Liberals in for the next twenty years. There's little point in fighting. He has his majority and we can't shake it."

They broke off, seeing Disraeli coming toward them. "Good evening, gentlemen," he said pleasantly. "Strange, how easy it is to tell that one has just been the subject of conversation. Do I interrupt?"

"Not at all," Manners assured him.

"Is something wrong?"

There was a pause, each waiting for one of the others to speak. "We seem to face a lifetime in Opposition," Stanley said at last.

To their surprise, Disraeli smiled. "On the contrary, Gladstone has just played into our hands."

Manners wished to believe him, but was puzzled. "In what way?"

"He introduced his Bill like an Old Testament Prophet announcing moral truths!" Cecil stormed.

"Ah," Disraeli nodded, "but he has blinded himself by his own righteousness. And lost his grip on his supporters. He has infuriated the Radicals, while many of his own party would prefer merely to talk of reform, as they have done for fifty years. The thought of being elected by their own workers alarms them."

"That's true," Stanley agreed. They saw themselves having to ask for approval from their own operatives.

"So all we have to do is stimulate both groups and keep proposing amendments. And we shall see," Disraeli promised.

The house was crowded and noisy. Angry murmurs came from the Radicals and a section of the Liberal back benches. Gladstone was again speaking and had lost his temper. He turned angrily and glared up at his own side. "If this amendment is carried, the Government may feel it its duty to resign!" he threatened.

Cecil rose from behind Disraeli and called across, "Do it now!" The Conservatives cheered and repeated the shout, "Resign! Resign!"

Gladstone gazed across at them defiantly, contemptuous, the Ministers around him applauding vigorously. His head turned swiftly as the cry of "Resign!" was taken up by the Radicals on his right and some of his own nominal supporters behind. His eyes darted back to Disraeli. Over the applause and cheers, the steady shout was repeated, becoming louder, "Resign! Resign! Resign!"

Disraeli sat with his legs crossed, his face set, his eyes showing the merest suggestion of a smile, as he tossed his white handkerchief from one hand to the other.

Lord Derby was nearly as pleased as Disraeli by Mary Anne's reaction. He had no more reservations. There was trust, even affection between them.

"So I am once again the wife of the Chancellor..." she smiled.

"Unfortunately, my dear," Disraeli confirmed.

Derby was surprised. "Unfortunately?"

"I had hoped for something different this time," Disraeli told him. "The Foreign Office, perhaps."

"Yes, but the Exchequer gives you more power—and you'll need it," Derby said. Like Disraeli, he had no illusions. "We are still in a minority. Sooner or later, the Whigs and Radicals will close ranks against us, as they've always done before."

"We are used to it."

Derby grunted. He had aged visibly in the last two or three years. "I'll have to ask you to take on as much as possible."

"Does your gout still plague you, Lord Derby?" Mary Anne asked, concerned.

"It is torture, Ma'am," he grimaced. "Some days I can barely move. It exhausts me."

Disraeli had been thinking. "So who'll have the Foreign Office—Stanley?"

"I suppose so," Derby agreed reluctantly. There was still little love between father and son. "He's the best choice after you."

"Bulwer?" Disraeli suggested.

Derby shook his head. "He's more of an invalid than I am—or thinks he is. He can have the peerage he's always wanted."

"Lord Lytton..." Mary Anne savored. "He'll like that."

Derby chuckled. "Yes. Who do we pick as Secretary for India?"

Without hesitation, Disraeli said, "Robert Cecil."

Derby was as surprised as Mary Anne. "But he's one of your most open critics!" he protested. "Have you forgotten those articles he wrote?"

Mary Anne sighed. "Dizzy never bears grudges."

"I try not to. When a man offends me, I am sometimes angry for a minute, then I write his name on a piece of paper."

"Then what?" Derby asked.

"I put it in a drawer and forget about it," Disraeli said. "It is astonishing how often, opening the drawer after a year or so, one cannot recollect the reason why the name is there."

"Well, well . . ." Derby chuckled. He hesitated. "I needn't say how pleased I am to be in harness with you again. And I know someone else who will welcome you."

Queen Victoria could not hide her joy at having Disraeli back in the Government. Albert had always tended to favor Gladstone. Regretfully, she had come to disagree with that opinion. Gladstone alarmed and attempted to bully her intellectually. With Disraeli she felt much more safe. In widowhood, she had grown stouter, her face sallow and more pouchy. She had never stopped wearing her black mourning. "I cannot tell you how delighted I am to have you once again as my Chancellor, Mr. Disraeli," she declared. "These past years with Mr. Gladstone I have found very trying."

Disraeli had not made the mistake committed by some other Ministers in arriving dressed as for a social occasion. He, too, wore mourning. As he stood in front of the Queen in the Audience Room, he attempted to seem politely reserved. The Queen's relations with Gladstone must have been trying, if she was prepared to complain so unguardedly.

"He does not keep me fully informed as you do," she went on. She bridled. "He speaks to me as if he were addressing a public meeting! Then, instead of conversation, he lectures me—about Homer or the Hittites . . . or the Athanasian Creed!"

Disraeli knew better than to smile. "Allow me to say that I have too much respect for you, Ma'am, ever to lecture you," he murmured. "Especially not on the Athanasian Creed." Victoria's mouth leapt at the corners. She compressed her lips. "At the same time," he continued, "I trust you do not find my reports of Cabinet business too dull?"

"Far from it," she assured him. "You are the only one

who contrives to make them interesting—as my dear husband used to." At first, his reports had seemed startlingly descriptive. Now she looked forward to them. They made her feel she had actually been there, at the discussions.

Disraeli bowed. "As I have said before—I could ask for no surer guide, Ma'am."

So respectful, Victoria thought. Forever mindful of Him, whom so many others seemed to have forgotten. It was a comfort just to hear his expressive voice and to feel the reassurance of that unswerving loyalty. But there were points that had to be covered. "These are difficult times," she said. "With dear Austria crushed by the Prussian Army. The Prince Consort always saw Germany as a moral, stabilizing force in Europe."

Because he had been German, himself, Disraeli thought. And had never met Bismarck. "Unfortunately, Prussia seems bent on dominating the other German states and creating a new German Empire. The balance of power is shifting." He saw her stiffen. "Though there is no immediate danger."

Victoria had sworn to follow Albert's memoranda to the letter, to obey His wishes. The marriage of their daughter Vickie to Fritz, who would one day be King of Prussia, was only one move toward a permanent alliance. But if Prussia were to become a menace to peace. . . . She would not think of it. "Far more in these Reform riots which have swept the country!" she stated.

Disraeli agreed. The mob had torn down the railings of Hyde Park opposite his home. His had been one of the few houses of politicians which had not been threatened—perhaps because the rioters could tell that Mary Anne, who waved to them from the windows, was sympathetic. "They have been led to expect changes, Ma'am," he said.

"It is a question which can no longer remain unsettled," Victoria insisted. Her people had been promised the vote. They should be given it. "Various administrations have tried, and *all* have failed. You must do something about it, Mr. Disraeli—and at once!"

330

He knew she had already tackled Derby on the matter. He bowed. "I assure Your Majesty that my Government intends to." -

The riots were a symptom of a deep dissatisfaction in the country. Disraeli had, from the first, advocated emancipation for all responsible members of society. He hesitated now, because he remembered Gladstone demanding that the vote be granted to "our fellow-subjects, our fellow-Christians, our own flesh and blood," and a Conservative MP asking him why our flesh and blood stopped at seven pounds? Yet to give the vote without restriction to all workers, laborers and operatives was, potentially, to hand all political power in the country to one class, and that the least qualified to know how to use it. Yet Derby agreed with him that something had to be settled, as the Queen said. If the Conservatives did not bring in a sweeping Reform Bill and receive the credit for it, then the Liberal Opposition would reunite against them. Disraeli announced that a Bill would be drawn up and presented by him in the near future.

It was an extremely delicate business. Even inside the Cabinet, opinions were sharply, violently, divided. Predictably, those who fought to restrict the numbers enfranchised were led by Robert Cecil and General Peel. The pattern was repeated throughout the party. The first version of the Bill satisfied no one, and in the following months so many people had to be reassured by different provisos and amendments that it began to look unwieldy and unworkable. Yet many Conservatives and Liberals were still prepared to support it, to put an end to the agitation and the years of uncertainty. Gladstone was furious. He realized what Disraeli was doing, gradually involving nearly everyone in the framing of the Bill and conditioning their minds to pass it in whatever final form it was presented. He brought in a series of wrecking amendments, but so spoiled his case by his naked hatred of his rival that Disraeli was able to have them decisively thrown out as a party attack, by "a candidate for power who had forgotten he has had his innings."

All this time, Disraeli was assessing and calculating,

balancing one suggested clause against another, taking note of the opinions of each group. If the Liberals had been able to resolve their differences, there would have been a majority of seventy against him in the House. He had to keep a sufficient number of them convinced that only his Bill would satisfy their demands. He was almost completely sure now of his own party. They had accepted that a Reform Bill must be passed, once he had pointed out that the Reform Act of 1832 had kept the Whigs in power for over thirty years and that any change must be to their advantage. The final Bill had to be put to the House. At the last moment, Robert Cecil resigned in protest from the Cabinet with two other members and announced his total opposition, although he had previously agreed to the proposals. He objected to the way he and everyone else, from Derby down, had been manipulated by Disraeli.

Late at night, Disraeli met Derby and Stanley in the Prime Minister's study at 10 Downing Street. After the resignations, Derby had been in despair. "This is the end of the Conservative Party," he had said. Disraeli knew better. In fact, the Cabinet was stronger without these constant critics of the Bill. Many of the fancy clauses which had only been included to keep them happy could now be scrapped, and the final proposals toward which he had been working all along put to the House.

As he outlined them, Stanley was shaken. He backed reform, like many others, provided it was contained within certain limits. "A domestic vote?" he queried.

"Why stick at artificial limits?" Disraeli said. "Why not grant one household, one vote—whatever the rent. Instead of a few thousand new electors, we will enfranchise a million."

Derby was the first to realize the implications. "It is not only necessary and fair," he agreed excitedly. "It will smash the Liberals!"

"But will our own side support it?" Stanely wondered. "It will be far too radical for many of them."

"That is the great danger," Disraeli admitted. "But we

have a week or so to work out the details and during that time I must—if I may put it so—continue to educate the party. When the mood is right, we shall call them all together and explain the principles involved."

"To the whole party?" Stanely exclaimed. "That's never been done before!"

"It will be now," Disraeli said quietly.

The innovation of bringing the whole parliamentary party together and taking the members into their leaders' confidence was a striking success. It immediately created a new feeling of confidence. The members readily saw that Disraeli's proposals were the only guarantee of the Ministry staying in power, if they were passed in the House of Commons. Their agreement gave him the opportunity, for which he had always longed, to establish the Conservatives as the truly national party. "For what is the Tory party unless it represents national feeling?" he asked. "The Tory party is nothing unless it represents and upholds the institutions of the country."

Mary Anne drove to Westminster with him in their carriage on the final night of the debate on the Reform Bill. It had been viciously attacked by Gladstone, Cecil, General Peel and many others and that he would win the final vote was far from sure. Yet, whatever happened, his own position was safer than it had ever been. He had revealed himself to his party as a leader of whom they could, at last, be proud. His ascendancy was remarkable. Even he was unaware of how complete it was. The entire House, friends and enemies, were astonished by his apparent ability to answer every question, meet every crisis, soothe feelings or rouse his followers to the highest pitch of determination, as he chose. He was never taken by surprise. Day after day he had been in his seat on the Front Bench, ready to sound the offensive or to defend. He had spoken over three hundred times.

Mary Anne held his arm tightly as the carriage jogged down toward Parliament Square. Win or lose, she was infinitely proud of him, yet her pride could not lessen

333

uneasiness. "All those months of preparation," she said. "I'm so excited for you! You must not be nervous."

"Even if I am I shall not look it," he assured her.

"What does it matter if Robert Cecil and those others resigned? The rest of the Party will support you."

"They have proved themselves surprisingly intelligent," he murmured. "In fact, they have realized that, by humanity and commonsense, we can achieve what the rest of the world has only brought about through bloodshed and revolution."

"You see?" she declared. "The Liberals must vote with you, if they've any political consciences at all!"

"The Radicals certainly must. This Bill will give them more than they ever dared to ask."

"And Gladstone?" she asked.

He paused. "In a frenzy. Still, tonight, he may rally his supporters in his last speech."

Mary Anne was indignant. "Surely they can see that it's not the Bill itself he is objecting to, but the fact that he's not presenting it himself. That *you* are?"

"It has been noticed," he told her drily.

The carriage stopped. Outside was the dark bulk of the House of Commons with its Gothic traceries limned against the lighter sky. A footman hurried to open the carriage door.

"Well, tonight will settle many things," Disraeli said quietly. He climbed out, Mary Anne leaned toward the window. The footman slammed the door shut and stood back. Disraeli turned, looking at Mary Anne, who was silent and motionless. "Thank you for coming with me, my dearest. Wish me luck."

"That and all my love, whatever happens," she whispered. Disraeli looked at her for another moment, touched his fingers to his lips and left. As soon as he had gone, Mary Anne's eyes closed and she gasped in agony, unable to hide it any longer. Her fingers had been caught in the door, when the footman had slammed it shut. Blood oozed from the edges of her fingernails. She had endured the pain in silence, showing no sign, so as not to worry him unnecessarily on this night.

The House was packed, with Members even sitting in the gangways. They had been shocked by the violence of the speech which Gladstone was just finishing at the Opposition front bench. At each phrase, he smashed his clenched fist down on the Treasury table, making the papers and pens on it jump. His speech thundered to a close.

"Never let it be said that the Commons of England passed a Bill such as this, an invitation to mob rule and the corruption of the electorate. We must reject, and utterly reject, this gigantic engine of fraud—cynically conceived for the purposes of the hour!"

He ended with a final, smashing blow that scattered pens and papers like straws and sat down, to an awed, stunned silence.

Everyone looked from him to Disraeli, who sat with his head bowed, pale and motionless. He rose slowly, as if crushed, and moved forward to the Treasury table. He leaned on it as if for support and spoke very quietly in the hushed silence, apparently a broken man.

"The Right Honorable Gentleman has spoken with much passion, much eloquence and much . . . violence." He paused. "But the damage can be repaired." Slowly and painfully, he collected up the pens and papers and, with great precision, began to lay them back in their usual orderly positions. As he glanced up, the House broke into laughter, partly in amusement and partly in admiration for the way he had pricked the bubble of Gladstone's oratory.

Up in the Visitors' Gallery, Montagu Corry hugged himself, grinning broadly. He could see Lord Derby laughing among the peers.

The laughter continued into the Carlton Club. All the leading Conservatives were there, except Robert Cecil and his friends, talking jubilantly of Disraeli's triumph.

"There never was such a smash!" Stanley exulted.

"We have done it," Derby said. "We have done it! We have dished the Whigs!"

Lennox was with a group of younger Members. "Now tell me," he asked, "why is Gladstone like a telescope?"

"Why is he?"

"Because Disraeli draws him out, sees through him and shuts him up." As they laughed, they saw heads turning. All sound cut off. Disraeli was coming in with Corry, who hung back. As Disraeli came on alone, everyone surged toward him, surrounding him, cheering, applauding.

Sir Matthew Ridley raised his glass and shouted, "Here's to the man who rode the race, who took the time and did the trick! Dizzy!!" The other members took up the cry, drinking his health, shouting his name.

In the tremendous tumult of praise and admiration, Disraeli stood impassively, nodding slightly in reply. He could remember his earliest visits to the Club with Lyndhurst. When his protector was not with him, no one would speak to him. He had stood apart, deliberately ignored. Now, he was almost mobbed by people trying to shake his hand. Manners and Edward Stanley rescued him and brought him over to Bulwer Lytton, who had become Lord Lytton. He was pouring a glass of champagne, which he handed to Disraeli, smiling. More than any of the others here, he was aware of the added irony of the triumph. "The Carlton's never seen anything like this," he said. "You are the hero of the hour—and well deserved."

Disraeli sipped the champagne gratefully and nodded. "Very welcome."

Manners, usually so reserved, was restless with excitement. It was a vindication of all his years of belief in Disraeli. "It is a night that should go on forever!" he exclaimed.

Disraeli saw Northcote smiling to him and raised his glass in answer. Philip Rose was with Northcote, grinning broadly. With Manners and Stanley, they were part of his own personal "Cabinet," those he could trust implicitly. And Corry, who with the loss of his assumed solemnity had become the perfect secretary.

"You'll stay to supper?" Stanley said.

Disraeli paused. It was hard to leave one's own triumph. "No, I'm sorry," he decided. "I must get home."

"But it's nearly m-morning!" Lytton protested. "Mary Anne will be asleep."

"This is a historic occasion," Manners insisted. "You can't disappoint all your friends and supporters."

Disraeli shook his head. "Tonight of all nights, I shall be expected at home."

All the lights in every room were on at Grosvenor Gate. Not a blind was drawn. The house shone like a beacon in the darkness of Park Lane.

In the drawing-room, a fire was blazing in the hearth. Mary Anne was sitting up, bright and expectant in her prettiest dress, freshly made up. Her right hand was bandaged, but partly covered by the lace at her wrist. Hearing the outer door open and close, she took off the shawl that was wrapped round her shoulders and dropped it behind her chair. She rose, delighted, as Corry opened the door and Dizzy came in. Corry bowed to her and left, and she hurried to Disraeli. He held her and kissed her, spinning her round a little.

She was laughing and breathless. "Monty sent me word—I knew it!" she said. "I knew you would do it! Oh, I'm so proud. . . ." She laid her head on his chest.

"Many of the Opposition voted with us," he told her. "Many abstained. I don't think—"

She drew back, stopping him. "No, dearest. You've thought and talked enough for tonight. You can tell me tomorrow. Come and sit down."

He gave in and let her lead him to the fire. On a small table beside his chair was a raised pie from Fortnum and Mason's and a bottle of champagne in an ice bucket. He pretended surprise and sat down. She arranged a napkin over his knees. A slice of pie was already cut. She laid it on his plate. As she poured him a glass of champagne, he noticed her bandaged hand and was concerned. "Mary Anne, what's happened to your hand?"

"Nothing," she assured him. "Just a little graze."

He took a corner of the pie, sipped the champagne appreciatively, then toasted her and drank off the glass.

She hovered over him, watching anxiously. In spite of her age, she was tremulously in love, like a young girl. "Delicious," he commented.

She was thrilled. As she made to pour him another glass, he took her hand gently and raised it to his lips. He kissed her fingertips. "My dear...." he murmured. "My dear, you are more like a mistress than a wife."

chapter two

Before the end of the year, a breakdown in Mary Anne's health alarmed Disraeli. She became so desperately ill that he was afraid he might lose her.

During the recess, they had gone on a tour of the north and Scotland. His public appearance in Edinburgh, where everyone expected him to be given a hostile reception, turned into another triumph. He was presented with an honorary degree by the University and the Corporation conferred on him the freedom of the City. Irrationally, many north of the Border had resented him for his habit of referring to "England," meaning the entire United Kingdom, including Scotland, Wales and Ireland. In the series of meetings at which he spoke, they began to catch the glimpse of the poetic, almost visionary, concept of the nation and the empire, which inspired him, and of which they were all an integral part. And they began to take more seriously his claim to be speaking for the truly national party.

He converted them as much by his humor as by his

arguments. An attack on him in the Whig *Edinburgh Review* and another even more bitter in the Tory *Quarterly Review,* written by Robert Cecil, had caused much comment. He disposed of them in his speech at the Conservative banquet. "Really, these *Edinburgh* and *Quarterly Reviews,* no man admires them more than myself," he said. "But I admire them as I do first-rate, first-class post-houses, which in old days—for half a century or so—to use a Manchester phrase—carried on a roaring trade. Then there comes some revolution or progress which no person can ever have contemplated. They find things have altered. They do not understand them and, instead of that intense competition and mutual vindictiveness which before distinguished them, they suddenly quite agree. The boots of the Blue Boar and the chambermaid of the Red Lion embrace, and are quite in accord in this—in denouncing the infamy of railroads." His critics were silenced with laughter.

Mary Anne stood up well to the excitements of those twelve months and the exhausting stay in Scotland, even dancing a jig with Dizzy in their hotel room after he was unexpectedly cheered by an audience of working men, who had come to boo. But after their return to London, she collapsed. She had her stomach pains again and, when her doctor diagnosed ulcers, she was put to bed on a strict diet. She was nearly seventy-six and had used up too much strength. The sight of her every day weaker and more wasted nearly overwhelmed Disraeli. Sympathy poured in from many sources. The Queen, who admired and trusted him more than ever, sent anxiously for news. Gladstone, who had never lost his regard for Mary Anne, called nearly every morning. To everyone's relief, she slowly began to recover.

Early in the new year, 1868, Disraeli was invited to spend a few days with the Queen at Osborne. It was a highly successful visit. He was impressed by the palatial, Italian-style house and its spacious grounds, and the Queen was kindness itself. She was grateful to him for conducting the Cabinet in Derby's absence and for his continued consideration to her. She was better placed than anyone to realize that the undoubted success of the Derby Ministry was due to Disraeli. She had also been angered by Gladstone who had used the Clerkenwell Outrage to make a speech offering concessions to the Irish. Many in his own party, thought it disgraceful. But, as Victoria pointed out, Gladstone had "a bee in his bonnet" about Ireland.

Before Disraeli left Osborne, the Queen's Private Secretary came to his room and told him something that he must not pass on to anyone else. It was everything Disraeli could have wished or hoped. In the event of Derby's retirement, she would accept no one but Disraeli as Prime Minister.

No reference was made to it as he said his goodbyes. She had been amused and stimulated by his company and was genuinely sorry that he had to leave. She had to admit to herself that, in his presence, she felt more alive, more sure of herself, cleverer and, somehow, more womanly. She was always very neat, but took more care with her appearance when they were to meet. She felt she could tell him anything, everything, and he would understand. The ease and lack of formality when they spoke was so refreshing. Like talking to Brown, only on a loftier plane. And she had noticed—unlike *some,* Mr. Disraeli showed no prejudice toward her Highland servant, accepting his plain, honest ways for what they were, a devotion to her as complete as his own. "I must say I am grateful to you, Mr. Disraeli," she confessed, "for explaining everything so clearly."

Disraeli bowed. "It has been not only my duty but my delight to render the transaction of affairs as easy to Your Majesty as possible. In smaller matters, I hope I may always succeed. It is in the great affairs of state that I venture to trust Your Majesty will never withhold from me the benefit of her guidance."

Victoria warmed with pleasure. She did, indeed, try very hard to be of use. From Albert she had learned the knack of cutting through to the essentials in any argument, but her shrewdness was natural to her. Since Albert died, she had not felt so appreciated by anyone. "In all things, I try to make out what opinion my beloved husband would have had—and act according to that," she said, almost shyly.

"His spirit watches over us still," Disraeli agreed. "Yet Your Majesty's Government has an even surer counsellor." Seeing her frown, he went on, "In Your Majesty's own accumulated experience. Your life has been passed in constant communion with great men, and the knowledge and management of important transactions. Even if Your Majesty were not gifted with these abilities, which all now acknowledge, this rare and choice experience must give Your Majesty an advantage in judgment which few living persons, and probably no living prince, can rival."

He had spoken so sincerely and matter of factly that Victoria could not take it as flattery. For a second, she had a vision of herself as he saw her, enthroned in wisdom and majesty. Where others made her doubt herself and her powers, he confirmed them. It was irresistibly satisfying and exciting.

When he returned to London, one of his first meetings was with Lord Derby, who had struggled out of bed against medical advice. He moved very slowly, in constant pain. "I am glad Mary Anne has recovered," he said.

"It is an indescribable relief."

"To us all, to us all. Gladstone, I hear, was sympathetic. A strange man . . . the Queen, too, told me she was most anxious."

"Her Majesty's sympathy has been a great comfort," Disraeli said. "But then, she is very attached to Mary Anne."

"And to you," Derby added, quietly. "I'd say she appreciates you more than any other Minister I can remember. You even got her to come out of her seclusion to open Parliament."

"I hoped the people's enthusiasm might induce her to lay aside her mourning. But . . ." Disraeli shrugged. The excitement had been tremendous. The country's first sight of the Queen in six years. Very valuable at a time when many had begun to criticize her in their ignorance of how much work, how many hours she spent every day on State business, reading despatches, writing, questioning, advising her Ministers. Yet she still would not take up her public life again, shutting herself away at Osborne or Windsor or Balmoral, and travelling by private train and closed carriage between them.

"Well, she wouldn't have shown herself for anyone but you," Derby said. It had been more than useful as a gesture of confidence in the Government. "How do you do it?"

Disraeli had grown a small tuft of beard under his chin. He stroked it, reflectively. "Everyone responds to flattery. With royalty, one has to lay it on with a trowel." He could see that Derby was shocked. "It is a kind of game we play," he explained. "Which does not alter the fact that I profoundly admire her."

"And she you," Derby grunted. He paused. "Which is just as well, in view of what I am going to say." Disraeli had tensed. He waited, while Derby collected his thoughts. "A year ago, when I suggested I might have to resign because of my health, you begged me to carry on. I no longer have any alternative. My doctors have told me that, if I stay in office, I have no hope of recovery."

"My dear Lord Derby—" Disraeli began anxiously.

Derby stopped him. "A year ago, I hesitated because I was afraid the party might still not accept you as Prime Minister."

"That is still far from certain," Disraeli pointed out. "They would agree to your son, Lord Stanley."

"No, it is you the party and the country need," Derby told him. "I know you have had a constant struggle against prejudice and malice throughout the thirty years you have been in Parliament. Now you have fairly and most honorably won your way to the highest rung of the political ladder."

Disraeli's mind was racing. He knew his rise had only been possible because, with Derby as unquestioned leader, the party had been prepared to accept him as second-in-command. As late as a year ago, if Derby had resigned, the party would have split and his own career would have been over. Had anything really changed? Had it changed enough, even with the Queen's backing? Faced with the final step he had always longed for, it seemed almost too high to take. "... I am entirely content with my present position," he said. "I am grateful, and honored by your confidence. But you must take time to consider, Lord Derby."

"I already have. I have informed Her Majesty that I shall retire at the end of this session."

Derby was reluctant to retire. He was only in his sixties, much younger than Russell and Palmerston had been. But he soon had no choice. He was not even present for the start of the new session. He had had a relapse and was again crippled and bed-ridden at Knowsley. He wrote to Disraeli: "Parliament sitting, and I still lying here, like a useless leg!" He knew he was unable to continue. Disraeli replied that he would do everything he could to maintain Derby's interests and influence. Derby's answer was that he had already sent in his resignation to the Queen and that it had been accepted.

Queen Victoria's Private Secretary came to Grosvenor Gate to deliver to Disraeli her summons to Osborne. He was General Grey. To Disraeli, it was another link in the chain of fate, for it was the same Charles Grey who had defeated him all those years before in his first election at High Wycombe.

The train journey down to Portsmouth was cold and the channel between the port and the Isle of Wight shrouded in dense fog. The boat provided for Disraeli made slow progress, but, by a trick of the weather, when he arrived, the skies over the island were clear. He was driven straight to Osborne and shown into the Queen's study. While he waited, many things revolved in his mind, thoughts, memories, words and faces from the past. Now that he was here, that it was happening, it scarcely seemed real. Thirty or forty years ago, it had seemed a foregone conclusion. But it had taken so long and he had endured and learned so much, since then. He was sixty-three. Sixty-three, he told himself. All that struggle and

344

effort, the scheming and flattery and backbreaking work, had it been worth it? There was only one answer he could give. He would change places at this moment with no one in the world. And no one living at this moment, not even Mary Anne, could know how it felt to be Benjamin Disraeli.

When Queen Victoria came in, she was animated and smiling. She was radiant as she held out her hand and advanced toward him, and he bowed. "You must kiss hands," she said.

He knelt stiffly on one knee before her. As he kissed her hands, he murmured, "In faith and loving loyalty."

Victoria could not remember when she had been so pleased and excited. "It must be a proud moment for you to feel that your own talent and labors in the service of your country have earned the high and influential position in which you are now placed."

He admitted his sense of the honor which had been conferred on him. "And of Your Majesty's most gracious kindness. I can only offer devotion." He noticed with amusement that she sat while she talked with him, as he was now her Chief Minister. Although his expression remained as carefully schooled as ever, he felt extraordinarily light-hearted. His own happiness was buoyed up by the Queen's, which she neither wished nor tried to hide.

Disraeli knew he had won over the Queen, yet was still uncertain how his appointment would be received by the public and by Parliament. He found out the next day when he arrived back in London. A crowd quickly gathered at the station to cheer him. Many more people waited at Westminster Hall, hoping to see him. He had fought so hard and won so fairly against all the odds, that his position at the head of his party and of the country was taken as inevitable and right, where once it had seemed unthinkable. His rise from obscurity, from derision and universal distrust, had made him a hero. Mixed with the enthusiasm was more than a hint of guilt for the past. The lobbies were packed and the cheers continuous as he walked through toward the Chamber.

Lord John Manners was among those waiting. He

stepped forward and bowed. "I accepted you as Young England's leader many years ago. As I was the first then, let me be the first now," he said with feeling.

As they shook hands, Disraeli held his tightly. The mask of his face was more set and remote than ever. Only the telltale flush at his cheekbones betrayed his emotions.

A little further on, he met James Clay, with whom he had once toured the Mediterranean and explored the Valley of the Nile. He had become a leading Radical M.P. and had helped Disraeli secretly over the Reform Bill. Clay also wanted to shake his hand, and smiled. "But who'd ever have thought, all those years ago, that one day you'd be Prime Minister!"

"Yes," Disraeli agreed quietly, "I have climbed to the top of the greasy pole."

In the Chamber, John Stuart Mill was speaking, but had to break off when Disraeli appeared and both sides of the House rose spontaneously to give the new Premier a thunderous, affectionate welcome. Slowly, Disraeli walked to the table, bowed to the Speaker and took his seat on the Government Front Bench. The members esteemed him as an outstanding parliamentarian and a great leader and the cheering continued for several minutes, wiping out the slights of many years. He looked across the table. Gladstone's seat was empty.

It was customary for the wife of the Prime Minister to give a reception. It was suggested tactfully that, in view of Mary Anne's recent illness, it need not be held. She would not be cheated of a celebration she had dreamed of, living it over and over in her imagination, actually to be present and taking a leading part, when all society honored her husband.

There was not sufficient space at Grosvenor Gate. She inspected 10 Downing Street and discovered it to be dingy and decaying. No Premier had actually lived there for decades. Lord Stanley solved the problem. The building of the Foreign Office was not finished, but the reception rooms had been completed and he lent them to her. The evening of March 26, 1868, was one of sleet and rain, with biting winds scouring the street, but the superb rooms of the Foreign Office blazed with lights. Inside, hundreds of distinguished guests from politics, the fashionable and diplomatic worlds, the Church and Court, created a pageant of splendor. Through it all moved Disraeli, escorting Princess Alexandra. Frail and haggard despite her make-up, but very proud, Mary Anne was on the arm of the Prince of Wales.

One night about a month before, William Gladstone had knelt in his study to pray for guidance. He was racked by self-doubt and feelings of envy which he knew were unworthy, yet could not suppress.

Oxford Street and Piccadilly, curling in wisps of vapor through the railings of Green Park. Although nearly sixty, he had lost none of his vigor and, with his heavy stick, did not fear the ill-lit, roughly paved backstreets where the fog was thickest, teeming with rogues, cheapjack peddlers, thieves and cheap whores. He decided to try there. He had given up the Haymarket. Most of the flashy women had disappeared inside because of the cold and rain, into the oyster shops and gin palaces, the better dressed crowding the long promenade bars of the music halls in Leicester Square. Those who were still out were miserable creatures, half-starved and desperate. Even so, not one would come home with him.

One had seemed promising. A thin, large-eyed young woman with the pallor of a consumptive, from the West Country by her accent, he had spoken to her first in Soho, then followed her at a distance as she cut through the alleys to Piccadilly Circus to try her luck in the brighter lights. Though pretty, the lights revealed how pathetic she was, in her broken shoes, bedraggled bonnet and grubby dress, and the men she smiled to hurried past with only a glance. He had lost her for a time, then came on her again, huddled in a doorway in Jermyn Street, shivering and clutching her sodden, woollen shawl round her narrow shoulders. She had brightened as he approached her, tossing her head flirtatiously but, when she recognized him, her smile faded and she pressed back into a corner of the door, turning her face away. He had spoken to her gently and soothingly and she had seemed reassured, yet, when he stepped forward to take her arm and she saw him more clearly, something about his set face and the heavy, ash stick he carried frightened her. She pushed him away and ran off, vanishing among the dark shadows.

He had persevered for another two hours before giving up and returning home to confess failure. Mrs. Gladstone was disappointed. It was the second night running that he had not found a girl to bring back. She kissed him and went to bed.

Passing the end of Burlington Arcade that evening, he had seen busts of Disraeli in the window of the shop nearest the Piccadilly entrance. The lined, sardonic face and heavy-lidded eyes of that magician haunted him. He could never forget how he had blandly accepted every amendment, every check and safeguard suggested to make his Reform Bill acceptable to his party and the House, then, when he had lulled them into security, had sheared the amendments all away and passed a Bill far more radical than any ever contemplated. Household suffrage! It was an irresistible rallying cry and Gladstone's own attempt to sabotage it had nearly lost him the trust of his own party. It was only the disarray of the Liberals that kept that cunning devil in office. To think of him, sitting at the table in the Cabinet Room of 10 Downing Street, in the center chair once occupied by Melbourne and Peel and Wellington and Canning, was almost unbearable. Even more unbearable was the thought that the Jew had been first in the race between them, wearing the olive crown that should by any right of natural justice ... It was an unworthy thought, and Gladstone asked forgiveness for it. Disraeli must be brought down, but not part of a personal vendetta, rather as an example of the inevitable fall of the ungodly when challenged manfully by the spirit of revealed Truth. As his mind turned and turned, Gladstone remembered the reaction to his speeches after the Clerkenwell outrage. Ireland—there was an emotional issue to which his party *and* the new voters might respond. To settle the ills of Ireland would appeal to the right-minded, the liberal masses and the taxpayers. Gladstone suddenly realized that the Almighty had spoken to him. As clear as a trumpet call. He would lead an Irish Crusade.

Disraeli was too experienced not to know that his tenure of 10 Downing Street might be one of the shortest on record. Yet even he was surprised when Gladstone rallied his party so swiftly with his proposal to disestablish the Protestant Church of Ireland and to reform the Irish educational and land systems. Disraeli had been discussing with Cardinal Manning a plan to build a Catholic University in Ireland and steps that could lead to Catholics receiving a share of the church endowment. It could mean an end to centuries of religious hatred and mistrust. Naturally, in view of the Liberal proposal, Manning broke off the discussions. Why share, when his Church could at last take control? It was useless to point out that Gladstone had never been to Ireland and had no special knowledge of conditions there, nor that he had often declared it his sacred duty to preserve the Protestant Irish Church. The man was a spellbinding orator when roused and blinded his listeners to the opportunism that sometimes lay behind the cause he preached. Gladstone's Resolution was passed by sixty-five votes in the Commons and, within a month of coming to office, Disraeli was faced with a demand for his Government's resignation. Obviously, he could not carry on with such a minority in the House and so he had to inform the Queen. She was horrified at the possibility of losing him so soon, but he saw a way out. The new electoral registers would not be ready until later in the year, when there would be a General Election. To Gladstone's fury, he announced that he would continue as Her Majesty's Chief Minister until then.

It was March. He would have approximately eight months of power. Not long, but enough, provided he avoided an outright confrontation between the parties, to make some mark on the country, to make improvements in education, the law system and the condition of lower paid workers, as he had always promised, and he began to bridge the gap that opened between Britain and America during the Civil War.

The months passed all too quickly. Some of his colleagues, Lord Stanley in particular, were despondent, but Disraeli put his faith in the new electors. His party must have won their undying gratitude. He was fairly confident when he spent some weeks at Balmoral in the autumn as Minister in attendance and Queen Victoria felt happier than she had done all summer.

She loved Balmoral more than any of her other homes. The castle had been designed and built for her by Albert as the perfect retreat, and she dearly wished Disraeli to like it as much as she did. For their walks to see her favorite views, accompanied by John Brown, he dressed in the clothes he normally wore in the country and the added touch of informality delighted her. In return, he praised the dignified simplicity of the Scottish baronial castle in its wooded setting and the scenery which he was sure could not be surpassed, not even in Switzerland. Every day, they spent an hour or two in serious talk and the rest of the time chatted and gossiped like old friends. She was able to spot possible problems in any situation with uncanny accuracy, although she was often guided by her emotions. He found her remarkably sensible and confided his thoughts to her almost completely. In her isolation it was like water in the desert. Never before had she felt that she had been told everything. That year appeared a small book of reminiscences she had written, *Leaves from the Journal of our Life in the Highlands,* a copy of which she had sent to him, rather nervous of his reaction. But he had been charmed by its freshness and simplicity. After a strong hint she had dropped, he had sent her the collected edition of his novels. Thereafter, he sometimes discussed literary subjects with her, beginning with a slight bow and the words, "We authors, Ma'am," which thrilled as much as it amused her. She could still surprise him. One day on a picnic, he looked round to see the Queen and her daughters, Princess Beatrice and Princess Helena, unconcernedly puffing cigarettes, as they explained, to keep away the midges.

Several days after he returned to London, as he sat in his study in 10 Downing Street one afternoon, he found his mind wandering. It was a time of suspended animation. The General Election was only six weeks away and he was glad to be back. Running the country six hundred miles from Westminster had doubled the difficulties. And Mary Anne's health was causing alarm again. She had recovered from her collapse, but it had left her permanently weak, although she insisted on carrying out all their social engagements. Fellow guests were sometimes startled by her appearance, for she often wore dresses from an earlier age, combining features of several in total eccentricity. Over a bell-shaped gown of the 1830s, she might wear a frogged hunting jacket and a Georgian lace cap. Often she arrived for dinner wearing a crimson velvet tunic with a miniature of Dizzy pinned like a medal on her left breast, the whole topped off by a silk turban with an enormous feather. Her chatter was as amusing as ever and her sympathetic interest in everything and everybody never flagged. People adored her and were touched by the way she caressed Disraeli's face and hair as they talked and thought first of him in everything. For the first time, he kept some of his worries from her, to make her life as peaceful as possible. If only they could escape for a while to Hughenden and she could rest.

He was really unable to concentrate and wanted nothing more than to be at home with her, sitting quietly by the fire. He looked up to see Montagu Corry watching him from his smaller desk nearer the door. Dear Monty . . . he had never known a truer friend, nor more loyal helper.

Corry was sorting through the pile of general correspondence. "There's a letter from a clergyman in Slough, Sir," he said. "He demands to know why you have not moved into 10 Downing Street, now you are Prime Minister."

"Because it is drafty, uncomfortable and too expen-

351

sive to decorate for the few months I may have the right to live in it!" Disraeli answered tetchily, then paused. "No, don't tell him that. Tell him Mrs. Disraeli and I are too attached to Grosvenor Gate to consider moving."

"Yes, sir," Corry smiled.

Disraeli grimaced. "Really! Why does one have to— They never seem to think that my mind may be on the cost of the war in Abyssinia or the cotton famine in the north, or how to squeeze unpopular Bills through Parliament while leading a minority Government."

Corry shook his head sympathetically. He watched as Disraeli looked at the papers in front of him, dropped them back in to the despatch box and locked it.

Disraeli rose. "I can't do any more today. I've been at these since six o'clock this morning." He moved to the door. "I shall be at home. Don't bother me with the routine work. Attend to all of it, yourself." He opened the door and stepped out, then looked back. "But, of course, if there is any really important decision to be made . . . make it." He closed the door.

Mary Anne had to go to Hughenden without him. Her doctors would not let her delay her return to the quiet of Hughenden any longer. He was in the middle of the election and could not accompany her.

Due to his age, Lord John Russell had resigned, leaving Gladstone undisputed leader of the Liberals, and the election became a straight fight between him and Disraeli. Because of the difficulty of organizing balloting, and collection and counting of votes over wide areas, it was spread over two to three weeks, and the strain of waiting for the final results to come in was considerable. Indications were that the Conservatives were picking up seats in the southern counties, although not doing nearly so well in the north, Wales and Scotland. These were the regions where Gladstone had concentrated his forces and begun to preach his own fiery crusade. He had presented his call for justice and liberty in Ireland with messianic fervor and the newly emancipated voters responded with enthusiasm. At the same time, he banged the party drum, claiming that Disraeli had only brought in Reform because he had forced him to do so.

Toward the end of the second week, the inner core of Disraeli's cabinet met after dinner at Grosvenor Gate. It was not an official meeting. One by one his closest colleagues had drifted in, as if needing the reassurance of one another's company. For a day or two, they had been elated, when a telegram from Lord Derby announced that Gladstone had been defeated in his own constituency in South-West Lancashire. He had already covered himself, however, and had also been nominated for Greenwich, which he won easily.

Disraeli sat at the desk in his study. He was deathly tired and already knew that not even a miracle could save his party from defeat. At least, in one respect, it had been a clean fight. His Bill to put an end to bribery and intimidation at elections had seen to that. Never again would the man with the deepest pocket be bound to win. Never again would unscrupulous candidates and their local sponsors be able to turn ballot day into a drunken carnival of feasting and marching bands and hogsheads of ale broached in the streets, with paid voters reeling into the polling booths and gangs of hired bullies armed with clubs terrorizing their opponents.

None of his worries showed, as he tried to hearten his companions. Stafford Northcote was reading out a report by an eminent statistician from Manchester, which gave the Liberals a handsome majority, if trends continued. "That may be so," Disraeli murmured. "I, myself, used to be most impressed by statisticians, until I attended the Statistical Congress some years ago."

"Used to be?" Manners queried.

Disraeli nodded. "It was held at Cambridge House by Lady Palmerston. We were all prepared to be awed by their deliberations. I found myself in a strange gathering of men with bald heads, and all wearing spectacles. You associate these traits often with learning and profundity, but when one sees a hundred bald heads and a hundred pairs of spectacles the illusion is impaired."

As the others laughed, Corry came in to join them. He

glanced round, seeing how the atmosphere had lightened. In those past weeks, he had come to admire Disraeli even more. He had taught them all how to lose with grace.

"No further news from the Doctors?" Disraeli asked.

"Not since this afternoon, Sir," Corry said. "Mrs. Disraeli is resting."

"No more word from the Midlands?"

"No, Sir. Only that the early returns suggest things are not going well for us."

Edward Stanley had been trying to copy Disraeli's example of detachment, but could not keep it up. "Hang it, it's so unfair!" he exclaimed. "In the eight months you've been Prime Minister, you've done more positive good than the Liberals in eight years!"

"The electorate is fickle," Disraeli said with a shrug. "The first thing a politician must learn not to rely on is gratitude. If I said to them—in that time, I have federated the North American colonies into one Dominion, Canada, restored justice in Abyssinia, ended bribery at election, improved the school system and the Post Office, brought in sanitary laws and put a stop to public executions, they would say, Yes, but what have you done today?"

At the end of the following week, he travelled to Windsor to inform the Queen of his resignation.

It was an unhappy meeting for them both. Try as she might not to be partisan, Victoria had been in despair at the final results. As she told her eldest son, the Prince of Wales, "I think it a defect in our much famed constitution to have to lose an admirable government such as Mr. Disraeli's for no great matter of principle—merely on account of the number of votes!" She could not understand why he smiled. Not since dear Lord M had said his goodbye had she felt so reluctant to part with a Minister.

Disraeli waited patiently, while she composed herself. He saw how her small hands gripped the carved lions' heads at the ends of the arms of her chair. Her face was turned toward the window, her head lifted, her mouth pursed with disappointment, as he realized, with real sorrow. "I had looked forward to a long and increasingly fruitful association," she said at last.

"The Liberal majority in the House of Commons has been nearly doubled, Ma'am," he told her quietly. "There is no possibility of my continuing."

She sighed. "Then I must accept your resignation although with much regret." She glanced at him as he bowed. She frowned. "I suppose I shall have to send for Mr. Gladstone."

"He is the undoubted leader of his party now, Your Majesty. A man of . . . singular talents."

Victoria's lower lip turned down. The violence of some of Gladstone's speeches that she had read had shocked her. At least, up till now, he had been restrained by Palmerston or Russell. To think of him at the head of *her* Government, preaching at her, with his interminable explanations which only grew more and more confusing, and his even more unintelligible memoranda. A pedantic demagogue. And now he had been taken up by the lower half of society as a kind of savior . . . What was it they called him? "The People's William," she muttered, distastefully.

She was so little able to hide her feelings that Disraeli had been able to follow her line of thought by her expression. He did not feel it correct for him to comment. He coughed. "May I confess, Ma'am, that due to Mrs. Disraeli's continuing ill-health and the strain under which I, myself, have been for the past few years, I shall not be so reluctant as I might have been to lay down the burden."

All other thoughts were driven out of Victoria's head by her sudden alarm. "You would not think of retiring?" she protested.

Again Disraeli was gratified. "Merely for a period of rest, Ma'am," he assured her.

Victoria relaxed. "I am relieved to hear it." She considered him. Yes, he definitely looked older. Not exactly stooped, yet not so erect and vital as he had been. If only the country could know how tirelessly he had labored and how much better he deserved of them all. It was in her power, to show her own gratitude. "I have been concerned, myself, Mr. Disraeli, about your health," she said, "the strain, as you say, of conducting daily business in the House of Commons. The simplest answer would be for you to lead your party, as others have done, from the Lords—and for that purpose, and in recognition of your services, I would like to offer you a peerage."

He had realized at once what she was going to say. In fact, it had already occurred to him that the offer might be made. Others had been ennobled whose services to the country had been much less than his. It was a great thing, another dream of his youth come true. He bowed deeply. He already knew what he must answer. "I am deeply sensible of the notice Your Majesty has taken of my efforts," he said, "and the favor which Your Majesty is prepared to bestow. Regretfully, I feel, for the sake of my party and the better to serve Your Majesty, that I must decline."

He was so clearly decided that Victoria did not argue. The answer was a credit to him and she should have expected it. He could not desert his followers in the Commons in their hour of need. She nodded. "If that is your wish."

He could tell that his reply had pleased her. To keep faith with himself and his party, he could have made no other choice. He paused, before saying, "There is, however, someone to whom I might humbly request Your Majesty to grant an honor."

Mary Anne lay on the sofa in the drawing-room at Hughenden. She was shrunken, having lost so much weight that she looked almost like a waxen doll dressed in clothes far too large for it. Her eyes were shut and her hands lay on the silken quilt that covered her, withered and motionless, yet she had touched up her hollow cheeks with rouge and she wore her newest dress to welcome Dizzy home. Her eyes opened as the door clicked and saw him looking at her. He came to her quickly. "Dizzy . . . forgive me. I was lying listening for your carriage. I must have dozed off." She smiled apologetically. He had met Corry outside, who told him how she had defied everyone and refused to stay in bed. He kissed her and sat on the edge of the sofa. Her voice was weak. "Did the Queen accept your resignation?"

"With regret—I was happy to see," he told her. "She was most complimentary."

Mary Anne pushed herself up to lie with her shoulders against the cushioned arm. "What did she say?" she asked eagerly. "Tell me everything that was said."

"Oh, many things. She thanked me for my services, and my consideration toward her. And she asked after you. But most important, she offered me an earldom."

Mary Anne caught her breath. It was what she had most wanted for him. In becoming Prime Minister, he had reached the height of his ambition, higher even than she had even dared hope for him. This would put the perfect seal on his career.

"I told her that, if I had been able to accept," he went on, "I would have chosen the name of Beaconsfield from our neighboring town."

She was puzzled. *"If you had been able?"*

"I had to refuse," he explained. "Many people say it is my fault we lost this election. Now Gladstone is returned with an overwhelming majority, he will be twice as dangerous. I loathe the thought of spending the rest of my days in hopeless Opposition, but I cannot leave it to others. I must be there to do battle with him in the Commons."

Mary Anne's excitement faded, but she understood. "Yes, of course." She stroked his hand. "But I'm so disappointed for you, my darling."

He caught her hand, raised it gently and kissed it. "Oh, I am far from disappointed," he reassured her, smiling. "You see, the Queen has been graciously pleased to transfer the honor to my most trusted and constant helper, whose courage has always been my spur and whose love my inspiration." She gazed at him as he rose and stood looking down at her. "The greatest privilege I have ever been given," he said, "is to tell you that you are now, my dearest, in your own right, Viscountess Beaconsfield."

Proud and moved, too overcome to speak, Mary Anne still gazed at him as he bowed to her.

chapter three

William Gladstone was at last Prime Minister and, by
the grace of the Almighty, in a much stronger position
than his rival had ever been. The British people had risen
at his call and removed the ungodly from the seats of
power. He had no need to conciliate nor maneuver. Even
the Queen could do no more than register her dismay at
the sweeping nature of his proposals and decline, on
grounds of poor health, to attend the official opening of
Parliament. Within six months, in the teeth of bitter
protests, he brought in a Bill to disestablish and disendow
the Irish Church, and prepared to follow it by another to
legalize the rights of Ireland's tenant farmers and their
landlords.

Disraeli was once again in his customary place to the
left of the Speaker, on the Opposition front bench. There
was little he could do except to warn against the probable
consequences of the Irish Bills and suggest amendments
to improve their chances of success. Since the fall of Peel,
the balance of the parties had been so delicate that he

had had to be in his seat every day, ready to take advantage of any split in the combined ranks of old-fashioned Whigs, Liberals and Radicals that faced him. Now there was no hope of toppling the large, Liberal majority and he could relax at last. When his followers urged him to attack, he told them that he saw no point in leading a frontal assault on an impregnable position. It was far better to give Gladstone as much rope as he wanted, and trust that he would hang himself.

He spent longer and longer periods quietly at Hughenden with Mary Anne. Incredibly, she seemed to be recovering. He was with her constantly and she gained strength from his presence and loving care. Although seldom without pain, she was soon well enough to drive her pony cart and accompany him in walks through their woods, up the hill behind the house to the wild area of woodland he had planted, which he called his German forest.

Leisure was such a novelty to him that at first he was content to do absolutely nothing except walk a little, sit with Mary Anne, pretending to read while she dozed, and attend church on Sundays. In the evenings, when she had gone early to bed, he sat in his library, rediscovering his earliest friends, his books. As he sat alone, thinking, owls would come and tap at the lighted windows with their beaks. Keeping him company, he fancied. Gradually, an idea began to revolve in his mind, becoming more and more appealing, until he could resist it no longer and reached for his pen.

A year after his election defeat, the whole country was startled by the announcement that shortly there would appear a new novel, *Lothair,* by Benjamin Disraeli. It was not only the general public and his oppenents who were surprised. He had written the book in complete secrecy, without telling anyone, not even Montagu Corry, only Mary Anne. The sensation it produced was immense. It was his first book in over twenty years. The first novel by a former Prime Minister. Those who expected his style to have changed were astonished. It was not serious or solemn, but light, amusing and satirical, the story of a noble young man who is disillusioned by society and his own wealth, flirts dangerously with Roman Catholicism, secret societies in Italy and the international revolution, and finds love and happiness at the end with a pure woman. Again, it covered recent events and many of the characters were drawn from life, and everyone guessed and wondered on whom they were based. His enemies gleefully predicted that it was the ruin of his career as a serious politician. The critics found it lightweight and flippant. Many in his own party were scandalized and his friends wished he had never written it, but demand for it was so enormous that five editions were printed before publication. Everyone read it and discussed it. Songs, waltzes, horses, ships and streets were named after Lothair and the heroine, Corisande. Edition after edition came from the press, in spite of the scathing reviews, because the public adored it. It was translated into every European language and demand abroad was as great as in the United Kingdom. In America it was even greater. The first 25,000 copies were sold out in three days. In six months, 80,000 were sold. Sales in England continued at a thousand copies a day. It was the most widely read book of the century and enabled Disraeli, for the first time in his life, to put money in the bank.

He had taken a considerable political risk in publishing it, as his leadership was again under pressure. He was more vulnerable than ever, for Lord Derby had died. They had become close friends and colleagues and, while Derby lived, his prestige had protected Disraeli from criticism within the party. Shortly before, another old friend, Lord Salisbury, had also died and his son, Robert Cecil, succeeded to the title. When a group of Conservative peers asked him to take the position of leader in the House of Lords, he made a well-publicized show of refusing because he would not be acceptable to Disraeli. Disraeli pointed out that the new Lord Salisbury was not even eligible, as he had resigned from the party. However, that Robert Cecil had even been approached was a warning of serious dissatisfaction in the Lords. For the time being, any damage he might do could be countered by

Edward Stanley who had also gone to the Upper House, succeeding his father as 15th Earl of Derby.

A select number of guests were invited to Hughenden for a weekend in early summer. The first to arrive were Lord John Manners and his younger, very pretty wife, Janetta. Shortly after, Lady Chesterfield's carriage rattled up to the portico of the north entrance. Like them she was surprised to be greeted by Mary Anne, and relieved to see her looking so much better.

By late morning all the guests had arrived. Chief among them was a neighbor, Lionel de Rothschild. His younger brothers had both bought estates in Buckinghamshire near Aylesbury, Anthony at Aston Clinton and Mayer at Mentmore.

Lunch lasted until well after three. A walk to the lake, where descendants of Hero and Leander still nested, had been proposed, but a light shower kept everyone indoors. They all gathered in the drawing-room.

"There is only one topic of conversation in town at the moment," Lady Chesterfield said. "Everyone is Lothair mad."

Corry was standing slightly behind her. "The bookshops are still besieged," he said.

Disraeli shrugged. "Well, I expect people are curious."

"You're being too modest, Dizzy," Charlotte objected.

"Yes, I must admit I am," he agreed amidst laughter.

"The critics weren't too kind to it, though, were they?" Rothschild commented.

"Critics—who are they?" Disreali inquired, blandly. "Only men who have failed in literature and art." As the others laughed, he turned to Mary Anne, and saw her pressing her hand to her stomach, unable to conceal her distress.

"I'm perfectly all right," she whispered, but she was nearly fainting with pain. She looked round, seeing the concern of others, who had noticed this time. She managed to smile. "Please . . . It is only a little twinge I get, when I do not keep to my diet." She hesitated. "If you will excuse me . . ." She tried to rise, but could **not.**

Disraeli stood, helping her to her feet. She patted his arm. "I'll be—I'll be all right, if I lie down for a minute."

"I'll see you to your room, my dear," he told her.

"No, no," she protested, and smiled to the others. "He will fuss ... We mustn't both leave our guests. Monty will come with me."

Corry had stepped forward. He helped Disraeli lead Mary Anne to the door, then took over when she insisted that the guests must not be left alone.

Disraeli watched as Corry supported her, helping her slowly up the stairs. He could not return to the drawing-room without a few minutes to compose himself. He turned and went out on to the terrace.

The shower had stopped, though the sky was still threateningly gray, with dark rainclouds further down the valley. He crossed the terrace and stood looking down over the lawn toward the lower grass terrace, but he saw nothing. The mask he wore in public slipped and his eyes were haunted with despair. Hearing footsteps on the gravel behind him, he blinked and turned. He was angry at the intrusion, but held himself in check when he saw it was Lady Chesterfield.

She came to him, pausing as she saw the anxiety he could not hide. "I hope you will forgive me," she said.

"No need." He shook his head.

"Why did you not warn us?" she asked gently. "Mary Anne is clearly much sicker than any of us realized." He nodded, needing all his self-control not to break down. "What is it?"

He did not answer for some time, then began, "I need not ask you to repeat ..." He looked away, back toward the garden. "Monty and I know. Only us. We have known for nearly five years."

"Known what?"

"That Mary Anne ... is suffering from cancer of the stomach."

Lady Chesterfield was shocked. She took a step nearer to him. "Oh my poor ... can her doctors not do something?"

"I have begged them—but it is incurable," he told her

363

quietly. "She thinks . . . that I do not know. And to save worrying me, has always tried to pretend that her illness is slight and temporary."

Lady Chesterfield nearly wept for them both. All those years, with no one suspecting . . . "But Dis—she must be in agony."

"At times."

". . . and she still tries to keep it from you?"

His head moved slightly. "It is kindest to let her think she is deceiving me."

"Yes," Lady Chesterfield agreed, then added compassionately, "I know how you must feel."

"No one can," he said simply. "To see her wasting away day by day, in constant pain, is almost more than I can bear."

The other guests were pleased to see Lady Chesterfield and him come back in. She showed nothing of what he had told her and he, himself, was again perfectly controlled, inscrutable. They stopped by Manners, Northcote and Rose.

"I hear that Mary Anne has had to lie down," Manners said, concerned.

"A forlorn attempt to introduce the siesta to Buckinghamshire," Disraeli murmured and they laughed. As Lady Chesterfield smiled and moved on, he saw a look pass between Manners and Northcote. "Have they been badgering you, Philip?" he asked, faintly mocking.

Rose smiled. "Probing, more or less delicately, I would say."

"Ah . . ." Disraeli shook his head. "They should know better than to attempt to worm secrets out of a lawyer—especially mine."

Northcote drew himself up. "I assure you—"

"No need, Northcote," Disraeli interrupted. "I can guess your complaints exactly. But I have not been writing another book. Philip and I have been discussing a plan—for the total reorganization of the Party." Northcote and Manners were alert at once. "The formation of a central office to define policy and to consult and advise local constituencies."

"In short," Rose said, "the creation of a party machine."

"There is a desperate need for it," Manners put in, excitedly. "But it would take years!"

At a nod from Disraeli, Rose explained, "We have already set it up in outline. Local party associations are to be encouraged and, where necessary, developed. Their members to be drawn from all classes of society. Wherever possible, they will choose local candidates, with knowledge of their special needs and problems. The central office will co-ordinate, distribute information and also select and train promising candidates, who can be sent to fight elections wherever the local associations have found no one suitable."

"All that remains is to work out the details," Disraeli said. "For that, we shall engage some younger, legal minds. Our party is weak because we are unorganized. There must be a strong, central directing force."

It was an astonishingly simple, but revolutionary concept. Northcote saw the advantages at once, yet hesitated before welcoming it. It would require the constant inspiration and support of the party leader. "It cannot be run from here," he objected.

"Which is why I am returning to London tomorrow," Disraeli said blandly. He smiled very faintly as they reacted. "After all, we must not let William Gladstone have it all his own way in the House of Commons."

"He gains in authority every day," Manners complained. "No one dares to stand against him."

"I half thought I might try," Disraeli murmured.

The inevitable and immediate result of the Government's policies had been to increase religious rivalry and hatred in Ireland. To Gladstone's dismay, instead of dying out, violence there had flared up to an unprecedented level, with riots, intimidation and murders almost a daily occurence. The announcement of his Land Act, which should have completed the pacification, only made the situation worse. Up to now, a type of feudal system had existed, where the landlord would often not press his tenants for

365

rent in bad years and, if a tenant gave up his holding, he would be paid for any improvements he had made to the land and farm buildings. Legalizing the rights of tenants and landlords destroyed the unwritten balance. In any of the lean years of near famine, instead of being assisted by his landlord, a tenant could be evicted from his holding for nonpayment of rent, without compensation. It caused fear and hardship. At the same time, seeing the compulsory purchase of church lands and property, many people thought the Act meant that land would also be taken from Protestant farmers and given away free. The new Act was meant to give tenants protection against excessive rents and security in their holdings. It proved completely ineffective.

Gladstone's attitude to the rise in violence had been to deplore it and pray that it would stop. He would never accept the view that one cannot reason with fanatics. One day, he was convinced, the people of Ireland would awake to the rightness of his policy. Then, in an election for Tipperary, the Government candidate was beaten by a convicted Fenian and a wave of crime and outrages followed. The Government sent troops to suppress it. It was the moment Disraeli had waited for.

As Prime Minister, Gladstone had grown in personality and presence. No longer handsome, his hair gray and receded, his face deeply lined above his high, old-fashioned collar, his look dominated the House of Commons. When one of the Opposition argued against him, he would chime in with an ironic "Hear, Hear!" at the end of each phrase, interrupt with requests for figures or quotations to be verified, make copious notes for his reply, sending for blue books and reference books continually, so that his opponent frequently lost his line of thought. Often, the piercing glare of Gladstone's eyes was enough to reduce an opponent to flustered silence.

He had become indifferent to Disraeli's presence or absence. His old rival spoke so mildly and reasonably nowadays, when he spoke at all. He had revealed his essential shallowness by writing his catch-penny novel, which Gladstone had attempted to read but had thrown away as flippant trash. Obviously, the Jew had one real talent. He knew when he was beaten. So, it was with some surprise that he saw that Disraeli had risen in his place across the Treasury table and was beginning to discuss the Irish question.

The Members on both sides, who always enjoyed hearing Dizzy, listened with interest. They did not expect sparks. So helplessly outnumbered, Disraeli had shown no wish for a fight. But they were soon on the edge of their seats, as Disraeli's review of the causes of the disorders in Ireland developed into a scathing criticism of the Government's policies, and their lack of firmness in dealing with the wave of crime and sedition until now. "So the Irish people thought: is it not a natural consequence that if you settle the question of the Irish Church by depriving the bishops of their property, you will settle the question of the land by depriving the landlords of *their* property?"

Hearing that calm, ironic voice again, Gladstone had a nightmare memory of times he had heard it in the past and of the effect it created. Those who watched him saw that his face had completely drained of color as he stared across at Disraeli. After months of despondency, those in the benches behind Disraeli began to take heart. They wanted him to make them laugh and cheer again, but his speech was deadly serious, despite the irony, as he finished.

"Horrible scenes of violence had been occurring in Ireland, but the Government would never move. Landlords were shot down, farmers beaten to death by masked men, bailiffs shot in the back, policemen stabbed. Households were blown up, and firearms surreptitiously obtained. All this time the Government would not move; but the moment the Government candidate was defeated at the hustings—a Government candidate pledged to confiscation—the moment that occurred there was panic in the Castle, there was confusion in the Council. The wires of Aldershot were agitated, troops sent across from Liverpool to Dublin, and concentrated in Waterford, Tipperary and Cork . . ." He paused. "I remember one of Her

Majesty's Ministers saying, I think last year, 'Anyone can govern Ireland with troops and artillery.' So it seems ... even that right honorable gentleman." His tone was contemptuous.

When he sat down, looking impassively back at Gladstone, there was loud, sustained Conservative applause. On the benches opposite, the Members were tense and silent, watching Gladstone and waiting for his reaction. The Prime Minister forced himself to appear indifferent to the reaction. He glanced along his front bench, but none of his Cabinet would rise to answer. He, himself, needed time. Like everyone else, he knew that Disraeli had just made a declaration of war.

Any hopes his party may have had that Disraeli was about to lead them in a swift, victorious campaign were disappointed. He had given notice that he was prepared and still able to attack when necessary, and that was all. His policy was unchanged, to wait and see. In any case, he was not fit enough to lead a long and bitter campaign in his former style. Just as he had begun to feel rested after a few months of less strenuous work, he had been struck down by an attack of bronchitis, which left one of his lungs badly affected. All winter he had struggled on with clogged and labored breathing, waiting for the summer weather to be cured. He had now learned that his lungs were permanently damaged. The effort of long speeches exhausted him and there were days when he could only sit silent, letting others speak for him. With Edward Stanley gone to the Upper House as Lord Derby and Stafford Northcote in Canada, as Chairman of the Hudson Bay Company, to negotiate in the disputes between the Canadian Government and the company, Disraeli had to depend more and more on younger Members whose careers he had helped along, particularly Gathorne Hardy. Hardy was a boyishly handsome man, with short, curly brown hair and extravagant whiskers, whose puckish smile hid an incisive and highly capable mind. Suspicious of Disraeli at the start, he had slowly come to appreciate and understand him, responding to his progressive ideas, and with understanding had come trust and willing cooperation. He had been Disraeli's most able lieutenant in the Reform Bill debates and now became his "sword-arm" in the Commons.

Meanwhile, abroad, Bismarck had completed his masterplan by goading France into war. Europe braced itself for a prolonged and bloody conflict between the two great military powers, but the Prussian army, the most powerful in the German Confederation, rigidly disciplined and equipped with modern weapons, smashed through the ill-prepared French. French forces under Marshal Macmahon resisted with desperate gallantry, but in seven weeks it was virtually over, following the Prussian victory at Sedan, when Napoleon the Third was captured. The terrible siege of Paris lasted for another four months, until acute starvation forced surrender. Napoleon was deposed and France became a Republic. In January, 1871, in the Hall of Mirrors at Versailles, Bismarck proclaimed the King of Prussia first Kaiser of a united German Reich, with himself as Imperial Chancellor.

Gladstone, who wanted to prevent the war or at least to keep it short, discovered that by cutting back on armaments and reducing the army and navy to dangerously low levels he had made England so weak that other nations could not be made to listen to him. Bismarck, calling him "Professor Gladstein," laughed at his appeals for peace and moderation. Disraeli saw that the war was an even more important event than the French Revolution, with consequences that lay far in the future, and warned that none of the principles that once guided foreign affairs any longer existed. The balance of power had been entirely destroyed and the country most in danger was England. When he criticized the Government for its lack of readiness to meet the crisis and deliberate reduction of Britain's strength, Gladstone's reply was self-righteous and unconvincing. Almost immediately, the Government blundered again. The Russians, realizing that England was powerless and that Germany and France would not interfere, repudiated the treaty which they had been forced to sign at the close of the Crimean War, by which the Black Sea had been declared neutral territory. The Foreign Secreatry threatened war if Russian naval ships entered the Black Sea, but Gladstone did not back him up and asked, instead, for a Conference to decide on a compromise solution. To Disraeli, it was obvious that the Tsar had never given up his ambition to take Constantinople.

In the midst of this, Gladstone's Irish policy was proving a disaster. In some counties, there was almost a state of anarchy and he arranged for a secret Committee to examine the problems.

It was the opening for which Disraeli had been waiting. He had been prodding and pricking Gladstone all along, though restraining himself while the Prime Minister's prestige and popularity were still high. Now the signs were that people's eyes were opening. Even among Gladstone's followers, many had begun to resent his arrogance in debate and inability to accept any contrary opinions. They had only been bearable, until he had been proved not to be infallible. For the first time, Disraeli turned the full force of his irony on his rival and had the satisfaction of hearing the House respond. Gladstone experienced humiliation and fury by turns as the speech went on, sitting pale and tight-lipped while the House of Commons laughed as his most cherished beliefs and earnest proposals were ridiculed. He winced when Disraeli, standing facing him, elbows tucked into his sides, gestured negligently toward him.

"The right honorable gentleman persuaded the people of England that with regard to Irish politics he was in possession of the philosopher's stone," Disraeli drawled amidst laughter and appaluse. "Well, Sir, he has been returned with an immense majority, with the object of securing the tranquillity and content of Ireland. Has anything been grudged him? Time, labor, devotion—whatever has been demanded has been accorded, whatever he has proposed has been carried." He paused and drew his handkerchief from the rear pocket of his frockcoat, passing it to his other hand. "Under his influence and at his instance we have legalized confiscation, condoned high treason. We have destroyed churches, we have shaken property to its foundation, and we have emptied jails. And now he cannot govern a country without coming to a Parliamentary Committee!" He stopped the swell of laughter with a slight motion of the handkerchief. "The right honorable gentleman, after all his heroic exploits, and at the head of his great majority, is making government ridiculous." He dabbed his mouth, replacing his handkerchief in his pocket and sat, to a roar of applause and cheering.

The effect of his speech was even more dramatic than he had expected. While he rested in his study in the Commons, Gathorne Hardy came hurrying to warn him there was to be a vote. In the present temper of the House, roused by his words, it was more than likely that the Government would be defeated. Considering the state of the parties, Disraeli had no wish to force the Vote of Confidence which would have followed. Hardy and he rounded up about fifty Conservative Members on whom they could depend and left the House to prevent a catastrophe. The time was not yet right for a confrontation.

There was widespread antagonism to the Queen.

Sympathy with her over her bereavement had turned to impatience and, as the years went on, to exasperation. It was nearly twenty years since Albert's death and her isolation had become more impenetrable, her refusal to appear in public more determined. The vast amount of work she accomplished and her dedication to duty had no effect on mass opinion because they were unreported and unknown. What mattered was that she seemed to consider the wishes of her people of less importance than her private grief. The outward show of monarchy, the great ceremonials, the investitures, the pageantry and processions had ceased. At times of national rejoicing or sorrow or pride, the people needed the physical presence of the sovereign as a focus for their emotions and that was what she denied them. She had become the remote and selfish

371

figure of a woman in black who demanded the obedience and homage of more than half the world, yet gave nothing in return, the Widow of Windsor.

Discontent changed from grumbling to demands for action. It was not only radicals who began to question the state payments for the upkeep of her palaces and household, and the sums voted annually by Parliament for herself and the many members of her family. Republican Clubs were founded in many cities and the movement grew in strength and vehemence. What use is she? they demanded. Placards were hung on the railings of the largely disused Buckingham Palace, "Desirable Premises To Let—Owner About To Retire," and scurrilous stories were told of her relationship with her blunt, Highland servant, John Brown. It was whispered that he had deluded her into believing he was a medium, in touch with the departed spirit of Albert. How else could the son of a mere Scottish crofter, a man of no polish and education, become so close to her? She would go nowhere without him. Unless she were mad and he was her keeper. Of course, he was sturdy and handsome. Perhaps they were secretly married? And they ridiculed her as "Mrs. Brown."

For a while, the discontent had been kept down by the popularity of the Prince of Wales, known familiarly as Bertie, and his Princess, the lovely, gentle-natured Alexandra. They were seen everywhere, at parties, theaters, concerts and race tracks. Their home at Marlborough House off Pall Mall took the place of the vanished Court. The Prince presided at meetings, opened Town Halls, dedicated statues, attended civic receptions and visited hospitals. His frank, straightforward manner charmed everyone he met. Yet, in time, whatever he did was not enough. He had no serious occupation nor interests. The fact that he had begged his mother to be allowed to take some useful employment in his country's service was not known. His life was all play. And rumors began about his affairs with women, his gambling and extravagance. The moral middle classes adored Alexandra and disapproved of him, and the disapproval became national when he was subpoenaed to appear in court in the unpleasant Mordaunt Divorce. Although cleared of adultery with young Lady Mordaunt, he was booed afterward in the streets and theater and when he drove around the course at Ascot.

The agitation became so dangerous that Gladstone had to take notice. He had tried to avoid grappling with the problem of the monarchy. His relations with the Queen were polite, but strained. "To speak in rude and general terms," he confided to his Foreign Secretary, "the Queen is invisible and the Prince of Wales is not respected." As he thought about it, he convinced himself that, next to Ireland, his mission in life was to restore the moral prestige of the Crown. First, the Queen must come out of her isolation.

The idea horrified Victoria, as much as his direct approach and involved lectures on how to fulfil her duties offended her. It was unthinkable that he should make such demands. To her, her mourning was no ritual formality. It was as sincere and as poignant as on the dreadful moment it began. Not a day passed but she thought of Albert and longed to be laid by his side. Only the needs of her country had forced her to go on. Every member of every Cabinet knew how hard and conscientiously she had worked, and now this man was attempting to bully her into making an exhibition of herself, merely to gratify some people's ignorant curiosity, to abandon the only way of life that was bearable to her. She flatly refused. Her nerves, she told, would not stand it.

Gladstone directed all the force of his powerful personality on her and, running full tilt against her indomitable will, retreated bruised. He was discouraged, but did not give up. If she would not attend state functions, then the Prince of Wales must be deputized to take her place. Her reaction was icy. The Prince was not entitled to be her representative. No one had ever had that right, except her beloved husband. She would not grant it to Bertie.

If Gladstone had understood women even slightly better, he might had realized sooner that she was jealous. She deplored Bertie's love of luxury and frivolity, his relaxed morals and dubious friends, in stark contrast to his late father, but she had burned even more with jealousy at the joyous welcome of her people to him and Alexandra, at the crowds who applauded them, when their sole loyalty and devotion should have been hers. That Bertie had lost his popularity was unfortunate, but she would by no means help him to get it back by letting him appear in her name and behaving as if she no longer existed.

The agitation which Gladstone had tried to calm was reaching an explosive level. Republicans talked openly of the deposition or forced abdication of the Queen. Gladstone was coming slowly to the conclusion that her abdication might be the only solution. Then something happened which confounded all the political theorists and made all the revolutionary schemes and manifestos and plans for counter measures so many pieces of paper.

After staying for a week with Lady Londesborough at Londesborough Lodge, near Scarborough, the Prince and Princess of Wales returned to Sandringham, their home in Norfolk, to spend the two months before Christmas with their children. Usually robust and energetic, the Prince complained of headaches and tiredness. Developing a feverish cold, he was put to bed, protesting. His sister Alice, who was visiting, sent for a leading physician, Dr. Gull. She had nursed their father in his last illness and Gull's diagnosis confirmed her fears. Bertie had the symptoms of typhoid. Even the word brought terrible memories. As his condition worsened, the children were sent away and his brothers and sisters began to gather at Sandringham. Finally, the Queen, weak and ailing as she was, arrived from Balmoral.

News of the Heir to the Throne's indisposition had caused little interest, but, with the announcement of the true nature of his illness and the Queen's arrival, the public felt stirrings of anxiety. It was reported that the drains at Londesborough Lodge were infected and other guests who had been at the house party were struck down, including Lord Chesterfield. When he died on the first day of December, anxiety turned to alarm. The

Prince, friendly and approachable, had his failings, but who had not? The nation read the accounts of his desperate fight for life and of the Queen and Princess Alexandra's vigil by his bedside, stunned by the thought that he might die from the same disease that had killed his father. As the anniversary of Albert's death came nearer and the Prince was reported to be sinking, the demand for news became insatiable. Special editions were published. Bulletins had to be pinned up morning and night outside post offices and police stations throughout the country.

On the eve of the fatal anniversary, many churches stayed open. The Disraelis prayed with their tenants in the church at Hughenden, as countless thousands prayed throughout the nation and the colonies. The next day, when it was announced that the final crisis had come and that the Prince had survived it and was sleeping peacefully, the sense of relief was indescribable. It seemed he had been saved by a miracle of prayer. People wept in the streets. Sympathy poured out to the family, to the Prince and Princess, and to the Queen in her ordeal.

A few months later, a service of National Thanksgiving was held at St. Paul's. Victoria had been against it, but had let herself be convinced by Alexandra that the public had shared their grief and should be permitted to share their joy. Dense crowds wept and cheered the open carriage taking Bertie and Alix and the Queen in procession through the streets of London. The Prince was pale and still not fully recovered, and all hearts went out to him. The tumultuous shout that greeted the moment at Temple Bar when Victoria took his hand and kissed it signalled the end of the Republican movement for ever.

A congregation of thirteen thousand attended the service, the nobility, foreign representatives, dignitaries from every institution in the country, and the officers of State led by Gladstone and Disraeli. Gladstone remained coldly aloof. Disraeli knew that the Queen had rejected his Irish plan for the Prince and, having suggested a similar scheme himself and having had it turned down, was not surprised. Yet Gladstone was lucky. The feeling of national rejoicing would undoubtedly lead to greater stability and fewer problems for his government, already in an invincible position with its substantial majority.

After the service, there was a delay while the carriages for the congregation were driven up in order to the foot of the steps outside the Cathedral, and the crowds waited to cheer their favorites. Disraeli, talking to Lord Derby and Mary Anne, glanced round at a noticeable silence, broken by a few boos. To his amazement, he saw that the hostile reaction was for Gladstone. The jeers mixed with a scattering of half-hearted applause continued as the Gladstones' carriage swung away down to Ludgate Circus. Others had noticed and watched with interest as Disraeli helped Mary Anne up into their barouche and the crowd cheered. Mary Anne was thrilled. Disraeli seemed abstracted and unresponsive, but Mary Anne kept on waving to the people thronging the forecourt and the sides of the streets, as they drove away. And the cheering continued, swelling in volume and enthusiasm, turning their journey through the City to Waterloo Place into a triumph. The signs were unmistakable and the politicians driving behind them took note. The cheers and shouts for Dizzy came from all classes and conditions of men and women, and carried on without stopping even after their carriage turned off from the official route and drove up Regent Street, along Oxford Street and down Park Lane, where he dropped Mary Anne, and on to the Carlton Club.

In the club, he sat for a long time in the morning room, answering greetings in such a preoccupied way that he was left alone. Those who saw him through the glass door wondered at his expression. He had been resigned to unremitting struggle and small victories, with no hope of ever achieving office again. The unexpected demonstration of his popularity that day and the coolness to Gladstone sent all his calculations spinning. Out of it, some new probabilities emerged. People had expected too much from Gladstone. Having hailed him as a Messiah, they were becoming disillusioned. When he spoke to them, his speeches were so tortuous and involved, they could not understand him. They resented his concentration on Ireland to the exclusion of affairs at home, and for all his efforts the situation there had only grown more serious. He had alienated many of the new voters by complaining that reform had altered the composition of Parliament for the worse, by refusing to allow peaceful picketing in strikes, and by forcing through unpopular Licensing Laws to regulate the opening times of bars and public houses. Most of all, by backing down in every international dispute and by his inability to act firmly at moments of crisis, he had lowered national prestige and seemed indifferent to the loss of Britain's position as leading world power. Disraeli's patriotism and courage, and the truth of his warnings, appeared all the more admirable by contrast.

He had had an indication at the end of the previous year, when the Liberal students of Glasgow University had surprisingly elected him Rector, in preference to John Ruskin. Putting that and his ovation today together ...

chapter four

Two weeks later, he was sitting at his desk in his study at Grosvenor Gate with a towel draped round his shoulders, while Mary Anne snipped at his hair with scissors and a comb. He hunched forward, trying to write.

"Sit still, Dizzy!" she ordered. "I've nearly done."

"I'm trying to make notes for my speech," he protested.

"Well, do so. Just pretend I'm not here."

"How can I?" He blew stray clippings of hair from the page. "Snip, snip, snip. I feel I have fallen into the hands of some female Sweeney Todd."

"Then you know what to expect," Mary Anne laughed, threatening him with the scissors. "Do sit still. I will not have you going to Manchester looking like an out of work scarecrow."

He sat quietly for a moment, looking at what he had written, then laid down his pen. "I am not sure I will go to Manchester."

"Why on earth not?" Mary Anne exclaimed. "There's

to be a great parade of all the Conservative Associations, then your speech in the Free Trade Hall—"

"Precisely. Only one of three monster rallies in the North. And at each I will be expected to make a speech lasting several hours."

"Think of the effect it will make!"

He grunted. "I am thinking ... nowadays, with my asthma, I can only stay on my feet talking, if I drink brandy and water non-stop. So I'll lose the Temperance and Churchgoers vote straight away."

She smiled. "Then put white brandy in the water jug—and the audience won't know a thing about it."

She laughed as he swivelled round and looked up at her. "Lady Beaconsfield," he said admiringly, "you are as fair as an angel and as devious as a serpent."

As she kissed him, the door opened and Corry came in. He stopped, embarrassed. "Quite all right, Monty," she assured him. "We weren't doing anything naughty. I'd just finished." She took a last snip at Disraeli's side curls and gathered up the cut ends in the white towel.

Corry came forward. "May I get rid of that for you?"

"No, no," she told him. "I'll take it out with me." She hobbled slowly to the door, which Corry held open. She looked back. "Now, dearest," she warned, "don't work poor Monty too hard."

She went out, patting Corry's cheek as she passed. He was like a son. He smiled, closing the door. When he turned, he was concerned to see Disraeli's distress.

"Her fingers are so swollen, she could scarcely hold the scissors," Disraeli told him.

Corry remembered how upset she had been, when she had had to take off her wedding ring for the pain it caused. In thirty-two years, it had never been off her finger. "I thought Lady Beaconsfield seemed a little better," he said.

"She will not give in," Disraeli muttered. He looked at Corry. "She insists on travelling to Manchester with me."

Corry was worried. "Could you not advise against it, sir, because of the appalling weather?"

"She will not listen. Though I am afraid the journey will be too much for her."

"For her own sake, sir," Corry urged, "could you not refuse to let her come with you?"

"How can I?" Disraeli said quietly. "When I know that every time she hears me speak now, she is afraid it may be the last."

Disraeli's reception in the Midlands was a scene from one of his most romantically extravagant novels come alive. No one could have predicted or imagined it. Manchester and the county of Lancashire were Liberal and Radical strongholds, an industrial area, the home of Free Trade. Both Gladstone and John Bright had been born in Lancashire and, over the years, had visited it again and again to make impassioned appeals for the support of its independent-minded working men.

Disraeli and Mary Anne arrived in Manchester on a cold, wet Easter Monday, to be met by a huge crowd of workers on holiday, who would not let their carriage leave the station yard, until Disraeli spoke to them. Laughing and cheering, they unharnessed the horses and teams of men took turns to draw the carriage through the streets to where they were staying.

The climax of the week was the giant meeting on the Wednesday evening in the Free Trade Hall. With Derby beside him, surrounded on the platform by all the Conservative MPs for the county, Disraeli spoke for three and a quarter hours to an enormous audience. It was the most significant speech of his life, setting out his party's program, defending and defining his belief in the Constitution, the Church and the Monarchy, setting out the need for continued social reform. It was an astonishing performance, lucid and uplifting, received with immense enthusiasm. Within minutes the audience was rapt, cheering and applauding, laughing or utterly silent, as he willed.

Accompanied by Montagu Corry, a rug over her knees, Mary Anne sat in the front row of the main gallery with a perfect view. She felt the power that flowed out from the platform and the response of the audience excited her.

Even she had never seen or heard Dizzy like this. She gazed short-sightedly down at him as he stood at the table, pale and intent, one last, dyed lock of hair curling over his forehead, his gestures almost superhumanly restrained. There was no hint of difficulty or weakness in his rich, full voice, even after three hours.

He had answered the criticism of the Government that his party had no ideology or program. Now he turned to the Government's own record and history and his voice became more ironic and biting. The administration, he declared, was formed on the principle of violence and had begun with the despoiling of the Irish Church and the plundering of landlords. There were shouts of "Hear! Hear!" and a long burst of applause. While he paused, he poured colorless liquid from the decanter beside him into his glass. As he sipped it, he raised the glass in a small, secret toast to Mary Anne up in the gallery. To stay on his feet and keep his throat clear, he had got through nearly two full bottles of white brandy. He lowered his glass and the crowd fell silent. "All along," he said, "Her Majesty's new Ministers have proceeded in their career like a body of men under the influence of some deleterious drug." There was laughter. "Not satisfied with the rape and anarchy of Ireland, they have begun to attack every institution and every interest, every class and calling in the country!"

During the roars of agreement and the applause, he sipped again from his glass. "I have watched them," he went on. His tone hardly changed, yet already the audience was smiling. In every, tiny pause, the laughter was instant and growing. "As time advanced, it was not difficult to perceive that extravagance was being substituted for energy by the Government. The unnatural stimulus was subsiding. The paroxysms ended in prostration ... some took refuge in melancholy—and their eminent chief alternated between a menace and a sigh. As I sat opposite the Treasury Bench, the Ministers reminded me of one of those marine landscapes not very unusual on the coasts of South America. You behold a range of exhausted volcanoes. Not a flame flickers on a single pallid crest. But the

382

situation is still dangerous. There are still occasional earthquakes . . . and ever and anon the dark rumbling of the sea."

The laughter which the audience had been trying to suppress burst out in renewed applause and cheering. Disraeli took another sip from his glass, smiling very faintly. In the gallery, Mary Anne nearly doubled over with sudden, excruciating pain, but forced herself to sit erect, smiling and nodding down to him.

He could not finish without mentioning foreign affairs, although he knew the difficulty of discussing a subject which the average Englishman was convinced did not concern him. "Unhappily," he said, "the relations of England with the rest of the world, which are 'foreign affairs,' are the matters which most influence his lot." He condemned the weakness of Gladstone's Government in its negotiations with both Russia and America, although they must understand that he favored firmness at the right moment rather than aggressive diplomacy. He knew that the relations of England to Europe had undergone a fundamental change. At the same time, the Queen had become the head of the most powerful of oriental states, and sooner or later the new establishments on the other side of the world would demand a voice in international councils. And now, the United States of America was throwing a lengthening shadow over the Atlantic. "These are vast and novel elements in the distribution of power. I acknowledge that the policy of England with respect to Europe should be a policy of reserve, but proud reserve. And in answer to those mistaken statesmen who have intimated the decay of the power of England and the decline of her resources, I express here my confident conviction that there never was a moment in our history when the power of England was so great and her resources so vast and inexhaustible. And yet, gentlemen, it is not merely our fleets and armies, our accumulated capital and our unlimited credit on which I so much depend, as on that unbroken spirit of her people, which I believe was never prouder of the Imperial country to which they belong."

As he ended, the entire audience rose to its feet. After the grey and uncertain years that had passed, his words had given them a pride in their country and a belief in its future that was as dignified as it was glorious. In feeling himself a part of the invincible empire that spanned the globe, each man seemed to share in its power and majesty. The wine he poured for them was heady after the water they had been used to drinking. They called for him again and again, pledging their trust, their affection and their loyalty.

As Mary Anne peered at the people around her, who were cheering and craning forward to see him, inspired, she bit her lip and thanked her Maker that she had lived to see this day.

Corry waited until the hall had partly cleared, to avoid the crush as he helped her out. The group from the platform had already moved off. Policemen were holding back a large, enthusiastic crowd at the foot of the stairs. When they saw Mary Anne come slowly down on Corry's arm, they began to applaud. She paused, surprised, and the applause mounted.

"For me?" she breathed.

"Their admiration is as much for you as for him," Corry told her quietly. "They all know of your devotion to each other, a marriage of true affection."

"Disraeli married me for my money," Mary Anne said. She saw that he was shocked, and added shyly, "But I think if he had to do it again, he would marry me for love."

Corry was moved and nodded. She smiled to the crowd and straightened, releasing his arm. He stood back and let her carry on down the stairs alone. As she moved haltingly towards them, the applause became even warmer, with shouts of "Mary Anne! Mary Anne!" The crowd parted, forming an avenue, and she walked through the mass of applauding, affectionate people, cheering and calling her name.

Disraeli and she were staying at the home of the chairman of the meeting. She was there first and waited,

384

almost breathless, for him to arrive. There were more people outside the house, but she was not aware of them. When his carriage drew up, she ran to the door and down the steps. He opened his arms and she held him, trembling, flushed and excited, weeping at last. "Oh, Dizzy . . . Dizzy . . ." she whispered. "This pays for all."

When they returned to London, Mary Anne was desperately weak and could not hide her suffering any longer. Disraeli asked Sir William Gull, the doctor who had saved the Prince of Wales, to examine her, but Gull could give him no comfort. He could not even guess how long she had to live. The cancer should have killed her years before. All he could do was make her last weeks or days as comfortable and painless as possible, but the pain could only be deadened for short periods, after which it came back worse than before.

The torment for Disraeli was in still having to pretend that he did not know. She was always cheerful, scolding herself for being a nuisance to him, and would not let him cancel any of their social engagements. She even went with him to one of the Queen's infrequent afternoon Courts at Buckingham Palace. Victoria was very pleased to see her and paused to ask after her health, as she circulated. Mary Anne assured her she was never better. Just after she moved on, Disraeli felt Mary Anne sag against him, about to collapse. All eyes were on the Queen, so he managed to hold her and lead her to the side, unnoticed. By now he knew the palace fairly well and, with the help of two ladies-in-waiting, carried her down side passages to the courtyard and their carriage.

In the Whitsun recess, the weather improved and they were able to go down to Hughenden for a few days, where she was certain she would get better. The lilacs and rhododendrons were out and the valley was filled with late blossom. Always before, the country air and the peace of her own home had revived her, but the miracle did not happen this time. Her sufferings increased. She could scarcely walk and any unguarded movement caused a spasm of pain, but she had herself pushed in a wheel-chair by Disraeli and his valet, up the hill behind the house to the German Forest to see her views again.

Back in London, she still would not give in. She refused to be treated as an invalid. Concern that she might be a burden to him was more distressing to her than her illness.

She insisted on accompanying him to a party at Lady Loudoun's, where she charmed everyone by her sprightliness and courage, but her forced vitality did not last the evening. The worst attack she had ever had paralyzed her and she had to be taken home. She had hardly reached Grosvenor Gate, when she had a hemorrhage. It was the last invitation she would ever be able to accept.

In the days that followed, he sat with her, reading to her, helping her with her letters. She apologized for being a nuisance and worried about him not working. He would only leave her when she pretended to fall asleep. At last, he had to attend the Commons for an important debate, but he could not settle for the thought of her lying alone and the fear of what might happen. Always before, he had sent her word of any interesting developments. At the end of the second hour, he scribbled a note and sent it home by messenger. It read, "I have nothing to tell you—except that I love you, which, I fear, you will think rather dull." The messenger brought back a reply. "My own Dearest—I miss you sadly. I feel so grateful for your constant tender love and kindness. I certainly feel better this evening. Your own devoted Beaconsfield."

Every August, when the Parliamentary session ended, they headed straight for Hughenden to rest. They had been counting the hours. This year, because the hemorrhages continued, they had to stay in the city. For months, Mary Anne had been unable to take any nourishment, even though friends like the Rothschilds sent delicacies from their kitchens to tempt her. Gull could not understand how she still survived. She even seemed cheerful and, on sunny afternoons, would not stay indoors. Disraeli went out with her for leisurely drives round

London, exploring the new suburbs, from the endless, southward spread of houses into Surrey to the villas of Highgate in the north. They pretended they were abroad and Dizzy turned each trip into an amusing adventure.

By the end of September, there was a definite improvement in her health. She still could not eat, but the constant pain had stopped. Nothing could keep her from Hughenden. They had missed the summer, but there were still some climbing roses on the terrace and the whole valley glowed with the rich russet and bronze and gold of the autumn leaves.

It was as well that Disraeli had not dared to expect a permanent improvement. Although at first she seemed stronger and even ate a little, the gnawing, agonizing pains began again. Even so, her spirit was unbroken and she fought back. The weather was not kind. Winter set in early and the ice and snow stopped her from paying the calls on neighbors she had planned. Disraeli could not think of work any more. All political business he left to Hardy and Northcote. All his time and thought were for Mary Anne. And she surprised him by insisting on their giving a houseparty at the end of November. John and Janetta Manners, the young Lord Rosebery, Sir William Harcourt and Lord Ronald Gower came to spend a few days, wondering if they should have accepted. It was unforgettable. They found Disraeli grave and hospitable, and Mary Anne emaciated, weak and shrunken, but brimming with life and curiosity and as playful as ever. She took such care to see they were all comfortable and constantly amused, and was so high-spirited herself, it was only when the men were alone with Disraeli and he told them how much she suffered that they remembered she was seriously ill.

A week after her guests left, Mary Anne developed congestion of the lungs and the specialist, Dr. Leggatt, had to be sent for urgently from London. He saw at once it was all over. Even with her courage, there was no chance of recovery. Montagu Corry arrived to give what help and comfort he could. She would not see him, nor

Philip Rose when he called. Her shattered body still fought, but her mind had escaped into delusions. Knowing she was dying, she fought against being put to bed and sat, wrapped in quilts, in her armchair. Her doctor, the servants, became enemies in her imagination, determined to kill and rob her. For eight days, Disraeli sat with her, tending to her, calming her, when she was able to understand him. She could not bear him to leave the room. He thought he had plumbed the depths of suffering, but, watching over her, listening to her ravings, was the most harrowing ordeal of his life. There was worse to come.

One day she seemed calmer. She was dying of dehydration and starvation and he tried to get her to take a mouthful of audit ale which Harcourt had sent for her. She sipped it, then demanded to see Corry. She became agitated and Disraeli finally handed a note to the servant who waited outside. When Corry came in, Mary Anne clung to him for protection, accusing Disraeli of trying to poison her, of scheming with the doctor to steal her house and all her money to pay his debts. They could not reassure her and, as she grew more agitated, Disraeli had to go out. He sent the servants away and waited in the narrow hall outside the bedroom, lost, anguished by the fear that she would die estranged from him. At last, Corry came out to tell him he had soothed her.

Mary Anne sat quietly in her chair. The pain had vanished in these dying moments. Her head lay to the side and she did not have the strength to raise it. She was watching a dancing flicker of sunlight on the ceiling that glanced from the silver-backed mirror on her dressing-table. She became aware that Disraeli was with her as he touched her hand. He was kneeling by her chair. Her eyes moved to him and her lips trembled as she tried to speak. She looked so peaceful that, for a moment, he had a wild hope that again she had cheated death, but her hand was cold and bloodless and her breathing so slow and shallow that he felt he could count minutes between each breath. He bowed his head over her hand. When he looked up again, he saw she was smiling to him, tenderly and lovingly. "My own darling... my Dizzy..." she whispered. "Forgive me ... How will you ever get along without me?" Her eyes closed.

She was buried in the churchyard at Hughenden.

Almost the first letter of condolence Disraeli received was from Victoria. "May God support and sustain him is the Queen's sincere prayer." Many others followed, from other kings and queens, from princes and friends and strangers who only knew of Mary Anne's courage and devotion. One letter which touched him was from Gladstone. "You and I were, as I believe, married in the same year. It has been permitted to both of us to enjoy a priceless boon through a third of a century. Spared myself the blow which has fallen on you, I can form some conception of what it must have been and be. I do not presume to offer you the consolation which you will seek from another and higher quarter. I offer only the assurance which all who know you, all who knew Lady Beaconsfield, and especially those among them who like myself enjoyed for a length of time her marked though unmerited regard, may perhaps render without impropriety; the assurance that in this trying hour they feel deeply for you, and with you."

Many would have attended the funeral, but Disraeli was too overwhelmed to face a mass of people, even sympathizing friends. Only the household and tenants, Corry, Philip Rose, Dr. Leggatt and himself were there, when her coffin was lowered into the vault by the east end of the church to join the body of Mrs. Brydges-Willyams.

It was a day of biting cold and drenching rain. When the service was over and everyone had gone, the gravediggers stood huddled against the wall of the church, waiting to fill in the earth. Bleak and desolate, Disraeli stood bareheaded, staring down at the vault, unable to make himself turn away for many long minutes.

When they came back to the house, Disraeli changed,

then sat alone in the library. He did not even notice a servant who came in to build up the fire. It was evening before he stirred.

He had asked Corry to collect all Mary Anne's papers and put them in the study, to be sorted out. He dreaded it, because of the memories it would bring back, but was afraid to put it off. He made himself climb the stairs. When he opened his study door, he found that Corry had already begun.

There were papers everywhere. The sheer volume was staggering. On the desk, chairs, the mantelpiece and bookcases, were bundles of letters tied with ribbons, scrap-books, piles of cardboard boxes, document cases, heaps of photographs and theater programs, engraved invitations and guest lists. Diaries, books of household accounts and paid bills. Corry was attempting to put the piles in some kind of order. He had adored Mary Anne and was clearly distressed. "There's so much, Sir," he faltered. "Not only her own correspondence, but every letter from you, every scrap of paper—since you first met."

Disraeli nodded. He had steeled himself not to show any emotion. If anything, his expression was more set and impenetrable than ever. ". . . Thirty-three years," he said. "And never a moment that was not filled with love and loving-kindness."

Corry watched as he crossed to his chair, lifted some cardboard boxes which lay on it and laid them on his writing-table. "Perhaps we should leave it to later, Sir," he suggested. "To another day."

Disraeli shook his head. "If I do not do it now—I shall never do it. Although it is like burying her again." He looked slowly round. "All our past is here." He untied the ribbon round the top box.

Corry took up another bundle of letters and started to lay them out in order, going by the postmarks. For now, there was no time to arrange them by contents. He paused, turning one over. "This letter seems to be un-opened, sir," he said. He read the envelope and turned, surprised, but hesitated.

The box Disraeli had opened was filled with small paper packets. He had undone one and was gazing at it. He held it out. "Look, Monty . . . every two weeks of our life, she cut my hair. From the beginning, she has preserved what she cut—in these little packets. All dated—all—" He looked again at all the boxes and bundles still to be opened, and could scarcely go on. "Forgive me," he muttered. "It is unfair of me to make you go through this. I should be alone."

"As you wish, Sir," Corry said quietly. "But this letter is addressed to you, from. Lady Beaconsfield." He handed it over. "From the date, it was written over sixteen years ago."

"To me?" Disraeli wondered. "Thank you, Monty." He was puzzled and troubled as he took the letter. Corry went out, closing the door softly behind him.

Disraeli studied the envelope. It was dated June 6, 1856. His hands were unsteady, when he opened it. He sat at the writing-table and cleared the space in front of him before taking the letter from the envelope. There was only one sheet of paper. He paused, then unfolded it. The writing was clear, though the ink was slightly faded.

"My own dear Husband," he read. "If I should depart this life before you, leave orders that we may be buried in the same grave at whatever distance you may die from England. And now, God bless you, my kindest, dearest! You have been a perfect husband to me. Be put by my side in the same grave. And now, farewell, my dear Dizzy. Do not live alone, dearest. Someone I earnestly hope you may find as attached to you as your own devoted MARY ANNE."

It had been written under stress, at some time of danger to his health or to hers. As he read it again more slowly, his impenetrable mask broke down at last, and he wept.

chapter five

Disraeli had thought that he could sort out Mary Anne's "archives" in two or three days. Seeing the enormous bulk of the material covering his past and their entire life together, he had to revise his estimate to two or three weeks, but he was not allowed even to make a beginning. Other business became more urgent.

Mary Anne's income had died with her. It meant an instant loss of £5,000 a year and, at the age of sixty-eight, he was suddenly thrown back into the precarious financial position of his youth. His books still brought in a little money and there was more, though not much, from the Hughenden estate. Andrew Montagu, the Yorkshire businessman who had bought up most of his debts, helped him again by lowering the interest he charged from 3 to 2 percent. That saved him for the time being, but there was a more immediate problem. Wyndham Lewis had left the house at Grosvenor Gate to Mary Anne only for her lifetime. As soon as she was dead, his family informed Disraeli that they intended to take possession at once. He had to hurry to London to move out all his furniture and written records and belongings, and arrange for those that were not put into storage to be sent to Hughenden. Grosvenor Gate had been his London home for half his life. Now he had been turned out and had to look for somewhere else. Heartbroken, emotionally drained, there were days when he felt incapable of making the slightest decision. Montagu Corry proved his worth by staying close to him and taking over as many of the details and arrangements as possible. Then he, too, was called away when his own father became dangerously ill and Disraeli was alone again. As he took a last walk around the empty house at the corner of Grosvenor Gate and Park Lane, which for so long had been filled with laughter and loving companionship, he realized he was more alone than he had ever been. All those closest to him were gone.

However, one sincere admirer remained, the one at this moment with more power than any other to reanimate and inspire him. In answer to her summons, he presented himself at Windsor for a very private audience with the Queen.

In recent years, since he was out of office, they had only met at infrequent intervals, although they had exchanged letters and Victoria sent boxes of primroses and snowdrops to Hughenden every spring, because he had seen them in white and golden profusion in the grounds at Osborne and told her they were his favorite flowers. She had to admit to herself that she had missed him and she saw with compassion the deeper lines which sorrow had etched in his face. "I trust you did not consider the expression of my heartfelt sympathy an intrusion, Mr. Disraeli?" she said, almost shyly.

Disraeli was touched by her gentleness and understanding. He had sometimes suspected that her own mourning was exaggerated and had complained that it was overprolonged, but now he had learned to accept its sincerity. "On the contrary, Ma'am," he assured her. "I had thought to see no one for many months, to stay in seclusion, but Your Majesty's letter of condolence was so affecting and so gracious that I felt I had to express my gratitude, however inadequately, in person."

"It is impossible to see beyond your present grief, I know," she said quietly, "yet there may be some consolation in thinking of the peace and freedom from suffering which I, in time, have found."

He bowed. "Your Majesty's example shall be my faith and hope."

Victoria was grateful that she might be able to help him. No one was better qualified. It was an added bond, drawing them closer together. Disraeli concealed his reaction, when she turned to her chair and sat. It was a gesture to show her esteem for him as a former Prime Minister and that she did not wish the meeting to be formally short.

She folded her hands in her lap. "She maintained her courage to the end, I am told."

"To the very end," Disraeli confirmed. "She always believed that one only dies if one surrenders to death, and swore that she never would. In her final collapse, she refused to be put to bed, and died still fighting."

Victoria was moved. She had heard that that final struggle had been harrowing for him. "And you, Mr. Disraeli?" she asked. "These last years have taken a great toll, I fear."

"At times it has almost been too much, Ma'am," he confessed. "My party is demoralized. I, myself, bowed down by old age and ill-health. I have often considered making way for a younger man."

The Queen's back straightened. "I will not hear of it," she announced firmly. "I have only been able to bear these last four years through the hope that, one day, you will again head the government."

It was an admission of such partiality as Disraeli had never imagined he would hear. Yet he had to be honest. For all his efforts and the success of his public speeches, Gladstone and the Liberals were still unshakably placed. "There seems less likelihood of that than ever, Ma'am."

Victoria's look was very direct. "Nevertheless, and though it must seem like an intolerable burden," she said, "I depend on you, Mr. Disraeli, to check the fanaticism of ... the present Prime Minister, in Parliament."

The new session was about to begin. He had half decided to leave the opening moves and speeches to Hardy and Northcote. Now he saw he had no choice. "As long as I have the will and the strength, I shall continue the struggle," he promised, "since my Queen commands it."

Edward's Hotel in George Street, off Hanover Square, was medium-sized, middle-class and respectable. Baron Lionel de Rothschild came in through the door to the street and paused to let two elderly ladies pass him. His glance took in the porter's cubbyhole, the glass-fronted doors leading to the dining-room and the manager's office and the stairs leading to the upper floors. The furniture was heavy, dark mahogany, matched by the subdued brown and dark cream of the decor.

He crossed to the reception desk where a well-dressed couple had just registered. The day porter and boots followed them to the stairs with their cases and hatboxes. Rothschild gave his name to the young male receptionist, who was filling in the couple's registration details and did not hear. Rothschild rapped on the desk and, when the receptionist glanced up, repeated more loudly, "Baron de Rothschild to see Mr. Disraeli."

The receptionist's involuntary look of annoyance was replaced at once by respect. "Oh! Oh, yes, sir," he said, impressed. "If you will excuse me?" He rang the handbell and called, "Boy! Boy!"

The boots turned out of sight up the stairs.

"Never mind," Rothschild murmured and moved to meet Corry, whom he had just noticed crossing the foyer with a handful of letters.

Corry bowed, surprised. "Good day, Sir. I'm sorry, I didn't know you were expected."

"I am not," Rothschild told him. "I've only just heard he was here. Is he ... at home?" He looked round with some distaste.

"Why, yes, I'll take you through," Corry said. "See these are posted, will you?" He handed the letters to the receptionist, then motioned Rothschild toward a corridor at the side.

As they moved toward it, Rothschild lowered his voice. "What is he doing here?"

"It is comfortable and fairly convenient for Westminster."

Rothschild showed his impatience at Corry's discretion. "Yes, but couldn't he have stayed at Grosvenor Gate until he found somewhere more suitable?"

"He was given a month to remove his personal effects," Corry said with a touch of bitterness.

Rothschild stopped abruptly. His anger showed only in a small, rapid twist of his mouth. A maid was passing, carrying a bundle of linen, and he waited until she had gone. "You know that Gladstone's latest Irish Bill has been defeated," he said, frowning. "If he resigns, Mr. Disraeli will be asked to form a Government. Is the country going to be run from a room in an hotel?"

Disraeli had taken two rooms on the ground floor. They were enough for his needs and within his means. That was all that he could find to recommend them.

He had recognized that the Queen had spoken more truly than she knew. He could easily succumb to grief and brood away the remainder of his days. The best antidote as always was work. He consulted with Gathorne Hardy and Lord Cairns, another top aide, and although they did not admit it, they said enough to confirm something he had already heard from Derby. His periodic absences from Westminster had started off fears that, with the loss of Mary Anne, he meant to give up politics. Salisbury had used it to call a secret meeting of the Conservative leaders at Burghley, without his knowledge, to discuss replacing him at once with a younger man. The choice fell on Lord Derby, whose reputation for moderation and common-sense should appeal to the country and induce middle of the road Liberals, who distrusted Disraeli's radical leanings, to join them. Derby was not at the meeting and, when he was told, would have none of it, although of all the others only Lord John Manners refused even to consider appointing another leader. Nothing was decided, but Disraeli's decision to consult Hardy and Cairns was only just in time. They were relieved to learn that he meant to go on fighting and reaffirmed their loyalty. He was their only hope. The rest came into line, leaving Salisbury isolated again.

Disraeli had warned them that the game would still be long and with no certainty of winning, yet at the very beginning of the session Gladstone's majority exploded around him. After his Church and Land Bills, he decided to do what he had prevented Disraeli from doing, to found a Roman Catholic university in Ireland. It would be the coping-stone of his Irish policy and redeem the failure of his other two measures to pacify the Emerald Isle. He worked out safeguards and answers to every likely objection and presented it with supreme confidence in a flood of rhetoric. The new university was to be in Dublin and would contain Protestant as well as Catholic colleges. Certain subjects were to be excluded, to avoid giving offense to either side. He defied criticism and expected his scheme to be acclaimed, but he had not reckoned on the violence of religious prejudice. It was denounced both by the Catholics and the Protestants, who refused to share a university, and its utter lack of validity as a seat of higher learning was exposed by Disraeli, when he pointed out that the teaching of modern history, moral philosophy and theology was forbidden and that any lecturer who upset the religious convictions of any of his students could be dismissed. The whole proposal was ludicrous. In the stormiest debate for years, Gladstone thundered that it was the duty of Parliament to force people to accept what was right for them, even if they objected, and threatened that he would take the vote on the second reading of the Bill as a vote of confidence in his Government.

Disraeli would not be bullied, nor let the House be bullied. No one was seeking to force the Government to resign. It was simply a bad Bill and it was the duty of

Members to vote for or against it, in spite of Gladstone's threats. With the full power of his party behind him, the Prime Minister had had a free hand for four years to push through his unpopular policies. And what was the result? "You have despoiled churches. You have threatened every corporation and endowment in the country. You have examined into everybody's affairs. You have criticized every profession and vexed every trade. No one is certain of his property and nobody knows what duties he may have to perform tomorrow." Disraeli was cheered as he had not been cheered in Parliament since the victory of the expedition to Abyssinia. The division was taken at two o'clock in the morning and the Government was defeated by three votes. A small number, but in view of the size of their majority it was very significant. When the result was read out, there was a hush followed by a roar in the Chamber. The Irish members, on whom Gladstone had depended, had voted solidly with the Opposition. He stared across at Disraeli, who looked back impassively as a din of cheers and shouts of "Shame!" and accusations built up around them. Both knew that the tide was turning. Already Gladstone was thinking feverishly of the best way to stem it.

Disraeli sat at the table by the window in his room at Edward's Hotel. The afternoon light was fading and he peered at the paper, writing a note to Hardy to tell him he had just had a message from Queen Victoria, who had taken up residence at Buckingham Palace during the crisis. He stopped and raised his head. Subconsciously, he expected to see his old study at Grosvenor Gate and had a second almost of shock. He looked slowly round the dark panelled, unfamiliar room in which the few treasured objects he had brought with him appeared so out of place.

As he held his glass to his eye and bent again to the paper, there was a knock at the door and Corry came in "Baron de Rothschild, sir," he announced.

Disraeli rose, pleased, as Rothschild came in. "Lionel . . ." Corry went out, closing the door.

Rothschild smiled, taking off his gloves. "Good to see you, Ben. I have not arrived at an inopportune moment, I trust?"

"Of course not," Disraeli assured him, and they shook hands. It was a particular pleasure to see Lionel, one of the few persons left to whom he was *Ben*. It was rare nowadays that he saw friends in his new, anonymous existence. Old friends were even rarer.

Rothschild glanced round the room. "I couldn't believe it, when I heard you'd moved to an hotel."

Disraeli shrugged, but could not disguise his feelings. "I will confess it feels like a mockery, when I tell the coach-driver to take me *home*. Hotel life in the evenings is a cave of despair." He smiled and motioned Rothschild to a seat. They settled themselves.

"I am hurt you did not come to me," Rothschild told him. "Charlotte and I would have been honored to have you to stay with us."

"I could not impose."

"You would not be a guest!" Rothschild protested. "You'd have your own rooms, to come and go as you please. You need only join in, when and if you choose."

So soon after his loss, Disraeli was still easily moved. He had to pause before replying. "I am grateful to you both but, at any rate for the moment, I am better on my own." The offer was tempting, yet few of his supporters would understand how he could live in the home of a political opponent without being compromised.

Rothschild also knew the difficulty, but dismissed it. Their friendship had nothing to do with long noses at Westminster. "Very well," he grunted. "But remember— my house is yours." He considered Dizzy. "You'll have heard that Gladstone had a cabinet meeting that lasted most of yesterday, and another this morning." In a banking business the size of his, a change of government and a shift in policy could have an enormous effect. He saw Disraeli's slight nod. "Well, you're bound to be told sooner or later. Gladstone's decided to resign." He waited for a reaction of surprise, but there was none. "You realize the Queen is bound to send for you shortly?"

Disraeli's lips curved briefly. "She already has."

It was Rothschild who was surprised. "Then what have you decided?"

"I am sorry, Lionel," Disraeli said quietly. "Until I have spoken with Her Majesty and the other Conservative leaders, I cannot tell you."

Rothschild had to accept it. There was not even a hint in Disraeli's voice or expression of what to expect. Who could imagine that anyone could hope for influence or unfair advantage through being a friend of Ben? What a businessman, or a gambler, he would make ... Or were they really the same thing?

When the Queen came into the Audience Room at Buckingham Palace, she could barely restrain her excitement. She confirmed what her message had already told Disraeli, that she had accepted Gladstone's resignation. She now had no hesitation in asking Disraeli to form a Government. To her amazement, he told her that, although his party had never been more united behind him, he regretfully had to refuse. It would be useless for him even to attempt to carry on a Government with a minority of support in the House of Commons. Victoria had seen Gladstone's resentment at being defeated over his Irish University Bill and was doubtful that he would agree to resume office, having declared his total unwillingness and inability to continue. She agreed with Disraeli that it was merely injured pride, but what was she to tell him? Disraeli bowed. "That I, respectfully, decline to form a Government in the present Parliament, Ma'am."

Manners, Northcote, Hardy and Ward Hunt were waiting for him at the Carlton Club. In the absence of Derby and Cairns abroad, they were his inner core of advisers. All except Hardy were as shaken as the Queen, when he told them what he had decided.

"She must have been thunderstruck," Northcote said.

"I flatter myself she was. Yet she understood."

"I wish I did," Hunt muttered.

"It is quite simple," Disraeli explained. "Never since I have been in Parliament has there been a Conservative majority. We have always had to depend on the support

401

of other groups, often those with whom we least agree, and are therefore at their mercy. I shall never let myself be in that position again."

"So you think this is a trick of Gladstone's?" Manners said.

"What else?" Hardy told him. "We are offered power which the Liberals can snatch away at any moment."

"Exactly," Disraeli agreed. "You'll have noticed that Gladstone has resigned. He has not asked for a dissolution of Parliament and a general election. He wants us to take office, leaving him with his majority. Then he can play cat and mouse with us. His party's only split on this one issue. He can bring them together again, whenever he chooses, to make every step we take as difficult as possible and prove to the country that we are unable to manage the simplest business without his help and agreement. Then, when he has made us look incompetent, he can turn us out at a moment's notice."

"I see that, of course," Northcote said. "But you realize, if Gladstone stays in power, he will continue to give concessions to the lower paid and the new electors, so that they will always support him."

"Always?" Disraeli murmured. "We shall see."

General Grey, the Queen's Private Secretary, had died and her new Secretary was Henry Ponsonby, a former equerry to the Prince Consort. He was a military man in his late forties, very capable, with a sense of humor that was not apparent at first sight, a decided Liberal and a firm admirer of William Gladstone. When the Queen sent him to Carlton House Terrace to tell Gladstone that Disraeli had refused to form a Government, he was surprised by the fury with which the news was received. He had expected to be welcomed as the bearer of good tidings.

Gladstone had spent two days in intense discussion with his cabinet. His decision to resign had been taken, as the Queen suspected, in a fit of wounded pride, and he had been prepared to be talked out of it, when his followers showed themselves to be sufficiently chastened by his threat to throw them all out of office with him. As Prime Minister, he had sole responsibility for resigning or staying on, and for advising the Queen to call an election. As the discussions had gone on, he had gradually realized that his instinct to resign was the correct, the only course. Although it hurt him to acknowledge it, he could read the signs as well as Disraeli and he did not want a general election where he risked losing a substantial part of his majority. To force the Conservatives in and to watch Disraeli waste his days planning and scheming and maneuvering, and beginning to hope, and then to reach out a finger and topple him . . . It would be the finish of him, and of his party as a contender for government. His decision taken and the Queen informed, he had been able to relax. He had gone to church on the way home from the palace and given thanks.

But now Ponsonby's news had shattered his calm. The Arch Fiend had stepped over the pit he had dug for him and Gladstone was teetering on the edge of it, himself! Or was Disraeli playing a deeper game? "Is it a trick?" he asked Ponsonby.

Ponsonby was puzzled. "I don't think—I don't see how, sir."

"You don't know him, you don't know him," Gladstone muttered. "He knows I can't humiliate myself by accepting office again. But if I refuse, he can claim that he has only accepted through absolute necessity. So he makes himself and his party seem indispensable."

"I see," Ponsonby nodded.

"He wants to use the Queen as a lever. She must have a Government. If he makes a show of reluctance and only accepts for her sake, then, morally, having refused myself, I cannot turn him out for the remaining life of this Parliament." As his mind turned and turned, trying to work out which of the courses of action open to him would leave him in the stronger position, he became more than ever certain that Disraeli's refusal of office was a double bluff. "I must know exactly what was said," he told Ponsonby. "I must have it in writing, everything he said to Her Majesty."

403

With Victoria's consent, Ponsonby called on Disraeli that evening at his rooms in Edwards's Hotel. Disraeli willingly and genially agreed to write out the substance of his conversation with the Queen. He had said, he wrote, that he was prepared to form an Administration which he believed would carry out Her Majesty's affairs with efficiency, but not in the present House of Commons. And he was of the same opinion as Gladstone, that he could not advise Her Majesty to dissolve Parliament.

When Ponsonby tried to argue with him, he said, "How could I carry on a Government with a majority of eighty against me?"

Ponsonby felt himself floundering. From what Gladstone had said, he had been prepared for Disraeli to be wily and slippery. Instead, he was frank and straightforward, seeming reluctant to disagree. But Ponsonby had promised to try to end the crisis as Gladstone wished. "You have defeated the Government," he repeated. "Oughtn't you therefore to undertake the responsibility of forming one?"

"We did not defeat the Government," Disraeli answered patiently. "We threw out a stupid, blundering Bill, which Gladstone in his high-handed way tried to make a vote of confidence. It was a foolish mistake, but he has made up for it by resigning." He smiled. "He can now resume office with perfect freedom."

Back Ponsonby went to the Queen, who hoped that everything was at last resolved. But Gladstone read the two sentences which Disraeli had written and found a difference in shade of meaning between them. Was it a deliberate ruse? Perhaps he was not giving an "absolute refusal" after all? He asked Victoria to explain what Disraeli meant. She told him he meant what he said, he declined to form a Government. She now expected Gladstone with his secure majority to do so. In reply, to her exasperation, he sent her a complicated memorandum, proving to his own satisfaction that Disraeli had no right to oppose him and then not take the consequences. She thought, not for the first time, that he was crazed. The whole thing was becoming farcical, but she could not ignore Gladstone's memorandum, for the country could not be left without a Government. However, she could not answer for Disraeli, as she would then have been answering for the Opposition party. Nor could she demand further explanations from Disraeli, as she might then be thought to doubt his motives as much as Gladstone. Again with Gladstone's knowledge, she sent a copy of his memorandum to Disraeli, asking for his comments. She left Buckingham Palace and went back to Windsor.

Disraeli had been given a perfect opportunity and he took two days to construct his reply, consulting Derby who had returned from his trip to France. He thanked the Queen humbly for allowing herself to become a channel of communication. His answer was nearly as detailed as Gladstone's accusation, but much clearer and more amusing. Summing up Gladstone's argument, he wrote, "It amounts to this: that he tells the House of Commons, 'Unless you are prepared to put someone in my place, your duty is to do whatever I bid you.' To no House of Commons has language of this kind ever been addressed: by no House of Commons would it be tolerated. It is humbly submitted to Your Majesty that no Minister has a right to say to Parliament, 'You must take such a Bill, whether you think it a good one or not, because without passing it I will not hold office, and my numerical strength is too great to allow any other effective Administration to be formed.'"

The crisis was over. Gladstone had to admit with bad grace that "no further effort was to be expected from the Opposition towards meeting the present necessity." Reluctantly, he recalled his cabinet and resumed office. His political position had been damaged and his Government could never again count on the support it had once had.

On all sides, Ponsonby heard praise for Disraeli's patriotic unselfishness in refusing the temptation of power for the good of his country. Both he and his party gained much in credit and respect. And Ponsonby wondered if Gladstone would not have been wiser to accept Disraeli's refusal as final right at the start. It had put his judgment in question and estranged him further from the Queen. Had Dizzy guessed that might happen? Did he really have the Machiavellian cunning that Gladstone complained of? Gradually, Ponsonby began to suspect that the enigmatic Opposition leader had made use of him and had been playing with all of them, all along.

After the elaborate comedy of the Ministerial crisis, Disraeli did not have to work so hard. He had shattered Gladstone's confidence as well as his reputation for infallibility. All he had to do was to keep his own party alert and be ready himself to pounce on the inevitable mistakes made by the demoralized Government. In that year, there were seven by-elections and the Conservatives won them all from the Liberals. Not enough to change the balance of the House, but another indication of how the tide was running.

Without that, the emptiness of his life would have been unendurable. He suffered badly from his bronchitis and attacks of asthma, but the sense of anticipation kept him buoyant. Yet he was lonely without someone with whom he could share the excitements and the daily twists and turns of the game. Corry became indispensable, unobtrusively taking over the organization of much of Disraeli's private life. Their relationship was affectionately intimate. Disraeli's affairs and interests were Corry's and, apart from working together in perfect harmony, they enjoyed each other's company. Disraeli had had few really close male friends, none as close as the women in his life, and the warm frankness of their friendship was refreshing. Yet, much as he wanted to, he could not demand all of his secretary's time. Corry was a much younger man, still unmarried, and forever falling in love. "Monty is a dreadful Lothario," Disraeli sighed, yet there was a hint of envy in his amusement as Corry set off in the evenings on a long series of disappointments and misadventures.

The loneliness was worst in the evenings. For a man used to constant companionship, dining in a hotel room by himself was intolerable. There was no remedy, for he detested the masculine conviviality of club life and most of the hostesses who before had showered invitations on him hesitated to intrude on his grief. Those to whom he might have turned, old Lady Cork and Lady Londonderry, were both dead. He felt cut off, yet, paradoxically, refused the few invitations he did receive. Brightly-lit rooms, filled with people, laughter, music and sparkling conversation, only made him more conscious that he was alone. Occasionally, he spent a quiet evening with colleagues and their wives like the John Manners, who would ask only him and, at most, one other. "I require perfect solitude, or perfect sympathy," he complained, and could achieve neither. He engaged a competent artist, G.F. Middleton, to paint a life size portrait of Mary Anne from a miniature done shortly after their marriage and insisted on many alterations, until it was exact. He hung it in his rooms, where sometimes it brought comfort and, sometimes, drove him nearer to despair at the memory of how much he had lost in her. "Someone I earnestly hope you may find as attached to you," she had written. Who could ever take her place?

Several ladies tried. Some rich, wellborn, by whose attentions he would formerly have been flattered, hinted that they would be more than willing to share their fortunes with him. Some younger women flirted with him and were offended, when he did not respond. One, recently widowed, even invited herself to his rooms. But one was more persistent than all the others, Lady Cardigan.

A forceful, rather disreputable woman in her mid-forties, she had known Disraeli slightly since she was seventeen, long before she married the dashing Earl of Cardigan, a national hero since he led the charge of the Light Brigade at Balaklava. She had been Cardigan's mistress before the marriage, causing much scandal in polite society. His death five years before had left her extremely wealthy, though still not fully accepted socially. Disraeli was grateful for her kindness to him, when he first came back to London after Mary Anne's death.

407

Widowed herself, she seemed disarmingly sympathetic. Ignoring the warnings of more conventional friends, he even dined alone with her, until he discovered what lay behind her sympathy. Her ambition was to become a great hostess, with an influential political and literary salon. Disraeli was to be the bait. With him at her side, her invitations would not be refused. For him the association might be disastrous, but that did not concern her. Her own dream of fame obsessed her and, when he eased back from the relationship, she pursued him even more strongly.

In his loneliness, he might just have yielded, but he was saved by a chance meeting with an old friend, Lady Chesterfield. She had been one of those who had not wished to intrude in the first months of mourning, but, seeing how depressed and lonely he was, she realized that someone must help him. Wise, calm and compassionate, she offered him exactly the kind of female companionship he had always needed, and without which he felt incomplete. She was a widow and, nearly seventy, beyond having to worry that their intimacy would be misunderstood. To Disraeli, it seemed almost miraculous to be with someone again to whom he could open his heart and mind, in whose discretion and friendship he could rely unreservedly. To him, she had not aged. He still saw her as she had been, when she and her sisters, Mrs. Anson and Selina Forester, were among the acknowledged beauties and he had escorted them to balls and masquerades as part of his campaign to conquer the fashionable world. Before he had even known Mary Anne. Within a few weeks, their friendship was more intimate and more precious to both of them than it had ever been.

Through her, he naturally began to see more of her youngest sister Selina, now Countess of Bradford. In her early fifties, with a quick, lively intelligence, Selina had kept much of her beauty and was still a conspicuous figure in society. Her husband, the Earl of Bradford, had been a colleague of Disraeli's as Lord Chamberlain during his first Ministry. A sensible, capable man, he was a noted sportsman and in his frequent absences saw absolutely no harm in his wife entertaining Disraeli at their house in Belgrave Square as often as she chose. Soon Disraeli was visiting one or other of the sisters nearly every day and, when meetings or late sittings at the House prevented it, exchanged long, revealing letters with them. Their warm, affectionate interest in everything he did and thought brought him to life again. To himself, he said that they had saved his sanity.

His policy of not harrassing or challenging the Government, merely commenting ironically on its mistakes and misfortunes, proved highly effective. Since Disraeli had made him resume office, Gladstone had watched the earlier prestige of his Ministry gradually fade away. In his five years of power he had forced the Liberal party rigidly into his own mold, crushing resistance and treating all internal criticism with contempt. He *was* the new Liberal party and he took its loss of favor in the country very personally. He was more and more tempted to ask the Queen to dissolve Parliament and risk an election. His own popularity remained considerable and, by gambling on that and winning, he would ensure himself of at least another four or five years in power, even with a decreased majority. But he delayed, waiting for the most favorable moment. Then, to his horror, a number of scandals erupted over irregular use of Post Office funds, mail contracts and the extension of the telegraph service, involving his Chancellor of the Exchequer and two other Ministers. In public he defended them, but in private he raged, knowing he had delayed too long.

At the end of the session, because of the Government's disarray and his friendship with the two sisters, Disraeli felt in much better spirits and could even face the thought of returning alone to Hughenden. Before leaving, he attended an afternoon al fresco party at Gunnersbury with them and Corry. Escaping from the throng, they strolled in the sun round the ornamental lake. Disraeli paused with Corry, when Lady Chesterfield and Lady Bradford turned aside into the exquisite Japanese garden. "The more I think of it," he confided, "the more I realize that Mary Anne knew me best, Monty."

"Your very heart, Sir," Corry agreed.

Disraeli smiled faintly. How well Monty had come to know him, too. "Indeed ..." He moved on to join the two ladies.

Lady Chesterfield turned. "This is such a beautiful place, Dis," she said. "Baron de Rothschild must be very proud of it."

"With reason. The Japanese Ambassador told him they have nothing nearly so lovely in Japan." They laughed. "I, myself, like it almost as much as my Beech Walk at Hughenden—which, to be sure, is less exotic."

"When are you travelling down?" Selina asked him.

"The day after tomorrow."

"Do you not find it lonely now?"

Selina was much more direct than Lady Chesterfield, who would never have asked such a question. "There are times when one longs for the sound of a certain dear voice. But I have my owls and my trees and my books."

"And your peacocks," Lady Chesterfield added, smiling.

"Most certainly, my peacocks."

As they walked on, he thought Selina's smile the most unaffectedly charming he had ever experienced. One did not see or notice or warm to her smile. One experienced it. He was very fond of them both, but could tell that, insensibly, he was being drawn to the younger, although he tried to disguise it. "I am surprised at you being able to take time off just now," she said. "My husband thinks a general election could be called at any moment."

"The decision is not up to me, my dear Selina, but to Mr. Gladstone. He need not call one for another twelve months and will undoubtedly try to announce it, when he thinks I am least prepared."

"So you are leaving town to tempt him," Lady Chesterfield guessed.

Disraeli laid his hand on his heart. "Am I so transparent?" They laughed. "I had hoped to avoid all such disagreeable subjects today. My mind, you see, is entirely occupied with something much more important." They were curious, as he paused. "An affair of the heart."

"Ah, yes," Lady Chesterfield said. "I had heard a rumor that a very rich, very determined, titled lady has asked you to marry her."

"Surely not?" Selina exclaimed.

"Is it so unthinkable that any lady should wish to unite her life with mine?"

"Why, no . . . no. I didn't mean——" she began, confused. Then saw that he was teasing.

"The rumor, alas, is true," he said. Lady Cardigan had given up hinting how valuable she could be to him and rushed into a frontal assault. She was the wealthiest widow in England, she told him, and he the most brilliant man. Was it not politically and practically fitting that they should marry and aid each other to achieve their dearest ambitions?

"What have you decided?" Lady Chesterfield asked.

"The wealth is tempting but, regretfully, I have had to decline her generous offer," he said drily, and hesitated. "Although I have not told her the real reason why . . . that I have fallen hopelessly in love."

Selina had been listening, fascinated. She was not at all sure that she liked the idea of him belonging to another woman and was piqued, but more and more intrigued. "With whom?"

"In love, nothing is ever simple," he confessed. "I have fallen in love with two ladies at once."

"Is it possible?" Lady Chesterfield wondered.

"Perfectly possible," he assured her, "and I cannot decide between them. One is as wise and understanding as Athene, the other as fascinating and unpredictable as Aphrodite." He looked from one to the other. ". . . With the added complication——that they are sisters."

They laughed delightedly, realizing at last what he meant. He took one on one arm and one on the other and they strolled on round the lake, back toward the house.

411

He spent nearly two months at Hughenden on his own, without even Corry for company. At last having himself to tackle the task he dreaded.

The personal letters and material collected by Mary Anne were still unsorted. She had stored them haphazardly, keeping everything, but in no order. He found even more, in tin boxes and sealed packages that had been overlooked by Corry. The volume was daunting and it was exhausting and saddening work, but he made himself approach it systematically, starting with her own private papers. Reading again his earliest letters to her, he relived the excitement and uncertainty of his election at Maidstone, the shock of Wyndham Lewis's death, the pangs and exaltation of their courtship, hurried notes written to her during the fierce battles of his solitary fight against Peel. Her letters to him were stored in other boxes and packages. There were her diaries and accounts, letters from Wyndham and her mother, poems and love-letters from her first suitors. He kept discovering more and more, his own correspondence, letters from Henrietta, from Metternich and Smythe, D'Orsay's last pencilled scrawl, hundreds from Mrs. Brydges-Willyams and Lady Londonderry and Bulwer...Poor Bulwer, who had just died, not from any of his imaginary ailments, but from old age. Every twist and turn and scheme and hope of Disraeli's life was encapsulated in these boxes. He was not only haunted by the ghost of his own youth. It was as he had feared. Mary Anne had come to life for him and died again a hundred times, before he finished.

Yet it was done, and he left Hughenden to spend a week in a hotel at Brighton. It was the end of September, when the beaches were no longer crowded by summer visitors and he looked forward to long, invigorating walks. Physically, he was more fit than he had been for years. A dry summer had helped his bronchitis and for months he had gone without sugar and wine, which seemed completely to have cured his gout. He had wanted to relax and go about, unnoticed, but during the week there was a sensational by-election at Dover, a safe Liberal seat, which they unexpectedly lost to a Conservative.

People began to raise their hats to him in the street and, one night, a choral society serenaded him outside his bedroom window. It was satisfying, although he realized it would make it less likely that Gladstone would chance a general election.

During the recess, Gladstone had made a stir by re-shuffling his Cabinet, including the Chancellor of the Exchequer who had been mixed up in the Post Office scandals. He took over the Chancellorship, himself. It was meant to give the country confidence, seeing him once again in charge of the Exchequer, but it created a problem for him. By law, any Member of Parliament accepting Cabinet Office had to submit himself to his constituents for re-election. Gladstone claimed that, as Prime Minister, the law did not apply to him. The Tory lawyers contested that and gave notice that he would be challenged on it, when Parliament reassembled.

From Brighton, Disraeli went to Weston, the Bradfords' country house in Shropshire. He had missed Selina, although she had written to him once or twice a week, and was excited to learn that she had missed him, too.

From Weston, he went to stay with Lady Chesterfield at Bretby, near Burton-on-Trent, which was much more restful. She was not as gay or as stimulating as Selina, but the pace of her life suited him better. Still, his thoughts kept straying back to the younger sister. His letters to her became even more romantic and affectionate.

Before the end of the year, Disraeli visited the Prince and Princess of Wales at Sandringham, then Blenheim Palace and Knowsley, before presiding at a meeting of the Conservative leaders at Hardy's house at Cranbrook, where it was agreed to concentrate at the opening of the session on Gladstone's equivocal position. Since he had flouted the law on re-election, it was doubtful if he was even still a Member of Parliament.

Disraeli spent Christmas quietly, then visited Selina and Lady Chesterfield again at Weston and Bretby. Towards the end of January, he travelled from Bretby to London and was back in his rooms in Edwards's Hotel. It was a Friday and he meant to use the weekend to look for a house to rent, or more suitable rooms. Corry had arranged for him to see over various possibilities, before returning to Hughenden on Monday.

He woke early on the Saturday morning, but was still in bed when Baum, his valet, brought him *The Times* with some excitement. When he opened it, Disraeli saw to his amazement that Gladstone had advised the Queen to dissolve Parliament at once, two weeks before the start of the session. The same edition carried three full columns of his manifesto for the general election, which was to take place immediately.

It was superbly timed, to catch the Conservatives off balance and unprepared. Disraeli, as far as anyone knew, was still visiting Lady Chesterfield in Staffordshire. His secretary was staying with an uncle in Dorset. Lord Derby was at Knowsley, relaxing with his family and tidying up personal affairs before coming back to Westminster, like all the other members of the Shadow Cabinet in their homes throughout the country. It would take days to gather them together and more precious days, perhaps the rest of the week, before they could agree on a common policy to answer the Liberal leader's manifesto. By that time, arrangements for the poll would be well under way in most districts.

Disraeli recovered quickly from the shock. To panic would be to react as Gladstone wanted. The People's William had chosen cleverly to make his announcement at the start of a weekend, but had not reckoned on his rival being in London. Disraeli had no books or papers, no one to help him, but at least he was here. He made himself think calmly and rationally. The question was, why had Gladstone decided to dissolve now? Obviously, he was disturbed by the sequence of by-election defeats and afraid that, the longer he delayed, the more damaging they would become. Add to that his furious indignation over the charge that he had behaved illegally by refusing to stand for re-election. Dissolution had made the whole matter academic and saved him from the humiliation of having to defend himself in public. Probably even more important, the reshuffle of his Cabinet had produced no noticeable improvement. His Government's impetus had faltered and he had no spectacular measure in hand to redeem its credibility. That would become apparent as soon as the new session opened. But Gladstone could disguise it and still save the day by going to the country with a cry tempting enough to dazzle the electors. And that was what he had done.

Disraeli got out of bed. His valet, who had been laying out breakfast on a side table, brought him his ankle-length, red dressing gown. "Thank you, Mr. Baum," Disraeli said, punctiliously. Baum was a diligent, taciturn man whom he always treated with serio-comic gravity. "Just coffee, please—no sugar."

He sat at the small escritoire and wrote out a series of telegrams to Derby, Cairns, Hardy, Northcote and Corry. "Now, Mr. Baum, will you kindly take these to the nearest Post Office and see they are sent off without delay. On the way back, kindly purchase me a ream of foolscap paper." He gave Baum some money and, when he had gone, sat at the table and sipped his coffee, while he read and read again Gladstone's manifesto.

Its style was even more wordy and tortuous than usual, but what struck him most was its tone. Gladstone's appeal to the electors had always lain in his powerful ability to make political arguments seem to be moral issues, his knack of presenting his policies as the only true, righteous course to follow and his critics and opponents as being misled by error or deliberate sin. Although often difficult to understand and sometimes unintelligible, when he spoke, his evangelical appearance and passionate conviction in his God-given mandate had an electrifying effect. In a basically religious age, to people with a conditioned regard for virtue and to the politically uneducated the appeal was irresistible. They did not have to understand, only to respond to his soul-stirring voice. Yet without the voice the effect was minimized, the written arguments clumsy. And this time the moral arguments took second place to finance. The theme of his manifesto was money, the millions he had saved the country by his stringent economies, and his main plank was a sweeping promise

415

that, if his party was returned to power, he would abolish Income Tax. The appeal was not to the nation's heart, but to its breast pocket.

Disraeli knew he could not waste a minute, if the challenge was to be met. When Baum came back with the writing paper, he was already setting out the headings of his own party's manifesto, in the form of an address to his electors in Buckinghamshire.

Lord Cairns was the first to arrive, in the afternoon. He was worried and anxious, until he learned that Disraeli had already written out the first draft of their party's election address. It seemed incredible. "It is, of course, only the first draft," Disraeli explained, handing it to him. "Now you can help me to revise it."

"It is very strongly worded," Cairns said, doubtfully.

"We have nothing to gain by pulling our punches," Disraeli answered. "It is a strictly accurate summary of the history of Gladstone's Ministry. There is not an expression that cannot be justified by ample, even abounding, evidence."

"That is true," Cairns had to agree.

"Very well. Let us revise it, so that, at least, it is not as obscure as the epistle from the People's William. And let us ask the voters to join us in putting an end to this Ministry's career of plundering and blundering."

It was evening when Gathorne Hardy joined them. On his journey to London, he had tried to put together his ideas for a basic program, but had become more and more depressed. It was now Saturday, January 24. The first polling was due to start in exactly seven days and they could never be ready. He was as anxious as Cairns and as astonished to be showed the completed address, answering every one of Gladstone's points. It was perfectly judged, so near to his own elusive ideas that all he could suggest were changes to a few phrases. Montagu Corry arrived late at night and, next day, all four spent the morning and afternoon in Disraeli's rooms, writing out copies which Corry then took to Fleet Street. When Derby at last reached the hotel on Sunday evening, prepared to begin discussions, everything had been decided and despatched, with Disraeli accepting full responsibility. And that is why he is leader and I am not, Derby admitted to himself, ruefully. While I am still thinking what is best to do, he has done it.

That night, Disraeli dined quietly with Derby and his wife. She left them afterward to talk over their brandy, but both were silent and serious. They were both aware of the dangers of the next few weeks and neither had any illusions. It was the first time Disraeli had put himself forward directly as Prime Minister. If they failed, it would be because the country did not have faith in him. Rightly or wrongly, the contest was regarded as a straight choice between him and Gladstone. He had carried out his reorganization of the party and it had all its candidates in the field, all seen as an extension of himself. If the voters rejected them, they would be rejecting him. So at last would the party, and his long career would be over.

On Monday, his election address appeared in all the morning papers. And the fight was on.

chapter six

Selina Bradford had never lived through weeks of such excitement. Her family had always been connected with politics and, through her father, her husband and her elder brother who was an MP, she had met all the leading parliamentary figures. Politics had always been one of her keenest interests and it was small wonder that her sons had been infected. In this election, they were both standing for Parliament. Yet it was not their chances, nor her brother's, nor the usual tension in her family during a general election which so thrilled her. It was the delicious excitement of her friendship with Disraeli.

In her youth, she had been amused by him and had flirted with him, although she sensed it was playing with fire. The stories of his romantic adventures, his flamboyant and striking appearance, his wit and "foreignness," all combined to make him fascinating to the girls of her circle. But Selina was quite sensible. She would not be drawn into an affair with him and would as soon have thought of becoming his wife as of dancing naked in St.

419

James's Park. With his marriage to the extraordinary Mrs. Lewis and her own to Bradford, she had seen much less of him, although she had watched his rise in the party to which her husband belonged with admiration and some astonishment. She had got to know him again through Bradford's appointment as Lord Chamberlain during his short Ministry and, when her sister Anne told her how lonely he was after his wife's death, her sympathy had been swift and genuine. No one who had seen how wounded he was could have failed to pity him and his gratitude for her kindness had been extremely touching. He was still so amusing and so perceptive of one's moods and so skillful at making one feel witty and intelligent oneself and the only person in the world whose approval mattered to him that meeting him was like a drug. One could not wait to see him again, and then again.

He was so open and romantically old-fashioned in the way he responded to beauty, and she knew she was still attractive, and in the way he spoke of friendship as love and paid little, extravagant compliments that were funny and deeply affectionate. Such things had never been said to her before. She might have been embarrassed, except that she knew he also spoke and wrote in the same manner to Anne. It was really as if they shared a lover, but one who was satisfied with appreciation and sympathy. She could not deny that it was stimulating. There was round him an unmistakable air of power and self-sufficiency. It had made her quite afraid of him at first. For so long, to her and all the world, he had been an enigma. And now he had let her see behind the mask, to the vulnerable man who desperately needed affection and someone to share his thoughts and hopes and many problems. She was immensely flattered that he had chosen her and trusted so completely in her discretion. For he told her everything, holding nothing back, his worries and pleasures, his dealings with his colleagues and the Queen, his maneuvers against his enemies, his frankest opinions. It was as if he wanted her to see through his eyes and think with his mind, which sometimes she felt she had begun to do.

The sudden announcement that Gladstone was going to the country had sent her mind spinning. For all that her life had been passed among politicians, she had never known so much nor understood so well the issues involved. All at once, everything that Dizzy had told her was no longer abstract. There was an object—to win. And she knew that it was possible. The Conservative Central Office had estimated from the by-election results that the party might have a majority of three seats. The Liberals had always done so well at the polls that to expect any more would be foolish. Dizzy was disappointed. With such a small majority, he would never be secure; any dissatisfied group on his own side could topple him. Yet he told her to wait and see. This was to be the first election in which the voting was to be in secret, when the voters did not have to state their choice in public in front of their employers and landlords and workmates. "The ballot box will tell," he said. It was nearly unbelievable, just the suggestion that he might be Prime Minister again, which no one but him had every imagined. She would be the most intimate friend of the Prime Minister, who had sworn to her that he loved her and lived only to see her . . . He had been so busy, advising and encouraging his supporters, speaking and writing, that she had told him he need not send her a letter every day, as he did. "I am making no sacrifice in writing to you," he replied. "It relieves my heart; and is the most agreeable thing to me, next to receiving a letter from you. In the greatest trials in life, it sustains one to feel that you are remembered by those whom you love. I can truly say that, amid all this whirl, you are never for a moment absent from my thoughts and feeling."

As polling began, Disraeli found a house in Whitehall Gardens. He would have preferred to be nearer the Bradfords in Belgrave Square, but at least his new home was in easy walking distance of the House of Commons.

There was nothing he wanted as much as two days rest, preferably at Hughenden, or at Weston with Selina, where he remembered the long evenings they had sat and talked quietly in the garden until sunset had turned to moonlight, but he could not be spared. He had to give an example of tirelessness and energy. His party machine was in operation and for the first time Conservatives were contesting every seat, yet no one could discount the might of the Liberals, who had virtually controlled huge sections of the country for as long as anyone remembered, especially London and the most important manufacturing boroughs. From these areas, the local agents reported little chance of success. He, himself, had the annoyance of having his seat in Buckinghamshire contested by a Liberal. The challenge was insignificant and it was purely a tactic to distract him from the main contest, but he used the hustings to answer the flood of speeches which Gladstone was making in his own constituency at Greenwich.

At the end of the first week in February, the borough returns were coming in. In London, the first result was in Marylebone. Conservative hopes had been high, but it went to the Liberals. Immediately, Disraeli's critics sensed disaster and blamed him for granting household suffrage in his Reform Bill. "He has led the party to commit suicide," they declared. However, the group which met in his drawing-room at 2 Whitehall Gardens at the end of the week were in a much more confident mood. Every message from the London constituencies confirmed a definite swing to the Conservatives. It was greater than any of them had expected and they talked excitedly, Manners, Northcote and Hardy, while they waited. John Gorst, the young barrister who had been made Principal Agent, had arrived and was in the study with Disraeli. There was a ring at the front doorbell and, after a moment, Derby came in.

"You'll have heard the news," Manners said. "We've won seats at Chelsea, Greenwich and Finsbury, as well as in the City."

"And Hackney and Tower Hamlets," Derby added, with a slight smile.

As they reacted, Disraeli camed from the study with Montagu Corry. "Yes, I've heard," he said. "Things look interesting, do they not?"

"Is there any more news, Sir," Northcote asked.

"The Metropolitan returns—and some of the northern and Midlands boroughs. Gorst is about to favor us with his predictions."

He was giving nothing away, but Hardy knew him well enough now to realize that the news from the other boroughs was better than good. "From the London results," he suggested, "it looks as if we could have a majority of about seven."

Disraeli nodded. "Something like that."

"Gladstone is prostrate," Derby told him, smiling. Of the two seats at Greenwich, one had gone to a Conservative, who was top of the poll. Gladstone had come second and only escaped defeat by 403 votes. "He is so bitter, he says it is more like a defeat."

They all fell silent as Gorst joined them, carrying a sheaf of papers which he held out to Disraeli. Disraeli shook his head. "No, no, Mr. Gorst, it is your moment. You organized the party. Pray do the honors." He paused. "And I believe these gentlemen have not heard the northern results."

Gorst seemed flushed. He cleared his throat. "Well, gentlemen, Central Office reports that we have taken Manchester, Bradford, Sheffield, Leeds..." As the list went on, the others looked at Disraeli whose eyes were half shut as though he listened to a litany. "... Nottingham, Newcastle-on-Tyne, Wakefield, Warrington and Northampton," Gorst concluded. He hesitated. "If the trend continues throughout the country, my office predicts a possible majority of twenty."

The others broke out into an excited babble. It would be an astounding victory. Disraeli stopped them. "Yes, I almost think we can congratulate ourselves," he said. "However, there are all the Scottish and Irish and the county returns to come in. It is too early to predict anything. It still depends on which choice the British people makes—their pay packets or the Empire."

The answer was known at the end of the following week. The counties showed the same swing as the boroughs, only more marked. Even Liberal Scotland was returning Conservatives, and the Conservative lead rose from 20 to 40 and still higher as more results were declared. Disraeli was returned triumphantly for Buckinghamshire and was now certain to be the next Prime Minister. His letters to Selina became more exultant. All he needed was to have her by his side to have everything he wanted. "I am very well, but sigh for moonlight. I think I could live, and love, in that light for ever!"

Gladstone had not recovered from his own near defeat and the rejection of his party by the country threw him into numbing depression. Even former Cabinet Ministers lost their seats. He was convinced that it was the brewers who had brought about his defeat, because he had shortened the licensing hours. "I have been borne down in a torrent of gin and beer," he said bitterly. Everywhere sin was triumphant. He had to accept that he had been beaten, yet he could not bring himself to resign. One thing obsessed him, the five millions he had saved by his painstaking economies. They were to have restored his party's fortunes by doing away with income tax, or for use in some nobler purpose. The thought that Disraeli would now have the spending of them for his own schemes nearly made him distraught. His wife, Catherine, comforted him, when he could find no legal way to use it up that would not be blocked by Parliament, now controlled by the Conservatives. She wrote to their son, "Is it not disgusting, after all Papa's labor and patriotism and years of work, to think of handing over his nest-egg to that Jew?"

Until Gladstone had formally resigned, Disraeli could only wait, but he had to be ready to take over and began to form his Cabinet. There were other problems which he had to solve. One of them he mentioned as he strolled with Corry through Hyde Park. He believed in exercise and was to be seen walking in the parks in all weathers. He had taken to wearing a long, white, high-collared coat like Bentinck used to wear and that, together with his wide-brimmed velour hat, made him a conspicuous figure. People always stopped to gaze at him, the men bowing or raising their hats. Sometimes he nodded back slightly, but more often he took absolutely no notice. "I intend to keep the Cabinet as small as possible," he told Corry. "It will be more manageable. No more than twelve—six peers and six commoners."

"The perfect balance between tradition and democracy," Corry commented.

Disraeli grunted. "We are in the age of democracy. The party and the country must come to terms with that." He walked on in silence for a few steps. "With that in mind . . . I think I must bring Salisbury back into the fold."

Corry stopped, shaken. "But he is your most outspoken critic, Sir! Most of the right wing members take their lead from him."

"Which is why I'd prefer to have him as an ally."

Corry was worried and caught up with Disraeli as he moved on again. "It might drive him even further away, Sir. It could be very damaging, if we don't think of exactly the right approach."

"I have already made one," Disraeli told him, blandly. "Through his stepmother, Lady Derby."

Corry's mouth opened, and closed again. When would he learn not to be surprised? Mary, Countess of Derby, had been married to Salisbury's father for twenty years. A gentle, charming woman, she had been a dear friend of Dizzy's for all that time and was now married to his second-in-command. She must have been sorely troubled by the breach between them and her headstrong stepson. "Will he agree to a meeting, Sir?"

"She believes so. Oh, I expect he will mutter and search his conscience. But Mary is a very persuasive woman."

Disraeli was not quite as confident as he seemed, but he had suggested to Lady Derby that she might point out to her stepson the size of his majority, which was even now being confirmed. He did not fear Salisbury, who could either join him or languish in outer darkness. But it would be a waste. He had detected an ambition in him as driving as his own had once been, and he trusted to that. They had come out of the trees and he saw ahead across the green expanse the distant traffic of Park Lane. He turned aside abruptly. He did not wish to catch sight of Grosvenor Gate.

When they reached Whitehall Gardens, they found that Salisbury had already called and left again. It was unfortunate that they had missed him. Disraeli immediately sent Mr. Baum round to his house in Arlington Street with a note, inviting him to call back at his convenience. It was time they had a conversation on the state of public affairs, "a conversation interesting to me and, I think, not disadvantageous to either of us."

The next day Gladstone at last resigned, and the Queen summoned Disraeli to Windsor. He had heard from Lady Ely, his confidante among her ladies, that she was impatient to see him, but even he was not prepared for the warmth of his welcome.

Victoria almost ran into the Audience Room. In her happiness, she looked at least ten years younger. She took a quite personal pride in his achievement and, seeing him now bowing to her with just the right mixture of respect and friendly greeting, her pleasure at his return was immeasurable. He had not only returned, but in such a fashion that she would have him as her Minister and counsellor for the foreseeable future. "So you have not merely won, Mr. Disraeli," she said, "but with a substantial majority."

"The final total had just been confirmed, Ma'am," he told her. "A majority of one hundred and five seats over the Liberals. Fifty over all parties."

Victoria gasped and clasped her hands together. He watched her as she moved excitely about the room. "It is astonishing . . ." she muttered. "Unprecedented!"

Disraeli could only agree. "I confess I am still astonished myself, Ma'am." He had never really been doubtful, once his instincts had told him that the tide was running in his favor. He had expected to win and only wondered by what margin, hoping that it would be enough to let him govern for once without having to make compromises and petty concessions to every malcontent. The final result gave him such power as no peacetime Prime Minister had ever had. Even the political landslides in his novels had not been so tremendous.

Victoria turned to him, smiling radiantly. "You must kiss hands, Mr. Disraeli," she announced, advancing to him. He knelt stiffly and kissed her hand, holding it for just a moment longer than was strictly necessary. He felt her small fingers squeeze his in answer. When he looked up she was gazing at him so fondly that he had the distinct impression she might embrace him. She was aware of the impulse herself and stepped back to sit demurely, folding her hands in her lap, as he rose. "You have been triumphantly chosen by the country you have worked for so long. I know you will have no difficulty in forming a Government."

He took a list from his inside pocket and handed it to her. "I have taken the liberty of suggesting some names for Your Majesty's perusal."

She scanned the column of names quickly. "Lord Derby...yes. Sir Stafford Northcote, Lord Cairns...Mr. Hunt, Lord John Manners. Mr. Cross?"

"He is a lawyer from Lancashire, Ma'am, an extremely capable organizer, as he proved on my tour last year. I fancy he will make an outstanding Home Secretary."

"And he is another commoner," Victoria noted. "That is good. Yes, I approve. You have gathered a team of exceptionally able men."

"I am anxious to bring as much new blood into the Cabinet as possible. If I may say so, I have been grooming them for years."

Victoria smiled. "Well, with Lord Derby as Foreign Secretary, guided by you, our voice should once again be heard in world affairs."

"It is one of my most fervent wishes, Ma'am."

"One of them?" she queried.

"The guiding principles of my Government shall be those which I have established for my party," he explained. "The maintenance of our institutions, the protection of our Empire, and the improvement of the condition of the people."

427

Victoria nodded decidedly. "You may depend on my support. As I know I can count on your consideration in everything that concerns me." Her last words were just sufficiently pointed.

"Whatever Your Majesty wishes shall be done—whatever the difficulties," Disraeli promised. "May I assure you of my complete devotion and loyalty as unaltered as on the first occasion I gave it, the day of Your Majesty's coronation. I would dare also to offer my heart ... but, Your Majesty had that long ago." He laid his hand over his heart and bowed.

Victoria smiled very slightly with a mixture of deep satisfaction and hidden amusement. It was really too theatrical, but she found him so fascinating, she could forgive him anything.

He straightened. "I cannot resist mentioning that I would appear to be justified in declining to take office last year."

"Indeed so, Mr. Disraeli," she commented. "Mr. Gladstone tells me that he is so sickened by his defeat that he intends to retire from politics." Gladstone's reaction was nonsense, of course. She could recognize sour grapes, when she saw them. She had told him that Sir Robert Peel had said the same when he had been defeated, but had been unable to carry it out.

"I am afraid, Ma'am, that I do not place too much credence in the remarks of that gentleman," Disraeli said drily. "Even as regards his own retirement."

Victoria laughed, then considered him shrewdly. "One not inconsiderable result of your victory, Mr. Disraeli," she said, "should be that all serious opposition to you inside your own party should now have ended forever."

Manners and Northcote made their way with difficulty into the main room of the Carlton Club. The atmosphere in the club, which until recently had been defiant or despondent by turns, the scene of meetings of small cliques dissatisfied with the leadership, had completely changed. It was filled with members, all elated and noisy, talking at once. There were some here they did not

428

remember having seen for a decade or more. Manners nudged Northcote. He had just noticed Salisbury standing alone by the window. As they moved forward, it was refreshing to be greeted enthusiastically by people who had barely been civil, not so long ago.

Barrington and Lord Henry Lennox came to meet them, with William Hart Dyke, the Conservative Whip. "There's been nothing like it since Pitt!" Barrington laughed. "Not even Peel had a majority like this!"

"I hear from Brooks's that the Liberal Whip has fled town," Hart Dyke said, smiling. "We are in for years."

"And who do we owe it to?" Lennox demanded loudly. "One man. Every vote for us was a vote of confidence in him!"

Salisbury had moved forward. He heard Lennox and the murmur of everyone who stood round him. They had all surrendered. In spite of his father's admiration for Disraeli, he had never accepted the indignity of the party being led by such an outsider. Educated at Eton and Oxford, entering Parliament at the age of twenty-three, he had all the promise and qualities to fit him for a brilliant career, but apart from a brief period in the Cabinet under Derby, he had abandoned it to wage his long, implacable campaign against the Jew, who had destroyed the purity of parliamentary politics by his shameless manipulation of the House and his blatant jockeying for power. He had been convinced that ultimately Disraeli would lead the party to destruction and had sacrificed his career to prevent that. Listening to the voices around him, he wondered if in fact he had merely thrown it away? He was no longer a promising boy. He was forty-four. It was pride that had made him carry on the fight so long. The party had been so weak and divided that it had been natural to blame the leader. But what would the situation have been if Salisbury had supported him, instead? He had had his conversation with Disraeli at Whitehall Gardens and had heard his views on all the most important subjects that concerned the public interests. They had not been materially in disagreement with his own. Perhaps he should have listened to his afther more carefully. A tall, broad-shouldered figure with a full beard, his light brown hair receding from the dome of his forehead, Robert Arthur Cascoyne Cecil, third Marquess of Salsibury, began to admit that, perhaps, through all those wasted years, he had been wrong.

All eyes in the room turned to the door as Disraeli came in, leaning on Corry's arm. There was a second's hush, then a shout of welcome and a continuous, swelling cheer as the crowd parted and he walked slowly forward to join the other leaders. There was no pressing in on him. No one tried to shake his hand. He had become such an object of respect and authority that the ordinary members were in awe of him. He bowed his head to the group that now included Derby, Lord Cairns and Gathorne Hardy.

"Have you heard the latest news, Sir?" Hardy asked. Like the others, his manner was now much more respectful. "Gladstone's resigned from Parliament."

Disraeli shrugged. "I have heard something of the like. I do not believe it. He will not be able to stay away."

"One thing is certainly true, however," Derby told him. "Because he cannot face being defeated, he has told Granville that he no longer considers himself leader of the Liberal Party, and will resign formally, as soon as it can be arranged."

For almost a minute, Disraeli stood absolutely motionless and expressionless, then turned to speak to his supporters. With the liberty of an old friend, Lennox thrust a glass of champagne into his hand.

Hart Dyke stepped forward. "Gentlemen!" he called. "To the Chief!"

The shout was taken up and repeated all round the room. "The Chief! The Chief!"

As his colleagues and their followers drank his health, Disraeli had to pause. He smiled faintly in acknowledgment, nodding to them. Not one of them could possibly have read his thoughts.

Disraeli was back in the Prime Minister's study at 10 Downing Street. If anything, it was shabbier and more in need of decoration than before. He had filled all the principal posts in his Cabinet, except one which he offered to Lord John Manners. Loyal and capable, although not up to one of the great offices of State, Manners was his oldest and most trusted colleague.

"Postmaster General?" Manners repeated. "I am grateful and, of course, accept. Though I'm afraid I may be a square peg in a round hole in a business department."

Disraeli tapped his shoulder and moved stiffly to sit at the desk. "I have every confidence in your ability, John. And I should be able to give you time to learn."

Manners smiled. "Yes. You now have unlimited power." He was surprised to see Disraeli frown and look away.

The silence was broken, as Disraeli shifted at a sudden pain in his leg and rubbed his thigh. "Power?" he murmured. "It has come to me twenty years too late. If only I had your youth and your health."

Manners was concerned for him. "Still, there are things you can do now," he said, encouragingly. "Things you have always wanted to do."

Disraeli looked at him and suddenly smiled, a full, open smile, delighted and mischievous. His face was transformed. "I feel like a child in front of a giant toyshop window, holding a five pound note. Where do I begin?"

Manners laughed. The smile took him back to when they had first met. Then as now, he thought that Dizzy smiling was like nothing so much as the Joker in a pack of cards. "Well, have you chosen your Cabinet?"

Disraeli's face was masked again, although clearly something still amused him. "It is nearly complete, thanks to you. There is only one lesser post still to be filled, the Secretary for India. It must be a peer."

"What about the new Lord Lytton?"

Poor Bulwer's son . . . "No, I have other ideas for him," Disraeli said. "I have offered it to young Salisbury."

"Surely not?" Manners exclaimed. "You have always forgiven him—but this is too generous. A place in the Cabinet? In any case, he will never accept."

"I think he will," Disraeli contradicted gently. "And it is not generosity. I see real promise in Salisbury. He is highly intelligent, inquiring, balanced but forceful." He paused. "Besides, it will weaken the possibility of a revolt by the right wing of the party."

As Manners smiled and shook his head, Corry came in with a small box which he laid on the table. "Excuse me, Sir," he said. "This has just arrived from the Isle of Wight, from the Queen."

Manners caught his excitement as Disraeli cut the tape round the box. "Has she sent you a decoration already?"

They bent forward, when Disraeli opened the box. He parted the wax paper that lined it and, inside, were one small bunch of snowdrops and two of primroses. A card lay on them, in the Queen's handwriting. It read, "The first of our spring flowers, which you said you so much admired. V.R." Manners looked at Corry, puzzled.

"How charming . . . " Disraeli breathed. "I shall wear them on my breast, to show that I have been decorated by the Faery Queen herself—with flowers from her enchanted island." He laid a bunch of primroses on his lapel and looked up. Neither of the other two could be sure how serious he was.

The primroses pinned to Disraeli's lapel troubled Salisbury, too, at the first meeting of the full Cabinet that afternoon. They stood out against the black silk of the revers, disturbingly bizarre. He did not choose to comment on them, nor did anyone else, although he saw a few raised eyebrows, when the Chief came in. He, himself, did not plan to say anything that might even hint at criticism for a while. He knew he was still under sufferance and that some of the others, particularly Derby, the Foreign Secretary, Northcote, Chancellor of the Exchequer, Cairns, Lord Chancellor, and Manners felt uncomfortable at having to work with him. He held himself very stifly and correctly.

Disraeli sat in the Prime Minister's chair in the center of the long table with his back to the fireplace, with the portrait of Walpole hanging above it. He felt the polished wood of the table under his hands and the solid arms of the chair surrounding him. He felt cocooned with power, as all the links and vibrations of this room rushed in on him. He sensed them now more strongly than ever before. Perhaps, he thought wryly, because this seat is at last truly mine. And he thanked whichever of his departed predecessors had selected the center chair, for the warmth of the fire at his back on this raw day was distinctly pleasant. They were all watching him... "I shall not take up much of your time, gentlemen," he stated crisply. "You have your offices and departments to organize. In fact, I have only two specific requests. To ask you, Lord Salisbury, to look into the question of replacing the Viceroy of India."

Singled out, Salisbury kept his expression as immobile as Disraeli's. "Certainly, Sir. The Liberals' choice has proved unsuited to his position." Disraeli had passed on to him a report that the present Viceroy refused to use the Secret Service grant "on moral grounds."

"With Russian pressure on India and Afghanistan," Derby said, "we must have a man there with the ability to resist it effectively and yet, at the same time, not to provoke action."

"Quite so," Disraeli agreed, and turned to Northcote. "And I would ask the Chancellor to prepare for an early Budget."

"That might be tricky, Sir," Northcote suggested. "After Gladstone's offer to abolish the Income Tax."

"Well, in spite of the demands of social legislation," Disraeli told him, "I am in favor of an immediate reduction, say by one third. But we cannot cut it all together, not without further reductions in the Army and Navy, which I will not permit."

"It would be madness," Derby declared. "With Germany threatening France again. It could mean a war that would spread throughout Europe."

"Surely even Bismarck wouldn't risk that?" Hardy objected.

"He might," Disraeli said, "because these past years have taught him to discount any chance of British intervention. We must show the Iron Chancellor that the lion is not dead. He has only been sleeping." There was light laughter round the table. Then, as Disraeli began to collect together the papers in front of him, the members of the Cabinet glanced at one another, uncertainly. He moved to push his chair back.

"Is that all, Sir?" Cairns asked for all of them.

Disraeli seemed surprised. "I have too much respect for the intelligence of everyone around this table to give you directions at this stage."

Northcote coughed. "May I ask—what will be your main concern, Sir?"

Disraeli laid his papers back down. He had thought his role and his objectives would be obvious to everyone who knew him. "I intend to push forward the kind of progressive Conservatism which has been my ideal for forty years."

Something had been troubling Salisbury. "You mentioned 'social legislation.' Could you give us some hint of what you have in mind?"

Disraeli considered him, then looked to either side. Well, it had to come. "Nothing too much," he assured them, soothingly. "Let's say ... slum clearances, the setting up of savings banks, a shortening of the hours of work, legal equality between workers and employers— and the establishment of the rights of Trades Unions. Among others."

Salisbury clenched his hands in his lap to stop himself replying. There was a reaction of shock among most of the others. Manners hid his smile of admiration. Had they expected the leopard to change his spots?

"But that is more radical than anything ever proposed by Gladstone!" Lord Carnarvon blurted. He was Colonial Secretary and a friend of Salisbury.

"It certainly does not sound like Conservative policy," Salisbury agreed quietly.

Disraeli leant forward on the table and put the tips of his fingers together. "So that there is no mistake," he said seriously, "I shall repeat what I have said before. I wish this Government to represent the interests of every class, since it was every class that elected us—and not just one section of society." He looked at Salisbury, who was silent. "I admit that I am not completely sure how some of these ideas are to be achieved. But I intend to discuss them with the Queen at the earliest opportunity."

"If you discuss unformed ideas with Her Majesty," Derby put forward hesitantly, "asking as it were for her advice, will it not give her a false impression of her personal power?"

Disraeli sighed. "Let me tell you my attitude to the Queen. Quite simply, having been reared to sovereignty, trained by the Prince Consort and used to discussion with a series of brilliant Ministers, she has an understanding of British and international politics that few statesmen can equal. Anyone who ignores her advice is a fool."

"That may, indeed, be so," Cairns commented, unconvinced. "One must remember, however, that she is a woman."

Disraeli nodded. "Precisely." He picked up his papers and rose. "So added to everything else, she has feelings and intuition." He nodded to them again and left.

The weeks and months that followed were exhausting for him. The demands were unending. As well as Government posts, he had many others to fill, including the royal Household. He at least had the pleasure of making Lord Bradford Master of the Horse, for Selina's sake, but one other appointment caused bitterness. The charming Lord Henry Lennox had followed him loyally, but had never fulfilled his early promise, in spite of his many talents. He had no staying power. Disraeli wanted to reward his loyalty, although it was difficult, and finally offered him the position of President of the Board of Works with responsibility for the parks, palaces and public buildings of London. It seemed ideal. Although Lennox accepted and appeared happy, he was grossly offended that he was not in the Cabinet. While still keeping up a show of friendship, he was viciously abusive behind Disraeli's back. Philip Rose, however, was genuinely grateful for being made a baronet. He still handled Disraeli's financial affairs, but the running of the complex party organization had been taken over by Gorst and his team.

Letters, petitions, invitations poured in. Everyone, it seemed, had claims on the Prime Minister. There were speeches, Cabinets, debates in the Commons, reports and continual meetings with the Queen. He had always treated the Prince of Wales with consideration, Prince Hal, as he called him, and now became a favorite, which was flattering, though time consuming.

Meanwhile, there was the business of Parliament and Northcote's first Budget which he helped him to construct and to present. Even their enemies could find little to criticize. Undoubtedly, the atmosphere was calmer in the House of Commons, since Gladstone had gone home to Hawarden, declaring that he wanted "an interval between Parliament and the grave" to complete his religious studies and his critical analysis of Homer. Disraeli set Cross to work on the new Factory Act and, at last, could have a short rest with Lady Chesterfield at Bretby. He looked forward to a stay with Selina, but the Bishops lit a bomb under him by proposing a Bill to put a stop to the growth of Ritualism in the Church. It was essentially an argument between High Anglicans and Low Anglicans, who saw in embroidered vestments, incense and elaborate rites a movement toward Catholicism, and Disraeli had no desire to be involved in a religious controversy. He had no option, for the debate soon spread beyond Parliament and the country became sharply and bitterly divided. A wide division appeared in the Cabinet with one side led by the High Church Salisbury and the other by Lord Cairns, and the whole situation was made more inflammable when Gladstone stormed back to Westminster, attacking the Bill with all his eloquence in the name of Liberty. He had lost his hold on the House, however, and only twenty of his former followers backed him. Dismissed by Disraeli as a champion of the "Mass in masquerade," he gave up the fight as abruptly as he had begun it and hurried back to North Wales, before any more damage was done to his reputation among moderate churchmen. Working quietly and sensibly, Disraeli held his Cabinet together and saw the Bill passed in a modified form that saved the Church and the country from splitting apart. He was warmly congratulated, but he resented the bigotry on both sides which had kept him from more essential matters. The Queen, as Defender of the Faith, was more indebted to him than ever.

During this, another widescale war was threatened in Europe. France had made a brave recovery after her defeat by Germany. Bismarck's eyes were on the successful reconstruction of her industries and her army, and he had begun the troop exercises and self-justifying speeches that everyone now recognized. They were the prelude to his giving the order to attack again.

And all this time, Disraeli's heart was aching.

He could no longer hide from himself that he had fallen in love with Selina Bradford. To be with her, near her, to see her and hear from her when they were apart became an obsession. He had not forgotten Mary Anne, but all through his life he had needed the spur of love to drive him on. There had to be one special person who cared for him above all others and to whom his deeds were dedicated as by a medieval knight to his Lady. That was the nearest parallel. He did not desire Selina physically, although he could gaze at her face, watching her changing expressions, and admire the grace of her body by the hour. He had known fierce sexual love and found a contentment with Mary Anne that had forever satisfied that part of him. From Selina, he needed total admiration and sympathy and the assurance that his feelings were returned. He did not even wish to take her from her husband. All he had to know was that that portion of her love that was free to give was his.

It was a pity that he had not concentrated his affection on Lady Chesterfield. She was not as vivid, nor as intellectually alive as her sister, but she would have been more understanding and gentle with him. Selina was more capricious. She accepted Disraeli's adoration of her at one level and responded to it, yet his intensity disturbed her and sometimes she backed away and would not answer his letters nor agree to meet him. But she always weakened and so he lived in hope, which was more painful than rejection.

He was seventy and suffering all the passions and heartbreak of youth. He knew it was absurd and that he was in danger of becoming ridiculous. Yet he did not care. He saw life without love as a black and desolate wasteland. Tortured by gout and asthma, he escaped for two days to Brighton, only to return at once, when he heard both Lady Chesterfield and Selina were in London. But he missed her. She had already gone, when he reached Belgrave Square. He hid his despair behind a mask of polite indifference. Later he wrote to Selina, "To love as I love, and rarely to see the being one adores, whose constant society is absolutely necessary to my life; to be precluded even from the only shadowy compensation for such a torturing doom—the privilege of relieving my heart by expressing its affection—is a lot which I never could endure, and cannot. But for my strange position, which enslaves, while it elevates me, I would fly forever . . ."

Then the wasteland burst into flower, as suddenly as little paper Japanese blossoms dropped into water. Selina and Bradford accepted an invitation to join a houseparty at Hughenden.

The Bradfords and the few Cabinet colleagues and their wives who were their fellow-guests were delighted with the arrangements made for their comfort. Disraeli was the ideal host, making sure that only the choicest food and wines were served and that there was always something to keep them amused, yet allowing them just to sit and talk, if that was what they wished. He wanted everything to be perfect for Selina and her husband, who were the last to arrive. With the others, he showed them around and was tremendously relieved when Selina said she was enchanted with everything, the house and garden, the woodland walks, the little lake with its island, where a colony of swans had now established itself. The boys from the neighborhood stole the eggs, he explained, or there would be more. They all had tea on the terrace and laughed at the raucous cries and strut of the peacocks.

Selina had never seen him so relaxed. The sense of power was even stronger. Of course, he was now internationally famous, there was no denying. When they heard she was coming to Hughenden, all her friends had been envious. She had wondered if she ought to. She had made some foolish promises to him in the past, because she was so fond of him and because he looked so hurt, but she hoped he would not try to hold her to them. Then, when she had implied she might not come, he had said he would be very happy to accept Bradford on his own. Had his feelings changed? He was certainly different, not exactly distant to her, but reserved. He did not gaze at her, in that way that used to trouble her so much. And he seemed very attentive to Mary Derby.

Disraeli was controlling himself with the greatest difficulty. To have her here, under his roof, gave him a sensation which was practically unbearable. He heard every word she said, and yet he forced himself not to look at her, unless there was a reason to turn in her direction. He knew that, somehow, he must come to some kind of terms with her. He had read and re-read her letters of a year ago. One phrase from them had burned into his memory. "Have confidence in me, believe in me, believe that I am true—oh! how true" she had written. He could no longer believe the words, but it was something to have had them written to him once. He had tried to stay away from her, and failed. Clearly, she still wanted to see him, or she would not be here. But he had realized that, if he went on trying to force her, he would drive her away from him, permanently. He had three choices. He could either hide his feelings altogether, which he knew he could never sustain, or disguise them as mere romantic playfulness, spicing a platonic friendship, which was just possible—or give up seeing her completely, which was unthinkable.

He did not manage to be alone with her until the evening before dinner. Some of the others were talking quietly in the garden room. Disraeli joined them and, when Selina came in, he contrived to lead her out into the drawing-room on the pretext of seeing the portrait of herself which Lady Chresterfield had sent him. "Bradford promises to send me one of you, since you will not," he told her. She laughed. "That's better." He wanted to tell her how incredibly lovely she was in her pale lilac silk evening gown, the draperies of the bustle and skirt frilled with silver, but he restrained himself. "How delightful to have you to myself for a moment."

"I have looked forward to it," she said, smiling. It sounded sincere and his heart leaped. "I wanted to congratulate you on the way you forced Bismarck to back down."

"Oh, no, Selina!" he protested. "I did not invite you here to talk politics."

"It is you who have made me so interested in them. How did you do it?"

"Influence you—or Bismarck?"

Selina laughed again. "Bismarck . . . Everyone is saying that a European war has been avoided—all due to you."

It had been astonishingly simple. To make sure that France could not find an ally for a war of retaliation and to protect Germany from attack from the east, Bismarck had set up a treaty of mutual co-operation between Germany, Austria and Russia, the League of the Three Emperors. Under Liberal leaders, Britain had become so isolationist that her possible involvement was not even considered. Having insured against interference by the other two major powers, Bismarck prepared to launch a final, crushing offensive against France, to remove her forever as a threat to German supremacy.

The war fever had steadily mounted, since Disraeli took office. The French desperately wanted to ask for his help, but could not do so openly in case it gave Bismarck the excuse for which he had been waiting. More and more, Disraeli realized that in some way the German Chancellor had to be checked, to protect the independence of all the smaller nations of Europe. Unexpected information from the Ambassador to St. Petersburg gave him his chance. During his state visit, the Czar had spoken of his desire to preserve peace. Now, on the eve of a visit to Berlin, he had apparently sent a despatch to the

Kaiser insisting that no warlike action was taken against France before their discussion. Immediately, Disraeli authorized Derby to telegraph to St. Petersburg, assuring the Czar's Foreign Minister that Great Britain would back his stand to prevent another Franco-Prussian War. At the same time, he induced the Queen to write to both Emperors also expressing her resolve to preserve peace.

Suddenly faced with a concerted move by Britain and Russia, Bismarck's plans were thrown out of gear. He could not find out how far their agreement extended. The new British Government under Disraeli was an unknown factor, disturbing all his calculatons. He himself had no military alliance with Russia. Had they signed a secret treaty with the British? Would either have taken this stand without it? Did it include the French? His immensely devious mind saw every possible combination. He decided, for the time being, to take no risk and wrote to the British and Russian Foreign Ministers, protesting that his intentions had been misunderstood. However, as they had relieved the unfortunate tension between his country and France, he congratulated them on their contribution to the cause of peace.

Czar Alexander had made the first move, but it would have had little effect without Disraeli's intervention. By one swift move, at no cost and no danger, he had reasserted Britain's claim to have a voice in European affairs. Once again the smaller nations, who had been powerless against German domination, looked to Britain for protection and Disraeli had stepped on to the international stage.

"I am so proud of your friendship," Selina said.

They were words he had waited to hear and he could not stop himself as he answered, "You must know that what I feel for you is not friendship."

Selina was troubled. He was going to spoil everything. "Please—I beg you not to say any more. You must not keep saying you love me." She had spoken more sharply than she meant, and smiled. "Someone might believe it."

"But it is true," he told her simply. He saw her glance

away, that anxious look with its hint of impatience that he had come to fear. But he still could not stop himself trying to make her understand. "I cannot help it. I am even conscious of being ridiculous, but at heart—I feel like a boy feels. I live for the moments I see you. I accept all invitations to receptions and dinners and parties, only in the hope you might be there. Although to see you alone and with others is the difference between the sun and the moon."

"No, please!" she begged him, distressed. "You must not go on. I should not have encouraged you."

"It happened before you even smiled at me."

She knew it was her fault. She should have been firmer from the beginning and they could still have been friends. This time, she had to end it, however much it hurt him, however much she would miss him. "Don't you see? I was flattered. But I am a married woman. We—we played a charade that became too real. I was selfish. Perhaps I led you to hope too much, and I am sorry. But I think it best that we do not meet again." She made for the door.

"Selina—please, not without hearing me! Surely, at least, I deserve that?" he pleaded. She paused and, as soon as she had done so, regretted it, but it was too late and he had followed her. His voice was more gentle. "I honor you too much ever to do or say anything in public that would embarrass you. But the thought that you could cut me out of your life so simply would be unbearable." It was his voice she could not resist. She tried to steel herself against the pain she heard in it and, even as she did so, began to relent. "You are never for an instant absent from my mind," he told her. "I can remember every word you have said every time we have met."

For a long moment, she did not speak, then she sighed. "Well . . . I know I can rely on your honor." She turned, although she still did not look at him. "But at least we must not meet so often," she insisted, "and you must not write to me so often—nor shall I."

"Without love, one does not live. One merely exists in a gray world," he said quietly. He moved closer. "What I

442

told you is true. To see you, or at least to hear from you, every day, is absolutely necessary to my existence."

"It is impossible ..." she protested, but much more faintly. She looked at him at last. His dark, compelling eyes were fixed on her and she smiled, giving in. "At least—not more than three times a week."

Relief flooded through him, when she smiled. He had not compromised. He had not dishonored either of them by disguising his true feelings. And now, if he could only prevent himself from being possessive, if he did not frighten her by being too intense, she would still be his.

chapter seven

Disraeli almost laughed aloud at Salisbury's expression, at the raised eyebrows and the mouth quirked in surprise. He had been to Windsor, and then to Marlborough House, and come straight to the India Office to catch Salisbury before he left at the end of the day.

Salisbury had recovered his composure. "India?" he queried. "The Prince of Wales is going to India?"

"On a state visit, it seems," Disraeli confirmed. "He told his mother that it was my idea and, since her Government approved, she reluctantly gave her permission."

Salisbury blinked. His massive brow lowered ominously. "And yet, sitting here, I knew nothing about it. Would you mind telling me, Prime Minister, why I have not been consulted till now?"

"Because, until now, I knew nothing about it, myself." This time, he did laugh. "It appears that our Prince Hal dreamed it up all on his own, as a means of strengthening the Subcontinent's loyalty to the Crown."

"His irresponsibility is incredible!" Salisbury splut-

445

tered. "Naturally, you told Her Majesty that we have definitely not authorized such a visit!"

Disraeli hesitated. ". . . No. That would have placed the Prince in an impossible situation. I merely said I had not discussed the details with you."

"But we must put a stop to it, before it's too late."

"I am not sure that I wish to put a stop to it. In fact, I wish I had thought of it, myself."

About to object, Salisbury paused to think. He had developed a considerable respect for the Chief and learned when his most casual remarks were not to be taken lightly. All at once, he saw what he meant. The Queen was seen as an abstract, almost mythical figure in India. A visit by her eldest son, the future King, would demonstrate her actual existence and personal care for her people. That could have a significant effect. The Liberals' neglect had led many Indians into thinking that Britain meant to abandon them. They had the example of Afghanistan. There, the Amir had watched his neighboring states being conquered one after the other by Russia and, with the Czar's army poised on his borders, had appealed to the British Government for protection. Gladstone's answer had been so negative and indefinite that the Amir had had no alternative but to reject his friendship with Britain and accept Russian political advisers in Kabul. Nearly all the present troubles and uncertainly in India were a direct result of that.

"Yes, I see," Salisbury said. "But can we really entrust such a visit to someone as lightweight as the Prince?"

"Most definitely," Disraeli answered, surprising him. "He appears indolent, but only because he has never been allowed to work and has not the habit. But he is a born diplomat, with a sincere desire to serve his country. Don't look so worried. When he was only seventeen, he carried off his visit to Canada and the United States triumphantly. And he's prepared. He's been studying Indian affairs secretly for months."

Salisbury was not entirely convinced, yet saw that for the trip to have its maximum effect it had to be made by the Heir to the Throne. "It will require an immense amount of organization. And in what style are the Prince and Princess to travel?"

"His wife's not going," Disraeli said. "He has not even told her. That will be an explosive moment, when she finds out."

Salisbury grunted. "Well, he is bound to get into scrapes with women, whether she is with him or not. So I suppose it's marginally better that she isn't."

Disraeli nodded. The Prince's indiscretions were notorious. "Much will depend on the character of the staff he takes with him. The Faery insists on reverend gentlemen and others of high moral tone—who might not abound in the Prince's entourage. However, I have undertaken to manage the entire affair, and she trusts me."

"What about the cost?"

"That is the problem. He does not have a shilling—and she will not give him one. As you say, he must travel on an imperial scale, so we shall have to raise the money from public funds."

In spite of Radical opposition, Disraeli had much less difficulty than he anticipated in persuading Parliament to vote sufficient money for the trip. Unable to bear the sight of his rival in power, Gladstone had finally resigned the Liberal leadership and his appearances were extremely rare. The new Liberal leader was the tall, shambling Marquess of Hartington. Always shabbily dressed, though one of the richest men in England, Harty-Tary was well-balanced and politically intelligent. He raised no objections to the state visit to India, except that the money voted was not enough.

There were innumerable problems connected with the visit. While Salisbury and he coped with the thousands of detailed arrangements to be made for a tour of six months, Disraeli became involved in endless wrangles and discussions between Windsor and Marlborough House.

Somehow, Disraeli emerged from it all without losing the respect or confidence of anyone. The Prince was especially grateful for the opportunity to do something useful at last and promised to inform him if he came across any matters which he thought might interest him particularly. Disraeli said goodbye to him that October with a profound sense of relief.

It had been a tiring, though tremendously productive, session in Parliment. The whole country was astonished by how much Disraeli's Government had accomplished. Encouraging each of his Departments to propose measures on the lines of social reform which he had laid down, he passed a series of Acts on the Trade Unions, making employers and workmen equal before the law and "conspiracy" in trade disputes no longer a crime, Factory Acts shortening the hours of work and ending the exploitation of women and children, empowered local authorities to pull down slums and build decent, lower-priced housing, founded the Friendly Societies to protect savings, improved sanitation and took steps to prevent the pollution of rivers, among many others.

It was the vindication of his concept of Tory Democracy, with its principle that all government exists solely for the good of the governed, that all public institutions are to be maintained only so far as they promote the happiness and welfare of the people and that all who are entrusted with any public function are trustees, not for their own class, but for the entire nation. His only regret was that it had taken so long. He would have passed many of the measures years before, if he had been given power. Now he could only make a beginning. Yet, and for the first time, he was satisfied. Although he still looked for the stroke that would reaffirm Britain's position as a world power.

When he reported to the Queen at Osborne after the session, she was concerned to see how tired he was. She was seated on a chair in her study, while he leaned on his cane, half crippled by gout and made breathless by asthma. They had been talking about how Russia had re-established her power in the Black Sea and was more openly encouraging the Slav Provinces to revolt against

448

Turkey. He paused, catching his breath, and shifted in discomfort.

"I am distressed to see you unwell, Mr. Disraeli," she said.

"A touch of gout, Ma'am," he told her. "The lower limbs reminding a youthful heart that they are not so young as they were."

She smiled, but was worried. "You must take more care of yourself. You should not be standing." She paused. "It is a pity that no one may sit during an audience." She paused again. "No one has, you know ... ever!"

"No one would dream of such a breach, Ma'am," he assured her.

She struggled with herself, and decided. ". . . You shall have a seat."

Disraeli was touched, knowing the effort it cost her to go against a lifetime of rigid protocol. And he was tempted, but shook his head. "I could not accept such an honor."

Victoria drew herself up. "Nonsense! I insist."

He bowed humbly. "Much as it grieves me to disobey Your Majesty, I must, out of respect, decline your gracious offer." His left leg really hurt abominably and, if she had continued to insist, he would have yielded gracefully. But he could tell that she was secretly relieved.

"Well—if you are determined . . ." she said quietly. She admired him all the more for not taking advantage of her daring. "I must thank you again for keeping me so fully informed, unlike your predecessor. Particularly in foreign affairs."

"Mr. Gladstone," he began delicately, "I fear, frequently underestimates their importance." She snorted. "Our standing abroad is not merely a question of prestige but, ultimately, also of economics. However much he prides himself on that subject, he has not mastered it."

"Exactly," she nodded. "Our overseas markets and our trade depend on our international influence."

He wanted to bring her back to the specific matter of

Russia. He had made many attempts to follow up the joint action for peace with the Czar, but Alexander and his Chancellor, Prince Gortchakoff, had always replied that they could not endanger their league with Austria and Germany. Reluctantly, Disraeli had come to realize that they were preparing for a clash between Russian and British interests. "In the case in point," he said, "a Russian fleet in the Eastern Mediterranean would menace Egypt and the Suez Canal, threatening our direct route to Australia and British India."

Victoria's thought echoed his own. "It has been perfectly obvious for years that, despite the Czar's protestations of friendship, the real design of the Russian push to the East has been to take control of India."

"That we shall never allow, Ma'am," he assured her. He was now on sensitive ground. "It is why I supported His Royal Highness, the Prince of Wales', current state visit there—so that the Indian peoples could demonstrate through him their unswerving loyalty to yourself."

Victoria frowned, yet it was true that Bertie had been received in Bombay with unparalleled enthusiasm, a rapturous welcome from all classes and castes. The gifts he had received on her behalf from the Indian princes were staggering, gold and rubies, whole baskets of diamonds. "You know I am strongly opposed to the Prince being considered as my representative—until he has learned to control his rashness and frivolity. However, in this instance . . ."

"It is only one of several steps I plan on taking, to make India the brightest star in Your Majesty's crown," Disraeli said smoothly. He waited until there was no danger of an outburst. "Yet, nearer to home, I received a letter from His Royal Highness, written as he passed through Egypt. He observed that one of Britain's most serious mistakes was in not buying shares in the Suez Canal Company at the beginning. His exact words were, I think, 'If we don't own it, we might be forced one day to take it.' "

"That is unusually perceptive of him," she said.

Disraeli bowed. The Prince's powers of observation were, in fact, proving extremely useful. "His Royal Highness also mentioned that the ruler of Egypt, the Khedive Ismail, appears to be almost totally bankrupt."

He was speaking very casually. Like others who had come to know him, Victoria realized that he was not talking aimlessly. She tensed, as her thoughts again locked on to his. "He was certain?"

Disraeli knew he had her. "I have had it confirmed by our agent in Cairo," he said. "I have also had inquiries made discreetly in Paris. It seems that the Khedive has let it be known that his shares may be for sale. Three French groups are already bidding for them."

"I see . . ." Victoria's mind was racing. It would be a— "Is there a possibility?"

Disraeli's head turned slightly to one side. "No more than that, Ma'am. But I shall do everything in my power," he promised. "It must be done."

"It must, Mr. Disraeli."

Disraeli sat with his entire Cabinet. He sat upright, his elbows close to his sides, his hands folded in his lap, his immobility concealing the tautness inside him. The Cabinet members, summoned to Downing Street, although Parliament was not in session, were agitated and uneasy, some unable to grasp what he had just told them.

"The Canal . . .?" Northcote questioned. "Buy the Suez Canal?" The canal, linking the Mediterranean and the Red Sea, had been open for five years. Built by a Frenchman, De Lesseps, and administered by a largely French company, it cut the sailing time to India by several weeks and was one of the most significant strategic factors in the world.

"The 177,000 shares owned by the Khedive," Disraeli explained.

When no one else spoke, Manners asked, "Is there any certainty that he will sell?"

Disraeli nodded. "After years of colossal extravagance, he has brought his country to the edge of ruin. He is desperate for money. According to our agent in Cairo, he has given an option on his shares to a French syndicate."

"For how much?" Cairns asked.

"Eighty-five million francs. Say, three million, four hundred thousand pounds," Disraeli said quietly.

There was a reaction of shock and surprise. "Then there's no point," Northcote declared, with relief. "The French have it."

Disraeli was still impassive, his voice controlled. "Not yet. It is November 23rd. They have until Friday the 26th to decide. What they are offering the Khedive is a mortgage at exorbitant rates." He looked at Derby whose office controlled the Cairo agent.

"Khedive Ismail would sell at once to us for a higher sum, and for cash," Derby confirmed. "He must have the money by the end of the month, or his country is bankrupt."

"A higher sum?" Cross asked, after a pause. He looked at Disraeli.

"Say, four million pounds."

The argument broke out again. Disraeli knew that Derby had been convinced and would support him. So would Manners, Hardy and Hunt. But with Parliament not in sitting to approve the amount, the Cabinet decision had to be unanimous.

"It is out of the question!" Carnarvon protested.

"It is an international waterway," Cross, the lawyer, put in.

"We have a greater interest in it than anyone else," Derby told him. "Four fifths of the ships that use it are British."

"But why do we have to buy it?" Northcote asked.

"To make sure that no one prevents us from using it," Salisbury said flatly. The others looked at him, surprised at him supporting Disraeli. "The possibility of that link being cut is an enormous threat to India—with Russia already too close to its northern borders. If Russia manages to block the canal, and at the same time the Amir of

452

Afghanistan opens his mountain passes for her army . . ." He shrugged.

"That may be true," Cross admitted. "But we must not make a hasty decision."

"In any case, the Khedive's shares are less than half," Northcote argued. "We would still not control it."

"We would have by far the largest holding," Disraeli said. "With the few shares we already own and more we may acquire, we shall have a controlling interest."

Northcote shook his head. "It's too big a step."

"I shall quote the Prince again," Disraeli said patiently. "If we do not buy it now, one day we shall have to take it."

Salisbury agreed. "Nothing is more certain."

Disraeli was still motionless, his voice under strict control, but all could feel the strength of the conviction that flowed from him. "If the French are allowed to buy the shares, the majority will be held by France who is already trying to extend her influence in Egypt. If nothing is done, in a few days Bismarck will hear of it and throw the resources of Imperial Germany into the bidding. And there is the Russian menace in the Middle East. Britain must have a stake in the canal!"

Cross was aware that, from a diplomatic viewpoint, the Chief's conclusions were probably incontestable. What concerned him was the absolute legality of what they were doing, to answer the flood of criticism that was bound to come, both at home and from abroad. "For such a sum as four million pounds," he stressed, "by law, the decision must be taken by Parliament."

"Parliament is not in session," Disraeli said. "To recall it would take too long—and in any case, speed and secrecy are vital. The decision is up to us, to the twelve of you sitting here."

Northcote hated to go against him, but as Chancellor of the Exchequer he had to think of how the money was to be raised. Most of what had been available was committed to the social program. "You said yourself, it's a matter of urgency Prime Minister. Even if we approach the Bank of England, they will not have such an amount available. Even if they are willing to act as agents for the Crown without Parliament's authority."

"And what if the House refuses to confirm the purchase?" Cross put in. "The Bank must be satisfied. There will be endless inquiries and committees to go through."

Disraeli shook his head. "It must be decided now."

"There's nowhere we can raise it quickly enough," Northcote protested. "It is simply impossible!"

Disraeli's expression did not alter by a fraction. "That is the next consideration. First, we must reach agreement here. Do I have it—yes or no?"

Derby's, Salisbury's and Manners' hands went up at once, then others round the table, one by one, until only Northcote and Cross were left. Disraeli looked at them. Slowly, they raised their hands.

Everyone watched Disraeli. There were no outbursts or congratulations. Everyone was too conscious of the insurmountable difficulties to come. His fingers separated and he rose without speaking. They still watched him, puzzled, as he limped to the door and opened it. Montagu Corry was waiting outside. He turned quickly and Disraeli nodded to him.

In the Partners' Room of his financial headquarters at New Court in St. Swithin's Lane, Lionel de Rothschild was finishing a light meal. His three sons, Nathaniel, Alfred and Leopold were with him. He glanced round as Montagu Corry was shown in and advanced to the table. He selected a Muscatel grape, as he nodded in greeting. ". . . Mr. Corry."

Corry bowed, aware of the sons, all so different, yet all cool-headed and acutely intelligent, all watching him. "You will forgive my interruption, Baron. I have come from the Cabinet Room on an errand for Mr. Disraeli." Rothschild nodded again and put the grape in his mouth. Corry hesitated. "He needs the sum of four million pounds."

"When?"

"By tomorrow."

Rothschild took the skin of the grape from his mouth and laid it on his plate. "What is your security?"

Corry had his instructions. "The British Government."

Rothschild finished the grape and reached for another. "You shall have it," he said.

Queen Victoria would not allow her Secretary to open the despatch box. Her fingers trembled with excitement as she unlocked it and took out the letter from her Prime Minister. Her heart leaped at its opening words. "Mr. Disraeli with his humble duty to Your Majesty: It is just settled. You have it, Madam. The French Government has been out-generalled . . ."

Her hopes, and Disraeli's, were triumphantly fulfilled. The sensation which the news caused throughout the world was immense, creating exactly the desired reaction. The French comforted themselves with the thought that British co-operation would make the canal more secure, and more profitable. The leaders of the smaller nations hastened to congratulate Disraeli, realizing all the implications of the purchase of the canal shares. In Berlin, the Russian Chancellor, Gortchakoff, had just begun a meeting with Bismarck. Their intention was to reach agreement on how to solve the Eastern Question, in their own interests and sharing the political and territorial pickings. The news stopped them in their tracks. Nothing could be settled, they now knew, without consulting Great Britain, which meant Disraeli. Gortchakoff returned in fury to St. Petersburg. Bismarck, however, was a realist and accepted the inevitable. He had merely been fishing, implying that, if Germany gave her approval to any action Russia took in the Middle East or in Asia, he would expect something in return. He remembered meeting Disraeli very well. He had been correct to be impressed. He wrote, adding his congratulations.

At home, public opinon came out strongly in favor. Not even Disraeli could have foretold how popular the reaction would make him. He had kept his promise to restore Britain's prestige. Predictably, Gladstone fiercely denounced the purchase of the shares, having seen no value in a similar offer made to him some years before by De Lesseps. He rushed to Westminster, but Hartington and most of the other Liberal leaders had already approved the purchase and would not support him. It was galling to find himself more than half ignored in the midst of all the acclaim for Disraeli.

The Prince of Wales's state visit to India was another diplomatic triumph. The enthusiasm shown by the dense crowds at the beginning only increased as the weeks went by and more and more people came under the spell of his handsome appearance and his friendly, approachable manner which did not detract from his dignity. The fervor and the mass loyalty expressed through him to the Queen proved to the world, and to Russia in particular, that the ties were not to be broken. Even those who agitated for independence were silenced. The Empire was more secure than ever.

The Prince had every reason to be proud of his achievement. He had not only carried the visit off well, far beyond expectations, but he had helped to cure a great injustice by protesting against the insolence of some British administrators to their native assistants, and even to the Indian princes they advised. His protest, acted on by Disraeli and the new Viceroy, Lord Lytton, led to a dramatic improvement in the relations between the officials and the people they governed. The only unpleasantness on the tour had been the letter one of his companions, Lord Aylesford, known as Sporting Joe, had received from his pretty wife, Edith, to tell him she meant to run away with Lord Blandford, another friend. Blandford, a son of the Duke of Marlborough, was married, too, and was going to leave his wife. The Prince thought his behavior disgraceful and gave Aylesford permission to return home to sort things out. Then, dismissed it from his mind.

As he travelled home, he had other matters to concern him. He learned from the newspapers that Disraeli planned to proclaim his mother "Empress of India." He was wounded and Disraeli wrote to apologize, regretting that through pressure of work he had neglected to inform him.

He had naturally expected that the Prince would have heard of it from the Queen.

Ever since India had been transferred to the Crown, Disraeli had dreamed of an addition to the Queen's style and title. Victoria, herself, became passionately keen as soon as the suggestion was made. It seemed to her that to be India's Empress was the perfect way for her to unify its many different races and show her personal concern for them. For Disraeli, the concept went much further. The Empire had existed in fact for over two hundred years. With this title, he would make it a reality. Although occupied by the business of the Suez Canal and continued and more violent uprisings in the Balkans, at the beginning of the new year he had introduced his Royal Titles Bill. He was prepared for criticism from those who resented change, but he muzzled it at first by persuading the Queen to open Parliament in person, almost as spectacular a feat as buying the shares. Her appearance in public after so long produced extraordinary scenes of emotion and awe. Afterwards, however, a strange mixture of traditionalists and Radicals started an uproar. Seizing the opportunity to attack Disraeli and all his works, Gladstone yet again stormed back to Westminster to fulminate against the bill, and the arguments raged on needlessly for months. Victoria was deeply hurt. Disraeli listened incredulously to some of the accusations, that the Queen would become another Czar, that the un-English title of Empress would destroy loyalty to the Crown and that the very word was immoral because it suggested persecution and debauchery.

Gladstone had not forgotten that Hartington had allowed the vote on the Suez Canal to be passed without a division. This time, he forced divisions at every stage. Although he caused much trouble, he damaged his own case by the excessive ferocity of his arguments and his undisguised malice toward Disraeli. Members became ashamed to support him and, in the country, sympathy developed for the Queen. Again, having lost the applause of everyone except a small group of Radicals, he abruptly abandoned the contest. Disraeli won every vote by an overwhelming majority, explaining over and again that the title of Queen still had precedence and would still be used exclusively in the United Kingdom and all the colonies and dominions, except India.

The burden of the whole struggle had fallen on him and should have been enough, but, during it, he became embroiled in an extremely delicate matter that could have affected the whole future of the monarchy.

The sporting Lord Aylesford had returned to London and announced his intention of divorcing his wife and ruining Blandford by citing him as co-respondent. Blandford's family was horrified and his younger brother, Lord Randolph Churchill, took on the role of mediator, for which he was temperamentally unsuited. Blandford would only give up the idea of eloping, after Lady Aylesford panicked at the thought of the social ostracism that would follow. But Aylesford refused to stop his preparations for the divorce, and a scandal developed which could convulse society. Churchill, a promising, Conservative MP, and his strikingly beautiful, American wife, Jennie, were members of the Prince of Wales's circle like the others. Relying on his friendship, Churchill telegraphed to the Prince, appealing to him to use his influence to have the divorce proceedings stopped. The Prince replied that he had no right to interfere in other people's private lives. Churchill was incensed. Excitable, and anxious over his elder brother's impending disgrace, he began to think of the Prince as responsible for the whole situation. He accused him irrationally of forcing Edith and Blandford into each other's arms, by taking Aylesford with him to India.

Disraeli had heard of the affair as a friend of the Duke of Marlborough, father of Blandford and Churchill, and was disappointed that no one seemed able to resolve it. He became alarmed, when Ponsonby came to him on behalf of the Queen. The story that unfolded was so sensational that he doubted, if he put it into a novel, that anyone would credit it. Frantic now to prevent the divorce, Lady Aylesford confessed to Blandford that the Prince of Wales had been her lover some years before and gave him some indiscreet letters which the Prince had written to her. He handed them to Churchill, who went straight to Marlborough House. Arriving unannounced, in a state of excitement, he forced himself on Alexandra, Princess of Wales, and told her that he "had the Crown of England in his pocket." Alexandra was unwell and did not understand. He ordered her to tell the Prince to stop the Aylesford divorce or he would publish the letters and make sure he "never sat on the Throne of England." Not knowing what else to do, Alexandra went to the Queen, who was shocked and sent to Disraeli for advice. Now everyone was involved.

Before Disraeli could even contact Churchill and the others, Lord Hardwicke, another member of the Marlborough House set, arrived to represent the Prince of Wales. He informed Disraeli that, infuriated by the gross insult to his wife, the Prince had challenged Churchill to a duel with pistols somewhere on the north coast of France. Disraeli summoned Churchill to Downing Street, but he haughtily refused to back down. The letters gave him the top hand, he said, and the Prince's challenge was cowardly, only made because he knew that no one could accept it. Disraeli urged Lord Hardwicke to persuade Aylesford to reconsider, as the only way out of the problem, but Aylesford was determined. The Prince defied Churchill, but relied on Disraeli's advice and was prepared to stay out of the country for as long as he thought best.

The scandal was assuming colossal proportions and Disraeli became worried. The Queen and the Princess were depending on him, but none of those concerned would listen to reason, especially Churchill. The worst was that the Prince of Wales had already appeared as a witness in the Divorce Court and had narrowly escaped being charged with adultery. If he appeared again, this time cited by Blandford as a co-respondent in a cross-petition, his position as Heir, all the good of his state visit, and probably the Royal Titles Bill, itself, would be in jeopardy. Disraeli made one last appeal to Churchill and Aylesford, which was turned down, then decided on a gamble. He advised the Prince to return home exactly as

459

planned. As he hoped, the popular imagination had been fired by the tour of India and the Prince was given a tumultuous welcome. All London turned out to cheer him, wherever he went. Aylesford was shocked into realizing how nearly he had betrayed his friendship and agreed to separate quietly from his wife, instead of divorcing her. Lord Randolph Churchill was forced to realize that to attack the Prince publicly now was to commit political suicide and the end of his career. Cut by most of society, he sent a curt apology to Marlborough House and left for America with Jennie, till it blew over. The Duke of Marlborough was given the post of Viceroy of Ireland and took Blandford with him to Dublin. The Prince would not acknowledge Churchill's apology, until he was compelled to by Disraeli and the Queen, and then only when it was rewritten by the Lord Chancellor, Cairns, and ratified by Disraeli and the leader of the Opposition, Lord Hartington. The ladies and gentlemen in Disraeli's stories behaved in a much more noble manner. In the entire melodrama, he recognized that he was the only romantic figure, with the exception of the sad Princess. He was the despised outsider become the Man of Power, directing the destiny of nations and preserving the honor of Kings.

In the early summer, he invited his charming, elderly confidante, Lady Chesterfield, down to Hughenden. As always, he found her company restful and her interest in all the events of his life unaltered. She had inquired often about his health in this past year and he was glad to see her in the country, where he usually felt and looked better. His asthma had been particularly bad, making him feel that he was strangling, and the gout in his left leg and foot made him suffer the indignity at times of attending the House of Commons in carpet slippers. There had been more rumors that he was thinking of retiring.

"Would you?" she asked.

"Perhaps. Sometimes I long to do nothing but sit in my library and look at the sun on the bindings of my books. But always the question—or do I flatter myself?—who would take my place? Derby will not even discuss it. Neither will Northcote. Nor anyone. I am the man in the saddle who cannot get off." She laughed. "The gallop is exhilarating, even the trot. But I admit I find the daily amble of business in the House more and more tiring." Despite his other preoccupations, somehow, he had made time to pass a Bill to provide Elementary Education and others to protect merchant seamen, to control the vivisection of animals and to limit the enclosure of common land.

He took Lady Chesterfield into the drawing-room to see his portrait of Selina, which had finally arrived. She was touched to notice her own portrait by Landseer, much younger and very lovely, seated in her box at the Opera, hanging near it. They were on either side of a portrait of Queen Victoria, by Von Angeli, rather stern and forbidding. She had had it painted especially for him. He was very proud of all three.

"We spoil you," she said, smiling. "Well, perhaps you spoil us—especially the Queen." He shook his head. "Oh, you know you do, Dis! You have a way with her. You handle her better than anyone has ever done. What is the secret?"

"I never argue. I never contradict," he told her. "Sometimes, I forget." He offered her his arm to lead her out. "Also, she knows that I love her—and am not afraid to say it."

"You never were," Lady Chesterfield murmured.

Disraeli showed her ceremoniously to a white-painted chair and sat near her. For a long moment, they kept a companionable silence, looking out at the lilac and chestnut, the pink and white thorns and the line of beeches beyond. Then Lady Chesterfield asked him to tell her more of the details of how he came to buy the canal shares, how long he had planned it without telling anyone and what part the Rothschilds had really played. As he told the story, dramatizing and embroidering it for her, she marvelled. "And to buy it from under the noses of three governments and half the financiers of the world . . ."

461

He smiled. "All the gamblers and capitalists, organized and platooned. Secret agents in every corner—and we were never suspected! It would have given France virtually the control of Egypt."

"Which is now yours?"

"That remains to see," he said carefully. The best kind of conquest, bloodless. And the best kind of colonization, by influence. Of course, the French considered Egypt as within their sphere of influence and a clash must be avoided. Yet British financial advisers were already assisting the Khedive. "The Faery is particularly pleased."

"No wonder she values you so highly. And now you are to turn her into an Empress."

"She insisted," he whispered, and she laughed. "But it was not entirely for her. It fulfilled a dream." He paused. "There are not many left."

"I suppose not," she said gently. She could tell there was something on his mind, and hoped it was not bad news about his health. She had heard that sometimes he had gone to the House intending to speak, but his asthma had been so bad he had been unable to get to his feet. Physical weakness in a first Minister had to be hidden. At long meetings and after dinners, he could only survive by smoking cigarettes saturated with menthol and laudanum.

His head was partly turned, looking down the valley. "I was pleased to do the Queen this last service." Again he paused. "I cannot delude myself that, at my age, there will be many more opportunities to play a really important part in world events."

You have played it nobly, my dear, she said to herself. Then spoke it aloud.

He glanced toward her, grateful. He hesitated, then said with an unusual hint of shyness, "I must confess, my dear Anne, that I had an ulterior motive for asking to see you alone."

"Yes?"

"We have been friends for many years and I have come to admire your delightful company and judgement, and to depend on it for a large portion of any happiness there is in my life."

462

She smiled. "As always, you are too kind."

"I only speak the truth. I flatter myself that you have a similar appreciation of me. And, you know, in many ways we are very similar. Both alone, both married to loneliness." She nodded, agreeing. He took her agreement for a sign. "In short . . . in spite of being half-blind, half crippled and almost unable to breathe, I am asking you to do me the honor of becoming my wife."

Lady Chesterfield was surprised, but only for a moment. There was no one in the world of whom she was more fond than Dizzy, but . . . She smiled. "Dear Dis, I care for you far too dearly ever to marry you." She stopped him as he made to speak. "Not because of your age, or failing health—but because you would only be marrying me to be closer to Selina."

He was stricken, unable to deny it. The face and voice of her younger sister still haunted him. He had made himself be more restrained in her presence and of the many letters he still wrote some were never sent. He did not walk through Belgrave Square, nor call at her house unless invited. And since he had made himself pretend not to love her so passionately, she had been more tender and more kind, more open in her pride at being close to him. He had accepted that she never could belong to him and that she spared him all the time and thought she could. Yet the need for her was as strong as ever and only lessened when he was caught up in great events. Or when he was with Anne. Her sister. By marrying her, he would be part of Selina's family, involved in everything that concerned her, an automatic member of all family celebrations. With Anne, whom he cared for, and who cared for him, perhaps even more than Selina. She was looking at him, indulgently and understandingly. "Am I so ridiculously obvious?" he muttered.

"No, never that, my dear," she said quietly. "But you are a young Byron who has lived into the Age of Steam. And pure Romance has vanished."

He shook his head. "If I believed that, it would no longer be worth living."

She smiled "You must be practical." She took his

463

nearest hand and shook it lightly. "Think—Selina and myself are both grandmothers."

"Wise as ever . . ." he sighed. He raised her hand and kissed it. "You are right. Though I am certain there is no greater misfortune than to have a heart that will not grow old."

Like Africa, there was always something new from the Balkans. The peasant revolt against their Turkish rulers spread from Herzegovina to Bosnia and, incited by agitators from the Russian-backed secret societies, there were sporadic riots and uprisings in other provinces. The movement toward independence for the Slav peoples grew and, through lack of resource and their own indolence, the Governors of the decadent Ottoman Empire were unable to suppress it. The rule of the Sultans, from their capital of Constantinople, had lasted for five hundred years, but in the last forty they had had to give freedom to Greece and lost effective control of Rumania and Serbia. Russia stood to gain most by the destruction of the Turkish Empire in Europe, but, after her defeat in the Crimean War, had been forced to renounce her claim to protect Christian subjects in the Sultan's territories, which had been her pretext for causing the war, while Britain, France, Austria and Italy guaranteed the integrity of the remaining sections of the Turkish Empire. The Pan-Slavonic movement which inspired the uprisings was the spearhead of Russia's latest attempt to gain control of the Balkan Peninsula.

Britain had enormous financial and territorial interests in the Middle East and to protect them was Disraeli's responsibility. His entire policy was based on the treaty which excluded Russia and upheld Turkey. The problem of independence for the remaining provinces was perplexing. They were made up of many races and creeds, even more antagonistic to one another than they were to the Turks. Freed from the Sultan, disunited and squabbling, they would become as easy prey for the Czar. Already Disraeli had seen how the previous Government's weakness had allowed Russia to re-establish her naval power in the Black Sea. He could not permit any further advance in that power, even though it meant taking on himself the whole obligation to protect the empire of Turkey. Germany and Austria were leagued with Russia, so he could expect no help from Bismarck. France was still struggling to recover from her defeat, Italy torn by the problems of unification. America had no reason to intervene. Look where he might, he could find not a single ally. He had boasted of the ability of the British Empire to stand alone, if necessary. Now he had to prove it.

Almost daily the situation became worse. The Sultan was discovered to be nearly bankrupt, which explained why reinforcements had not been sent to put down the revolt. If the Governors had had common energy, or even pocket money, Disraeli said, it could have been settled in a week. Serbia and Montenegro prepared for war in support of their fellow Slavs. Then, during Mohammedan riots, the German and French consuls were murdered in Salonika.

Bismarck, Gortchakoff and the Austrian Foreign Minister, Andrassy, met at once and drafted a memorandum to end the crisis. A copy was sent to Disraeli for his agreement. He had already agreed to two sets of proposals issued by the League of the Three Emperors, although angered that Great Britain had not been invited to join the discussions and was asked merely to give automatic consent. But, in those cases, the Imperial Powers had offered Turkey assistance in keeping peace in the provinces, in return for a series of reforms to remove all reasonable cause of discontent in the Sultan's Christian subjects. On this occasion, however, most of the proposals had come from Gortchakoff and the memorandum was really an ultimatum. It insisted on an armistice of two months, during which the rebels were to remain armed, Turkish troops were to be withdrawn, relief supplies and materials for the reconstruction of Christian houses and churches supplied and the agreed reforms carried out. If not, at the end of the two months, the Imperial Powers would take steps to see that they were.

Many reforms were needed in the corrupt, repressive regime, but none of the terms could possibly be met within two months. The memorandum provided a perfect excuse for the Imperial Powers to take over the administration of Turkey and dismember its empire. They would put a stranglehold on the entire Middle East. Disraeli saw the threat behind the apparently justifiable proposals immediately. He called his Cabinet together, obtained a unanimous consent to reject the memorandum and sent a British fleet to the Dardanelles.

His action sent shockwaves round the world.

In England, once he had explained his decision in the House of Commons, the mass of public opinion was strongly on his side. The Liberal leaders, Hartington and Sir William Harcourt, agreed that the memorandum was unacceptable. He told them that he had sent the fleet to protect the interests of the British Empire, not the Turkish, that his policy toward the civil war was one of strict neutrality, provided other nations remained strictly neutral, and that he had insisted on the Sultan carrying out the reforms affecting his Christian subjects, which he had promised.

In Europe, there was consternation. Gortchakoff had promised the Czar that there would be a Russian garrison on the Bosphorus within two months. He had taken Disraeli's offers of friendly co-operation over the past two years as proof that England could not act single-handedly. He was raging. The Austrians had been deciding what share of Turkish territory they would accept and felt robbed. France had reached an understanding with Russia and begged Disraeli to reconsider. The smaller nations were paralyzed. They had agreed to the memorandum, as they agreed to everything signed by Bismarck. Bismarck, as always, played his own game. Germany had no claim to any part of Turkey and no liking for independence movements, but settlement of the Eastern Question on these Russian terms would have greatly extended his influence. He, too, had discounted the possibility of England acting alone. He remembered how Disraeli and the Czar had made him abandon his plan to

466

attack France. Now, in turn, Disraeli had thwarted the Czar. He actually laughed at Gortchakoff's frustration. He would not make the mistake again of leaving England out of his calculations. Disraeli had asserted Britain's right to police the Middle East and European Turkey in the interests of everyone. And the fleet showed he was not bluffing. A secret despatch had reported a remark of Disraeli's, when warned that England might be drifting into war. "Whatever happens," he had said, "we shall certainly not drift into war, but go to war, if we do, because we intend it, and have a purpose which we mean to accomplish. I hope, however, Russia, at the bottom of the whole affair, will be sensible. And then we shall have peace." The memorandum was dead. The only difficulty was how to bury it without losing face.

Undoubtedly, events helped Disraeli. Even as Bismarck locked himself away to think, refusing to speak to anyone, there was a palace revolution in Constantinople. The unstable Sultan Abdul Aziz was deposed by his nephew, Murad, and allowed to commit suicide. The new Sultan accepted the need for constitutional reform and agreed to co-operate with the foreign Powers. Bismarck laughed again at the luck of the old Jew's timing. He wrote to London to say he would follow any policy Disraeli wished to suggest and sent German warships to Salonika to assist in the policing of Christian property.

Disraeli was leaning on Derby's arm as they came into the Carlton Club. He was still in some pain, but feeling better. Dr. Gull had insisted on his drinking nothing but port. With his gout, it had nearly killed him. It left him so infirm, he had offered to resign as leader, but Derby, his chosen successor, refused to hear of it. It had forced him to make another decision, however, urged on him by the Queen, and which no one else must know.

He liked Derby, as a loyal friend and colleague. And he was more satisfied with him now, because of his firmness over the Turkish business. As a Foreign Secretary, he was often too cautious and too unimaginative. "So you agree with me about Bismarck?" he asked.

"Absolutely," Derby answered. "He wants us just now, but he is not exactly the person in whom one can implicitly confide. He offers us assistance and an unreserved interchange of ideas. I'd like to see more clearly what assistance we are expected to give in return."

"Quite so," Disraeli panted. He paused to catch his breath. "But we'll find out more quickly by displaying an absolute lack of suspicion."

"What about Gortchakoff? He has sworn to follow our policy of non-interference."

"And we shall hold him to it," Disraeli said. "Though there's no acting with people when you can never be sure they're telling the truth. He won't give up his game easily."

Derby smiled. "Well, at the moment, everybody is at your feet."

"That may be so. The thing is to keep them there." With Derby in the Lords, Disraeli was Foreign Office spokesman in the Commons, an ideal arrangement, making him the voice of Britian's foreign policy as he had always wished.

As the porter helped him out of his long white overcoat, Rose came to them, carrying a folded newspaper. Manners was with him and both seemed worried.

"Sir Philip's just shown me this report in the *Daily News*," Manners said.

"Have you read it, Mr. Disraeli?" Rose asked.

"I have been told about it. I don't rely for my facts on the Liberal press." Always something new out of the Balkans . . . Two months before, roused by Russian agitators, Bulgaria had joined the revolt with a savage massacre of local Turkish officials. In a central province commanding the main routes to the west, his rebellion was potentially more serious even than the others. Now the *Daily News,* the leading Liberal journal, had published an account of the suppression of the Bulgarian revolt by a force of regular Turkish troops and armed irregulars, the ferocious Bashi-bazouks. Disraeli took out his glass and held it to his left eye, as Rose handed him the paper. In lurid detail, it told of the slaughter of 25,000 unarmed peasants in scenes of inhuman barbarity, whole communities butchered, villages burnt, women impaled, children roasted alive, girls sold into slavery, rape, sodomy, torture. The story was graphic and fearful, but too over-colored. Many of the details were obviously invented.

"It's horrifying, isn't it?" Rose commented.

Disraeli handed back the paper. "Yes, it would be, if it were true."

"I had a search made of all Foreign Office despatches," Derby said. "There's no mention of anything. And since it is supposed to have taken place nearly two months ago, our Ambassador to the Porte would be bound to have heard."

Manners breathed out. "Thank Heavens . . . then none of it's true?"

"In the name of humanity, I wish I could think so," Disraeli told him. "No, I'm sure there's been great ferocity on both sides, but nothing of this nature."

"I hope not," Rose muttered. "People have been shocked by this report. There's bound to be reaction against our support for Turkey."

"Which is why the *News,* printed it," Derby said. "They'll publish anything that could be damaging to the Government."

They moved toward the stairs. Disraeli took Manners's arm. "One thing we may be certain of—the Russians will use it. We must never forget that the Turks are not fighting a few simple peasants. It is a full-scale revolution, organized by St. Petersburg."

The reaction of horror throughout the country increased as more descriptions of the atrocities were published, and continued to grow as no firm denial of them was made. Disraeli urged Derby for firm information from the British Ambassador to the Sublime Porte, the Sultan's Court in Constantinople, and finally it came. The Ambassador assured the Foreign Office that none of the stories could be confirmed. Questioned in the House, Disraeli answered that he hoped, for the sake of human nature itself, when all the facts were known, "it will be found that the statements are scarcely warranted." Civil wars were always the most terrible, especially when put down by irregular, undisciplined troops. "I cannot doubt that atrocities have been committed in Bulgaria; but that girls were sold into slavery, or that more than 10,000 persons have been imprisoned, I doubt. In fact, I doubt whether there is prison accommodation for so many, or that torture has been practiced on a great scale among an Oriental people who seldom, I believe, resort to torture, but generally terminate their connection with culprits in a more expeditious manner."

As humor was expected of him, everybody laughed when he sat down, and the tension eased. "What is there to laugh at?" he muttered to Northcote. He had not meant it to be humorous.

Only a few days later, at the Foreign Office, he discovered a despatch from the British Consul at Rustchuk on the Danube, referring to rumors of massacres and giving details which suggested that the newspaper reports were partly true after all. He was extremely angry, both with Derby and his Department. The despatch had been received two weeks before and laid aside. If it had been shown to him, his reply in the Commons would have been very different. A check on the Ambassador to the Porte revealed that he had made no noticeable effort to investigate.

Disraeli had been placed in a very difficult position. As it was, he was being accused from all sides of callous flippancy. He sent a special envoy to Constantinople to uncover the true facts. He could have extricated himself by throwing the blame on the incompetent Ambassador, but it was never his way to crucify subordinates, when he himself stood to gain by it. The man could be quietly removed. At least, the despatch from Rustchuk intimated that the newspaper stories were grossly exaggerated and the massacres involved much smaller numbers. Nevertheless, they were massacres of Christian peasants and public feeling would turn inevitably against the Turks. The end of the session was approaching and the final debate on his Eastern policy. He had been warned that Gladstone was planning to attend and make his most slashing attack yet on the Government. He had to be ready for him.

He had already had many anxious meetings with the Queen, appalled by the current horrors, and had had to answer her queries over whether Britain could not justify her defense of Turkey. She listened to his arguments, but was only finally convinced when Serbia suddenly entered the war. Victoria understood as well as her Prime Minister that Serbia had only taken this step with Russia's promise of support. Russian officers and volunteers were the backbone of the Serbian army. He would use in the House the same arguments he had used to the Queen, that Great Britain could not alter her traditional policy simply because a revolt had been put down with severity, that the horrors complained of had taken place under the previous regime and the Powers were now pledged to help the new Sultan to implement promised reforms. On the other hand, if sufficient reforms to make life tolerable for the Sultan's non-Muslim people were not put into operation and only bloodier war and confusion prevailed, then Britain was fully prepared to fulfill the duty she owed to civilization and impose a general peace.

Gladstone, fiery and eloquent, made a swinging speech received with enthusiasm at first, which gradually died away as he moved from defending his membership of the Government which helped the Turks during the Crimean War to an attack on Disraeli for rejecting the Berlin Memorandum, and lastly to a demand for "prompt interference," unspecified, that would at once preserve the territorial integrity of Turkey and give her subject races self-government. No one could quite understand how that was to be achieved. He had also made a bad tactical mistake by rising imperiously on the first night of the debate, which gave Disraeli the chance to consider his reply and to dismiss his charges with delicate irony, as he had so often done before. His arguments were so positive and incontestable that, at the end of the debate, Hartington declared that the Liberal leaders had no quarrel with the conduct or policy of the Government. They recognized the dilemma of Disraeli's situation. To interfere in the civil war on behalf of the rebels and to carve up the Turkish Empire in Europe would be directly against British interests. Gladstone called for a vote of no confidence, but his party refused to support him.

The size of Disraeli's victory was unlooked for and he hoped he could relax, but confirmation of the atrocities from his special envoy fanned the flames of indignation again. Although they invloved only half the reported numbers as Disraeli had predicted, several prominent Liberals joined together to denounce him for maintaining the alliance with Turkey. The first really concerted attack came on August 11, 1876, just as the session ended. Gladstone had been offended by the lack of response on his last appearance and did not take part.

Throughout the long and often passionate speeches, Disraeli sat absolutely motionless in his place on the Government Front Bench, his dark frockcoat buttoned across his plush waistcoat, his arms folded, one knee over the other. His head was lowered as if he was about to go to sleep. It was his custom when under attack, but this night he was so tired he had to fight against real sleep. By no sign or any change of expression did he show any consciousness of the appeals and accusations that were hurled across the floor at him, not even when Harcourt beseeched him to "redeem Christendom from the shame by which she had been too long dishonored." Although he tried to concentrate on every word, his mind kept slipping away, far away, not in place but in time, to the first moment he had taken his seat on this bench and to the days when he had sat defiantly behind it, behind Peel. Wyndham Lewis, Bentinck, Edward Stanley, O'Connell, Palmerston . . . by listening intently, he could just catch the echo of their voices. Fanciful. He shifted and tugged at the wrist of his shirt. His eyes were wet and he kept them half closed in case anyone noticed.

Because it was the close of the session and Dizzy was to speak, the House was full. Sir William Harcourt finished to cheers, "and then, I hope to God we will at last have done with the Turks!"

There was a stir of expectation as Disraeli rose. His voice was solemn and measured, its effect calming the House. No one had ever had such mastery. The slaughter of 12,000 individuals was certainly a horrible event which no one could think of without emotion, he said, but was it sufficient reason to make the British Empire denounce its treaties? Britain was not the only ally of Turkey. So was Russia and Austria and France, all with linked and separate agreements. If all their treaties were to be considered as idle chaff, then statesmanship would become a mockery. The Opposition claimed that the Government's duty was to drive the Turks out of Europe. "What our duty is at this critical moment is to maintain the Empire of England. Nor will we agree to any step, though it may obtain for a moment comparative quiet and a false prosperity, that hazards the existence of that Empire." It was a calm, positive speech, unremarkable, but he finished to the usual loud applause.

At the end of the debate, instead of going straight out, Disraeli limped down the House to the bar, where he turned and stood for a while with his glass to his eye, looking slowly around the Chamber from the galleries to the benches on both sides. Then he walked back up the center, passed the massive wooden table and the Front Bench and went out behind the Speaker's chair. Afterwards, members saw him in the lobby in his long, white coat and lavender kid gloves, shaking hands with nearly everyone who passed.

The next morning, the reason became known. The Queen had created him Earl of Beaconsfield and Viscount Hughenden. It had been his last speech in the House of Commons, which he had championed and commanded for so long.

Besides the Queen, only a few of his most intimate colleagues had known it was to happen. Because of his declining health, he had realized the impossibilty of continuing as leader of the party and the Cabinet with all the work and strain redoubled by daily attendance at the Commons. His eyesight had deteriorated so much that he could not even see the expressions of those on the Opposition front bench. Neither Queen Victoria nor the Cabinet would hear of his resignation and the only alternative was to move to the Lords, where he could still lead and the need for him to speak would be much less.

Since so few had been told of his decision and he had feared the emotion of a ceremonial leave-taking, the news shocked every member of the House of Commons. Small groups gathered that first morning, as though for comfort. Everyone on both sides, from the Speaker to the newest member, felt a sense of loss. Some even wept. Never to see that immobile figure again, or to hear that rich voice as it swelled, filling the Chamber. Disraeli had been the House.

Hart Dyke wrote to him, "All the real chivalry and delight of party politics seem to have departed. Nothing remains but routine." Manners was inconsolable. "It terminates for me all personal interest in House of Commons life. I cannot bear to think of the future." An opponent, Harcourt, wrote, "You have made the House of Lords much too rich and you have left the House of Commons by far too poor. Henceforth, the game will be like a chessboard when the queen has gone—a petty struggle of pawns. I hope the new ease will add long years to a life which is the admiration of Englishmen and is dear to those who have tasted your friendship. To the imagination of the younger generation your life will always have a special fascination. For them you have enlarged the horizon of the possibilities of the future."

By tradition, a new Lord had to be introduced by two members of the order of the peerage to which he had been raised. He chose Derby and Selina's husband, Lord Bradford. The Upper Chamber was crowded and the galleries filled with gorgeously dressed peeresses and distinguished visitors to see him in his robes, escorted by his sponsors and preceded by the Garter King of Arms and the chief officers of state, as he completed with great dignity the ancient ceremony of introduction. The occasion was without equal. He had become Leader of the House of Commons without ever having held office, and now became Leader of the Lords the moment he was introduced.

As he moved to take his seat between Derby and the Earl of Richmond, Lord Cairns whispered to him that he hoped he would not miss the daily excitement and the cut and thrust of the Commons too much. "I am dead," Disraeli murmured. "Dead . . . but in the Elysian fields."

chapter eight

William Gladstone went home to Hawarden Castle at
the start of the parliamentary recess. He was restless and
discontented, unable to find that relaxation with his family which so often consoled him for the disappointments of
his life and his failure to reach that ultimate state of grace
for which he strived.

His thoughts kept turning to the way he had been
humiliatingly brushed aside by Disraeli in the policy debate, the shame of the discovery that his own party would
not follow his lead.

And Disraeli was more secure than ever, draped in
ermine, degrading the Upper House by his presence.

As his thoughts churned, all at once, Gladstone had a
revelation. More. He experienced an explosion of the
mind. It was there! Put into his hands by the Almighty,
the great cause capable of stirring the moral passion he
needed, universal and clamorous, but as yet without a
leader. Why had he not seen it before, when he felt his
stomach heave and his rage fire up at reading of the

horrors in Bulgaria? Horrors which the sneering Disraeli had encouraged—fostered! Here was his crusade.

He had a subject for which he needed no notes, no facts, only the burning, intuitive truth of his imagination. He saw the Bashi-bazouks, ragged, subhuman, lice-ridden, bristling with weapons as they charged into a defenseless hamlet, screaming with lust—burning brands thrown into the thatched houses, children's brains smashed out against stones, young maidens howling for mercy as brutal ravishers threw them to the ground, men spitted on stakes...His brain was afire. It was a Thursday evening. He shut himself away, with his family forbidden to interrupt. His pen raced over many sheets of paper, indicting the Turks and their abominations....the one great anti-human species of humanity...the very people whose vile outrages Disraeli had shamelessly condoned...fell satanic orgies...bestial lusts...no criminal in a European jail, not a cannibal in the South Sea Islands, whose indignation would not arise and overboil at the recital of what had been done! "Let the Turks now carry away their abuses in the only possible way, namely by carrying off themselves. Their Zaptiehs and their Mudirs, their Bimbashis and their Yuzbachis, their Kaimakams and their Pashas, one and all, bag and baggage shall, I hope, clear out from the province they have desolated and profaned..."

He finished four days later on the Sunday and, that night, left for London, taking his pamphlet which he had titled *The Bulgarian Horrors and the Question of the East.* His publisher, Murray, had it printed in two days. Its effect on the public was shattering, with its recklessly violent language, vivid, terrifying images and its demand for a moral crusade to force the Government to sever its connection with the fiends who had committed such repulsive crimes. "No Government ever has so sinned; none has proved itself so incorrigible in sin." Within a few days, 40,000 copies were sold; in a month, 200,000. The vast conscience of the Victorian public was roused and frenzied mass meetings were held, insisting on the expulsion of the Turks from Europe. Gladstone was automatically at the head of the huge, popular movement and kept its vehemence at fever pitch by speeches and constant appearances.

Disraeli had no illusions over the reasons for Gladstone's campaign. It was a direct statement that, now that Disraeli was out of the Commons, Gladstone intended to make a bid to return to power, although by now the People's William would have convinced himself that only his conscience drove him on, not ambition or vindictiveness. The directness of the challenge had been made quite clear, when Disraeli received a complimentary copy of the pamphlet on the first day of publication. He had read it with mounting anger and incredulity. It would make his next moves in the long, diplomatic duel with Gortchakoff and the Czar infinitely more difficult and more hazardous. He wrote to Derby, "Posterity will do justice to that unprincipled maniac Gladstone—extraordinary mixture of envy, vindictiveness, hypocrisy and superstition; and with one commanding characteristic—whether Prime Minister, or Leader of Opposition, whether preaching, praying, speechifying or scribbling—never a gentleman."

His one grain of comfort was that the Turkish army had fought surprisingly well against the Serbians, inflicting a series of defeats, and was pushing them back. Yet even that now could prove disastrous. He moved back to London and called a Cabinet meeting. Before it, he scouted the views of its two most influential members, Derby and Salisbury.

They met in his study at 10 Downing Street. Both were perturbed by the public reaction to Gladstone's crusade. He had been cheered, when he announced at an open-air meeting that he hoped the Russians would march into Bulgaria.

"Have you read his pamphlet, Prime Minister?" Salisbury asked.

Disraeli shrugged. "Yes—it is possibly the worst of the Bulgarian horrors."

Salisbury's mouth twitched, but Derby was irritated. "It is no laughing matter!" he exclaimed. He had been

479

profoundly disturbed by the discovery that the reports were true. It did not affect his determination to uphold British interests in the Eastern Mediterranean, but his ideas on how they could best be achieved had begun to alter. "Our whole policy has been based on the concept that, if Russia attacks Turkey, we shall intervene. I cannot see how that is possible now."

"Because of the agitation?"

"Yes."

"That is the worst aspect of Gladstone's campaign," Salisbury said. "The more noise it makes, the more support it gets, the less the Czar will believe in our determination to protect Turkey. How could we, with the bulk of public opinion against it?"

"Especially if the Czar's intention is only to protect the Christian Slavs," Derby added.

"The Czar would put on a turban tomorrow, if it meant he could build a Kremlin in Constantinople," Disraeli said.

"Not according to the Russian Ambassador," Derby insisted. "Schouvaloff has assured me over and again that his country has no designs on the Bosphorus or the Dardanelles. Which is all that concerns us, or should do."

"He's said the same to me," Salisbury confirmed. "Gortchakoff wants a settlemnt in Turkey and reforms and freedom of worship. That is all."

The good-looking, aristocratic Count Schouvaloff had become a favorite in London society. He dined with all the leading politicians, Derby, Salisbury, Hartington, was always to be seen at the Opera and at fashionable balls, where he was very popular with the ladies. Too popular, many said. Within a few years, he had acquired an amazing knowledge of the intricacies of English political and social life. Behind a charmingly casual manner, he was sharply observant. He was so frank and confiding in his approach that, naturally, his acquaintances were confiding in return, not realizing that what he got were facts, valuable gossip and information, what he gave were compliments and professions of friendship. "Schou is charming, I grant you," Disraeli said, "and his assurances are the most convincing I have ever heard. But surely you remember, only three years ago, how he swore to everyone that the Russian advance in Asia had stopped and that they would never annex Khiva? It was less than a week later that the news came that it had been taken and the Turkomans slaughtered—a massacre fully as horrible as any that happened in Bulgaria."

Derby flushed. "Then what do we do?"

"I have learned one thing—that we gain nothing with Russia by conciliation and concession."

"What do we do?" Derby repeated.

"Stand by our agreements."

"I suppose we must," Salisbury said. "But what happens if the Czar calls our bluff?"

"There is some danger of that," Disraeli admitted. "Especially with the country divided as now. He may well step in to stop Serbia being defeated."

"Precisely."

"Which is why I have called this Cabinet," Disraeli told them. "We must arrange an armistice between Turkey and Serbia, to take effect at once."

Derby and Salisbury were both startled, then realized simultaneously what he meant. Salisbury smiled. Russia would have to give her consent, and would have lost her excuse to enter the war. Except— "Will the Sultan agree, when he's so near to winning?"

"He will have no choice. He must be made to think that, if he does not, we shall withdraw our support."

Derby saw the possibilities, too. It would defuse a dangerous situation. But for how long? "It will give us more time," he agreed. "But an armistice will only be a temporary measure."

"We shall try to make it permanent," Disraeli told him. "As Foreign Secretary, you must call a Conference, representatives of all the major Powers, to meet at Constantinople. We shall work out the details in Cabinet."

"If we compel the Sultan to accept," Salisbury put

forward, "will we not appear to have been made to change our policy by the agitation?"

"There is a world of difference," Disraeli said, "between persuasion, coupled with a warning that he might forfeit our support, and the use of armed force, which the agitators and their Russian allies would prefer. But we shall draw Gladstone's sting by means of the Conference."

Derby hesitated. "What are the objects of the Conference?"

"To establish local self-government and freedom of worship in Bulgaria, Herzegovina and Bosnia, on the pattern of Serbia, under the Sultan."

The normally stolid and undemonstrative Derby showed a trace of excitement. "By that, we would both satisfy the movement for independence *and* preserve Turkey in Europe!

Salisbury smiled. "And stop the agitators in their tracks. What could they complain of?"

"More important," Disraeli stressed. "If we reach agreement with the other Powers on this we shall permanently remove the possibility of Russia acting on her own."

News of the armistice and the acceptance of the talks by the leading Powers steadied confidence in the Government in the country, shaken by the atrocity campaign. The choice of Salisbury as British representative was widely approved. The confidence increased, when it was discovered that Russia had been preparing to occupy Bulgaria. Disraeli had acted just in time. He did not have great hopes for the Conference, itself, but depended on the presence of the other Powers to make both Czar and Sultan see reason. The one uncertainty, and the most unfathomable, was the attitude of Bismarck, who had shown no inclination to take sides. With his involvement the whole business might be much more simple. Disraeli had suggested a treaty between them, not an offensive and defensive alliance, but a treaty by which, together, Britain and Germany would guarantee peace in Europe and maintain the *status quo*. The Queen had liked that. It had been one of Albert's most cherished projects. Bismarck had seemed responsive and prepared to be friendly, but would not commit himself.

Why the German Chancellor avoided discussions and would never commit himself was that he could not make up his mind. It seemed to him far better to stay silent and watch the moves.

The banquet that New Year's Day at Windsor Castle was one which Disraeli had looked forward to with the keenest anticipation for many months. Perhaps all his life had been a prologue to this night. Seated on the Queen's right hand, with her youngest daughter, the nineteen-year-old Princess Beatrice, on his other side, he delighted in the pomp, the gold plate, the gold and crystal centerpieces and candelabra, the wigged and liveried footman behind each chair and, beyond them, the Yeomen of the Guard in their scarlet uniforms and black caps, lining the walls. Never before had he felt the sense of destiny so strongly.

Further down the table, young Lord George Hamilton, Under-Secretary for India, in charge of the India office during Salisbury's absence at the Constantinople Conference, caught his glance and smiled, but was afraid the Chief had not seen him. He leaned forward to catch his eye, then sat back quickly, in case the Queen thought he was peering up the table at her. He was conscious of the honor Lord Beaconsfield had done by bringing him and did not want to be remembered for unintentional rudeness.

Next to him, the Queen's favorite Lady of the Bed-chamber, old Lady Ely, noticed his look. "Her Majesty is very happy tonight," she smiled. "I don't think I've ever seen her in such high spirits."

On her other side, Ponsonby grunted sourly. "She's being tickled by her Court Jester."

Lady Ely laughed. "Oh, come now . . ."

"She's so different from how I expected," Hamilton whispered. He risked another glance down towards the center of the table. Lord Beaconsfield was murmuring to the Queen and she laughed, out loud, the sound high, clear and girlish.

Hamilton need not have worried. Almost the entire table was looking at the Queen. There had been astonishment, when she made her entrance. Tonight, instead of the usual black mourning, she wore a silk evening gown of imperial purple with low neck and frilled shoulders. Securing her white tulle veil was a small diamond crown, across her breast the ribbon and Star of India. Round her neck were loop upon loop of superb pearls, and her bodice and corsage, even the material at her shoulders, glittered with orders and Oriental jewelry, diamonds, rubies, emeralds, many of them uncut and of unusual size. No one had ever seen her like this. On anyone else, the mass of gems, glowing, sparkling in the lights of the thousand wax candles, would have looked garish, even grotesque, but with her enormous dignity the effect was to increase the aura of majesty that surrounded her. The gems were gifts of loyalty from the Princes of India when control had passed from the East India Company to the Crown. They were appropriate tonight.

Another surprise was the Queen's manner. Normally, solemn and slightly detached on public occasions, this evening she was animated, smiling radiantly. And most of her smiles were for her Prime Minister. The dream of the Empire was one they shared and Victoria could only love and honor the man who had fulfilled it for them both.

Lord George Hamilton had found it exciting. He told Lady Ely and she confessed that she, too, had felt it. She broke off, seeing heads turn and hearing a whisper of astonishment. She looked and saw Disraeli rising as the footman behind him drew back his chair. "Is something wrong?" she wondered. "Is Lord Beaconsfield not well?"

"He's going to speak, I think," Hamilton said.

"He can't be!" Ponsonby protested. "It's not done!"

The whisper turned to consternation, followed by deep silence as Disraeli bowed to the Queen, then glanced down the table in either direction. In his gold-embroidered, high-collared court tunic, the pallor of his face emphasized by the blackness of his newly dyed hair, the last curl still falling over his right temple, his appearance was almost theatrically striking. Aware of the effect he had caused, he prolonged the pause and, when he spoke, his voice was richly dramatic. "Your Most Gracious Majesty—Your Royal Highnesses, my lords, ladies and gentlemen," he said, "I rise with trepidation, aware that time-honored custom forbids unscheduled toasts and speeches at the Sovereign's table. Yet I have had so many instances of Her Majesty's gracious forbearance that I have no fear of being granted her indulgence as I speak to you on this day—this very special day. Today, the peace of Britannia stretches across the globe. On every continent, in every clime, her flag is unfurled. Races of every hue, of creeds without number, assured of freedom and of justice, secure behind her mighty shield, acknowledge her rule and daily praise her name in the person of our beloved Queen—as members of the greatest Empire the world has ever known. Which today became reality." He paused for the statement to sink into everyone's consciousness. "On this first day of January, 1877, in Delhi, at the first Imperial Durbar, the reigning Princes of India have hailed Her Majesty as Shah-in-Shah Padshah, Monarch of Monarchs, and the Viceroy, Lord Lytton, has proclaimed her Kaiser-i-Hind—Empress of India. As Prime Minister in her Imperial Majesty's Government, may I propose the most loyal of toasts—The Queen-Empress!"

The next morning, Disraeli took his farewell in the Blue Closet, the small room that had been Prince Albert's favorite and where his desk and chair, his pens, paper and paperknife still lay, exactly as he had left them. The Queen was dressed, more normally, in black mourning.

She was concerned when she saw Disraeli's limp. After the excitements of the night before, he was drawn and tired. For a second or two, he could not catch his breath to speak. "For—forgive me, Ma'am . . . I crave your pardon . . ."

485

"Lord Beaconsfield," she said, anxiously, "I thought you were so much better."

"I have been, Ma'am."

"Is it your asthma?"

"I am afraid so," He shrugged. "It is like the sea at Brighton. Always there."

Victoria's mouth twitched, but she looked at him reprovingly. "Then you must promise me you will not sit in hot rooms. The change of atmosphere when you go out can be most harmful."

He bowed. "I promise, Ma'am."

"You must take more care of yourself!" she scolded. She watched him for a moment, decided and turned away. To his amazement, she picked up a gilt chair and moved it out from the wall. "This time you *shall* sit."

"Please, Ma'am!" he protested. "I could never presume—"

"Nonsense!" she interrupted. Once her mind was made up, she would hear no refusal. "Who is to see? I command you." She smiled and sat on the little sofa near the desk. "There, it is settled."

Disraeli bowed with grateful humility. "Your Majesty knows well that I could never disobey her command." He shifted the chair nearer to her, bowed again and sat.

"Is that not better?"

"Much," he assured her.

She could swear that he was smiling, yet it was so fugitive, only a lightening of the face, a warmth in the eyes. She smoothed her dress over her knees and folded her hands, demurely, with a fleeting touch of embarrassment at her thought. What it was she would not confess, not even to herself. "I shall long remember the words you spoke last night," she said.

"They have waited nearly forty years to be spoken," he told her. "From the day on which, as the newest Member of Parliament, I watched Your Majesty's coronation at Westminster Abbey."

"I shall never forget that day," she said quietly. She looked at him. "I am sorry that you cannot stay longer. Here at Windsor you could rest."

486

He raised a shoulder. "The offer is gracious, Ma'am, but, at only an hour from Westminster, Ministers of State would beat a path to the castle gate. I must be readily available.

"Are affairs still so uncertain?"

"Even more every day, Ma'am," he sighed. "I had hoped, at the opening of Parliament, to be able to announce that peace had been obtained in the Balkan Peninsula. I have to confess, it seems no more likely than ever."

"Perhaps if you had been able to act as our representative," she began.

"No one could have done more than Lord Salisbury, Ma'am. Without him, the Conference would have broken up long ago. Yet even he is powerless against the obstinacy of the Turks. And against the endless intriguing of the Russians. Their man Ignatyev is cunning and unscrupulous, and seems to anticipate every move we make—as if he had read the minutes of the Cabinet meetings."

"He must be made to deal straightforwardly. You should tell his superior, Prince Gortchakoff, that unless we are assured of the honesty of their intentions, the consequences will be serious!"

"Unfortunately, Ma'am, we cannot afford to threaten."

She bridled. "If the Turks and the Russians will not listen to reason, they must be made to! We have the strength to make them."

Disraeli hesitated. "Unfortunately, Ma'am . . . we do not." She stared at him. "Our Army and Navy were so run down by the previous Government that we have only just begun to make good the deficiencies. Before we are ready to face a war, we need time and money—a great sum of money, which we will have to ask Parliament for. In the present climate in the country, to ask a penny for a Russian war could start up a tremendous protest. It might bring down the Government. It certainly would let our enemies know—which they are not yet certain of—that any warlike action we take does not have the common consent of our people. We dare not move."

"It cannot be so bad," Victoria argued, disbelievingly.

The people might rally to us," he admitted. "I dare say they would. But if they did not? We can only have our bluff called once, Ma'am." He paused. "It will be long before the mischief the 'atrocity agitation' has done us on the Continent will be remedied. Only last June, we dictated to Europe, and now every Power looks askance."

Victoria raised her clasped hands and shook them in frustration. "And all because of that firebrand, that half madman, Gladstone! Not to mention the Duke of Westminster, *and* Lord Shaftesbury! Cannot the Attorney-General be set at them? Their behavior cannot be constitutional!"

"It is the price we pay for free speech, Ma'am."

"So what now?"

"We must bide our time. And be sure that when we do act, we are able to act with firmness. There are signs that the people are coming round. The news that the Russians are mobilizing shocked many to their senses."

"What of Lord Derby?" Victoria asked.

Disraeli hoped he did not show his concern. Derby had been an excellent Foreign Minister. Stolid and unimaginative as he was, he was utterly determined in carrying out agreed policies. His stolidity recently, however, amounted almost to obstructiveness and had become irritating. Disraeli always excused his lack of energy as caution and made up for his shortcomings, himself, as much as possible. "Lord Derby refuses to panic, Ma'am. As always, we decide everything between the two of us, in complete agreement. And, most usefully, he is in constant, I might say daily, touch with the Russian Ambassador, Schouvaloff."

"Count Schouvaloff," Victoria frowned. "A most disarming person."

"And that makes him all the more dangerous."

"My opinion, precisely," she said. "I found him a touch too ingratiating." She saw Disraeli shift slightly. "You are impatient to be off, Lord Beaconsfield."

"Oh, no, no, Ma'am . . ." he denied. "Although—the despatch boxes will be ready for me at twelve, and I expect a cypher telegram from Lord Salisbury."

She smiled. "But you hesitated to dismiss yourself. You will let me know what he says?"

"Instantly, Your Majesty. And any comments I may have."

Victoria frowned again. "It is a pity they will have to go through Ponsonby. Having to deal with so many confidential matters, it is unfortunate that he has such a great liking for Mr. Gladstone."

"I will admit, Ma'am," Disraeli said, "I always feel a trifle more at ease, when Your Majesty communicates with me through Lady Ely."

Victoria nodded. "Then that is what we shall do. We must have a private channel for anything that is particularly confidential. Private or secret matters I shall send in cypher."

"It might be best, Ma'am," he agreed. "Not that I question your Private Secretary's discretion."

"Of course, not. But I envy you your Mr. Corry."

"He would be most gratified."

"And he will be waiting," she added. "That is what you would say." As he made to deny it, she smiled. "Oh, run along! Run along directly."

Disraeli rose and bowed his thanks. "My only consolation in leaving is that it is in Your Majesty's service."

Victoria stood and held out her hand, smiling. When he touched it lightly from below and kissed it, she caught hold of his hand and gave it a little shake. She was so clearly reluctant to let him go that it created a moment of embarrassment.

He broke it by stepping back. "With your permission, Ma'am—" He took up the chair on which he had been sitting and replaced it carefully against the wall. He turned. "So that no one will know I had the effrontery to sit in the presence of my sovereign." He backed to the door.

"Now be sure you wrap up well," Victoria ordered.

"I shall cosset myself, Ma'am," he assured her. "On your orders." He bowed again slightly at the door and went out.

Victoria watched him leave, smiling. She turned and looked at the chair on which he had sat. How appropriate it should be in this room. She had not sat with anyone in here since Albert. She moved to the door leading to her private apartments. "Always there . . ." she murmured, and gave a short burst of her girlish laughter.

A few weeks later, the country reacted with excitement to the news that she was to open Parliament in person for the second year running. It was a sign of her approval of her Government's actions and policies. The support of many people swung back to Disraeli because of it, as she intended. He was very nearly unable to be present. After leaving Windsor, "that Castle of the Winds," as he called it, he was stricken with rheumatism and bronchitis and had to keep to his bed. Victoria was disappointed, yet offered to release him from having to take part in the ceremony, in which, for the first time, he would be carrying the Sword of State. Nothing would keep him from it. "He would not like to miss so great an incident," he wrote back. "It is a chapter in life."

After the royal procession, when the members of the Commons were summoned, they jostled and crowded their way into the Lords. They were eager to see the Queen in her robes of state and to hear the Speech from the Throne, but even more eager to see the figure on her left, in scarlet and ermine, grave and motionless as he held on high the great sword, Her Majesty's First Minister and Leader of the House of Lords, Benjamin Disraeli, Earl of Beaconsfield.

Salisbury returned from Constantinople, empty-handed. The Sultan, even faced with being abandoned by all the Powers, refused to make any concessons. No one regretted it more than the Czar's representative, General Ignatyev. Ignatyev, a subtle, sociable man, made a point of being friendly with Salisbury, who was amused by his inability to let a chance of intriguing go by. He made no secret of despising the Turks and it was largely through the offense caused by his attitude that the Conference failed to reach a settlement. The representatives left Constantinople. The only progress they achieved was to get the armistice extended, so that the door was not fully closed.

In spite of various medicines and regimes tried by his doctors, Disraeli did not improve. There were long periods when he could not leave Whitehall Gardens and he had to have a camp-bed set up next to his study at 10 Downing Street, so that, after long Cabinet meetings, he could lie down and, if necessary, stay the night.

The campaign, calling for Britain to launch a Holy War to free the Balkans, did not slacken. It had lost many of its supporters in London and the southern counties, but it was given a further impetus by Gladstone's return to the House of Commons. His speeches attacking the Government and Disraeli were reported in the newspapers week after week and kept the movement alive. His extremism had alienated Hartington and most of the other Liberal leaders, but he would not lessen the virulence of his language. It brought a new and disturbing violence into politics.

Struggling against illness, Disraeli had to devote most of his available time to diplomacy to counter Derby's apathy. His attempts to rouse the Foreign Secretary to win back the diplomatic initiative for England failed. There were even times when he was tempted to replace him. Then Ignatyev arrived unexpectedly in London and events took a new turn. Expansive and sociable as ever, he was welcomed by the pro-Russian groups in society. Disraeli could not make up his mind whether to receive him, but finally gave a banquet for him and his attractive wife. The purpose of his visit turned out to be a series of draft proposals which he had brought with him from the Czar and Gortchakoff, again on the settlement of the Eastern Question. The proposals, when Derby presented them to the Cabinet, were extraordinarily mild, compared to previous Russian demands. If the Sultan promised to reduce his army to a peacetime force and agreed to proceed with the reforms, Russia would also disarm. The Ambassadors of the Powers would keep a watch to see that the Sultan's promise was kept. If not, the Powers would consider the best means to "secure the well-being of the Christian populations and the interests of the general peace." The proposals were immediately accepted by those members of the Cabinet who were against any thought of war with Russia in defense of Turkey, Salisbury, Derby and Lord Carnarvon, the Colonial Secretary. Apparently, the Czar had abandoned his insistence that the question could only be settled by force and had adopted Disraeli's veiwpoint. Although the Queen was suspicious, the proposals were signed by Derby and the Ambassadors in London of all the Powers, and Ignatyev went back to St. Petersburg.

Exactly a month later, the Russian army marched into Turkish territory.

It had been brilliantly conceived. Ignatyev had destroyed the Constantinople Conference by his insolence to the Turks and by developing an atmosphere of intrigue and distrust. The phrasing of the proposals was mild enough to tempt all the Powers, particularly England, but containing just enough hint of insult, coupled with the way Ignatyev presented it, to make the Sultan reject it. Gortchakoff claimed that the Russian army was only fighting to impose the proposals signed in London. Britain could not deny she had signed the proposals. Not with thousands of people throughout the country cheering Russia and the Czar. "Go on and prosper!" Gladstone had cried. Gortchakoff had found the perfect pretext to keep England out of the war. Disraeli could only accept it.

The Queen was alarmed. She saw as clearly as her Prime Minister the inevitability of a Russian victory, giving them control not only of Constantinople, but of Egypt and the Suez Canal. With England's routes to the Indian Ocean blocked, India itself would be the next objective of the Czar. "Was anything ever so deceitful as those Russians!" she declared. "If England is to kiss Russia's feet, I will not be a party to such humiliation and would lay down my crown!" Disraeli had to convince her, regretfully, that the new policy of watchful neutrality was the only one open to him.

Now that the moment had come, he might have risked going against public opinion and challenging Russia, but his Cabinet was hopelessly divided. The only agreement he could make them reach was for Derby to send a note to Gortchakoff, insisting that British rights in Constantinople, Egypt and the Red Sea must be respected. He could get no general agreement on what action should be taken, if they were not. Derby was more obstructive than ever, seeming determined on "peace at any price."

Seeing his chance, Gladstone tabled a series of resolutions in the Commons, condemning the Government for not joining forces with Russia in the Czar's noble bid to liberate the Christian races of the Balkans. Fortunately, for Disraeli, Hartington understood his difficulties and was alarmed by Gladstone's blind partisanship of Russia. He compelled him to withdraw most of the resolutions and, on the remaining two, Gladstone was heavily defeated, and realized that, if he persisted, he would split the Liberal party and be left at the head of only a small faction.

It was a grain of comfort for Disraeli. There were few others. The Russian advance swept on over a wide front, crossing the Danube, capturing northern Bulgaria and probing down into Thrace. He pressed Derby to make an approach to Austria, but, even as they waited for the reply, whispers came of the secret negotiations between Andrassy and Gortchakoff. Bismarck, impressed by success as ever, swung more noticeably toward Russia. It seemed that nothing could not prevent a Russian thrust to Constantinople.

In Britain, more and more people were becoming uneasy. Russia was a traditional enemy and, gradually, all the old fears came flooding back. Disraeli could sense that public opinion was turning, but was still hampered by the wrangles of his Cabinet and threats of resignations. Count Schouvaloff was more friendly, coming back from St. Petersburg with assurances from Gortchakoff that

Britain's rights would be protected. Patiently, laboriously, Disraeli worked to convince his Cabinet that only strong, concerted action could answer all their doubts and end the war. And all the time, he was bombarded with letters and coded messages from the Queen, "Pray act quickly!," "Be bold!," "The language—the insulting language—used by the Russians against us! It makes the Queen's blood boil!" Through it all, he made his own plans, knowing that one day they would be needed.

His health showed no improvement, but, somehow, he hung on. Then news came that the Russians had been thrown back twice at Plevna. In the third battle, they suffered a shattering defeat. The Czar would need time to move up reinforcements and, probably, would not be able to mount a second campaign until the following spring. Until then, Constantinople was safe. It was the tension which had been holding Disraeli together and, without it, he collapsed. His friends were worried and Cairns arranged for him to see a new doctor, Dr. Kidd, a homeopath who specialized in bronchial cases. Disraeli had only been able to sleep, sitting in one chair and leaning over the back of another. Kidd quickly realized that he was suffering from a disease of the kidneys, as well as the bronchitis and asthma, and that some of the medicines he had been given were actively harmful. With new medicines and a controlled diet, Disraeli's health rapidly improved and he was even able to speak at the annual Lord Mayor's banquet. He used it to make a review of his whole policy and to repeat his determination to fight, if necessary, to protect British interests. It was a speech that people needed to hear and he was loudly cheered. One phrase he used was repeated everywhere. "Cosmopolitan critics, men who are the friends of every country save their own, have denounced this policy as a selfish policy. My Lord Mayor, it is as selfish as patriotism."

In early December, Plevna was captured and the Russian advance began again without waiting for the spring. Disraeli had failed to get his Cabinet to agree to a note warning the Czar that a second campaign would end British neutrality. Now, encouraged by his reception at the banquet, he proposed to recall Parliament early from the Christmas recess, to ask for a massive increase in forces and armaments and that Britain should step in as mediator between Russia and Turkey. He had a new ally in the Cabinet. The overweight Ward Hunt had died and, in his place as First Lord of the Admiralty, he had promoted W.H. Smith, of the famous bookstalls, whose political career he had fostered. Smith supported him, along with Manners, Hardy and Cairns. Salisbury and others hesitated. Derby and Carnarvon opposed him, and the Cabinet had to be adjourned.

The next morning, a large crowd gathered at High Wycombe station and the Mayor waited nervously with Lord Beaconsfield as the royal train drew in. The Queen had come to visit her Prime Minister.

Accompanied by Princess Beatrice, an equerry and two ladies-in-waiting, Victoria drove through cheering streets to Hughenden, with Disraeli by her side. The news was headlined in every newspaper in the country. She had only once before visited the home of one of her Prime Ministers, thirty-five years before, when Albert and she had been guests of Lord Melbourne.

The visit was an adventure for Victoria. She had wanted very much to see Disraeli's home and found it even prettier than she had imagined. The little church on the slope below the house, the broad lawn before the portico, the quaint old chimneys. With Corry escorting Beatrice, Disraeli showed her his library and the dining-room where they were to have lunch, and where he had carefully rehung her portrait by Von Angeli. She was delighted. The same artist had done a portrait of Disraeli for her and she told him she would have it hung in her dining-room at Windsor to keep her company.

She saw many more portraits, in the hall and up the main staircase. That was his Gallery of Friendship, he told her, all the people he loved and who had influenced his life.

At last, they reached the drawing-room and she looked round, approving every detail. "Most charming," she said. "It is exactly as I knew it would be, Lord Beaconsfield, and as you have described it." Disraeli bowed. She moved toward the fireplace, but stopped as Beatrice followed her. She was impatient to talk to Disraeli alone. Corry had remained just inside the door with the equerry and the ladies-in-waiting. "Since the sun has come out, Beatrice," she suggested, "perhaps Mr. Corry would care to show you all the garden."

The order was unmistakable. Beatrice curtsied.

Corry bowed. "I should be honored, Ma'am." He bowed again to Beatrice and went out with her, followed by the others.

Victoria relaxed, and continued to the fireplace. Above it, the portrait of Mary Anne now hung and she paused, realizing who it must be, although the face was much younger than the one she remembered.

Behind her, Disraeli said, "May I offer you my heartfelt thanks again, Your Majesty, for the honor you have conferred on me of visiting my home?"

She turned. "I have wished to do so for a long time." There was one very unfortunate fact she had just learned. "But I am very concerned that I fixed this day for it, the anniversary of poor Lady Beaconsfield's death. Believe me, I only found out when it was too late to alter it."

"It will only serve to make the recollection of this day more hallowed, Ma'am," he said quietly.

She nodded. It was a sentiment she could perfectly understand. She glanced again at the portrait and sat on a brocaded sofa by the fire. When he did not move, she smiled. "I presume you will have no objection to taking a chair in your own home, Lord Beaconsfield?"

"It would seem to be quite fitting, Ma'am," he agreed with a faint smile. He bowed and lowered himself stiffly into a chair by the sofa.

"There. That is better. I am afraid this changeable weather is not good for your health."

"So my doctors tell me," he said. "Gull wanted to send me to Ems. Jenner suggested I go to Bournemouth. I should like to send them both to Jericho."

Victoria laughed. "But I understand you have a new physician."

"That is so, Ma'am. A quack, the orthodox would call him. But he has done me more good than any of them." He paused. "I confess I am overwhelmed by the condescension Your Majesty has shown me. To visit the home of your Prime Minister shows an exceptional confidence."

"Which is precisely what I wish to show—in this difficult time," she told him. The whole purpose of her trip today. "Was there ever anything so irresponsible as this behavior of Lord Derby?" she exclaimed suddenly. "Never to do nor agree to anything. I have never known a Foreign Secretary like him!" Disraeli moved his shoulders, but did not reply. "His behavior has convinced the Czar that he has a free hand, that whatever we threaten, we shall never be able to fight."

"It appears so, Ma'am," Disraeli said. He was saddened and, although he did not show it to the Queen, bitterly angry. A situation had arisen which he would never have believed possible.

He had been convinced for some time that the only way to stop the war before England had to intervene was for the Czar to be made to realize that every day brought them nearer to a bigger and even bloodier Crimea. A war now, fought between the British and Russian Empires with modern weapons, would be a holocaust without example in history. Even when watered down by Derby, his warnings sent from the Cabinet had been clear. The refusal of the Cabinet to agree to this latest warning against a second campaign had forced him, with the Queen's consent, to send a secret envoy to the Czar and Gortchakoff, without even the Foreign Office knowing, stating his position bluntly and irrevocably. The envoy had reported that the Czar paid little attention, knowing he had nothing to fear. Every move, every shade of opinion, the results of every meeting of the British Cabinet, were reported to him weekly by his Ambassador, Count Schouvaloff.

Instantly, Disraeli had realized the truth of what he had only suspected for some time, that there was an informant in the Cabinet. That there had been, since before the Constantinople Conference right up to the fall of Plevna. That was why all his moves, everything that might have prevented or shortened the war, had failed. Although he hated to believe it, there was only one person it could be. Derby's inertia and obstructiveness and his regular meetings with Schouvaloff were explained.

"For a Foreign Secretary to tell the secrets of the Cabinet to an unfriendly Power, with whom we may soon be at war—it's unheard of!" Victoria exclaimed. "Why has he done this?"

"I'm afraid there can be only one reason, Ma'am," Disraeli said slowly. "Because he does not trust me. Scouvaloff must have deceived Lord Derby into believing that Russia means to keep her word and that the only danger of us going to war is if I push us into it. By his own lights, he has been acting for his country."

"By betraying us! What is to be done?"

"The first essential is to put a stop to the meetings with Schouvaloff, and to do so without making any open accusation. It had best be handled privately, preferably by some third person. I would suggest Lord Salisbury."

"Salisbury!" Victoria snorted. "He is as obstructive as Derby."

"Only because he learned at Constantinople not to trust the Turks. But I think he will not allow it to be occupied by the Russians. Also, once he realizes that my intention is to give military aid to Turkey, only on condition that the Sultan carries out the reforms we have been promised for so long and permits freedom of worship and self-government to his Christian subjects, once Salisbury realizes that he will change his mind."

"Let us hope so," Victoria said. "It's about time he stopped behaving like a spoiled child! So many opportunities wasted! And in the meantime, Sophia has fallen and the Russian armies roll nearer and nearer to the Bosphorus. How are they to be stopped before it is too late? It worries me night and day!"

"There is still a card I can play."

"What?"

"To risk everything," Disraeli told her, "and hope to win round both the Cabinet and the country."

"You must, Lord Beaconsfield!" Victoria insisted. "And without delay!" She looked away, her face set. "Oh if I were a man, I would go and give those Russians such a beating!"

Looking at her, her small hand clenched, her chin tilted, Disraeli had the thought that, in this mood, a Russian brigade might well turn tail at the sight of the Queen.

Confronted by Salisbury, Derby did not deny that he had been passing information to Schouvaloff and refused to admit that he had acted wrongly. He was in a strange mental state, drinking heavily. He loved Disraeli as a friend and admired him, he said, but his duty was to save the country. Even when it became obvious that the main Russian objective was to seize Gallipoli and the Straits, he refused to believe it. Disraeli was gentle with him, not dismissing him, but not trusting him, either.

No one could mistake the mood in the country. Everywhere there was great alarm and excitement and fierce arguments over what should be done. At one meeting, the speakers demanded an instant declaration of war on Russia. At another, they condemned the Queen for going ostentatiously to eat with the Jew in his ghetto. When Gladstone continued to champion the Czar, a crowd broke the windows of his house in London.

Appealing for Salisbury's help in dealing with Derby was the wisest step Disraeli could have taken. As well as being flattered, the younger man had to look at his own arguments and when, with the Russian army at the outer defenses of Constantinople, the Sultan begged for help, he saw that the time for neutrality was over and that Disraeli's hands had been tied too long. With Salisbury's support, Disraeli now could carry the whole Cabinet with him, apart from Derby and the anti-Turk Carnarvon. He asked for a Vote of Credit of six million pounds to put the armed forces in a condition for war and ordered a fleet of ironclads to Constantinople. Derby and Carnarvon resigned. The shout that went up from the crowds assembled in Dowining Street waiting for the decision, and that was taken up throughout London as the news spread, sent Schouvaloff hurrying to telegraph to St. Petersburg that Disraeli was no longer bluffing and that the country had swung behind him.

The immediate result was a telegram from the British Ambassador to the Porte to say that Russia and Turkey had arranged a ceasefire and were discussing peace terms. The fleet could be recalled to the mouth of the Dardanelles.

For some weeks, there was utter confusion, conflicting reports from the war zone, constant alarms. There was now no real reason for Derby to resign and he stayed on nominally at the Foreign Office to preserve the appearance of a united front in the Government, but Disraeli took over full responsibility for foreign affairs. Both he and the Queen thought that the Czar had given in too easily and he went ahead with the Vote of Credit. The day it was passed in Parliament in spite of total opposition from Gladstone, the crowds were so dense that Disraeli had to walk from Downing Street to the House of Lords and was cheered all the way. Still trying to protest, Gladstone was jostled in the street and had to be given police protection.

The Queen and Disraeli had been right to mistrust the Czar's intentions. The sudden ceasefire was a ruse to allow General Ignatyev to force crippling terms on the Turks at gunpoint before anyone else could interfere. They amounted to the end of the Turkish Empire in Europe. Independence for all the subject provinces. Russia was to acquire huge tracts of territory in Asia and along the Black Sea, controlling the caravan route to Afghanistan. She was also to control a giant new state made out of north and south Bulgaria and stretching down to the Aegean, as well as rights in the Bosphorus and Dardanelles Straits. And all the time, even after the armistice had been signed, the Russian army kept up a stealthy advance towards Constantinople.

There was consternation in the capitals of Europe. Single-handedly, Russia was altering the entire balance of power. To prevent open criticism, Gortchakoff and the Czar announced that they would hold an international conference to discuss the peace terms at some date in the future. Austria was especially provoked. None of the secret agreements she had made with Russia were respected. Belatedly, Andrassy replied to the notes he had been sent by Disraeli.

In England, troop movements, activity at arsenals and dockyards, and the certainty that the routes to India were in danger, raised war fever to unimagined heights. In a speech of Disraeli's, he had said that, although the policy of England was peace, if she had to fight in defense of her independence or her Empire, she would use all her resources. "She is not a country that, when she enters on a campaign, has to ask herself whether she can support a second or a third campaign. She enters into a campaign which she will not terminate until right is done." It had inspired a patriotic, music-hall song that suddenly everyone was singing from end to end of the country.

We don't want to fight, but by Jingo! if we do,
We've got the ships, we've got the men, we've got the money too.
We've fought the Bear before, and while Britons shall be true,
The Russians shall not have Constantinople!

To the Queen, not one of the Russian terms was acceptable. She could not understand why Disraeli did not go to war at once and sent him so many letters, sometimes three a day, that he had to beg her not to tire herself out. "Lord Beaconsfield hopes that Your Majesty remembers her gracious promise not to write at night, at least not so much. He lives only for Her, and works only for Her, and without Her, all is lost." She need not have worried. Now assisted by Salisbury, he was taking the steps which he had always known would be necessary. It was perilous, but his head became more clear and his step more firm, the closer he came to the edge. The first step was to send the fleet, at last, to within sight of Constantinople. The ironclads steamed through the Dardanelles and anchored off the island of Prinkipo. The Russians had been about to occupy Gallipoli and, from there, take possession of the Straits. They stopped in confusion.

The Czar and his advisers had still been sure that England was not prepared to fight. If only they could be certain! Gortchakoff advised him to forget the Dardanelles, but he would not give up his dream of marching his army through Constantinople, whose towers and minarets gleamed in the sun just across the water. His commanders waited for the order and watched the ironclads, whose guns could smash the ancient city to rubble.

In London, Lord Salisbury hurried to Whitehall Gardens in answer to a message from Disraeli. He found him in his study, wearing his dressing gown and carpet slippers, but still working. Disraeli apologized for not rising. "You will forgive me, but the exertions of these past weeks have left me almost unable to move."

"Of course, Sir."

Disraeli laid his eyeglass on the papers he had been reading. "It appears the Austrians are at last ready to join us. They agree that Russia must submit its peace terms for international approval."

"But that's just what they refuse to do."

"So far." Disraeli paused. "You'll have heard that Lord Derby has finally resigned? Calling up the Reserves was the last straw for him—and other suggestions I made."

Salisbury took out the note he had been sent. "Do I understand you rightly, Sir? You wish me to become Foreign Secretary?"

"As of now."

"But I assumed that you would take charge officially."

"There's too much to do," Disraeli told him. "The Foreign Office handles so much business. I shall, of course, keep responsibility for these Russian-Turkish negotiations, but I wish a younger man to run the Department. Do you accept?"

Salisbury's hesitation was only momentary. "I shall be honored to, Sir." He would be in a subordinate position, but no one could expect to equal Disraeli. The more he had come to know him, the more he respected him and realized that they were really very alike. Yet he was puzzled that he had not chosen one of his other colleagues who had been with him longer. "If I may ask—why me?"

"Because I admire your intelligence," Disraeli said simply. "And you are one of the few men of real courage it has been my privilege to work with. It will take courage, at this moment, to back me."

Salisbury nodded stiffly at the compliment. Something else had occurred to him. "You mention other suggestions which had led to Lord Derby's resignation . . . may I know what they were?"

Disraeli's fingers tapped on the desk. Yes, he thought, I am definitely right about him. "Further moves which will be needed to break the Czar's nerve," he explained. "I have ordered seven thousand Indian troops to be sent to the Malta garrison."

"But we've never used Indian troops in a European war before!" Salisbury exclaimed.

"We shall now," Disraeli said. "To show I am determined to commit the whole might of the Empire, if necessary. We shall use them either to occupy the Dardanelles, or to seize a base at the eastern end of the Mediterranean, say, Alexandretta."

Salisbury's throat was dry. "But I thought—you assured me that your entire intention was to avoid war."

"Whatever anyone may think," Disraeli nodded. "And whatever the Faery may wish . . . but there must be no sign of weakening. If we are firm and determined, we shall have peace and we shall dictate its terms to Europe."

How sincere is he? Salisbury wondered. Is he playing the man of destiny, or *is* he the man of destiny? "What would be my part in this?" he asked.

"To draw up a total revision of the peace terms, which would make them acceptable to us. We must be fair.

Turkey has lost a war and must pay the penalty, to some extent, without being plundered. Austria must be satisfied. Russia has won a war and must have something to show for it. But she must not control the route to Afghanistan. She must not be allowed to dominate the Balkans, nor have direct access to the Mediterranean, nor have any control over the Straits. That will protect our interests, which is all I have cared about all along."

Only a conqueror, a Napoleon or Genghis Khan, could impose terms like that, Salisbury thought, and Disraeli was proposing to do it without having fired a shot. "I doubt if the Czar will agree to that, Sir," he said.

Disraeli's eyebrows rose. "He must be made to. The Queen—and our people—will be content with no less."

Salisbury knew they had come to a point from which there was no turning back. "I hope you realize you will be leading them over an abyss," he said.

"Well . . ." Disraeli murmured, "I have always had a good head for heights."

The brilliant circular which Salisbury drafted, setting out and justifying England's position and insisting that the peace Treaty between the Czar and the Sultan must be approved by all the Powers, established him as a major diplomat. Austria accepted it at once, seeing that she was to be given control of Bosnia. The Sultan embraced it, realizing that it let him keep more than he had dared to hope. Bismarck broke his silence and suggested that it was at least the basis for a conference.

The Czar's reaction was of fury and determination to fight rather than to submit to a dictated peace. But the arrival of the first contingent of Indian troops in Malta made him pause. Then came word that the Austro-Hungarian Army was massing along its border. He could not risk a war on two fronts and sent Ignatyev to hold urgent talks with Andrassy and warn him it would mean the end of the Dreikaiserbund. For all his subtlety and persuasiveness, Ignatyev could not convince the Austrains that the Czar was a more dependable ally than Disraeli. When he returned to St. Petersburg to admit failure, he was dismissed in disgrace and exiled to his estate in the country.

Another player who had been watching, but had not yet taken a major part, decided to make a move. Bismarck issued an invitation to all the chief Powers to meet at a Congress in Berlin, to decide the peace terms. He had seen the initiative pass to England and Disraeli begin to challenge his claim to be the leading statesman in Europe. By this, he meant to bring the attention back to himself. He made one condition—all major items of disagreement had to be worked out first by the Foreign Ministers, leaving only the final details to be ratified. He would not have the Congress breaking up in disorder.

Count Schouvaloff called on Disraeli at Downing Street, having heard that a second transport filled with Indian troops had arrived at Malta. "We are not at war," he protested. "How else is His Imperial Majesty to interpret their arrival, but as a threat? When are they to stop coming?"

"When we have enough," Disraeli told him.

It was obvious to Schouvaloff that his master, the Czar, had lost his chance, and the longer he delayed, the more British troops would be stationed in the Mediterranean. He had also heard of secret negotiations between Beaconsfield and the Sultan of Turkey. He knew that the Imperial Chancellor, Prince Gortchakoff, favored accepting the invitation to a Congress, since it was to be at Berlin, where he was in no doubt of sympathetic assistance from Bismarck. Only the Czar and some of the Russian military had to be convinced. He offered himself as a go-between to end the deadlock and Disraeli took him patiently through Salisbury's circular, pointing out the areas where England might be prepared to give way and where she definitely would not. Schouvaloff travelled to Russia and was back within two weeks with the Czar's consent to the Congress.

Afterward, Disraeli explained to Salisbury, Manners and Northcote how it had been done. "When he left, I told him that it was only fair to say distinctly that we could not, in the slighest degree, slow down our preparations. And that they must go on, even if there were a Congress. So . . . the Congress is fixed for June 12. I arranged for confidential despatches to be sent to the Sultan, Andrassy and the Rumanian Government, announcing that, even if we were alone, we would be ready by May 3 to expel the Russians from European Turkey."

"But the Czar's agents were pretty well bound to hear," Northcote objected. He was puzzled when Salisbury and Manners laughed.

"I confidently hoped so," Disraeli said patiently. "In fact, I depended on the Sultan telling his Greek doctor, Andrassy revealing it to Bismarck, and Rumania, of course, to Russia."

"Can you hear that?" Manners asked. Acceptance of the invitation to the Congress by all Powers had been reported in the papers. Even at the rear of the building, the cheers of the people gathered outside could be heard.

"You will have to be prepared for a deal of hard bargaining," Northcote warned Salisbury. "You can't trust them. They're bound to go back on the terms you've agreed."

Manners smiled. "You'll be walking like Daniel, into the lions' den."

"I shall not be alone," Salisbury told them.

Disraeli coughed. "No . . . Prince Bismarck, himself, will be President of the Congress. Other heads of government will be there. I feel it only right, in spite of my health, that I should accompany Lord Salisbury to Berlin."

Rightly, Disraeli knew that the Congress would be a major diplomatic duel, which he could not leave to Salisbury. No entreaties nor protests from the Queen that his health would not stand it and that it was much too far to travel could make him change his mind. He answered her worries by taking four days for the journey, accompanied by Montagu Corry and their valets, and arrived as fresh as if he had just walked down the street to the House of Lords.

The Congress opened formally two days later, when

Bismarck welcomed the Plenipotentiaries to the great hall of the Radetsky Palace. Disraeli watched him as the others arrived. He had altered considerably since their last meeting. A great bear of a man with a florid complexion and full, beetlin moustache, at sixty-two he was nearly bald and the wasp waist had completely disappeared. Not only physically, but in personality, he dominated the assembly. As he moved from group to group with his aides and his huge mastiff, which accompanied him everywhere, it was easy to see by their deference how much most of the delegates feared him. At last, Prince Gortchakoff was announced, the man Disraeli most wanted to meet. Gortchakoff was carried in, with his arms on the shoulders of two Russian Guardsmen. He was small and shrunken, even older than Disraeli, crippled with rheumatism. With his white hair, little, round glasses and benign smile, he looked like a retired country schoolmaster, but Disraeli knew the mild appearance hid an extremely devious mind and an implacable intelligence. Their greetings were cordial and civilized, though brief, in the diplomatic language, French.

On the way to the conference table, a ludicrous incident happened, which might have been very serious. Gortchakoff was leaning on Bismarck's arm. Bismarck tripped and stumbled and Gortchakoff fell, bringing the giant down with him. As they rolled on the floor, the mastiff thought that his master was being attacked, leaped on Gortchakoff and began to worry him. Only strenuous efforts by Bismarck, himself, and his aides managed to prevent him from being badly savaged. The dog was banished for the rest of the conference.

At last, the delegates took their seats. The table was arranged alphabetically, starting with Austria on the left, then Britain. It was designed to put Germany in the center, and Bismarck. Disraeli had the most junior Austrian secretary on his left, Salisbury on his right. At the far end, he saw the Turkish representatives, stiffly uncomfortable next to the Serbians and Russians.

After the applause for Bismarck's opening address and

while the order of business was being sorted out, Salisbury murmured, "Well, the preliminaries seem to be going smoothly enough."

Disraeli nodded. "May they remain so." By now, he had assessed all the delegates from Caratheodory Pasha, the handsome, able, young Turk, to the impeccable Italian, Count Corti. None of them were a match for Salisbury and could be left to him. Bismarck and the combination of Gortchakoff and Schouvaloff was different. Bismarck intended to *be* the Congress and make its final decisions. The Russians planned to recover as much as possible of what they had been made to give up. There was certainly an understanding between Bismarck and the Austrians. At a guess, he also had one with the Russians. That was what Disraeli would have to deal with, himself. He had already brought up the withdrawal of Russian troops from Constantinople, but Bismarck had adjourned discussion of it to another day. Was that a proof of bias? If so, he would have to be doubly on his guard.

A few days later, Corry left Disraeli talking to Andrassy and Bismarck after a reception at the British Embassy, and went to find Salisbury. These days had been so hectic that Corry wondered how he could survive another three weeks. Apart from the meetings, there was a continuous round of visits, receptions and banquets. At the weekend, they had stayed overnight at Potsdam in the rococo New Palace with the Crown Prince and Princess. Then back to Berlin for more informal discussions. And all the time, Lord Beaconsfield kept writing to the Queen and to Lady Bradford and Cabinet Ministers back in London. How long could he keep it up?

"He's certainly stood up well to all the social events," Salisbury said. "He is the social lion of the Congress." Disraeli's books had been in all the shops, when they arrived. Now they were all sold out and the booksellers were clamoring for more. It was not only the diplomats who clustered round Disraeli. It was all the prettiest women, and the royalty. And everyone gossiped about him, about his early days and love affairs. And obviously he was enjoying every minute of it.

"I've seen the draft of his address to the Congress tomorrow," Corry said. "It's in French."

Salisbury could tell he was worried. "Why not? Lord Beaconsfield reads French fluently."

Corry hesitated. "Yes, but when he speaks it, he seems to have made up his own pronunciation. Ung treh bong jour, nace pas?"

"I see . . ."

"The other delegates will laugh, rather than listen to what he says," Corry went on, urgently. "The effect could be disastrous."

Salisbury glanced over to where Disraeli leaned on his cane, listening to one of Bismarck's scurrilous reminiscences. "Why don't you speak to him about it, Monty?"

"I think it would be much better, if you did, Sir," Corry said. As Salisbury looked at him, he smiled.

Salisbury had to admit that he would not relish tackling Dizzy about it, either. He did not have that kind of courage. He nodded to Corry and crossed to have a word with the British Ambassador, Lord Odo Russell.

They were going on to a banquet at the Italian Embassy. Lord Odo Russell offered to take Disraeli in his own carriage and, as they drove through the streets in the bright summer evening, he was impressed to see how people recognized Disraeli and waved or raised their hats. As a Liberal, Lord Odo had had strong reservations about Disraeli, but it was certainly true that, since he had become Prime Minister, he had put Britain firmly back on the political map. "You look well, Sir," he said.

Disraeli nodded. "This warmer weather is better for my asthma. Yes, I might say I am almost fairly well."

Lord Odo laughed. "And you are pleased with progress?"

"Relatively. We might have to give way a little more in Asia than I'd like, but at least the Russians have accepted the two Bulgarias." That had been the first stumbling block. Instead of the huge Bulgaria reaching down to the Aegean, wanted by Gortchakoff, Disraeli had insisted on the area being much smaller and split into two, the northern section having autonomy and the other, from the

Balkan mountains to the sea, still ruled by the Sultan. After a great amount of argument, Gortchakoff had yielded.

"Bismarck says you have kept Turkey in Europe. It is more than he ever thought you'd achieve." Disraeli's eyebrows moved fractionally. Lord Odo looked away from him. "I understand you have met Prince Bismarck before."

Disraeli sighed. "Many years ago. Of course, he was slim, narrow-waisted and handsome, then. Autre temps, autre moeurs . . ."

Lord Odo blinked. It sounded like, "Autre tems, autre moors." He shifted and said casually, "There is a rumor that you are to speak to the Congress tomorrow in French." Disraeli looked at him. "That would be a very great disappointment to the other delegates."

Disraeli's eyes narrowed. "How so?"

". . . They know you are the greatest living master of the English language," Lord Odo explained, "and have been looking forward to hearing you—as the intellectual experience of their lives."

He was attempting to look sincere and honest. Disraeli watched him expressionlessly for a long moment. "Very well, Lord Odo," he said quietly. "I shall consider it."

The next day, there was loud applause when Disraeli rose to address the assembly. It was followed by an expectant hush.

Salisbury, Russell and his other aides kept their eyes lowered, when he began, "Mon Prince—chers confreres . . ."

Lord Odo felt Salisbury tense beside him.

"It is with profound emotion that I rise today to address you," Disraeli said. He paused, his glance not quite reaching Salisbury, who covered his smile quickly with his hand. "Emotion," Disraeli went on, still in English, "and a sense of grave responsibility . . ."

In the break afterward, Disraeli paced slowly in the anteroom with Corry and Lord Barrington, who had come out to join his staff. "Really a superb speech, Sir,"

Barrington said. "I don't think anyone could have imagined that everything could go so smoothly."

"No. That's what Bismarck said," Disraeli murmured. It was something that vaguely disturbed him. Was it because of Bismarck's authority, his own prestige? The Indian troops still in Malta. The Russians had put only a token resistance, even to sharing Bulgaria with Turkey.

"Would you care to sit down, Sir?" Corry asked.

He shook his head. "No, thank you, Monty. No sign of weakness, when the most important points are so nearly settled."

"It's been an incredible week," Barrington smiled, admiringly. He had seen how Disraeli had come to dominate the Congress with his personality. And all so quietly, without the bluster that most of the others used. Even Bismarck deferred to him.

Disraeli raised his eyeglass. He had been trying to watch Salisbury who was talking by the door with Schouvaloff. They separated and Salisbury came straight to him. He was controlling himself and made himself turn and walk slowly by Disraeli's side as Barrington stepped away. He spoke softly, but urgently. "Prepare yourself, Sir. We had it settled. Russia and Turkey to share Bulgaria."

Disraeli's head lifted. "That's agreed. They can't change their minds now."

"They know that," Salisbury told him. "But I have just been talking to Count Schouvaloff. It appears that the Czar refuses to allow Turkey the right to station troops in its section."

Disraeli stopped, and the others paused around him, shaken.

"But that would leave the route to the Mediterranean still open!" Corry exclaimed.

"It is a deliberate attempt to undo everything we have negotiated."

Disraeli made no comment. He nodded slowly, thinking.

"The Russian Chancellor is coming, Sir," Barrington warned him.

Disraeli turned. Gortchakoff was coming toward them,

painfully, leaning on Schouvaloff's arm. He paused as Disraeli bowed. "My dear Lord Beaconsfield, I had to tell you how inspired I was by your speech this morning." Disraeli bowed again. Gortchakoff smiled. "Are you returning for our session?" The afternoon was to be devoted to a private Anglo-Russian meeting.

"This very moment," Disraeli said.

"Very good," Gortchakoff smiled. They moved very slowly through the door of the anteroom into the main hall, where the under-secretaries were checking the maps and documents on the long table. Gortchakoff paused, before Disraeli and he parted to go to their separate ends. "En verité, these last days have been absorbing. I only agreed to make the long journey from St. Petersburg for the pleasure of meeting you. May I say? My expectations have been more than fulfilled."

Once again, Disraeli bowed. "You honor me. I also must confess to more than a slight curiosity to meet one of the masters of European diplomacy." Gortchakoff smiled and returned the bow. "Particularly, one who understands that terms once agreed cannot be altered."

Schouvaloff glanced quickly at Gortchakoff. The Russian Chancellor's smile was mild. "There are always some areas of adjustment," he said smoothly.

"Naturally," Disraeli nodded, "and those we may leave to the Ambassadors after the main treaty is signed. All that remains for us to decide is the size of the garrison on the Turkish border of Bulgaria." Behind him, Salisbury and the others were tense. They saw Disraeli turn as if to move away.

"But there can be none!" Schouvaloff protested. "The Czar will never permit it."

Disraeli looked back at him. "Then, I fear His Imperial Majesty has been wrongly advised."

Gortchakoff had stopped smiling. "His Imperial Majesty will have the last word!" he snapped.

"He may do so in St. Petersburg," Disraeli told him. "Not in this Congress Hall."

Gortchakoff's head jerked. He held down his anger. "If

Turkey is allowed to arm her borders, we will have fought for nothing," he pointed out.

Disraeli seemed slightly surprised. "But you have liberated the Christian section of Bulgaria," he said, innocently. "Which was your declared intention."

The two Russians were gazing at him. "A hundred thousand men lost and millions of money—all for a dream?" Gortchakoff whispered.

Disraeli was silent.

Schouvaloff appealed to him. "You must see, Lord Beaconsfield, that we cannot possibly decide—only the Czar. And it will take time to send a messenger to St. Petersburg."

Gortchakoff could not yield. The memory of Ignatyev's disgrace and banishment was too recent. "That would solve nothing," he stated. "You must know as well as I do that he will never agree."

"I am very much afraid," Disraeli said solemnly, "that if he does not, and by the day after tomorrow, England will withdraw from the Congress."

That evening, at a banquet at the Italian Embassy, Disraeli spoke in confidence to Count Corti, a favorite of Bismarck's, and a confirmed gossip. He told him he took the gloomiest view of affairs and how sad he was to have to break up the Congress, if Russia did not adopt his proposals, because of the terrible consequences. The next day, Gortchakoff did not appear and Schouvaloff told Disraeli they had despatched a colonel to St. Petersburg, but he would not return before the end of the week. They spent the morning discussing Greece. Bismarck was said to be indisposed and did not show himself.

Afterward, Disraeli strolled with Corry in the Tiergarten, a thickly wooded park. It was an exceptionally fine day and, after days of sun, his gout had almost disappeared. The strain of the crowded days and late nights was beginning to tell and he panted, leaning on Corry's arm. "What a change, Monty . . . to breathe fresh air." Some children ran past them, bowling hoops, and he watched them as they were playing.

The tension was affecting Corry as much as everyone else who had heard. "Austria, Italy and Turkey have begged you to reconsider," he said. "They know the Czar will not give in." Disraeli nodded. "It will mean war between us and Russia, in which they would inevitably be involved. A war of an extent and horror unimagined since the days of Napoleon!" Disraeli nodded again and moved on. Corry caught him up. "All they ask is that you stay on for more talks," he pleaded.

Disraeli stopped. "Contact the German Railway Company and order a special train for tomorrow morning," he said casually.

"To go where, Sir?"

"To Calais. It will take us and the rest of the English delegation home. Be very discreet."

Corry was shocked. "But . . . Prince Bismarck is bound to hear of it."

"Yes," Disraeli agreed. "He hears everything. He is still convinced this is *his* Congress. Gortchakoff would never have acted without his support. You will order the train."

That evening, Disraeli had an urgent invitation to dine with Prince Bismarck. He was dressing for a dinner at the British Embassy, but sent his apologies to Lady Odo and drove to the Chancellor's Palace, instead. Bismarck was most agreeable. "I hope you don't mind," he explained. "We wanted to have you to ourselves for once."

At dinner, there was only family, his wife and daughter, his niece and two sons. The conversation was light and amusing. They drank a great deal, and never mentioned politics. Afterward, Bismarck showed Disraeli into his study, a panelled room, very masculine, rather spartan, with crossed duelling swords on the walls, silver cups and a portrait of Kaiser Wilhelm I.

Both were trying to seem relaxed, but they were watchful. "That's enough of the family," Bismarck chuckled. "My wife and daughter have been badgering me to invite you."

His wife was very plain, his daughter even plainer, the

514

niece so attractive she seemed to be there by mistake. But all of them were reading *Henrietta Temple*. And Disraeli had been surprised to learn that Bismarck had read all of his novels. He smiled. "I was delighted to meet them. And dinner was superb."

"Well . . . now we can talk a little," Bismarck grunted. He motioned Disraeli to an armchair and he sat, keeping himself very erect. "Brandy?"

"A suggestion," Disraeli answered. Bismarck nodded and moved to pour two glasses, ponderously, with great care. Disraeli watched him, then glanced round the room, seeing the portrait. "I am sorry not to have seen His Imperial Majesty, the Kaiser. He is recovering from his wounds, I trust?"

"Slowly," Bismarck told him. "Those damned Socialist Anarchists! It was one of them that shot him. A so-called Doctor of Philosophy."

"A philosopher with a gun," Disraeli commented.

"It's the coming thing in politics," Bismarck muttered. He brought Disraeli his glass and sat opposite him. They toasted each other silently. Bismarck drank and lowered the glass to his knee. "Now, what's all this business with the train?"

"Train?" Disraeli asked.

"The one you've ordered to stand by."

"It is to take my delegation home," Disraeli said candidly.

"You can't be serious?!" Bismarck spluttered. Disraeli did not answer. "You'd be prepared to break up the Congress?"

Disraeli sipped his brandy. "If necessary. As a matter of principle, I cannot continue unless I have a favorable answer from the Russians."

"By favorable, you mean giving in to what you demand!" Bismarck growled.

"I mean an answer that satisfies the conditons under which I came here. I told Count Schouvaloff what I would and would not accept."

"So everything has to be settled on your terms?" Bismarck's voice was harder. His eyes were fixed on Disraeli, menacing. "That would be an ultimatum not only to Russia, but to me and all the other Powers!"

Disraeli nodded calmly. "That is exactly what it is—an ultimatum."

There was silence for a full minute, while Bismarck still stared at him, considering him, searching for any sign of indecision. Was he bluffing or really determined? At last, he said abruptly, "Will you have a cigar?"

Disraeli hesitated only briefly. "That would be most agreeable."

Bismarck heaved himself up and fetched a carved, ivory cigarbox. He offered it to Disraeli and watched as he chose a cigar, crackled it by his ear, sniffed it and checked to see that its end was snipped. He took a box of sulphur matches from the box. Bismarck returned to his own seat and also took a cigar and box of matches. They both lit their cigars, Bismarck impatiently with clouds of smoke, Disraeli more delicately, not inhaling. The ritual over, Bismarck settled back, puffing on his cigar, watching him. Disraeli inhaled gently, then panted as it robbed him of breath.

"I'm surprised you smoke at all with your asthma," Bismarck said.

"I used to," Disraeli coughed. "But this is the first time for many years, It will probably be the last nail in my coffin."

"Then why did you take it?" Bismarck asked, puzzled.

Disraeli had recovered from the small attack of coughing. He puffed again, without inhaling. "Because when two men sit and talk together, if only one of them smokes, he cannot relax properly. The one who does not smoke is, somehow, like a spy taking down his conversation in his mind. Smoking together helps to put us at our ease."

Bismarck drew on his cigar, still considering him. All at once, he chuckled. "By God, I like you!" He laughed aloud and slapped his thigh. "You're not like those others. It's easy to do business with you. In quarter of an hour, you know exactly where you stand. The limits to which you're prepared to go are clearly defined. You're straightforward—not at all crafty, like they said."

"It's surprising how often complete honesty is taken for cunning," Disraeli murmured.

Bismarck shrugged. "Honesty's another matter."

"In politics, honesty is a matter of accepting the inevitable," Disraeli said. "For example, England and Germany exist. We must accept each other."

"Gladly," Bismarck smiled. "There is a natural sympathy between our two Empires. And great harm could be done, if we intrigued against each other."

Disraeli flicked the ash from his cigar. "I have a disgust for political intrigue."

Bismarck nodded. "It's a slippery slope, once you start."

"It fascinates the young, for it appeals to our invention and courage," Disraeli said, "a dazzling practice, but one which should really only be left to the second-rate. Great minds must trust to great truths and great talents for their rise, and nothing else. Like you."

Bismarck had listened, motionless, not even smoking. He grunted. "It's a rare thing to hear someone speak one's secret thoughts . . ." He rose and went to fetch the brandy decanter. "Why not? We've both risen by our talents—and always by service to someone else. And we can both be dismissed as soon as we no longer please—you by your electors, me by the Kaiser I created."

"That is hardly likely to happen."

"Likely?" Bismarck frowned. "No. But we are always and only judged by results." He had spoken with a touch of bitterness and shrugged it away, bringing back the decanter. He offered it to Disraeli who held his hand over his glass. Bismarck filled his own glass and sat again, laying the decanter on the floor beside him. He leaned forward, confidentially. "I tell you one thing, my friend. The Suez Canal is in your pocket. Turkey can't stop you. I don't understand why you don't take Egypt."

"Because of Prince Bismarck," Disraeli said.

Bismarck's eyes opened. "I don't want it!" he snorted. "I won't stop you. Egypt's of no interest to Germany."

"On the contary," Disraeli countered. "You would use it to drive a wedge between England and France, just as you have been playing us off against Russia. It is an old principle—'Divide and rule.'"

Bismarck stared at him for a second, then chuckled and shook his head. "Oh, we are well suited . . . if we were only twenty years younger! What things we could achieve together!" He sat back, puffing on his cigar, still chuckling. "By the way," he said casually, "I shall speak to the Russian Chancellor."

"I hoped you might," Disraeli replied, just as casually. "It is not for a man like you to preside over a Congress and see it come to nothing."

Bismarck smiled. "Exactly," he admitted.

"Oh . . . and, by the way," Disraeli told him, "Turkey has ceded the island of Cyprus to Britain, as a base from which we can guard the Suez Canal."

It had not happened often, but Bismarck was taken completely off guard. He was speechless with admiration for a time, then leaned back in his chair, shaking with laughter.

Four hours later, Schouvaloff was wakened with a coded answer to his despatch to St. Petersburg. The Czar had given in.

The signing of the peace treaty in the Congress Hall by all the chief delegates was a colorful ceremony, perfectly stage-managed by Bismarck's aides. It took place nearly three weeks later.

If Disraeli had been famous before the Russian capitulation and the announcement of the acquisition of Cyprus, giving England command of the entire Eastern Mediterranean, it was nothing to the adulation shown to him afterward. He seemed almost to be a wizard, all-powerful and inscrutable. He had won every point he said he would and had set his country at the apex of world Powers. Watching diplomats marvelled at the way he had won his long duel and acknowledged him as their master. The question of whether he had really been bluffing was argued over and over and remained unanswered, and unanswerable.

In the last two weeks of the Congress, the strain had become too much and it seemed as if his old body could take no more. The doctor wanted to take him home immediately, but he insisted on being at the final ceremony. Somehow, Kidd managed to patch him together and he went with Salisbury to the Radetsky Palace. He was cheered on the way and at the entrance to the palace and, in the Congress Hall, the delegates stood for him. During Bismarck's concluding speech, congratulating the delegates on having achieved peace for generations to come, most of the distinguished guests were watching Disraeli. Finally, Bismarck signed the heavily-sealed document and Prince Hohenlohe passed it to Gortchakoff and Schouvaloff. When it was carried along and laid in front of Disraeli, the witnesses burst into applause. Even the Russians applauded. Watching as he took up a quill pen with a gold nib and dipped it in the ink, Bismarck nodded. "The old Jew . . . ," he murmured. "He is the man."

On the journey home, he recovered sufficiently to be able to stand the excitements of his arrival. Queen Victoria had offered him a dukedom. He refused it, saying that to know he had served her was enough. She insisted on investing him with the Order of the Garter, but he would only accept on condition it was also given to Salisbury.

The platforms and concourse of Charing Cross Station were hung with garlands of roses, geraniums and the flags of all the nations at the Congress. A deputation of Dukes waited with the Lord Mayor and the Sheriffs of London to greet him, as he limped from the train with Salisbury supporting his arm. Stretching to the vaulted exit was an avenue of peeresses and peers and Members of the House of Commons. He did not see, nor expect to see, Gladstone.

The Queen had written to him, "High and low, the

whole country is delighted, except Mr. Gladstone, who is frantic." He damned the Treaty as "an insane covenant" and accused Disraeli of contriving it by "an act of duplicity of which every Englishman should be ashamed." To Disraeli it was the buzzing of a fly.

Dense crowds cheered and sang outside the station and packed Trafalgar Square, Whitehall and Downing Street. When his carriage drove out, with Salisbury sitting beside him, the delirium of the crowds turned the welcome into a victor's triumph. The cheering continued all through the Cabinet reception at Number 10, until, at last, he had to show himself. The mass of people jammed into Downing Street roared jubilantly as he came out on to the balcony, and the cheers increased, at the gesture, when he drew Lord Salisbury out to stand beside him. It was minutes before he could be heard and he waited, nodding down. He raised his hand and the sound died away. "Lord Salisbury and I have brought you peace," he said proudly, "but peace, I hope, with honor."

chapter nine

When the pony-cart drew up in front of the house, Disraeli was too stiff for a moment to climb out. Mr. Baum, his valet, had been waiting with an umbrella and ran forward to help him down. He had to put his arm round Disreli and half carry him to the front door. He looked so accusing that Disraeli almost apologized.

He had not meant to stay out so long, certainly not in this rain. He had been wearing his leggings and long waterproof coat. His hat was saturated. The rain had caught him two or three miles from Hughenden and, at first, had seemed fairly light. After ten minutes, it had become a downpour, and there was little point in stopping somewhere for shelter. It had set in for the rest of the day.

Mr. Baum helped him out of his coat and gave him his indoor cane. He limped through into the drawing-room, where there was a good fire. Standing in front of it, he rotated slowly, rubbing his hands to bring back the circulation. Everywhere the story was the same, the crops

521

washed out. It had been a glorious summer, followed by torrential rain through the whole of August and on into this month. The fifth ruined harvest in a row. Bad news for any Government, especially at a time when world trade was bad, many out of work or having to take lower wages. And everyone asking, what's the Government going to do about it? Build a giant umbrella and cover the whole island every autumn . . . He was very thankful that he still had over a year before he had to call an election. He could choose a better time than this.

In the eighteen months since the Congress, he had had more than his share of bad luck. Though everything was in a good state now, apart from the harvest and world trade, which no one could control. He had scarcely returned from Berlin, when the Russians had started to stir up trouble in Afghanistan, inciting the Amir to call for a holy war against the British. To do nothing was to hand over control of the northern passes into the Punjab and India to the Russians. At least, the campaign had been short, under a brilliant general, Roberts, ending with the Amir fleeing into exile and his son installed in his place, heavily subsidized by the British taxpayer, and a British Representative in residence at Kabul.

What a howl Gladstone and the Radicals had put up, calling it an unjust war. But all criticism had been wiped out by the news of Roberts' heroic march to the relief of Kandahar. Then, there had been an unnecessary and costly Zulu rising, fortunately also concluded successfully.

Mr. Baum brought him a glass of hot brandy and water with a slice of lemon. A kind thought. His spirits revived as it warmed him. Yes, affairs were generally much better, except for trade and the harvest. Not a single Russian soldier remained in the Balkans. The frontier of India was secure for the first time, the Zulus pacified. In this recess, he should at last be able to have a rest. And he had something special to look forward to. Selina and her husband were coming to stay for a day or two with their daughters.

The next morning, Corry came down from London with the despatch boxes and terrible news. The British

Envoy in Kabul and his staff had been massacred by the Afghans. He telegraphed to the Queen and had an instant reply. "We must act with great energy. No hanging back . . ." He was on his own, the Cabinet scattered. At least, there was a proper reason to take action this time. He sent for the new Secretary for India and sent a coded despatch to the Viceroy, authorizing General Roberts to advance on Kabul.

It was the end of the first week in September. By mid October, Roberts had routed the Afghan rebels and the Amir, who had fled to him for protection, abdicated.

Disraeli sat with the Queen on her terrace at Osborne. Over the balustrade, they could see the long slope of the grounds down to trees and the sea. After all the rain of the previous months, the grass was lush and green and the spring flowers seemed more numerous than ever. In their sheltered corner, it was like an early summer day. They talked quietly, like old friends. Lady Ely had shown Victoria his letter and it had touched her deeply to think she had hurt him. It was a fault, she knew, in herself. Sometimes, she was sharp, when she meant only to be firm. She had not lost a minute before writing as affectionately as she dared, to let him know she still valued him above all others. Now the cloud between them was all forgiven and forgotten. At sixty-one, her hair was quite gray and rheumatism had partly crippled her hands. There was no longer such a noticeable difference in age between them, although he was fifteen years older, when he sat quietly, resting, as he was now. To her, he had always had the same dark, rather Oriental agelessness.

"There is almost nothing in life to which I look forward more keenly than to my visits here," he said, "to this enchanted isle."

"I must ask you here," she said, "since you will not come to Balmoral."

He could not abide Balmoral. It was even draftier than Windsor. "I dare not be too far from Westminster these days, Ma'am."

She was not deceived. "My children are just the same.

They make every excuse not to come. I do not understand it. Albert and I so loved it."

"But then, you created it together, Ma'am. It was built with your love."

"There is not a day that passes but I still remember him—and miss him," she said. "Do you not find the same, dear Lord Beaconsfield?"

"I have been thinking of that," he told her. "Sometimes, when I try to remember Mary Anne, it is difficult. All I sense is a presence. Yet, there are occasions when, without thought, I will open a door and expect to find her there. Or look up from a favorite book and be surprised she is not sitting, smiling to me."

"Yes," Victoria agreed. "That is how it is."

"It is the little things," he went on. "Just as a gift of tiny primroses from the hand of my Queen may suddenly remind me there is a life, another life of open sky and green pastures, outside Parliament."

She frowned. "You work much too hard. Perhaps after this election, you should choose a deputy to take over some of your duties."

"That may be the answer, Ma'am."

"I still remember how exhausted you were, when you came back from Berlin." She smiled. "That was a time! I have never known such excitement."

He nodded. "Indeed, Your Majesty, it almost appeared the whole world had gone mad."

"And all due to you. I often wish you had let me give you a dukedom."

"I have no desire for further honors," he assured her. "Except the supreme one, to be allowed to serve Your Majesty to the best of my ability, for as long as I am spared."

"You are an example of service to us all, Lord Beaconsfield," she said quietly. "All your triumphs abroad —and the social progress that has given a better life to so many of my people."

"We have only one duty, Ma'am," he said. "To make the world a better place for our passing through."

He had made her, made everyone, aware of so much.

"I am proud to have you as my friend and Chief Minister."

He bowed where he sat. "Then I have all the thanks I shall ever need." He hesitated. "However, I must point out that I may not be Your Majesty's Prime Minister for much longer."

She tensed. "But you told me you had called this general election because it was a favorable time."

"We have won the last three by-elections, which is unusual for a Government that has been in for six years," he explained. "And the latest, in London, was quite unexpected. So this would seem to be a good time for my party, although there have been signs that the electorate is turning against us."

She was shocked. "After all your triumphs?"

"Five bad harvests in a row have forced up the price of food." He smiled faintly. "The triumphs of a Minister are forgotten, when he is found to be unable to control the weather."

She smiled, but her anxiety was growing. She rose, appalled by a sudden thought. Disraeli pushed himself to his feet. Victoria moved away, then turned back. "But if I lose you as Prime Minister, I may have to accept . . . You know who!"

"It would, indeed, be a sad day for both of us, Your Majesty," he admitted.

"It is unthinkable!" she exclaimed. "How could I work with that half-mad, opinionated, fanatical old man!"

"I am inclined to agree with Labouchere," Disraeli murmured, "who says he does not so much object to Mr. Gladstone always having the ace of trumps up his sleeve, as to his conviction that God Almighty put it there."

Victoria smiled briefly, but was too anxious to be laughed out of it so easily. "His speeches and letters get worse than ever," she complained. "I cannot make head or tail of them."

This time, she did laugh. "How unhappy he must be," Disraeli murmured, then gave the smallest shrug. "But he has been a ceaseless Tartuffe from the beginning. That sort of man does not go mad at seventy."

The result of the election could not have been foretold. No one looked for a dramatic change, but the by-elections turned out to be the exceptions. Out of the first 69 seats declared, the Government lost 15. And the pattern was repeated thoughout the country. Largely through Gladstone's incessant repetition that Disraeli had wasted the nation's resources by plunging needlessly into foreign adventures and that he represented moral corruption both at home and abroad, the position of the parties was nearly exactly reversed and the Liberals won a resounding majority.

Disraeli was bitter. He had expected, at worst, a small majority either way, but he behaved with dignity and handed over without rancor. He still would not accept any further honors. All he asked for was a peerage for Montagu Corry, who had some claim, anyway, as the grandson of an earl on both parents' side. He had just inherited Rowton Castle in Shropshire. The Queen consented and raised Corry to the peerage as Lord Rowton.

She was heartbroken at losing Disraeli, but he promised still to give her his loyalty and advice, as he had already given his duty, and his heart. Her only consolation was that Gladstone had resigned the Liberal leadership, but, when she sent for Lord Hartington, he told her that Gladstone had such a strong position in the party now, after the elections, that he had threatened to bring down any Government that was formed without himself at its head. After checking with Disraeli that it was true, she finally had to accept Gladstone as her Prime Minister for the second time, under protest. The audience she gave him when he came to kiss hands was brief and icy.

Disraeli went immediately to Hughenden, after taking leave of the Queen. She gave him a bronze statuette of herself and, when he kissed her hand, she took his and shook it. From now on, she said, they must not write to each other formally, but as friends, in the First Person. The goodbye was distressing for both of them.

At Hughenden, Disraeli found the consolation he needed. He had never been there as spring turned into summer, always having been busy at Westminster. Until the new Government was established, there was no real need for him and he could rest and watch the slow growth of his trees and the change of each day in his garden, as he had longed to do ever since he had bought the house for Mary Anne. Where the bustle of town made him more conscious of his age and infirmity, he found the country moved at his pace. And the peace and routine he developed caused a dramatic improvement in his health. Even when he had to go up to London on business, he caught the night train home. His friends and colleagues thought he had accepted that his work was done and was withdrawing from the world in which he would make no more stir. But they were wrong.

Montagu Corry, now Lord Rowton, came to Hughenden for a few days at the end of the summer. He was still Disraeli's private secretary in spirit and handled business for him in London. He was still unmarried and devoted to his old chief.

One day a package was delivered from Balmoral and he took it straight up to the study where Disraeli usually spent half the morning and all afternoon, reading and writing letters. Corry was touched to see him hunched over his writing table, which had been moved nearer to the window to catch the best light, wearing his long red dressing gown. He had not heard Corry come in and started, throwing one arm across the papers on his desk.

"I'm sorry, Sir," Corry said. "But this has just arrived —from Her Majesty."

Disraeli peered at the box. He was nearly blind in one eye. "She is spoiling me again. What is it?"

"I don't know, Sir. But it's quite heavy." Corry laid the package on the end of the table and opened it. Inside was a magnificent salmon, with a note from the Queen to say it had been specially caught for Lord Beaconsfield by John Brown.

"What a good thing I was always polite to him . . ." Disraeli murmured. Corry laughed. "Well, what do you say, Monty? Shall we have some for supper?"

"It could feed a regiment," Corry said.

"Well, we'll take what we need and ask some country-woman of Mr. Brown's to kipper the rest." Corry smiled. "Talking of supper reminds me . . . Prince Hal told me a friend of his had been at a supper for the Gaiety Girls."

"A friend?"

Disraeli shrugged. "Well we know what that means. However, it seems that the young ladies were asked whom they would prefer to marry, myself or Mr. Gladstone. Flatteringly enough, only one chose Gladstone—and the others booed her. 'Wait a minute,' she said. 'I'd like to marry Gladstone, then get Disraeli to run away with me, just to see Gladstone's face!'"

Corry laughed. "You see how the Sex admires you, from the Queen to chorus-girls." Disraeli smiled and sat back. Then quickly sat forward again, but not before Corry had seen what was under his arm. He had supposed Disraeli was composing one of his letters to Lady Bradford. Instead, there was a pile of manuscript. "Are you writing something, Sir?" he asked.

Disraeli showed a flash of annoyance, then sighed. "I didn't want anyone to know, until it is finished."

"What is it?"

For a second, Disraeli looked quite impish. "I couldn't find anything I wanted to read, so I thought—I'll write another novel." Corry was startled. "I'm calling it 'Endymion'."

"What is the subject?"

"The usual," Disraeli smiled. "A romance—about a penniless young man who owes his rise all to women and, on the last page, becomes Prime Minister."

Corry smiled, but felt a twinge of jealousy. Barrington had been acting as the Chief's secretary. Did he know? "But you didn't tell me."

"I was not sure I could finish it. I didn't tell anyone, not even Selina. Not even Mr. Baum."

Corry chuckled, seeing how pleased he was with himself for having duped everyone. "So that's why you have been staying down here so much. You are sure it is not too great an effort, Sir?"

"It's nearly done," Disraeli told him. "Good thing, too. It might bring in some money. I was going to ask you to handle it."

Again, instead of the serious work one might expect from an aged statesman, it was a light, satirical romance, full of epigrams and odd turns of fate, with many of the characters based on real people, like Louis Napoleon and Bismarck. Disraeli thought that Monty should do rather well in his negotiations with Longmans, the publishing company. It was all managed in strict secrecy. Then, on an afternoon in early August, Corry took his seat beside Disraeli in the House of Lords and slipped him a note. It told him that Longmans had agreed an advance of £10,000 for the rights of *Endymion*. Disraeli was astounded. It was the highest advance ever given up to that time for a work of fiction. "I know no magic of the Middle Ages equal to it!" Disraeli told him. "And you are the magician." Apart from the success, it meant that all his remaining financial worries were over. If he was to die, he would die solvent.

Until the book was published, Disraeli continued to live at Hughenden. He had given up the lease of Whitehall Gardens, but Alfred de Rothschild, Lionel's son, put a self-contained suite of rooms at his disposal in his mansion at Seamore Place, now that he was once again an idol of society through the record sale of his new novel. "Nothing succeeds like success" had been one of his phrases and, again, he had proved it. He had refused, at his stage of life, to ask people to take pity on him as a failure.

Victoria wrote to him constantly, asking for his advice, worried over his health, excited about his book. She invited him to Windsor and he went again on her return from Balmoral. She made no secret now of her affection for him, seating him next to her at dinner, spending so long talking to him in her study that one of her daughters would have to come and knock on the door to remind her

529

that all the other guests were waiting. She was so happy when she was with him, she told him, for then she could pretend that "what has happened is only a horrid dream." She had written, "Oh! if only I had you, my kind friend and wise councillor and strong arm to help and lean on! I have no one." The only time her guests ever saw her laugh now was when Lord Beaconsfield was with her. Ponsonby, for the first time, honored Disraeli, realizing how easy it would have been for him to take political advantage of the Queen's affection and seeing how discreet and impartial his advice always was. As for Disraeli, on every visit, Victoria seemed prettier and younger to him, and more endearing.

Next to his affection for the Queen, his chief pleasure in visiting Windsor now was to see his portrait hanging in the dining-room in a place of honor. It was not mere vanity. Gladstone had to be invited from time to time, despite the Queen's antipathy. It gave Disraeli the keenest possible relish to think of him seated at that table, unable to digest his food because that portrait's eyes were fixed on him.

After the election defeat, at a full party meeting, he had offered to step down for a younger man. The party's answer had been to cheer him for a full three minutes. After the book was finished, he attended debates more often, although he could only speak now in public by using drugs to ease his throat. Once, the effect of the drugs wore off before he could rise. From then on, he prepared notes to pass to others who could speak for him. The most notable speeches of some lords' careers were made at that time.

Just before the novel was due to appear in November, asthma, bronchitis, rheumatism and gout attacked him all at once and left him virtually in a coma. The drugs and medicines needed to treat one illness were dangerous when used with the others and for ten days he suffered dreadful agonies, until the asthma cleared. Dr. Kidd visited him at Hughenden, but told him that he could only treat him properly in London. With the money from *Endymion,* he took a nine-year lease on a house in

Curzon Steet from which he could walk to the House of Lords on a clear day, or to Selina's, if she came to London.

He was to move in the New Year and spent Christmas absolutely alone. Even Monty had gone, taking a critically ill sister to Algiers to recuperate. Lord Barrington was to assist him again in January, but until then he had to cope with life and work on his own. And there was suddenly as much work as if he had still been in office. His prophecy that the change of Government would be disastrous for the country was coming true even more quickly than he had feared. Gladstone's unrealistic policies had provoked a revolution in Ireland and another in South Africa. His declaration that his sole aim was to destroy "Beaconsfieldism" had added to the slump in world trade. Knowing they no longer had to deal with Disraeli, the Russians had begun their push again in Asia and Afghanistan was in revolt. Not even Gladstone could control the weather and the sixth harvest had been the worst on record. Everywhere the condition of the people was desperate and Disraeli was swamped with appeals for him to fight, to write, to rally his party.

He moved to Curzon Street in January and his very presence so near Westminster gave many people hope. His voice was heard again in debate. The Queen, anxious for the country, offered to arrange meetings between Liberal and Conservative leaders to co-operate during the crisis, but Gladstone would not agree.

Disraeli, himself, sensed that his time was running out. From the end of January, the weather was icy and his asthma returned worse than ever. For some weeks, he struggled on, working and joining in society. He even gave a splendid dinner party in his new house. It was to be for Selina, but she was not in London, although her husband and Lady Chesterfield came. He was holding on, hoping for milder weather to bring relief, but it never came. March was a month of bitter winds. After an especially violent seizure, a week after his dinner party, he had to be put to bed.

His condition was so serious that Kidd could no longer

help. Philip Rose came to see Disraeli in his sickbed and was shocked to see how ill he was. He consulted with Barrington and they agreed to call in a leading chest specialist, Dr. Quain, with Kidd's approval. But because Kidd was a homeopath, Quain would not consult with him. Only pressure from the Queen ended the deadlock and, from then on, Quain led a team of doctors who were on call night and day and two nurses were engaged.

Any exertion or excitement caused agonizing spasms and the doctors would not permit visitors. Disraeli knew it would make no difference. Whatever they said, he knew it was the end, and refused to be denied the comfort of his friends. He wrote confidently to the Queen, but she heard from Barrington and Rose that there was little hope and was in despair.

One day at the end of March, Dr. Kidd came to see his patient and found the sickroom empty. Barrington and Rose had both now moved into the house and he hurried to look for them. He found Barrington in the red and gold drawing-room. "Why is he not in bed?" he demanded.

"He keeps saying he will not be treated like an invalid," Barrington told him.

"He must realize that he is!" Kidd insisted. "He will seriously weaken the little strength he has left."

"Dr. Kidd, you can't tell him," Barrington said. "He's even begun another novel after the success of *Endymion*."

Kidd was completely thrown. Did no one understand? Barrington was a thoughtful man, conscientious, but with no real authority. Rose would die himself rather than upset his idol. "There must be someone here with enough influence to make him stay in bed," he protested.

"Soon, I hope," Barrington said. "Monty—Lord Rowton—is abroad, but I have sent for him."

Kidd had left the door open and they could hear Disraeli's voice outside, scolding his nurse. "Am I not to be permitted even the most intimate of functions without supervision!"

Kidd turned as Disraeli came in, wearing his slippers

and dressing gown and supported by a fair-haired young nurse, who clearly adored him, even though he made her slightly afraid. "Doctor!" Disraeli panted. "This young woman is tyrannical!"

Kidd controlled himself. "She is trying to get you to rest, Sir."

"I can rest just as well by the window, where at least I can see the world still turning," Disraeli said. The nurse tried to steer him to a couch, but he pointed sharply. "No, no . . . over there." Kidd helped her to take him to a chaise longue by the long windows, overlooking the street. As Kidd settled him, the nurse fetched a rubber air-cushion, shaped like a ring, which she slid behind his back. "What is it?" he asked.

"An air-cushion, Sir," Kidd explained.

The nurse froze as Disraeli's eyes fixed on her. "Take away that emblem of mortality," he ordered, imperiously. She snatched up the air-cushion and retreated.

Philip Rose had come in and was whispering to Barrington, who said, "No, no, it's out of the question. He can't see anyone."

"What was that?" Disraeli asked.

"A visitor, Lord Beaconsfield," Kidd said.

Disraeli hesitated, then shook his head. He had made his stand, but he knew he should not be exposed to anyone from outside. He looked out of the window. It was a blustery, cold day with no break in the dark cloud. I live only for climate, he told himself, and I cannot get it. He heard no sound behind him and glanced round. His eyes opened and he felt his whole body tense.

Selina Bradford had come in and stood, motionless, looking at him. He could not speak.

At a sign from Rose, Kidd and Barrington went out. He waited for the nurse and followed them, closing the door.

Disraeli was still gazing at Selina, whom he had not seen for so long. He had tried to write to her only that morning, but had not the strength to hold the pen. As she came toward him, he tried vainly to rise.

"No, my dear, please——" she said, gently, stopping

him. He tried to tell her it was only the surprise of seeing her, to apologize, but still could not speak. "I know," she assured him. "You must not try to get up. I have only come to sit quietly with you for a little while." She sat near him. She could have wept at the change in him, but she smiled. That was what he would want.

Her smile seemed to warm him. "I have ... have missed you," he whispered.

"And I you," she told him.

He tried again to speak, but even to whisper was an effort. "I . . . cannot find words . . . " He should have something, something special to say to her that she would remember, that would sum up all he still felt for her.

She understood and took his hand. "There's no need," she said, quietly. "Not any more."

She kissed his hand and laid her cheek on it for a moment. He settled back, gazing at her and they sat quietly, just looking at each other, with Selina still holding his hand.

In her study at Windsor, Victoria sat and gazed at the small bust of himself that Disraeli gave her, when she visited Hughenden. It was as if, through it, she was trying to will strength and life back into him. She was drawn and anxious. Each day she prayed for an improvement, but he was only weaker. She had written to the doctors to ask if there were any possibility of seeing him, perhaps for the last time, but she had known their answer before it came. Even Lord Rowton, his closest associate over many years, had come back all the way from North Africa and Lord Beaconsfield, himself, had refused to see him, until he was used to the idea of him being there.

She took her pen and began to write. Did they even let him read her letters? There was so much she wanted to say, but not for others to read. She looked again at the bust and, laying down her pen, put out her hand and touched its cheek.

Disraeli lay in bed, his shoulders raised by pillows. His eyes were nearly closed and he was very tired, not really in pain any more. His mind had wandered to Hughenden and he felt a great sadness that he would never see it again. The swans would sail in white splendor and the peacocks strut and scream for others. The leaves would come soon on his trees again, and fall, and come again . . . never ending. He would like to have seen his library, with his books and his father's, the silent companions of so many hours. For a book, even if you do not open it, is a companion . . . Most of all, he would like to come down the stairs again, lined with the portraits of all his friends, his Gallery of Friendship . . . Smythe and Lyndhurst, Byron whom he had never met, but who had transformed his youth, John Manners and Edward Bulwer . . . and George Bentinck . . . Selina. Endymion was the lover of Selene, untouchable Goddess of the Moon. Had she understood? Anne Chesterfield . . . D'Orsay and Lady Blessington. Now even their house was gone, Gore House, and where it had stood was a concert hall in memory of Prince Albert, the Albert Hall . . . Sarah, dear Sa. And turning the corner into the drawing-room, there over the fireplace, Mary Anne. Dearest, unforgettable Mary Anne . . .

What had made him think of Hughenden? Oh, yes. Monty had come. Strange, he had been so afraid of seeing him. But now that he was here, he felt so much safer. He opened his eyes. Monty was sitting by the bed, watching him, so concerned. And Philip was over by the door. How long had they both been sitting there? Philip was asleep.

Corry sat forward when he saw his eyes open.

"I am sorry to interrupt your holiday, Monty," Disraeli said. His voice was stronger suddenly. "Your sister will never forgive me."

"She insisted I came at once," Corry told him. He blamed himself for not having been here. "I should never have left."

"Nonsense . . ." Disraeli smiled. He could see that Monty was near to tears. That would be embarrassing for him. Young men are so ashamed of tears. He began to push himself up, breaking the atmosphere. Corry rose quickly and helped him to sit further up the bed. Disraeli nodded decisvely. "Well, now you are here, we may as well do some work."

Corry was astonished and forgot his emotion in his surprise. "Work?"

He saw Disraeli point to a pile of proof sheets on a tray on the bedside table. "The proofs of my last speech in the Lords. I fear it may truly be my last."

Corry fetched the tray automatically, then paused. "You should not, Sir," he protested. "You will tire yourself."

"I would rather live. But I am not afraid to die," Disraeli told him. He pointed again and Corry laid the tray over his knees. Disraeli took up his pencil. "I will not go down to posterity talking bad grammar."

Corry smiled as Disraeli began to work, bending over the proofs, peering at them with his eyeglass. He passed each sheet to Corry after he had made his correctons.

The nurse came in and Rose woke as she touched his shoulder. Disraeli was intent and did not notice. She had a small basket of flowers which she gave to Rose, then she whispered to him and went out. He pushed himself stiffly to his feet and came to the bed. "Sir—from Windsor," he said.

He laid the basket on the bed and uncovered it. It was filled with primroses. Disraeli was touched and sighed. He gazed at them for a time. "Windsor?" he wondered, at last. "I thought Her Majesty was at Osborne."

"She has come to Windsor to be nearer you, Sir," Corry told him.

Disraeli looked again at the flowers.

Rose was troubled. "Sir—the messenger was to ask if you felt well enough for Her Majesty to pay you a short visit?"

Disraeli glanced up and his eyebrows lifted. "No . . ." he murmured. "No, she would only ask me . . . to take a message to Albert." Corry and Rose were shocked, but laughed in spite of themselves. Disraeli shook his head. "No . . . It would—I would dearly love to see my Sovereign for the last time—but the strain would be . . . I could not support it." The effort he had been making to seem normal was proving too much. He lay back on the pillows, panting.

Corry had seen the corner of the envelope in the basket. "There's a letter, Sir," he said and lifted it out.

Disraeli coughed. His throat felt as if it was closing. "Open it, would you, Monty?"

Rose took the tray from Disraeli's knees. Corry opened the envelope, took out the letter and passed it to Disraeli. He peered at it, but even with his eyeglass he could not read it. He tried harder, but it was useless. Wavering lines. Suddenly, it became unbearably important. "The Queen's writing...I cannot—cannot make it out now . . ." He was growing agitated.

"Shall I read it to you, sir?" Corry suggested.

Disraeli was distressed. There were rules. "I—I do not know what it contains," he muttered. "It can only be read by a Privy Councillor."

"Lord Barrington," Rose said. He left quickly.

Disraeli lay back again, panting. Corry leaned nearer. "Oh, Monty . . ." Disraeli whispered, "I have suffered much, and yet . . ." He held up his hand. Corry held it, until Barrington came in.

Disraeli gave Barrington the letter, and Corry went out, leaving them alone.

Disraeli nodded, and Barrington unfolded the sheet of paper and read, "Dearest Lord Beaconsfield—I send you a few of your favorite spring flowers—this time from the slopes here. I will send more from Osborne. I would come to see you, but I think it far better you should be quite quiet. You are very constantly in my thoughts, and I wish I could do anything to cheer you and be of the slightest use or comfort.

With earnest wishes for your uninterrupted progress in recovery.

Ever yours very affectionately, V.R.I."

When Barrington stopped reading, Disraeli took the letter from him, gazing at it, although he could not make out the words. Barrington bowed and left.

Disraeli sighed very gently. He lay back, holding the letter to his heart, and his eyes closed.

In a crowded, hushed House of Commons, many of the Members were in tears. On the Opposition Front Bench, Sir Stafford Northcote sat covering his eyes with his hand. Lord John Manners gazed blankly at the Treasury Table.

At the Treasury Bench, Gladstone stood, paying tribute. His speech had cost him many heart-searching hours. He doubted if he even had the right to make it. Disraeli's desire to be buried at Hughenden, with no national ceremony, struck him as pure theatricality. He had said to his secretary when he heard. "As he lived, so he died—all display, without reality or genuineness." He could not praise what his entire conscience considered worthy of the highest condemnation. Yet he had to speak the truth and praise those things which no one could dispute. "... His strength of will, his long-sighted persistence of purpose, his remarkable power of self-government; and last, but not least of all, his great parliamentary courage."

Although the nation called for a State funeral at Westminster Abbey, Disraeli was buried in obedience to his clear instructions in the vault of his church at Hughenden, next to Mary Anne and Mrs. Brydges-Willyams.

His coffin was carried by tenants of the estate. Although he had asked for his burial to be as simple as Mary Anne's, the Prince of Wales and his brothers, the Duke of Connaught and Prince Leopold, all the Conservative and Liberal leaders, except Gladstone, all his aides and personal friends, followed the coffin, his remaining brother, Ralph, and his nephew to the tomb.

Four days later, the royal carriage drew up outside Hughenden House, where Corry was waiting. In deep mourning, wearing a mourning cap and black veil, Queen Victoria was helped out by her Highland servant, John Brown. Taking Corry's arm, she followed the path down which Disraeli's body had been carried to the church-yard.

The vault at the east end of the church had been opened for her and when they reached it, Corry paused, letting her go on alone.

Disraeli's coffin was covered with a mound of splendid wreaths and bouquets. As she approached it, she raised the veil which covered her head and shoulder and body, nearly to the waist. Under it, she was holding a small spray of primroses, and she laid them down at the very end of the coffin in the gap between two wreaths of white lilies.

Alone and desolate, she stood gazing down.

On a card with the spray of primroses was written, "His favorite flower."

PROVOCATIVE CONTEMPORARY FICTION
BY TOP-RANKED AUTHORS

THE PERFECTIONISTS
by Gail Godwin   (92-207, $2.25)

The relentless sun of Majorca beats down upon a strange group of vacationers: a brilliant English psychotherapist, his young American wife, his small, silent illegitimate son and a woman patient. In the blinding light of the sun, they begin to look at one another and themselves to see with unflinching clarity the unsavory shadows that darken their minds and hearts.

VIOLET CLAY
by Gail Godwin   (91-079, $2.50)

The brilliant tale of a woman becoming an artist. Violet Clay is "about the integrity of work, the responsibility of the artist to his talent . . . we find ourselves inextricably a part of Violet's world as she reveals herself in a voice at once colloquial, artistic, familiar and elusive."   —Book World

GLASS PEOPLE
by Gail Godwin   (92-089, $2.25)

Francesca was flawless, a perfect cameo: beautiful, delicate —her husband's most prized possession. But lethargy has so engulfed Francesca that even her husband recognizes that she needs a change—perhaps a trip east to visit her mother. But Francesca needs more than a change. She needs an identity, a purpose, secrets of her own. And she will discover them on the trip east . . . in her own way.

THE ERRAND
by Francis Casey Kerns   (90-175, $1.95)

"I don't believe this; it's not really happening!" Chris thought. But it was real. They were in the hands of kidnappers, and one of them was insane! A tale of terror and truth, love and hope, discovered under the shadow of a kidnapper's gun.

CANA AND WINE
by Francis Casey Kerns   (81-951, $2.50)

Secrets . . . everybody has them. The Magnessen family and friends keep their share. From the author of THIS LAND IS MINE and THE WINTER HEART comes the compelling story of a midwestern family, respected and loved, until the past's dark horror is exposed in the brilliant Idaho sun.

THE BEST OF BESTSELLERS
FROM WARNER BOOKS

DESIRE AND DREAMS OF GLORY
by Lydia Lancaster   **(81-549, $2.50)**
In this magnificent sequel to Lydia Lancaster's PASSION AND
PROUD HEARTS, we follow a new generation of the Beddoes
family as the headstrong Andrea comes of age in 1906 and finds
herself caught between the old, fine ways of the genteel South
and the exciting changes of a new era.

A PASSIONATE GIRL
by Thomas Fleming   **(81-654, $2.50)**
The author of the enormously successful LIBERTY TAVERN is
back with this gusty and adventurous novel of a young woman
fighting in the battle for Ireland's freedom and persecuted for her
passionate love of a man.

PHILIPPA
by Katherine Talbot   **(84-664, $1.75)**
If she had to marry for money, and Philippa knew she must, then
it was fortunate that such a very respectable member of the
House of Lords was courting her. It was easy to promise to
"honor and obey" a man she so respected. It would be difficult,
though, to forget that the man she loved and did not respect
would be her brother-in-law . . . A delightful Regency Romance
of a lady with her hand promised to one man and her heart lost
to another!

LADY BLUE
by Zabrina Faire   **(94-056, $1.75)**
A dashing Regency adventure involving a love triangle, an enfant
terrible and a bizarre scheme to "haunt" a perfectly livable old
castle, LADY BLUE is the story of Meriel, the beautiful governess
to an impossible little boy who pours blue ink on her long blonde
hair. When she punishes the boy, she is dismissed from her post.
But all is not lost—the handsome young Lord Farr has another
job in mind for her. Meriel's new position: Resident "ghost" in
a castle owned by Farr's rival. Her new name: LADY BLUE!

THE FIVE-MINUTE MARRIAGE
by Joan Aiken   **(84-682, $1.75)**
When Delphie Carteret's cousin Garth asks her to marry him, it is
in a make-believe ceremony so that Delphie might receive a small
portion of her rightful—if usurped—inheritance. But an error has
been made. The marriage is binding! Oh, my! Fun and suspense
abounds, and there's not a dull moment in this delightful Regency
novel brimming with laughter, surprise and true love.

ROMANCE...ADVENTURE...
DANGER...

MORE OUTSTANDING BOOKS
FROM WARNER BOOKS

A CAPTIVE OF TIME
by Olga Ivinskaya (85-968, $2.75)
A CAPTIVE OF TIME is the story behind "Doctor Zhivago"—the extraordinary romance that inspired it—the passion between the genius poet and the woman who shared his life and his work and who went to prison for loving him. It is the story that only Olga Ivinskaya could write, revealing the man she alone knew.

RASPUTIN: THE MAN BEHIND THE MYTH
by Maria Rasputin & Patty Barnham (82-480, $2.25)
Was this Russian "holy man" and manipulator of the Czar and his family really evil? Was he really a drunkard and a devil . . . a seducer of the faithful . . . a conductor of vast orgies that shocked even the Russian court? Now his daughter tells the true story of those years, as she saw it and as she remembered it. A tender, revealing, but always shocking memoir.

CHANGE LOBSTERS AND DANCE
by Lilli Palmer (89-085, $1.95)
A life touched by suicide, scandal and sorrow, yet packed with triumph. From the day she fled Hitler's Germany to her marriage to Rex Harrison to her close friendships with Noel Coward, the Duke and Duchess of Windsor, Helen Keller—Lilli Palmer's life upstages even the great roles she has played. A poignant and revealing story that takes place in all the capitals of the world.